Jute No More

JUTE NO MORE

TRANSFORMING DUNDEE

Edited by Jim Tomlinson
and Christopher A. Whatley

Dundee
University
Press

First published in Great Britain in 2011 by
Dundee University Press

University of Dundee
Dundee DD1 4HN

http://www.dup.dundee.ac.uk/

ISBN: 978 1 84586 090 5

British Library Cataloguing-in-Publication Data
A catalogue record for this book is available on
request from the British Library

Typeset and designed by Mark Blackadder

Printed and bound in Britain by MPG Books, Bodmin, Cornwall

Contents

List of Figures and Tables

List of Illustrations

List of Contributors

Kenneth Baxter was awarded a PhD by the University of Dundee for a thesis entitled '"Estimable and Gifted"?: Women in Party Politics in Scotland *c.*1918–1955' in 2008. He teaches on the University of Dundee's History Programme and he has also taught at the School of History, University of St Andrews. Publications include *A Dundee Celebration* (Dundee, 2007) (with David Swinfen and Mervyn Rolfe) and 'Florence Gertrude Horsbrugh: the Conservative Party's forgotten first lady' in *Conservative History Journal* (Winter 2009/10). He also assisted with the research, production and writing of C. McKean and P. Whatley, *Lost Dundee: Dundee's Lost Architectural Heritage* (Edinburgh, 2008).

Sarah Browne is a teaching associate in History at the University of Nottingham. She completed a PhD at the University of Dundee on the Women's Liberation Movement in Scotland *c.*1968–*c.*1979. She has a number of forthcoming publications and has had published a booklet, *Making the Vote Count: The Arbroath Women Citizens' Association, 1931–1945* (Dundee, 2007).

Rob Duck is Professor of Environmental Geoscience at the University of Dundee. A geologist in general and a sedimentologist in particular, he has published extensively on Earth surface processes and the science that underpins the management of lake, coastal and estuarine environments, notably the Tay Estuary. He is the author of a forthcoming book, *This Shrinking Land: Climate Change and Britain's Coasts*.

Ruth Forbes studied History at the University of Dundee where she gained a PhD for her dissertation 'Patterns of Cultural Production in Dundee, 1850–1900'. Her research interests are in culture and identity and she has published on musical activity in nineteenth-century Dundee.

Matthew Jarron is Curator of Museum Services at the University of Dundee, with responsibility for the University's historic collections of art and artefacts. He also teaches film history for the University's Continuing Education department. He is the author or co-author of various University of Dundee Museum Services publications, including *David Foggie: The Painters' Painter* (2004), *The Artist and the Thinker: John Duncan and Patrick Geddes in Dundee* (2004), and *D'Arcy Thompson and his Zoology Museum in Dundee* (2010). He is chairman of the Scottish Society for Art History and secretary of the Abertay Historical Society.

William Kenefick is a Senior Lecturer in History within the School of Humanities, University of Dundee. He has published widely on Scottish maritime and labour history, the impact of the First World War and the Russian Revolution on the Scottish working class, and Irish and Jewish relations in Scotland from *c.*1870 to the present. His latest book is *Red Scotland! The Rise and Fall of the Radical Left, c.1872 to 1932* (Edinburgh, 2007).

Bill Knox is Senior Lecturer in Scottish History at the University of St Andrews. He has published widely on modern Scottish historical development, including books on class and gender, and has also carried out extensive research into the impact of American multinational firms on industrial relations during the period 1945–70. Currently he is working on a project dealing with homicide and Scottish society in the eighteenth and nineteenth centuries.

Charles McKean, FRSE has been Professor of Scottish Architectural History at the University of Dundee since 1997. His books include *The Scottish Thirties: An Architectural Introduction* (Edinburgh, 1987), *The Scottish Chateau: The Country House of Renaissance Scotland* (Stroud, 2004), and *Battle for the North: The Tay and Forth Bridges and the 19th-Century Railway Wars* (London, 2006). He was joint editor of *Dundee:*

Renaissance to Enlightenment (Dundee, 2009), of which he wrote or co-wrote three chapters, and he contributed a chapter to L. Miskell, C.A. Whatley and B. Harris (eds), *Victorian Dundee: Image and Realities* (East Linton, 2000). He represents Scotland on three European networks on medieval and Renaissance architecture, and is chairman of Edinburgh World Heritage.

Alan McKinlay is Professor of Management at the University of St Andrews. He has written extensively on Scottish business, labour and political history. He has also written about the French philosopher Michel Foucault.

Jim Phillips is Senior Lecturer in Economic and Social History at the University of Glasgow. His published work mainly examines employment relations, labour and industrial politics in twentieth century Scotland and the UK. He is the author of *The Industrial Politics of Devolution: Scotland in the 1960s and 1970s* (Manchester, 2008), and is currently writing a history of the 1984–5 miners' strike in Scotland.

Gordon Stewart is the Jack and Margaret Sweet Professor of History at Michigan State University, where he teaches World History and Imperial History. He has written on topics ranging from religion and politics in eighteenth-century North America to economic and cultural developments in British India, including his *Jute and Empire: The Calcutta Jute Wallahs and the Landscapes of Empire* (Manchester, 2008), which analysed the Dundee–Calcutta relationship from the 1830s to the 1950s. His most recent book, published by Cambridge University Press (2009), is *Journeys to Empire: Enlightenment, Imperialism, and the British Encounter with Tibet, 1774–1904*.

Jim Tomlinson is Bonar Professor of Modern History at the University of Dundee. He has published widely on the historical political economy of modern Britain, most recently articles on subjects including Keynesianism, financial credibility, the balance of payments and the 'moral economy'. He is the author (with Carlo Morelli and Valerie Wright) of a forthcoming book on managing the decline of the Dundee jute industry.

Christopher A. Whatley is Professor of Scottish History at the University of Dundee, where he is also Vice-Principal. Although an instigator of the History of Dundee project, for this volume his role has been to guide, advise and assist with the editing rather than contribute any substantial new material.

Valerie Wright was awarded a PhD by the University of Glasgow in 2008 for a thesis entitled 'Women's Organisations and Feminism in Interwar Scotland'. In 2008–10 she was a post-doctoral researcher at the University of Dundee, working on the Leverhulme Trust funded project on the decline of the jute industry. She is joint author (with Jim Tomlinson and Carlo Morelli) of the forthcoming book arising from that project.

List of Abbreviations

Advertiser	*Dundee Advertiser* (merged with the *Courier* in 1926)
Courier	*Dundee Courier* (and *Argus* until 1926, when it merged with the *Advertiser*)
DCA	Dundee City Archives
DCC	Dundee City Council
DOHP	Dundee Oral History Project
DSU	Dundee Social Union
DUA	Dundee University Archives
DWCA	Dundee Women Citizens' Association
LHC	Local History Collection, in Dundee City Library
NAS	National Archives of Scotland
TNA: PRO	The National Archives: Public Record Office (Kew)

Acknowledgements

The editors are grateful to the William Harvey Trust for financial support for the preparation of this volume, and to contributors to a workshop held in 2009, especially George Peden, Esther Breitenbach, Bob Morris and Billy Kay. They are also grateful to Michael Bolik from Dundee University Archives for help with the illustrations

Introduction

Christopher A. Whatley

Dundee is one of Scotland's best-known but least understood towns. This book, the third in a series of three, attempts to change this. Perceptions and realities of Dundee are, and often have been, in conflict. In most people's eyes a jute manufacturing centre – and a grim one at that – Dundee's heritage as a major religious centre in medieval times, with a bustling maritime quarter that had much in common with the Baltic ports then and thereafter, has been largely overlooked. So too has the fact that in early modern times Dundee was Scotland's second burgh (it was only in the later nineteenth century that it was accorded the rank of city), ahead even of Glasgow. It is still one of Scotland's biggest towns. The catch-phrase 'Jute, jam and journalism' is often applied to Dundee, but jute has all but disappeared. Keillor's – the firm associated with Dundee marmalade from the eighteenth century – abandoned Dundee a long time ago; much 'Dundee' marmalade is now made in Robertson's factory at Droylesden in Manchester. Whilst D.C. Thomson continues to keep the flag flying for journalism, newspaper sales – even of the *Sunday Post* – are no longer sufficient to sustain a company which has been moving strongly into IT. D.C. Thomson, however, is at the heart of an expanded publishing empire – selling some 100 million copies of its publications annually – which still include titles of what when they were launched were examples of sheer publishing genius: the *Beano*, *Dandy* and *People's Friend.* Remarkable, and almost certainly unpredictable if viewed from the perspective of an imagined crystal-ball gazer of the 1950s, is that a significant element of the self-image of early twenty-first-century Dundee is the so-called Cultural Quarter – an area to the west of the city centre that encompasses the highly regarded award-winning theatre company (the Rep), Dundee Contemporary Arts centre and Duncan of Jordanstone, the formerly independent art college which is currently a thriving part of the University of Dundee. Incredibly – at least to those either unaware of or unconvinced by Dundee's attempts to re-invent itself as a post-industrial city in which the creative arts are to the fore – was the announcement in 2008 that London's Victoria & Albert museum might open a £47 million venue in Dundee, in a prime waterfront location off the northern shore of the River Tay. As this book goes to print, the competition for the appointment of the architectural team to design what will undoubtedly be an iconic building is in its final stages. The target completion date is 2014, with hopes high that Dundee can benefit from the rise in cultural tourism and other spin-offs of the kind that have resulted from the spectacular Guggenheim Museum of modern art in Bilbao, opened in 1997. However, in this volume, in their chapters on music and art respectively, Ruth Forbes and Matthew Jarron reveal that long before the 1990s – when the creative arts began to be consciously promoted as agents of economic and social regeneration – these artistic forms played important parts in the cultural life of the city.

Yet even during the hey-day of jute, Dundee was far from being simply a colourless industrial workshop. There was much joy in the lives of Dundee's working classes, especially in the pioneering days of jute production when jobs were aplenty and high wages created new-found opportunities for those earning them to spend on more than just the basic essentials. Housing too was available, albeit often in sub-divided properties, but without the levels of overcrowding that later identified Dundee along with Glasgow as Scottish leaders in urban squalor. That Dundee had become a leading UK and even global centre for linen and then led the way in jute represented a major triumph for many of the town's thrusting and innovative merchant-manufacturers and businessmen – most of whom are unsung and now largely forgotten. William Topaz McGonagall and Dundee are now inseparable as far as external perceptions are concerned, rarely to the advantage of the reputation of either. Yet McGonagall was simply the worst (as judged by the standard literary canon) but the best known of an array of worker poets who abounded in Dundee. The city's social character was in the early jute decades shaped by paternalism. Outside the mills, factories and warehouses this often manifested itself in popular celebrations not only of monarchy and successes of British imperial forces overseas – several of which were captured in McGonagall's verses. Also celebrated – and mourned when they died – were some of the city's leading employers, but sources of local pride too were particularly large mills, clocks, chimneys – and Dundee's parks. There was much enthusiasm about the construction of the Tay rail bridges, and relief that the second, more robust version survived. The significance and impact of their mid-twentieth-century counterpart, the Tay road bridge, is assessed in this volume by Jim Phillips (Chapter 10). The course of the bridge's approach roads necessitated the filling in of some of the city's vast dock area; as Rob Duck shows in Chapter 3, this was not the only instance in the twentieth century where human intervention has altered the appearance of the riverside.

Dundee became known and attracted much comment, mainly unfavourable, as a 'women's town', the subject of two essays in the present volume by Sarah Browne and Jim Tomlinson (Chapter 5) and by Valerie Wright (Chapter 6), who looks at the changing nature of female employment in the city. The description of Dundee as a 'women's town' was applied largely on the basis of the sheer numbers of females employed in the staple industries, and also as mill lasses and their weaver counterparts forged a distinctive and hard-edged popular cultural life on the town's streets and in its wynds, closes and tenement blocks. Yet there was also a powerful male presence in the Victorian city, in the vanguard of which were men like the radically inclined preacher the Rev. George Gilfillan, whose adherents, largely drawn from the ranks of the 'respectable' working classes, were united in the fervour of their attachment to liberal values and liberal causes. These included the Liberal Party to which the city's electors remained loyal until the rise of Labour, a topic investigated in Chapter 8 by Billy Kenefick and Kenneth Baxter. Heroes for nineteenth-century workers in Dundee were many and varied, and from abroad included Garibaldi. At home, however, no-one could match Robert Burns in their estimation, not least for the part Burns' poems, songs and the example of his life – rising from 'heaven taught' ploughman to world-ranking poet – played in building their self-esteem. The unveiling of Burns' statue in 1880 attracted the biggest crowd central Dundee had ever seen (the largest in the vicinity was for the opening of Baxter Park, in 1863). The tens of thousands in the audience roared their approval when in his speech for the occasion the Liberal MP Frank Henderson declared that by furnishing the working man with 'the essential dignity of his labour and the possible nobility of his life – the Scottish working man became transformed'. It was from this base that organised labour took much of its strength.

The twentieth century too is probably misunderstood by those looking to Dundee from the outside. The dominant jute industry – along with other substantial employers in shipbuilding and engineering – long maintained a presence in the city. The long-term trend was of decline, however, but the process was slow (and uneven), and the social and political consequences were profound. Whereas a century earlier leading industrialists like Sir David Baxter had been feted by his workpeople and citizens alike, bitterness and bile were directed at employers and successive British governments for their failures, in the first case as wages reduced and jobs became fewer and in the second for alleged inaction. The chapters in this volume by Gordon Stewart (Chapter 2), and Bill Knox and Alan McKinlay (Chapter 11) bear heavily on these issues. Social problems including poor health, in part the legacy of rampant industrialisation in the nineteenth century, abounded, with housing quality and availability being one of the most pressing – although Dundee after the First World War was in the forefront in addressing these challenges. But neither in this nor in many other respects has Dundee managed entirely to shed the burdens of what has in effect been a process of de-industrialisation – and this following several decades when there was little diversification from a core industry in which wages discouraged significant investment in the city's social fabric. There are in Dundee individuals who, and even areas which, feel excluded from the re-fashioning of the city as a northern cultural capital, with teaching, learning and research as one of its major driving forces. Although less true now than was the case twenty years ago, it is argued that they have experienced relatively little direct benefit from the employment generated in academe but also in 'spin-out' bio-technical companies developed since the early 1970s as a result of the work of the University of Dundee's world-ranking Life Sciences research teams in molecular biology, biochemistry and genetics. The leading figures such as Sir Philip Cohen have been and are invariably recruited from beyond Dundee, but on the positive side they are now drawn to the city by its appeal amongst scientists as one of the best places in the UK to live and work, and the indirect benefits they generate for Dundee are immense. But from the later nineteenth century onwards efforts have been made by the town council and other bodies and key individuals to improve the city's social fabric, and enhance its reputation; the work continues. Some attempts have been flawed, although this is easier to see in hindsight, even if in Chapter 4 Charles McKean is inclined to be less forgiving of Dundee's city fathers in their cavalier attitude to the city's heritage.

But remarkably, a place which not much more than a hundred years ago had a higher proportion of its population in manufacturing industries – overwhelmingly coarse textiles – than any other Scottish town of comparable size, has re-invented itself as a major provider of education. Leading the way have been its further education college and two universities. Indeed late in 2010 the University of Dundee was included in a prestigious list of the world's top 200 universities. 'Juteopolis' no more, but Dundee is finding new ways to feature on the global stage. Raucous students have replaced promenading and frequently drunken, singing mill girls on Perth Road on a Saturday nights (although only during term-time; during the summer months the city's west end can seem eerily quiet). Instead of the processing of raw jute that resulted in a relatively low grade workaday textile, Dundee's output is of graduates. Many serve the professions – law, accountancy, teaching, social work, psychology, management and in IT, to list but a few – while others find employment in a host of other fields where graduate skills are required. There is substance in the city's claim to be one of the UK's leading centres of scientific research, notably in the bio-sciences and drug discovery and their application, but also, through the work of the Invergowrie-based Scottish Crop Research Institute, major strides forward have been made in agriculture, horticulture and food processing. There is much more to Dundee's transformation than this of course; the National Health Service is a major provider of state-funded employment, and not only of doctors, dentists and nurses. Albeit on a smaller scale, the role in the city of long-established firms such as Alliance Trust, Low & Bonar, NCR and others has been important. Alliance Trust for example, which dates back to 1873 when Robert Fleming established the Scottish American Investment Trust – the Alliance Trust was formed in 1888 – is the city's only FTSE 100 Share Index company. Based in premises which until the 1920s had been the Temperance Hotel, founded by the nineteenth-century Dundee antiquarian and businessman A. C. Lamb, in 2009 the Trust opened a new custom-built headquarters in the city's Marketgait. If the numbers directly employed are relatively few, the company's reach and impact are global – although, as Jim Tomlinson's opening chapter demonstrates, globalisation and Dundee have long been synonymous, and may even be less significant in 2010 than was the case in 1910.

How this transformation has been achieved is a major focus for this book. Important at this stage is to recognise that such a momentous change has happened. It was not a single moment, its causes were several and progress has been uneven, but the 1980s almost certainly represent a major turning point. It was then that the city finally began both literally and metaphorically to shake off the dust and stour associated with industrial textiles and worked harder to recreate the city not on the basis of the opportunity that had been lost of North Sea oil, but by exploiting brains rather than brawn – and certainly not the child workers who were recruited into the jute trade. Of more than symbolic importance was the return to the city in 1986 of the RRS *Discovery*. An inspired move, the capture of this iconic vessel associated with the exploration of the Antarctic by Captain Scott, Ernest Shackleton and others, that had been launched in Dundee in 1901, helped in providing a means by which the city could value and celebrate – and exploit – its history. With the *Discovery* centre and its splendid if under-sold textile history museum, Verdant Works, opened in 1996, Dundee has established itself as a tourist destination, with around 90,000 people a year attracted to Discovery Point alone. *Discovery* also provided the inspiration for the banner under which the town galvanised and presented itself to the outside world in the following decades, 'City of Discovery', an issue explored by Jim Tomlinson in the book's concluding essay. It is simplifying things to say that Dundee found a future and began to look forward with a greater confidence than had been the case earlier, but there is some truth in the observation. Unrelated to *Discovery* but adding to the sense of resurgence in the city was the success both domestically but even more notably in Europe, of the two professional football clubs, Dundee FC and Dundee United FC in the 1960s and 1980s respectively. In the 1990s there was the series of triumphs in world athletics of the Dundee-born runner Liz McColgan, including her win in the New York marathon in 1991, the year in which she also came first in the 10,000 metres race at the World Championships in Tokyo.

This is not to propose that Dundee has disconnected from its past,

or indeed that recent achievements were based wholly on new foundations. Both of the city's universities, for instance, have roots stretching
back to the era of Victorian manufacturing eminence, with the
University of Dundee being established as University College in 1881
with funding from Mary Ann Baxter, of the Baxter textile dynasty, whilst
soon after its foundation in 1888 the Dundee Technical Institute
(University of Abertay from 1994) was designated an 'industrial
university'. Dundee has long had a major hospital (the first of note in
1798), even if another late-twentieth-century development has been the
closure and conversion for housing of the Victorian, city-centre Royal
Infirmary and the concentration of medical services at the vast Ninewells
complex – effectively a medium-sized bustling town to which streams of
buses travel back and forth incessantly. To the west of the city, Ninewells
– a teaching hospital linked to the University of Dundee – opened in
1974. Nor is the transformation 'complete': economies and the towns of
which they are part are in a more or less constant state of evolution. Of
concern to Dundee in the economic downturn which followed the
global banking failure of 2007–8 was the announcement in March 2009
by NCR, one of the US companies that had been part of the city's post-
1945 economic revival, that it was to cease manufacturing operations in
Dundee. Perhaps even more disconcerting was the threat, in the late
summer of 2010, of company downsizing and even closure with conse-
quent job losses in the computer games sector, which it was anticipated
will be another platform for growth in the post-industrial city. Over 350
digital media businesses with a total turnover of some £185 million are
clustered in and around Dundee and within the Tayside region. Between
them in what has been a decade of remarkable growth, they have created
the equivalent of around 3,400 full-time jobs. It is salutary to note,
however, that this was less than some single jute manufacturing
companies employed in the nineteenth century.

It was to explore all of this in greater detail and to offer readers the
opportunity to understand Dundee at a deeper level that the History of
Dundee project was inaugurated in 1997. At that time a major study of
Glasgow had just been completed, the results of which appeared in two
volumes published by Manchester University Press. Aberdeen's city
council was in the process of launching a history project for Aberdeen,
which again led to the publication of two substantial books, under the
imprint of Tuckwell Press. Prior to these, and subsequently, a number of

histories of Scottish towns have been published, although urban history as a whole as a sub-discipline is less well-developed than in England and, arguably, Ireland. Certainly Dundee was lagging in terms of the attention paid to it by historians, albeit that some seminal studies of aspects of the town's history had appeared from the end of the 1960s and through into the 1970s and 1980s, including the late W. M. Walker's *Juteopolis: Dundee and its Textile Workers, 1885–1923* (1979) and, much more recently, Aileen Black's *Gilfillan of Dundee, 1813–1878: Interpreting Religion and Culture in Mid-Victorian Scotland* (2006). Two volumes so far have resulted from the History of Dundee project: *Victorian Dundee: Image and Realities* (Tuckwell Press, 2000), and *Dundee: Renaissance to Enlightenment* (Dundee University Press, 2009). This, the third volume, brings the story, and the analysis, up to date. The lead for the project as whole was provided by Professor Christopher Whatley, who with Bob Harris and Louise Miskell edited *Victorian Dundee*; Professor Charles McKean led with *Dundee: Renaissance to Enlightenment*; and this twentieth-century project has been initiated, managed and brought to fruition by Professor Jim Tomlinson. As with the previous two volumes, a team of historians was recruited and commissioned to write on topics agreed between them and the editors.

In one sense the publication of this volume marks the end of the History of Dundee project. But the series can also act as a stimulus for further work. We hope that, by having begun the investigation, others will be inspired to dig deeper, to tackle topics we have neglected and even ignored altogether, and to offer alternative explanations to those advanced in these three books. History may be about the past but the discipline itself is continuously developing, with new approaches and theories offering means by which we learn to see the past from new angles and in fresh light. The three books in the series present Dundee's history over a period of some five centuries from the perspective of historians working at the end of the twentieth century and the early part of the twenty-first century. In ten, fifty or even one hundred years from now, the city's past may look very different. Not so much however, we hope, to be unrecognisable from the picture we have portrayed in our three books!

CHAPTER I

Dundee and the World:
De-globalisation, De-industrialisation and Democratisation

Jim Tomlinson

DE-GLOBALISATION

Long a significant international port city, with especially important sea connections with the Baltic, Dundee by the beginning of the twentieth century was a highly 'globalised' city. Despite much twenty-first-century rhetoric about the novelty of global integration, the welfare of Dundonians was far more affected by international economic factors around 1900 than a hundred years later, a consequence of its distinctive economic structure. While Dundee has partaken of some elements of cultural 'globalisation', especially through the impact of modern mass media, in economic terms changes in that structure have made the century one of 'de-globalisation'.

While famous for 'jam, jute and journalism', the economic fortunes of Dundee around the turn of the twentieth century rested upon the jute industry, directly employing half of the local workforce at the industry's peak in the Edwardian period, and indirectly influencing the prosperity of many more.[1] Few if any cities have been so synonymous with one economic sector, so the title 'Juteopolis' has been aptly applied.[2]

Jute manufacturing was characterised by export dependence on worldwide markets, and a raw material entirely imported from Bengal.[3] This meant that the industry's, and much of the city's, short-term fortunes were tied to fluctuations in foreign demand for jute products and variations in raw jute prices. A stock market crash in the USA (such as in 1907),[4] or a sharp rise in jute prices (such as in 1901) could seriously reduce activity.[5] The longer-term trends in the industry were very much

I

affected by foreign, overwhelmingly Indian, competition, and it was this factor that meant the industry's employment reached its all-time high in 1908, and thereafter was in inexorable, if periodically slowed, decline, until it disappeared in 1999.[6]

But while the extreme dependence on jute gave Dundee a particularly exposed place in the international economy, the city shared other characteristics of the national economy, which have led economic historians to emphasise the globalised nature of pre-1914 Britain.[7] Central to the economic welfare of all wage-earning Britons in this period was the behaviour of consumer prices – especially in industries like jute, where money wages were held down by international competition.[8] For Dundonians, like all Britons, the average real wage rose very substantially over the last quarter of the nineteenth century because of the fall in world food prices, as the exploitation of the great temperate food-growing areas of the Antipodes and the Americas, combined with cheap transport by rail and steamship, brought a flood of cheap food.[9] The low-wage earners of Dundee saw the price of the staple food, bread, fall by 50 per cent, at a time when up to 25 per cent of their income was spent on this item, accompanied by major falls in the prices of other important foodstuffs.[10] A contemporary enquiry suggested that a weekly grocery order for a family earning 20 to 25 shillings per week would include four loaves of bread, half a pound of tea, and 3 lb of sugar – all involving imported commodities.[11] From around the turn of the century the global balance of agricultural demand and supply shifted, and prices tended upwards, a process that continued unevenly until the 1930s (with a sharp break in the early 1920s); but when low prices returned after 1929, this was accompanied by mass unemployment, depriving many Dundonians of the wages needed to significantly benefit from the price fall.

Dundee was also highly integrated into the world economy by the substantial outward capital flows, many of them, as elsewhere in Britain, to the countries supplying the influx of cheap imports, where British capital financed land purchase, railways and other infrastructure, which made the low-cost production and transport of food and raw materials possible. Investment Trusts, springing up in Dundee in the 1870s, and primarily concerned with channelling investment funds to North America, were not invented in the city, but under the leadership of Robert Fleming grew rapidly there from that decade, and the Alliance Trust continued as a significant presence into the twenty-first century.[12]

Dundee money (along with Dundee machines, skilled workers and managers) also initially helped to underpin its rival jute industry in Calcutta, beginning in the 1860s. Strikingly, the Dundee Stock Exchange, founded in 1879, was, before 1914, dominated by foreign stocks, in part because the local jute producers were largely private, not public companies.[13] Finally, Dundee participated heavily in the great international emigration flows of Britons (and other Europeans) in the pre-1914 era, an outflow, mainly of men, which helps to explain the lopsided gender demography of the city.[14]

Contrast the city at the end of the twentieth century, by which time the biggest employers in Dundee were the local National Health Trust, above all based in the teaching hospital at Ninewells; the universities (Dundee and Abertay), and the City Council. The largest private sector employers were Tesco, followed by NCR and D.C. Thomson.[15] At the time of the 2001 census, sectoral breakdown of employment gave the proportions of the city's workforce in health and social work as 16 per cent, education as 9 per cent and public administration as 6 per cent (manufacturing was 16 per cent).[16] Alongside NCR there is multinational manufacturing employment in companies such as Michelin, alongside a considerable number of small, local manufacturing companies, but in total 'global' manufacturing is very much a minor part of total employment.

By 2001 public sector employment predominated, so that Dundee's economic fate was largely determined by tax and spending decisions taken in London and Edinburgh. The contrast with the beginning of the twentieth century is stark. Direct comparison of public sector employment is not possible, but at the census in 1901, of a total employed population of 84,000, 736 were recorded as working in 'public service' with a further 347 in 'Gas, water, electricity and sanitary service'. It is likely that a significant proportion of the 2,225 denoted 'Professional' were also public sector workers (teachers and doctors). But if we make the extreme assumption that all of those in this category were employed in the public sector, we are still left with a total public sector employment under these three categories combined of 3,300, which is less than 4 per cent of the total of those employed.[17] (The national figure for 1900, including both local and central government, but excluding the armed forces, was 4.8 per cent.)[18]

Not only was state employment in 1900 very limited, so also was state expenditure, before the Liberals after 1906 inaugurated the rise of spending on welfare in all its forms. Today, therefore, Dundee's citizens are much more insulated from the vagaries of the international economy. Of course, since 1900 the expansion of education combined with greater longevity has meant for most people a much longer period in their life span when they are not in receipt of employment income, and have to rely on other sources. This shift has underpinned the rise of individual and collective (such as pension fund) holdings of financial assets, so that exposure to international fluctuations in asset markets is much more substantial today. In the early 1900s the savings of Dundonians were minimal; in 1901 29.5 per cent of the population had an account with Dundee Savings Bank, but of this minority, fewer than half had more than £10 (eight to ten weeks' wages for an average worker.)[19] On the other hand, for most people today, the exposure to asset price fluctuations is most evident in the price of housing, although Dundee has been notably slow to be converted to a 'property-owning democracy', with only just over a half of households being home-owners in 2001.[20] In sum, developments in British society in general, and Dundee in particular, have meant that, on balance, the economic fortunes of its citizens are linked much more to domestic political processes, and much less to events elsewhere in the world, than was the case a hundred years ago.

DE-INDUSTRIALISATION AND DEMOCRATISATION

This process of de-globalisation has also been a process of de-industrialisation, though the latter was far from a simple tale of the loss of jute. Dundee, like Scotland, had a successful period from the 1940s to the 1960s of attracting multinational manufacturing companies, successfully replacing much of the employment that had been lost in jute.[21] So the really striking de-industrialisation of the area was a feature of the years from 1970 onwards, especially when the 'Thatcher slump' after 1979 combined to drive jute into its final phase of decline, while speeding up the retreat of the multinationals.

Responding to the decline of jute is inevitably a large part of the history of twentieth-century Dundee. We might divide that response very crudely into three periods. While the industry's output and employment peaked before the First World War, the first serious decline was in the inter-war years, especially in the 1930s, when there was almost no policy response, and the city experienced unemployment levels unmatched by any large urban area in Britain.[22] From the Second World War down to the end of the 1960s, within a protected market, the decline was managed quite successfully, with, as noted above, jute job losses substantially offset by employment growth elsewhere in the city's economy, especially in multinationals.[23] From the 1970s Dundee suffered an exaggerated form of the de-industrialisation widespread across Britain, with a further slump in the early 1990s; jute underwent accelerated decline, and the multinationals contracted fast, and it was not until the mid-1990s, with jute now all but gone, that a degree of prosperity returned. This was very much aided by the long national economic upswing of 1992–2008, though by now the population had shrunk from its 1971 peak.

The de-globalisation and de-industrialisation of Dundee have coincided with a process of democratisation – the extension of the parliamentary franchise to all adults (men in 1918, women in 1928) and the struggle of parties, new and old, to operate within that new electoral environment. How did the parties respond to the decline of jute, which was the key issue for much of the century? At the famous by-election of 1908, which saw Churchill elected in Dundee, the three main political parties give three distinct responses to that already-perceived decline, all with long-term ramifications. Churchill won on a Liberal platform of the continuation of free trade.[24] This policy had been associated with the 'cheap loaf' slogan in the crucial general election of 1906, but while this message still had resonance, it was no longer quite as compelling in the face of the global reversal in commodity price trends. Two days before the Dundee election, the Liberal government's budget had sought to bolster the free trade case partly by cutting sugar duties (thus cheapening one of the few foodstuffs still not subject to free importation, and one which had substantial symbolic significance). More important in the long run was the other major budgetary measure, the introduction of old age pensions. Albeit initially on a very frugal scale, this heralded the huge increase in public spending on social security which increasingly through the twentieth century was to protect the population against the vagaries of international markets. Politically crucial for the Liberal cause was the demonstration that state welfare could be funded without recourse to tariffs.

Churchill's Unionist opponent in 1908 was Sir George Baxter, a linen and jute baron who stood on a protectionist platform, though perhaps wisely he focused his protectionist demands on Germany, rather than India, an Empire country against which it would be politically very difficult to impose protection.[25] An alternative strategy to protection against Indian jute manufacturers was to seek a duty on Indian exports of raw jute going to non-Empire countries, but this too ran up against the complexities of Britain's 'imperial mission' in India.[26]

The conversion of many of Britain's capitalists to protectionism was commonplace in this period.[27] In Dundee there had been such calls as far back as the 1870s, and there was strong support by the time of the Tariff Commission in the early 1900s.[28] (D.C. Thomson also made a rare personal intervention on this matter.[29]) But the jute employers were far from unanimous on the issue, certainly before the 1930s. While Baxter stood on a protectionist platform in 1908, James Caird, another important local jute proprietor, was a key financial backer of free trade propaganda.[30] Despite the strong political pressure for protection, the disastrous state of the industry in the 1930s, and the introduction of general protection in Britain after 1931, jute remained unprotected until 1939, when Jute Control was introduced as a wartime measure. Politically, Dundee never mattered enough to overcome the objections to using tariffs against a poor Empire country which in the 1930s was always on the verge of revolt against British rule. It was only the strategic necessities of war that made protection possible. Following this, the new social settlement of the 1940s, with its emphasis on full employment, made it impossible for government to quickly take this protection away in an area which had suffered so grievously from the absence of jobs in the 1930s. As a result, protection was only slowly reduced down to the 1970s, and subject to a satisfactory local employment situation; a situation, as already noted, that was greatly aided by the influx of multinationals, very much encouraged by both national and local government.[31]

The third political party in 1908, Labour, faced the problem of wanting to defend jute workers' jobs and wages, but on the other hand, and in the name of international solidarity, not wanting to do so at the expense of Indian workers. The proposed solution to this conundrum was better conditions for Indians, through imposition of the Factory Acts in the subcontinent, or, later, as unions argued in the 1920s and 1930s, by the strengthening of Indian trade unions and use of the International Labour Organization to raise labour standards.[32] Strikingly, this Utopian programme had long-term resonance on the Left in Dundee, and can be found, for example, in the platform of the Dundee Communist Party, who in 1945 anticipated that a soon to be independent India would rapidly raise Indian wage levels such as to end low-wage competition with Dundee.[33] This, of course, did not happen, and eventually the full force of Indian competition, along with competition from synthetic fibres like polypropylene, saw the end of Dundee jute in the 1990s.

When the then Liberal Churchill won Dundee in 1908 he joined a pioneer Labour MP in what was, until 1950, a dual-member constituency. The big electoral story of the next century was going to be the decline of the Liberals (Churchill lost his seat in 1922) and the rise of Labour in a two-party system with Conservatives, until the latter in turn gave way to the rise of the SNP, initially in the 1970s and decisively in the 1990s. This simple story has of course to be qualified. Churchill lost to Edwin Scrymgeour as well as the official Labour candidate in 1922. Scrymgeour had equivocal Labour support, but is above all to be remembered as Britain's only ever Prohibitionist MP. He was a one-off, though Prohibitionism was a serious political force in 1920s Dundee, receiving strong support both from churches and a large number of newly enfranchised women. There were three votes on Prohibition in the 1920s, and in all three cases a substantial minority voted for a ban.[34]

While much of the history of twentieth-century politics in Dundee could be written around the rise and consolidation of Labour, there was a major interregnum – from Labour's disastrous election of 1931, when a Conservative and Liberal were elected for Dundee, until the Labour landslide of 1945. This interregnum was common to much of Britain, but Dundee was atypical in that this period provided a space for the Communist Party, which from the 1920s until the 1960s was a significant force in city politics. This was above all the consequence of the unemployment crisis, in which the failure of mainstream parties to offer solutions led to support for the CP, which offered unqualified defence of the conditions of the unemployed. William Gallacher stood as candidate for the party in 1922 and 1923, Bob Stewart in 1924, 1929 and 1931, and on the last of these occasions won 10,264 votes. Dundee's inter-war politics were extremely complex, especially in 1931, at which time the Communists were virulently hostile to Labour, branding the party 'social fascists', and the divide in the Left vote between Labour and the Communists helped to deliver the seat to a Conservative and a Liberal.[35]

In the 1930s the party's activity was most evident in the National Unemployed Workers' Movement, and this Movement and other Communist-dominated organisations were associated with numerous outbreaks of unrest in the 1930s.[36] The CP was also heavily involved in the squatting campaign immediately after the war. In 1945 no Communist candidate stood against John Strachey, but thereafter down to the 1960s their candidate gained between 1,000 and 1,500 votes in Dundee West, with familial memories of unemployment crucial in this prolonged pattern of support.[37] The last CP candidate stood in 1987, giving the city probably an unrivalled record for the number of general elections contested by Communist candidates.[38] Dundee also had a notable woman Communist, Mary Brooksbank, though her relationship with the party was to say the least uneasy, largely because of its difficulties with gender politics, and the priority she wanted to accord to reducing household poverty.[39]

While the role of the Communist Party marks out a distinctive part of the Left's history in the city, the trajectory of the Labour Party is in many respects reflective of the national picture. The city (and Scotland's) first Labour MP, Alexander Wilkie, elected in 1906, was a solid, Lib-Lab trade unionist.[40] After 1922 his successor was the internationalist intellectual E.D. Morel, famous for his exposure of the atrocities of Belgian rule in the Congo (and who, until his suicide in 1924, had a very unhappy relationship with his fellow MP, Scrymgeour).[41] He was succeeded by the solid, middle-of-the-road Tom Johnston, later a highly effective Secretary of State for Scotland after 1941, and important in devising the regional policies which helped sustain Dundee's employment after the war.[42] After 1945 Dundee's two Labour MPs included John Strachey, intellectual inter-war Marxist, and post-war Minister of Food. He, along with George Thomson, Minister in the Wilson government 1964–70, were the last of Labour's twentieth-century MPs for Dundee of national stature, and in later years the local Labour Party ethos was against London intellectuals being adopted in Scottish seats.

The rise of the SNP in the last quarter of the twentieth century in part followed a pattern common across Scotland, though it was less usual in 'post-industrial' cities like Dundee than in rural and small towns areas away from the central belt. The rise of the SNP was mirrored by the collapse of support for Scottish conservatism. Crucial to this seems to have been the process of de-industrialisation from the 1970s, and the perception that London governments, especially under Mrs Thatcher after 1979, were little attuned to Scottish concerns about the consequences of this process.[43] Alienation from the Conservatives allowed the SNP to garner the anti-Labour vote, though its policies reflected the realisation that the consensus in Scotland is broadly social democratic, and that a wholly conservative opposition to Labour would not flourish. From the 1990s this ideological positioning led to the SNP eating into the Labour vote.

Politics is not just about elections. Women gained few elected posts in Dundee until late in the century, but behind the scenes in the political parties, and in their own political organisations, they played a powerful role.[44] (See Sarah Browne and Jim Tomlinson, 'A Women's Town? Dundee Women on the Public Stage', Chapter 5 below.) Looking at the sociology of Dundee politics, we can note that the rise of Labour was unsurprising in such an overwhelmingly working-class town. But politics can never helpfully be reduced to sociology. Dundee may have been a working-class city, but even when Labour consolidated its parliamentary position from 1945, its share of the vote hovered around the 55 per cent mark; a rough calculation suggests that this means that a third of Dundee's working class consistently voted Conservative down to the 1970s. We have no direct evidence on what shaped this affiliation in the city, though nationally we know that such attitudes as deference to those seen as traditional rulers played some part; but more specifically, what seems to be crucial is the Conservatives' ability to construct an appealing political message embracing family, monarchy and empire, while also pursuing significant expansions of welfare provision aimed at garnering working-class votes.[45]

Religion has played some part in shaping political allegiance, with clear evidence in the 1960s of the links between adherence to the Church of Scotland and Conservative voting, and conversely Roman Catholicism and Labour voting, which were probably long entrenched.[46] However, religious adherence has declined sharply since the 1960s, most obviously evident in the recycling of many of the city's churches into secular uses.[47]

Ethnicity has played a relatively small political role in twentieth-century Dundee, given the very small ethnic minority population. Dundee has not attracted a significant number of immigrants. Like all port cities, there has probably been a little-noticed Black and Asian population present for many years, and small numbers of new Commonwealth migrants have come to the city in the post-war period, but overall jute's decline was too early to attract large numbers of immigrants into the industry, as occurred, for example, in cotton.[48] As a result the ethnic minority population of the city remained small, under 4 per cent at the time of the 2001 census. As is the case for Scotland as a whole, the biggest immigrant group is English, though recently there has been an influx of East Europeans, especially from Poland.[49]

Labour voting has traditionally been closely associated with trade unionism. With its main industrial employment dominated by women for much of the century, and women's lower likelihood of trade union membership, Dundee never had the union strength of other major industrial cities. The story of jute trade unionism is of constant challenges to its effectiveness, not least those arising from the long-term decline of the industry.[50] In the years before de-industrialisation much of the local trade union dynamism came from (male) engineers in shipbuilding and engineering, and the influx of multinationals after 1945 on balance strengthened trade unionism in the city.[51] In recent years, in line with patterns elsewhere in Britain, unions have been strongest in the public sector, and this has been paralleled by the 'de-industrialisation' of the Labour Party, now also dominated by public sector workers.

On the right of the political spectrum, the well-known desertion of Liberal ranks by employers joining the Unionists is seen in Dundee, with many of the major local employers giving up their Liberal allegiance around the end of the nineteenth century. But this did not mean that they then played a very prominent role in local Conservative politics. For example, while there were some candidatures, no jute baron was ever elected to Parliament under the Conservative flag. Conservative politics on the City Council after 1918, as in much of urban Britain, was dominated by the 'shopocracy': small businessmen and *petits bourgeois*, with a key agenda of keeping the rates low. So the jute employers' local political presence declined as their industry contracted, and their interests became less and less tied to the city.[52] As individuals they had long since invested abroad, but after the First World War the creation of large, merged firms, especially Jute Industries (1920) and Low and Bonar (1924), meant the arrival of a more anonymous, corporate capitalism, opening the way for these 'jute' firms to increasingly spread their interests well outside the city, though this process does not reach its apogee until well after 1945, and as late as the mid-1960s Jute Industries' interests were still largely confined to textiles and textile products.[53] This diversification of economic interests, coupled with an inter-war Conservative politics now focused on capturing the votes of the newly enfranchised workers, discouraged the jute employers from an overt political role in the city, though, unsurprisingly, they long remained highly active on issues directly affecting their industry, such as discouraging competition for 'their' labour from multinationals in the 1940s and 1950s, or fighting for the retention of protection from the 1940s to the 1970s.[54] Indeed, we should not exaggerate the discontinuities: two of the 'Three Wise Men' who negotiated the decline of the industry in the post-war years were from old jute families, albeit now involved in the diversifying giants of the industry, namely William Walker, of Jute Industries and Hugh Bonar, of Low and Bonar.[55]

The notion of Dundee as a radical city is further qualified by the pattern of local government politics. The story prior to 1914 has been analysed in detail by John Kemp, who argues that even before the First World War there was a significant shift to the left.[56] But after the war such a shift was limited as, fighting under a 'Moderate' banner, Conservative forces on the city council, as in Westminster elections after 1931, scored considerable successes, with Labour in the inter-war period only having a majority for one year, 1936–37.[57] Local politics in these years was characterised by great bitterness, where the Conservative (Moderate) desire to hold local rate spending down was at odds with claims for adequate unemployment relief, an issue that retained a local component in the inter-war years, as the Poor Law and its successors continued to support those unemployed who were excluded from National Insurance benefits. Much of inter-war local politics was defined by these demands for adequate relief from mass unemployment on the one hand, set against the shrinkage of the local rate base brought out by depression, and the belief that low rates were part of the necessary route to recovery.[58]

After the Second World War Labour won control of the council in 1946, but did not consolidate its position as the dominant party until 1954, after which it held sway, with interruptions, to the end of the century. The trajectory of local Labour politics since 1945 broadly followed the national pattern, with 'moderate' Labour dominating down to the late 1970s/early 1980s, when a new, more left-wing tendency emerged. In Dundee this became especially associated with the figure of George Galloway, never a Councillor, but full-time organiser of the city Labour Party from 1977 to 1983.[59] Like other 'New Urban Left' Labour councils, Dundee's came into conflict with Thatcher's government, especially over housing (see below), but also on international issues. Most notable here was the twinning of the city with Nablus, a Palestinian town on the West Bank, a political gesture which sharply divided the city. This shift to the Left was short-lived, and from the mid-1980s, like the national party, Labour in Dundee eschewed previous radicalism and moved, albeit with qualifications, in a New Labour direction.

Over the century, across Britain, local government has lost power to the central state, though of course in Dundee that has meant a shift to a complex combination of Edinburgh's and London's jurisdiction. One consequence of this has been a shift in the major issues addressed by local politics. Before the First World War the broad area of social policy was largely a local matter, but from the Liberal reforms of the 1906 government onwards, much of this responsibility passed incrementally to the centre. However, a major exception to this, down to the very last decades of the twentieth century, was housing, and this was a key issue in Dundee throughout the century.[60]

HOUSING AND URBAN DEVELOPMENT

The poor condition of Dundee housing was already notorious before 1914, not least from the famous Dundee Social Union *Report* of 1905. This found, in a survey of 6,400 households, that only 31 per cent had the use of a toilet shared by fewer than twelve people, and that 72 per cent of the population lived in houses of one or two bedrooms.[61] Before 1914 the powers of local authorities in housing provision were extremely limited, 'largely an extension of sanitation legislation of the nineteenth century', and focused mainly on demolition.[62] But the war brought major changes, not least because of extensive unrest, including rent strikes, which hit much of urban Scotland, including Dundee, in 1915.[63] The Addison Act of 1919 for the first time provided central government subsidies for local authority building, and in Dundee (and under Moderate councils) a total of 8,177 houses was built in the inter-war period under this and successor Acts. Subsidies were also given to private housing, albeit on a much smaller scale. Much of this building was of high quality, but most was also beyond the means of many working-class Dundonians, though poorer tenants benefited from some of the slum clearance schemes.[64]

In the immediate post-1945 period there was a crash programme of housing construction which peaked in 1957, in which year 1,735 council houses were built, though the quality of these dwellings was often below pre-1939 standards. A further (and final) burst of council house building followed in the late 1960s, but from the mid-1970s, with sharp declines in capital spending finance by central government, building more or less ended. While battles over the balance between rent subsidies and ratepayer interests continued in these years, the balance for the time being had swung the rent-payers' way.[65]

Local authority provision up to the 1960s mainly took the form of new estates established around the edges of the city. This responded to the perceived need to move people out of the city centre slums, but also meant long travel distances to work for many, although this was mitigated to a degree by the establishment of 'new' industries around the outer ring road (the Kingsway), especially from the 1940s. The 1960s saw a shift in emphasis to building high-rise accommodation close to the city centre. This was seen as a cost-effective way of providing better-quality accommodation, closer to city centre employment and leisure activities. The results of this were highly controversial, with high-rise blocks quickly gaining notoriety for poor quality and as concentrations of fragmented and disrupted families. From a local authority point of view such buildings proved expensive to construct and especially to maintain, and by the 1980s they were beginning to be taken down, especially those located north of the Kingsway.

From the First World War onwards, central government allowed and to a substantial extent financed the expansion of local authority housing. Down to the 1980s there remained significant local autonomy in the policies pursued at local level, so, as noted above, in places like Dundee a central part of local politics was a slugging match between Left and Right over the degree of subsidisation of council housing. This culmi-nated in the fruitless resistance to the housing reforms of the Thatcher government, which in Dundee, as elsewhere, characterised the early 1980s.[66] So 'the 1980s saw a complete turnaround in relationships. Central Government steadily increased its influence over local authorities, paralyzing their power to act autonomously and crushing their independence in order to reduce public expenditure.'[67] From the 1980s through 'Right-to Buy' and the structure of incentives governing central government support for local housing activity, the role of local authorities in housing provision diminished. Having peaked at owning over 70 per cent of the local housing stock in the 1980s, in the last two decades of the century the local authority, urged on by central government, was seeking to shift much of that stock to housing associations, though tenants' views on such matters were very mixed.[68] Also, given continuing problems with the rates (council tax) base, the city council was keen to encourage the expansion of accommodation for the prosperous, rather than simply being the landlord of an increasingly residual housing stock. By 2000 a key notion of much twentieth-century British politics, that local government would have a prime responsibility for housing provision, had suffered major retreat. In Dundee, as elsewhere in Britain, the two major recessions of the early 1980s and 1990s fell disproportionately on public sector housing tenants, emphasising the close links between this tenure and labour market disadvantage.[69]

The high-rise building of the 1960s was not just an episode in housing policy, but also part of a broader, strident drive for 'modernisation' in that era, which extended to the physical structure of whole of the centre of city. Plans for radical reconstruction of the city's core can be dated back to before the First World War in the work of James Thomson.[70] (See Charles McKean, '"Beautifying and Improving the City": The Pursuit of a Monumental Dundee during the Twentieth Century', Chapter 4 below.) Such ideas were revived in the 1940s, a great decade of planning, leading eventually to both *Tay Valley Plan* of 1950 and the 1952 *Survey and Plan* of Dobson Chapman and partners. The former envisaged large-scale decanting of Dundee's population from the centre to surrounding areas, while the latter believed a significant rehousing could take place within the city centre by high-rise construction.[71] Initially such plans had little impact on actions, but in the 1960s a number of forces came together to bring about a radical redevelopment of much of the city centre. Belief in 'comprehensive redevelopment' was now joined with resources to pursue this goal, at the same time as money became available for the long-desired construction of the road bridge across the Tay. (See Jim Phillips, 'The "Retreat" to Scotland: The Tay Road Bridge and Dundee's post-1945 Development',

Chapter 10 below.) The bridge was brought directly into the city centre, and much of the Victorian as well as earlier building legacy was knocked down, to be replaced by a road-dominated environment and a massive new shopping centre at the Wellgate.

On aesthetic grounds it is difficult not to agree with the lamentations of those who see the 1960s rebuilding as the culmination of a century of problematic 'modernisation', which destroyed much of the city's architectural heritage.[72] But if the primary task of the historian is to understand rather than stand in judgement, we need to see how this development was perceived at the time. Commenting upon it in retrospect, on the occasion of the conviction of local politicians and developers for the corruption which accompanied it, the *Courier* noted that 'most councillors saw the period as a once-in-a-lifetime opportunity to act out their role as architects for the common good'. The result was that 'Dundee has more council houses and fewer slums per head of the population than almost any city in Britain. And in the Wellgate it has a shopping centre admired throughout the world and which has been a roaring success from the day it first opened its doors.'[73]

This analysis (from a Conservative newspaper), captures something of the 'modernising' spirit of the 1960s, which in Dundee envisaged an escape from a world of 'Dark Satanic Mills' to one of planned advance, involving new buildings and infrastructure and new housing, the whole area to be integrated by road travel, the latter seen as a source of both personal freedom and efficient transport. In the early twenty-first century this is a world view few sympathise with, but it was one which was widely shared across Britain at the time, though perhaps particularly strongly in Dundee, where the physical legacy of 'Juteopolis' was so much disparaged.

POVERTY

Understanding past world views is perhaps equally challenging when we turn to the issue of poverty in Dundee. The Social Union report of 1905, whose housing analysis we have already noted, was also a significant milestone in the public understanding of poverty. It may be set alongside the work of Booth in London and Rowntree in York as an element in the development of a new sense of poverty, stimulated by a range of ideological and political shifts in late-Victorian and Edwardian Britain.[74]

The report's empirical material includes detailed budgets for a (non-random) sample of working-class families, and of wage levels in the city. This evidence reinforces other material which shows Dundee as a low-income city, above all because of the wage level in jute.[75] Widespread poverty was, then, an inescapable result of being a 'one-industry city', where that industry generated largely low-paying jobs. Of course, poverty is never that simple. We have already stressed that prices as well as wages determine real incomes, and in Dundee these were much affected by internationally determined food prices. Also important were rents, which commonly absorbed around 12 per cent of working-class budgets, a proportion which helps us understand why housing was such a central issue in Dundee life. Beyond issues of the cost of living is that of household structure; poverty varies a great deal with how many wage-earners and dependants live in a household and share income and expenditure. One of the most striking tables in the 1905 report is that which shows how few households conformed to the stereotypical male bread-winner, dependent wife and children model. Only 25 per cent fit this pattern, whereas there are, for example, 156 households of two working women with no dependents, and twenty-six of three working women, making up about 6 per cent of the sample.[76] So while wages for women in jute were low, if their recipients were unmarried, they might live together in multiple-earning households, and thereby enjoy a degree of 'affluence', which, as always, their 'betters' were wont to regard as leading to unseemly extravagance in both consumption and behaviour.[77] More broadly, we need to note the prevalence of multi-income households of various types in Dundee, often, unsurprisingly, married couples with two earners; despite local lore to the contrary, there is no evidence of a significant number of 'kettle-boilers', that is, men who stayed at home doing domestic tasks while their wives worked. Dundee may have been a pioneer of the 'dual-income household'; it was not a pioneer in being populated by 'the new man'.

While the DSU Report offers compelling data on working-class economic life, it offers little in the way of remedies for poverty.[78] Contemporary public discourse tended to focus upon problems of social administration, rather than economics, in discussing poverty.[79] Increasingly it was recognised that labour markets were crucial to the generation of poverty (and this meant at least a partial shift away from perceiving poverty as a consequence of individual failings), but correction of faults in such markets was largely seen as an administrative task, rather than one requiring economic reform. Hence, for example, the Edwardian focus on labour exchanges.[80] Parallel to this was the campaign against 'sweating', that is, very low wages, and advocacy of minimum wages in particular trades. But a Trade Board, the body set up to administer such a minimum wage, was not established in jute until October 1918, and was much resented by the employers.[81] It continued in existence down to the 1960s, but its impact on wage levels was probably slight, especially after the defeat of a strike against cuts in 1923.[82]

Relief of the unemployed was reliant upon the Poor Law until the National Insurance Act of 1911 introduced a new national scheme for workers especially prone to unemployment in the trade cycle. But what was not envisaged in this legislation was chronic, long-term unemployment, precisely the problem to be encountered in many of the 'staple' trades, including jute, after the collapse of the post-war boom in 1920/21, and even more disastrously in the slump from 1929. This unemployment, and its consequences, constitute a key element in the history of twentieth-century Dundee, not only because it was the dominant feature of city life for most of the 1920s and 1930s, but also because memories of it shaped the politics of the city until well into the post-war period.[83]

National Insurance against unemployment failed to cope with the long-term joblessness of the inter-war period, and recourse had to be had to all sorts of other mechanisms to relieve the unemployed, including the Poor Law and its successors in the 1930s. But National Insurance data provides the basis for the most useful estimates of the scale of the problem. These figures record 4,119 unemployed jute workers in 1924, rising to 13,639 in 1930, and reaching a peak of 18,122 in 1931.[84] Unemployment was not, of course, confined to jute, and was very serious in the textile machinery and shipbuilding trades, the other big areas of manual employment in the city. Recorded unemployment reached 50 per cent in 1931 and 1932, but Eastham suggests that the real level of idleness may have reached 70 per cent because of widespread short-time working. In jute the gender impact of this unemployment was complicated by the fact that weak demand for labour there tended to favour a move towards higher levels of male employment, as night shift systems were introduced, from which women were barred.[85] (See Valerie Wright, 'Juteopolis and After: Women and Work in Twentieth-Century Dundee',

Chapter 6 below.) Women's liability to unemployment is obscured by the operations of the Anomalies Regulations Act of 1931, which made it harder for insured unemployed married women to claim benefit, and therefore led to undercounting.[86]

Falling food prices in the 1930s offered little relief to the unemployed, many of whom endured reductions in benefit levels from the public expenditure cuts of 1931, and the Public Assistance scales introduced in 1935. We do not have the detailed investigations for the city in the 1930s that the DSU produced in 1905, but it is difficult to believe that the consequences of unemployment on poverty and ill-health did not match that common in other high unemployment areas of the country.[87]

The Second World War radically altered local labour market conditions. Men were mobilised or found civilian employment readily available; for women many new job opportunities opened up in munitions. In jute, demand for the products of the industry stimulated by the war, and the introduction of protection under the Jute Control of 1939, transformed the employment position. By 1943 the industry could not find the controlled levels of labour it was allowed under wartime 'concentration'.[88]

The war inaugurated twentieth-century Dundee's closest approach to an economic 'golden age', which was to last down to the end of the 1960s. In 1950 Rowntree's last survey of York found a huge fall in poverty in the city since 1931, overwhelmingly due to full employment. While his precise estimates have been qualified, the general point stands and applies equally to Dundee; it was full employment, much more than the direct effects of the welfare state reforms of the Attlee government, that underpinned popular prosperity in the 1950s and 1960s.[89] Of course, poverty was not abolished in these years; there were plenty of 'forgotten Dundonians' to match the 'Forgotten Englishmen',[90] especially amongst the elderly.[91] But prosperity for the working masses there undoubtedly was, especially when contrasted with the disasters of the 1920s and 1930s. As already noted, the labour market underpinnings of this prosperity came from the slowing of jute's decline by protection and innovation in the industry, coupled with the influx of multinationals, which meant that in the 1950s and 1960s unemployment in Dundee was below the Scottish average. The sense of recent prosperity, but also impending problems, is brought out by comments made by the President of the local Chamber of Commerce in 1970: 'Over the last ten years, with the exception of one or two periods, there has been a general expansion in the area and if we may, without complacency, congratulate ourselves a little, it was a story of remarkable success . . . However, the situation today is less encouraging.'[92]

These concerns were fully justified, with unemployment rising significantly over the next decade, then shooting up from 1979. By September 1979 the official rate had reached 9 per cent, before peaking at 18 per cent in 1991.[93] But increasingly this official figure underestimated the real rate of joblessness, and this problem, and its links to de-industrialisation, are returned to in the concluding chapter below. Whatever data are used, the early 1990s do seem to represent a nadir in Dundee's fortunes, though the patterns were not radically different from those in much of Scotland. An indicative analysis of social security claimants in the mid-1990s found 35 per cent of households in Dundee in receipt of benefit, compared with a national average of 33 per cent, and with Glasgow at 52 per cent, using the unitary authorities as the unit of analysis. Other data on poverty levels suggest a similar story of a city facing major problems of deprivation, albeit by most measures less severe than some areas of greater Glasgow.[94]

Alterations in labour market conditions cannot explain all fluctuations in popular welfare. Changing family structures, demographic shifts and benefit regimes interact with such conditions to produce a complex picture of 'social exclusion', a term which itself is freighted with all sorts of historical twists and turns in understanding what for most of the twentieth century was known as the problem of poverty. Nevertheless, the basis on which, if at all, access can be gained to that market remains the single most powerful determinant of economic prosperity. At the beginning of the twentieth century Dundee employment for the mass of people was characterised by very high levels of insecurity, but a labour market in which some employment, even for the most minimally skilled, was readily available most of the time. At the end of the twentieth century, the expansion of the state, as both direct employer and provider of income, has greatly reduced income insecurity, but the labour market is much harder on those unable to adapt to its requirements and norms.[95] Wages fluctuate much less than before 1913, and the state provides a floor below which incomes cannot fall, but for most people access to the labour market remains central to well-being.

A CENTURY OF PROGRESS?

Dundee at the end of the twentieth century was cleaner and healthier than in 1900, its inhabitants more prosperous, better-housed and better-educated, and they lived much longer (not least because of the dramatic fall in infant mortality). Their livelihoods were more secure and less threatened by external events, with the rise of the state a key determinant of that outcome. That rise of the state can plausibly be seen as a consequence of the politics of democratisation, though conversely it has undoubtedly involved a reduction of *local* democratic control, as government has become more centralised in Edinburgh and London. In a city like Dundee this decline in local autonomy may well be seen as a cultural and social loss, though the nationalisation of public finance has undoubtedly benefited a city with a perpetual fiscal problem.

In a broader sense we can see 'cultural' democratisation leading to relations between the sexes, the generations and social classes becoming notably less hierarchical. Aided by the more liberal social attitudes generally prevalent in an expanding higher education system, deference and prejudice are much less features of everyday life than they were when the twentieth century began.

While the story of the city since 1900 does not fit into any simple story of progress, it would be perverse to suggest that, on most indicators of economic and social well-being, the mass of inhabitants of the city have not seen major improvements. In the round, we might see this result as a consequence of an imperfect but effective response from a democratised polity to the profound late twentieth-century challenges of de-globalisation and de-industrialisation, which together have been the major forces shaping the city's recent history.

ACKNOWLEDGEMENTS

I am grateful to Jim Phillips, George Peden and Chris Whatley for comments on earlier drafts of this chapter.

NOTES

1. DUA, KLoc/033: O. Graham, 'The Dundee jute industry 1828–1928' (unpublished manuscript, Longforgan, 1929). Another 'globalised' industry was whaling, though by

the early 1900s it was in its last phase, destined to disappear from the First World War: G. Jackson, *The British Whaling Trade* (London, 1978), pp. 130–40.

2. D. Reeder and R. Rodger, 'Industrialization and the city economy' in M. Daunton (ed.), *The Cambridge Urban History of Britain*, vol. 3: *1840–1950* (Cambridge, 2000), pp. 564–70.

3. In 1900 the industry exported 70 per cent of its output, though this had fallen to around 30 per cent by 1931: W.S. Howe, *The Dundee Textile Industry 1960–1977: Decline and Diversification* (Aberdeen, 1981), p. 13; J. Eastham, 'An economic survey of present day Dundee' in R. Mackie (ed.), *A Scientific Survey of Dundee and District* (Dundee, British Association, 1939), p. 97.

4. Dundee's exports of piece goods to the USA fell from 28.1 million yards in the first four months of 1907 to 17.7 million in the same period of 1908 – a fall of almost 40 per cent: 'Monthly Trade Supplement', *Economist* 66 (May 1908), p. 13.

5. B. Lenman, C. Lythe and E. Gauldie, *Dundee and its Textile Industry, 1850–1914* (Dundee, Abertay Historical Society, 1969), ch. 2.

6. G. Stewart, *Jute and Empire* (Manchester, 1998); *Courier*, 26 June 1999.

7. M. Daunton, 'Britain and globalization since 1850: I. Creating a global order, 1850–1914', *Transactions of the Royal Historical Society* 16 (2006), pp. 1–38.

8. The jute employers, though, clearly used the 'low wage competition' argument in an exaggerated fashion in bargaining with Dundee workers: T. Cox, 'Rationalisation and Resistance: The Imperial Jute Industries of Dundee and Calcutta, 1930–1940' (unpublished Fellowship dissertation, Trinity College, Cambridge, 1997), pp. viii–ix.

9. C. Feinstein, 'What really happened to real wages? Trends in wages, prices, and productivity in the United Kingdom, 1880–1913', *Economic History Review* 58 (1990), pp. 329–55; J. Tomlinson, 'The de-globalization of Dundee circa 1900–2000', *Journal of Scottish Historical Studies* 29 (2009), pp. 123–40.

10. DSU, *Report on Housing and Industrial Conditions and Medical Inspection of School Children* (Dundee, 1905), ch. 2; F. Crouzet, *The Victorian Economy* (London, 1982), p. 167.

11. DUA, MS 134: D. Lennox, 'Working Class Life in Dundee for 25 years: 1878 to 1903' (unpublished manuscript, 1928), Table 187.

12. B. Lenman and K. Donaldson, 'Partners' incomes, investment and diversification in the Scottish linen area 1850–1921', *Business History* 13 (1971), pp. 1–18; C. Schmit, 'The nature and dimensions of Scottish foreign investment, 1860–1914', *Business History* 39 (1997), pp. 42–68. For an important case study see Claire Swan, *Scottish Cowboys and the Dundee Investors* (Dundee, Abertay Historical Society, 2004); J. Gilbert, *A History of Investment Trusts in Dundee, 1873–1938* (London, 1939).

13. Stewart, *Jute and Empire*; stock market listings may be found in the *Dundee Year Book*. Records of this exchange may be found at DUA, MS 69.

14. J. Brock, *The Mobile Scot: A Study of Emigration and Migration 1861–1911* (Edinburgh, 1999), pp. 124, 133 analyses regional patterns of out-migration, noting an especially large outflow from Angus (in which county Dundee was by far the most populous town) in 1891–1901; for an overview of migration: M. Gray, *Scots on the Move: Scots Migrants 1750–1914* (Edinburgh, 1990), ch. 5. In 1901 Dundee had 127 women for every 100 men: General Register Office, Scotland, 1901, *Census of Population*, vol. 3: *Occupations of the People of Scotland in 1901*.

15. DCC, *About Dundee 2004* (Dundee, 2004), p. 20.

16. 2001 Census from www.scrol.gov.uk/scrol/common/home.jsp.

17. General Register Office, Scotland, 1901, *Census of Population*, vol. 3: *Occupations of the People of Scotland in 1901*, pp. 680–2.

18. R. Middleton, 'Government and the economy, 1860–1939' in R. Floud and P. Johnson (eds), *The Cambridge Economic History of Britain*, vol. 2: *Economic Maturity, 1860–1939* (Cambridge, 2004), p. 462.

19. DUA, MS 134: Lennox, 'Working Class Life in Dundee', pp. 264–5.

20. In 2001 55 per cent of households were in owner occupation in Dundee (compared with 63 per cent for Scotland as a whole): 2001 Census from www.scrol.gov.uk/scrol/common/home.jsp.

21. The desire to attract multinational companies, especially from the USA, can be seen as part of national policy in the 1940s to gain from US economic predominance, but also very much a local effort, spearheaded by Garnett Wilson, the Lord Provost from 1940 to 1946.

22. W. Beveridge, *Full Employment in a Free Society* (London, 1944), pp. 51, 54.

23. N. Hood and S. Young, *Multinationals in Retreat: The Scottish Experience* (Edinburgh, 1982).

24. J. Tomlinson, 'Responding to globalization? Churchill, Dundee and the election of 1908', *Twentieth Century British History* 21 (2010), pp. 257–80.

25. LHC, 1908 Election. One Unionist leaflet distributed in the 1908 election itemised the tariffs in European countries, and called for Britain to 'resume our power of fiscal negotiation with the view of trying to have such tariffs reduced'. Another called for Imperial Preference on jute goods in Canadian and Australian markets.

26. Dundee opinion was, unsurprisingly, hostile to a jute levy which did not discriminate in favour of exports to Britain, and was aimed solely at raising revenues in India: DCA, Dundee Chamber of Commerce, Minutes of Directors' Meetings, 4 August 1905; *Advertiser*, 28 December 1905. On the broader issue of imperial economic connections, see J. Tomlinson, 'The Empire/Commonwealth in British economic thinking and policy' in A. Thompson (ed.), *The Oxford History of the British Empire: Britain's Experience of Empire in the Twentieth Century* (Oxford, forthcoming).

27. A. Marrison, *British Business and Protection 1903–1932* (Oxford, 1996).

28. S. Masrani, 'International Competition and Strategic Response in the Dundee Jute Industry during the Interwar (1919–1939) and Post-war (1945–1960s) Period: The Case of Jute Industries, Buist Spinning, Craiks and Scott and Fyfe' (unpublished PhD thesis, St Andrews University, 2007); London School of Economics, Archives: Tariff Commission papers TC1 2/7, *Report of the Tariff Commission*, vol. 2. *The Textile Trades*, part 7: *Evidence on the Flax, Hemp and Jute Industries* (London, Tariff Commission, 1906). There was a crucial local debate in the Dundee Chamber of Commerce in January 1904, when a majority supported the idea of a 'bargaining' tariff: DCA, Dundee Chamber of Commerce, Minutes of Directors' Meetings, 15 January 1904; *Advertiser*, 16 January 1904.

29. GD/CC/4/8: DCA, Dundee Chamber of Commerce, Minutes of Directors' Meetings, vol. 8, 1895–1907: D.C. Thomson to Joseph Chamberlain, 'The jute industry of Great Britain', 10 September 1903, where the main emphasis is on an export duty on raw jute exported from India to non-Empire counties.

30. F. Trentmann, *Free Trade Nation* (Oxford, 2008), pp. 105–19.

31. J. Tomlinson, 'Managing decline: the case of jute', *Scottish Historical Review*, forthcoming.

32. See election address by the Labour candidate, George Stuart, *Advertiser*, 2 May 1908;

John Sime visited India in the 1920s with Tom Johnston, and focused much attention on Indian unions: Thomas Johnston, *Memories* (London, 1952), pp. 50–84; G. Doud, 'Tom Johnston in India', *Scottish Labour History Journal* 19 (1984), pp. 6–21. For the Indian government's rejection of the idea of imposing the Factory Acts on India, *Courier*, 4 September 1906.

33. D. Bowman, *The Future of Jute* (Dundee, Dundee Communist Party, 1945). Bowman was the CP candidate in Dundee West in each election from 1950 to 1964.

34. K. McGregor, 'A Question of Choice: The Leisure Activities of Dundee Women in the 1920s' (unpublished MA dissertation, University of Dundee, 2003), Appendix 2, records majorities of around 3:2 on a 60–70 per cent turnout in each poll in 1920, 1923 and 1926. For Prohibitionism, W.M. Walker, *Juteopolis: Dundee and its Textile Workers, 1885–1923* (Edinburgh, 1979), pp. 333–93.

35. W. Gallacher, *Revolt on the Clyde: An Autobiography* (London, 1936); B. Stewart, *Breaking the Fetters* (London, 1967). Stewart was a Prohibitionist councillor in Dundee in 1908, later breaking with Scrymgeour over the latter's religious views. There are substantial security service files on Stewart (as well as a copy of the local Party 1931 manifesto) in the public records: TNA: PRO KV 2/1180–1183.

36. Graham Smith, 'Protest is better for infants: motherhood, health and welfare in a women's town, c. 1911–1931', *Oral History* 23 (1995), pp. 63–70. In 1939 the Labour Party selected Krishna Menon, later Defence Minister in independent India, as its candidate, but he was forced to step down in 1940 because of his close links with the Communist Party: M. Sherwood, 'Krishna Menon, Parliamentary Labour Party candidate for Dundee 1939–1940', *Scottish Labour History* 42 (2007), pp. 29–48; TNA: PRO KV 2/2509 contains the intelligence files on Menon for 1929–41.

37. D. Denver and J. Bochel, 'The political socialization of activists in the British Communist Party', *British Journal of Political Science* 3 (1973), pp. 53–71. See also D. Denver, 'The Communist Party in Dundee: A Study of Activity' (unpublished B.Phil. dissertation, University of Dundee, 1971).

38. For examples of local CP post-1945 election manifestos, see LHC, Lamb Collection 367 (25). Note that Gordon Wilson, SNP member for Dundee East, emphasised the Communist past of his Labour rival, Jimmy Reid, in the 1979 election: LHC, 441 (9).

39. S. Tolland, '"Just ae wee woman": Dundee, the Communist Party and the Feminization of Socialism in the Work of Mary Brooksbank' (unpublished PhD thesis, University of Aberdeen, 2005). For the whole question of women and the Communist Party in Scotland, see N. Rafeek, *Communist Women in Scotland: Red Clydeside from the Russian Revolution to the End of the Soviet Union* (London, 2008).

40. E. Ross, 'Alexander Wilkie, Dundee' in A. Haworth and D. Hayter (eds), *Men Who Made Labour* (London, 2006), pp. 213–20.

41. LSE Archives: E.D. Morel Papers, F2/9. Morel also faced serious problems with his relationship with the CP. In the *Advertiser*, 30 October 1922, he was quoted as saying that if a Communist candidate were to run in harness with him he would 'retire from the field' as 'I am unalterably opposed to Communism'.

42. R. Galbraith, *Without Quarter: The Biography of Tom Johnston, the 'Uncrowned King of Scotland'* (Edinburgh, 1995).

43. Jim Phillips, *The Industrial Politics of Devolution* (Manchester, 2008); A. Brown, D. McCrone and L. Paterson, *Politics and Society in Scotland* (2nd edn, Basingstoke, 1998), pp. 152–7.

44. K.J.W. Baxter, '"Estimable and Gifted"? Women in Party Politics in Scotland

*c.*1918–1955' (unpublished PhD thesis, University of Dundee, 2008).

45. D. Jarvis, 'The shaping of Conservative electoral hegemony, 1918–1939' in J. Lawrence and M. Taylor (eds), *Party, State and Society: Electoral Behaviour in Britain since 1820* (Aldershot, 1997), pp. 131–52.

46. J. Bochel and D. Denver, 'Religion and voting: a critical review and a new analysis', *Political Studies* 18 (1970), pp. 205–19. This strong local Catholicism was a divisive issue on the Left during the Spanish Civil War in the late 1930s: Dundee Trades Union Council, *Dundee and the Spanish Civil War* (Dundee, 2008). Catholicism was also an issue in the Left/Right splits in the Labour Party in the 1970s and 1980s, with George Galloway beaten for a local council seat in 1977 by a Catholic candidate who attacked both his Marxism and his 'living-in-sin' with his partner in a Dundee council property: D. Morley, *Gorgeous George: The Life and Adventures of George Galloway* (London, 2007), pp. 31–3.

47. H. Henderson, 'Religious life' in J.M. Jackson (ed.), *The Third Statistical Account of Scotland*, vol. 25: *The City of Dundee* (Arbroath, 1979), pp. 632–77, which surveys the picture up to the beginning of the 1960s, shows little evidence of decline, except in the discussion of declining religious enthusiasm amongst young people: and when was such a sentiment *not* offered by the middle-aged?

48. It was estimated that there was a Pakistani community numbering 500 to 600 in the late 1960s: H. Jones and M. Davenport, 'The Pakistani community in Dundee', *Scottish Geographical Magazine* 88 (1972), pp. 75–85.

49. M. Watson, *Being English in Scotland* (Edinburgh, 2003).

50. We know far more about the early years of the century than later: E. Gordon, *Women and the Labour Movement in Scotland 1850–1914* (Oxford, 1991); Walker, *Juteopolis*.

51. LHC, Dundee Trades and Labour Council (renamed Trades Council from 1949, when split off from City Labour Party): 2290 and 2306, Minutes 1934–39; 2240–2243, Annual Reports 1945–49 and Annual Reports 1945–65. D.C. Thomson was wholly hostile to trade unionism, and fought an important test case against recognition in the 1950s: G. Rosie, 'The warlocks of British publishing' in G. Rosie et al., *Bumper Fun Book* (Edinburgh, 1976), pp. 17–18.

52. For comparison with the mid-Victorian period, L. Miskell, 'Civic leadership and the manufacturing elite: Dundee, 1820–1870' in L. Miskell, C.A. Whatley and B. Harris (eds), *Victorian Dundee: Image and Realities* (East Linton, 2000), pp. 51–69.

53. Based on research by Dr Valerie Wright in the records of Jute Industries, DUA.

54. C. Morelli and J. Tomlinson, 'Women and work after the Second World War: a case study of the jute industry, circa 1945–1954', *Twentieth Century British History* 19 (2008), pp. 61–82. Tomlinson, 'Managing decline'.

55. The other was a younger-generation man, Lewis Robertson. Hugh Bonar was also head of Jute Control, 1940 to 1948.

56. J. Kemp, 'Red Tayside? Political change in early twentieth-century Dundee' in Miskell et al. (eds), *Victorian Dundee*, pp. 151–68.

57. One of Labour's first moves in 1936 was to attempt to cut the number of council seats in Broughty Ferry, from the six which had been agreed when the two councils amalgamated in 1913: *Courier*, 14 November 1936, 19 November 1936. This was not successful.

58. For examples during various local election campaigns: *Courier*, 2 November 1925, 3 November 1927, 5 November 1929, 2 November 1931, 30 October 1935. Note that Moderates on the Council favoured council house building, but sought for it to be funded by central government: *Courier*, 28 October 1927.

59. Morley, *Gorgeous George*, chs 1–8.
60. This significance is rightly reflected in the weight given to this issue in C. Whatley (ed.), *The Remaking of Juteopolis: Dundee circa 1891–1991* (Dundee, 1992).
61. DSU, *Report*, pp. 1–23.
62. Joe Doherty, 'Dundee: a post-industrial city' in Whatley (ed.), *Remaking of Juteopolis*, p. 28.
63. Ann Petrie, *The 1915 Rent Strikes: An East Coast Perspective* (Dundee, Abertay Historical Society, 2008).
64. W. Edgar, R. Rowbotham and J. Stanforth, 'Dundee's housing: 1915–1974' in Whatley (ed.), *Remaking of Juteopolis*, pp. 41–4.
65. Ibid., pp. 47–54.
66. Morley, *Gorgeous George*, pp. 67–8.
67. A. Gibb, 'Policy and politics in Scottish housing since 1945' in R. Rodger (ed.), *Scottish Housing in the Twentieth Century* (Leicester, 1989), p. 181.
68. S. Glynn, 'Home truths: the myth and reality of regeneration in Dundee', Edinburgh, Institute of Geography Online Paper Series: GEO-132: www.geos.ed.ac.uk/homes/sglynn/Home_Truths.pdf
69. J. Wadsworth, 'Eyes down for a full house: labour market polarisation and the housing market in Britain', *Scottish Journal of Political Economy* 45 (1998), pp. 376–92.
70. B. Harris, '"City of the Future": James Thomson's vision of the city beautiful' in Miskell et al. (eds), *Victorian Dundee*, pp. 169–83; C. McKean and P. Whatley with K. Baxter, *Lost Dundee: Dundee's Lost Architectural Heritage* (Edinburgh, 2008), pp. 182–9.
71. R. Lyle and G. Payne (eds), *The Tay Valley Plan: A Physical, Social and Economic Survey and Plan for the Development of East Central Scotland* (Dundee, 1950); W. Dobson Chapman and Partners, *The City and Royal Burgh of Dundee: Survey and Plan*, 2 vols (1952).
72. G. Stamp, *Britain's Lost Cities* (London, 2007), pp. 55–61; McKean and Whatley, *Lost Dundee*, especially pp. 181–217.
73. *Courier*, 14 March 1980. This corruption case involved an ex-Lord Provost, Tom Moore, and an ex-Councillor, James Stewart, alongside John Maxwell, a developer. The charges related to the period 1959–75. All three were sentenced to five years' imprisonment, but both Moore and Stewart were freed on appeal. See *Courier*, 7 February 1980 to 14 March 1980, and 20 June 1980. Note that such corruption was not uncommon in this period, with parallels in the redevelopment of Newcastle, for example.
74. I. Gazeley, *Poverty in Britain, 1900–1965* (Basingstoke, 2003), p. 36 refers to the Dundee Report's 'rare and detailed' examination of family structure, labour market participation and earnings; for context, see G. Stedman Jones, *Outcast London* (Oxford, 1971).
75. Board of Trade, *Hours and Earnings Enquiry* (London, HMSO, 1906).
76. DSU, *Report*, pp. 24–7.
77. Norman Watson, 'Daughters of Dundee. Gender and Politics in Dundee: The Representation of Women 1870–1997' (unpublished PhD thesis, Open University, 2000), pp. 162–4.
78. Which is not, of course, to suggest it was not deeply imbued with contemporary ideologies. For example, it criticised married women's employment for causing high infant mortality, a common trope of the time, but whose empirical base is shaky: S. Szreter, *Health and Wealth: Studies in History and Policy* (Rochester, NY, 2005), ch. 9.

79. J. Harris, *Unemployment and Politics: A Study of English Social Policy, 1886–1914* (Oxford, 1972).

80. W. Beveridge, *Unemployment: A Problem of Industry* (London, 1909).

81. TNA: PRO LAB 2/842/TBM1 14/4/1921, Discussion at Jute Trade Board 16/17 February 1921 on complaint of AJSM (Association of Jute Spinners and Manufacturers): 'Many of the employers disliked the application of the Acts to the jute trade from the first; their dissatisfaction was intensified and steadily grew after the collapse of the trade last Autumn.' See also the discussion in Morelli and Tomlinson, 'Women and work', pp. 71–3.

82. C. Craig, J. Rubery, R. Tarling and F. Wilkinson, *Abolition and After: The Jute Wages Council*, Department of Employment Research Paper 15 (London, 1980).

83. Denver and Bochel, 'Political socialization'. Popular accounts include D. Phillips, *The Hungry Thirties: Dundee Between the Wars* (Dundee, 1981); Barassie History Group, *Work or Want* (Dundee, 1996); 'Frank McCusker' in I. McDougall (ed.), *Voices from the Hunger Marches: Personal Recollections by Scottish Hunger Marchers of the 1920s and 1930s*, vol. 1 (Edinburgh, 1990), pp. 29–38.

84. Board of Trade, *Working Party Reports: Jute* (London, HMSO, 1948), p. 44.

85. Eastham, 'Economic survey', pp. 101, 100.

86. Ibid., p. 100; J. Tomlinson, 'Women as anomalies: the Anomalies Regulations Act of 1931 and its background and implications', *Public Administration* 62 (1984), pp. 423–37. Such discrimination pre-dated the 1931 Act, with the 'genuinely seeking work' clause of unemployment benefit used against women: TNA: PRO LAB 2/1347/ED2947 3/6/1929, 'Evidence to Morris Committee on Unemployment Insurance' in 1929, where Sime argues that married women find it harder to show they are 'genuinely seeking work'.

87. These consequences are much debated: see B. Harris, *The Origins of the British Welfare State* (Basingstoke, 2004), pp. 197–218. For official comment on local housing conditions: TNA: PRO AST 12/36, Unemployment Assistance Board, *Dundee District Annual Report for the Year 1938*: 'Prior to the war, private enterprise helped to provide the working class with housing at economic rents but with rising costs after the war such building, practically speaking, came to a standstill. In Dundee, a city of low paid workers who could not pay the economic rents required by private builders, the conditions arising out of overcrowding can only be described as a disgrace to the city.'

88. Board of Trade, *Jute*, p. 45.

89. R. Lowe, *The Welfare State in Britain since 1945* (3rd edn, Basingstoke, 2005), pp. 114–34, 152–4.

90. K. Coates and R. Silburn, *Poverty: The Forgotten Englishmen* (Harmondsworth, 1970).

91. Poverty amongst the elderly in this period was in large part due to their inability to save during the inter-war mass unemployment: Gazeley, *Poverty in Britain*, p. 176.

92. DCA, Dundee Chamber of Commerce, Minutes of Directors' Meetings, 12 June 1970.

93. E. Ross and J. Hardy, *Unemployment in Dundee* (Dundee, Dundee Labour Party, 1979), p. 3; *Department of Employment Gazette*, various issues.

94. G. Bramley, S. Lancaster and D. Gordon, 'Benefit take-up and the geography of poverty in Scotland', *Regional Studies* 34 (2000), pp. 507–19.

95. The welfare case for focusing on unemployment is powerfully made in A. Clark and A. Oswald, 'Unhappiness and unemployment', *Economic Journal* 10 (1994), pp. 648–59.

PART I
Key Themes

CHAPTER 2

Endgame for Jute:
Dundee and Calcutta in the Twentieth Century

Gordon Stewart

In 1896 Sir John Leng, Dundee's Liberal Member of Parliament, made a visit to India and described Calcutta as 'the Indian Dundee'. In a series of detailed letters he set out the 'resemblances and contrasts' between the two cities.[1] It was jute that had brought these Scottish and Bengali urban centres together, and the Dundee and Calcutta jute mills were the prime focus of Leng's comparative commentary. No other two world cities were linked in such an intimate yet competitive embrace. Dundee's expertise in jute spinning and weaving had helped start the Calcutta industry in the 1850s and continued to shape it throughout the next one hundred years. But by 1900 the Calcutta industry dwarfed its Dundee counterpart. In 1911, the peak year for employment in the Dundee jute mills, the total labour force reached 37,000 workers. When Calcutta achieved its peak in 1928 there were 339,000 workers, almost twice as numerous as the entire population of Dundee.[2] In 1919 Ernest Cox, owner of the Cox mills in Lochee, and the first chairman of the Dundee Association of Jute Spinners and Manufacturers, warned of 'the probability of the home market being swamped by cheap Calcutta made goods'.[3] During a parliamentary debate on the jute industry in 1936, Florence Horsbrugh, the Conservative MP for Dundee at the time, spoke in apocalyptic terms of 'a new terror' for Dundee workers as imports from India surged 125 per cent higher than they had been in 1935. 'If something is not done, and done quickly,' she starkly warned, 'the jute trade of the United Kingdom will cease to exist.'[4] By the middle of the twentieth century Dundee's offspring on the banks of the Hooghly seemed about to devour its parent on the banks of the Tay.

In the popular imagination of Dundonians, their city was the senior party in the relationship. This self-image lay behind Leng's use of such phrases as 'the Indian Dundee' rather than designating Dundee as 'the Scottish Calcutta'. There were solid grounds for holding that view of the relationship between the two cities. The first jute mills in the world were started in Dundee in the 1830s, and from the time the first jute mill had been established in Calcutta in 1855 Dundee expertise played a major role in building and sustaining the Calcutta industry. When the British Association held its annual meeting in Dundee in 1912, a brochure produced to mark the occasion noted with pride that 'the overseers, managers, and mechanics in the Indian jute mills were almost wholly recruited from Dundee'.[5]

Every British traveller who went to India and commented on the jute industry invariably referred to the stalwart Dundonians who were keeping things going out in India. During his 1896 trip, as Leng made his way across country from Bombay to Calcutta, he stopped off at Cawnpore and visited a struggling jute mill; it was being brought into working order by the manager, 'Mr. Thompson from Lochee'.[6] When Keir Hardie, the founder of the Independent Labour Party, and the champion of the working class in Britain, went to Calcutta in 1909 to study conditions in the mills, he received a warm welcome from 'quite a few friends from Dundee, Arbroath, and around Manchester way [who] came to crack about old times. They were mostly from the jute and cotton mills.'[7] In 1926 Tom Johnston, the Labour MP for Dundee, and John Sime, the Secretary of the Jute and Flax Workers' Union in Dundee, led a delegation to Calcutta to inquire into the working conditions of the factories. They noted affectionately for their readers back in Scotland the overwhelming proportion of Dundonians among the European assistants and managers – 'about 900 hail from Dundee!' they declared with evident pride.[8] As the Indian Industrial Commission report of 1918 observed, 'the association of the Calcutta jute industry with the East Coast of Scotland has throughout remained intimate. The majority of the European staffs are of Dundee extraction, and most of the experts in the managing firms are Scottish.'[9]

Some sense of the type of young men who went out from Dundee can be seen in the letters of Sir Edward Benthall, a partner in Bird & Company in Calcutta, and a leading figure in the jute business, who made regular recruiting trips in Britain. In 1935 he was on a mission to find men for a range of posts in Calcutta, from an assistant editor of *Capital*, the business newspaper largely financed by Bird & Company, to accountants for the head offices on Clive Street in Calcutta, down to assistants in the jute mills. For the white-collar jobs in the Clive Street offices he looked for public school and Oxbridge-educated candidates. In the case of the assistant editor post for *Capital* he interviewed two men. The first, L.G. Newton, had been educated at Blundell's School and Sidney Sussex College, Cambridge, and was then on the editorial staff of the *Financial Times* in London. The second candidate – a Mr Boyce-Jones – had been educated at Lancing and King's College, Cambridge. For a possible job as an accountant in the Clive Street office Benthall lighted on G.K. Young, who had completed degrees in Chemistry and Geology at Cambridge. Benthall also found this candidate appealing because he was 'the brother of Mrs. Russell whose Husband is the Financial Secretary in Bihar and Orissa'.[10] So for head office jobs Benthall looked at a certain social stratum in English society, with decent but not precocious degrees (seconds and thirds), and perhaps some social connections with well-placed members of the Indian Civil Service.

For the jute mills it was a different matter. Benthall explained his criteria – he was looking for 'a good class of Scotch boy from the Dundee district'. Oxbridge degrees and good social connections were not needed in this endeavour. In August he interviewed a young man whom Benthall 'did not consider outstanding . . . [but] a good average type of boy with a good deal of common sense'. He subsequently interviewed several applicants at the home of a business friend in Dundee. One successful candidate was William Ure, who had been educated at Harris Academy, had worked in the jute mills since leaving school at sixteen years of age, and was now with the Victoria Spinning Company. Benthall sketched out Ure's profile: 'he plays tennis for the Lockie [Lochee] Tennis Club and is Secretary of the Belmont Swimming Club; he does not read, except in the winter when he reads chiefly thrillers.' Ure knew several Dundee men already out in the Calcutta mills and told Benthall that 'he always wanted to go to India as does every young man in Dundee as trade is not good and there are no prospects'. Benthall summed up Ure as 'just the normal type we take on in Calcutta'. A second successful candidate in Dundee that year was Alan Anderson, who was at that time a yarn delivery clerk in one of the Dundee mills. Benthall described him as being 'keen on photography, shooting and golf, and often drives about in the family car, going for hours . . . His reading is mostly Dornford Yates and P.G. Wodehouse etc.' Benthall added that Anderson wished 'to go to India because there are little prospects at home. He says that everyone who joins Jute wants to get to Calcutta.'[11]

A thick network of social, engineering and business connections linked the two cities. The Calcutta mills, for example, recruited mechanical and management staff almost exclusively from the Technical College in Dundee. In 1909 at a meeting of the Indian Jute Mills Association, representatives of the Calcutta mills agreed to take up a special collection to support the extension of the Dundee Technical College in recognition of its role as the main provider of skilled workforce for the Calcutta mills. They 'very gladly endorsed the appeal' and urged all the Calcutta mills 'to come forward to help an Institute which has meant so much to Calcutta in the past, and will mean much more in years to come. For the jute industry owes its inception to Dundee, and for those capitalists engaged in Bengal to make possible, by their subscription, the completion of the Institution where jute workers are trained would be a peculiarly graceful and appropriate act.'[12] They expected mill assistants to have had two or more years' training at the College, where they earned certificates in spinning and weaving before adding the City and Guilds qualifications administered from London. This dynamic relationship remained in place right down to the Second World War and Indian independence. A 1941 report of the Indian Central Jute Committee noted that mill clerks and assistants 'are recruited either from mills or offices of Dundee jute merchants . . . Most of them hold the certificates of the Dundee Technical College and have a sound working knowledge of mill procedure.'[13]

There were weekly exchanges between the two cities on such essential business information as the price of raw jute, labour and energy costs in the factories, and the state of markets round the world. Good crops in any of the world's agricultural regions meant buoyant markets for jute bags and wrappings, and both Dundee and Calcutta paid attention to relevant news. As G.B. Morton, a director in the Bird group, explained in 1935, as he tried to forecast sales and market prospects in the coming months, 'everyone was waiting for rain in the Argentine'.[14] Whenever crucial negotiations about jute production in Calcutta took place, news reached Dundee very quickly. For most of the 1930s Dundee watched anxiously as the Calcutta mills debated amongst themselves whether to cut production in order to keep a floor under prices, or whether to go all out on production to drive down prices and force new mills to throw in the sponge.

When H.A.F. Lindsay, head of the Imperial Institute and former Indian Trade Commissioner to the United Kingdom, visited Dundee in 1935, he noticed that political and business news from Calcutta was scrutinised with an almost desperate urgency. He described how James Robertson, of Thomas Duff & Company, and the Chairman of the Dundee Chamber of Commerce, 'showed me a letter recently received from Calcutta which is likely to cause considerable anxiety to the Dundee spinners and manufacturers of jute. It had been addressed to the Calcutta Jute Mills by the Government of Bengal.'[15] This letter described a recent decision by the Bengal administration not to intervene by legislating shorter hours for all the Calcutta mills. Edward Benthall was in Britain when these negotiations in Calcutta were taking place. He received a copy of the Government of Bengal letter at his country home in Devon just as he was about to set out for a recruiting trip to Scotland – he 'would study it on the train to Dundee'.[16] He understood that the policy decision in Calcutta was of momentous significance for the future of the Dundee industry.

In Calcutta the Dundee mill assistants and supervisors lived at levels they could never have achieved back in Dundee. They had spacious bungalows in compounds specially reserved for European workers, and a host of servants to attend to their daily needs. They worked hard in the mills but they had plenty of leisure time for tennis and socialising with their colleagues. Eugenie Fraser, wife of Ronald Fraser, who supervised Indian clerks in the Lawrence jute mill, described the spacious living quarters: 'the whole compound, including gardens, tennis courts and the swimming pool beside the back door of our bungalow was looked after by an army of gardeners and workers.'[17] As Mrs Fraser remarked in her memoirs, her husband was typical of the Dundee men who went out to India 'to improve their lot and make money'.[18] When Sir Alexander Murray, a director in Thomas Duff & Company, made his annual visits to Calcutta, he would lay on treats for the European workers. He began with a dinner at the Bengal Club for the staff at the head offices on Clive Street and 'then on to the pictures afterwards'. The next day he turned to the staff in the jute mills. They did not merit dinner at the Bengal Club, so Murray 'decided to have all the managers, assistant managers and Mill

Clerks, with wives, to breakfast on Sunday at Victoria House, where Mrs Whyte [wife of a fellow director] was good enough to arrange a very pleasant party'. Murray noted in reporting this back to Dundee colleagues that 'I may say the party was very successful and very much appreciated.'[19] It was a sweet life in Calcutta in spite of the social distinctions between men in Clive Street and the jute mills. No wonder all the candidates interviewed by Benthall on his recruiting trips to Dundee told him that so many Dundee men wanted to get out to India. For these jute men 'the magic of India beckoned'.[20]

It was all these features of the connection – convivial conversations about men who had gone out to India, newspaper reports, business news, shipping arrivals at Dundee docks and so on – that led Dundonians to see their city as the primary partner. But by the twentieth century that view was fundamentally flawed. A delegation from Dundee informed the Board of Trade in 1919 that 'only a very small percentage' of the Calcutta factories were owned and managed from Dundee.[21] By the 1920s there were eighty-four European-managed mills in Calcutta. Only nine of these were controlled from Scotland, and only six from Dundee.[22] By this time there were several Indian-managed mills under the control of Marwari entrepreneurs such as the Birla brothers. These were joined in the course of the 1920s by half a dozen new Indian companies. In 1921 American investors set up the Ludlow mills on the banks of the Hooghly.[23] By 1922 the majority of shares in all these Calcutta jute companies was held by Indian investors. Throughout the 1920s and 1930s it was estimated that as many as 70 per cent of the shareholders were Indian. At the end of the Second World War, H.V. Bonar, the wartime Jute Controller in the United Kingdom, commented that 'the extent to which Dundee capital is still involved in the Indian industry is a small percentage of the total, many other large British interests now being represented there, and an increasingly large share of the capital being Indian owned'. He added his own view that 'the baby which was originally fathered by Dundee capital has grown to a size which dwarfs and threatens its Dundee foster parent'.[24] In 1940 the Indian Central Jute Committee had calculated that there were 68,416 jute looms in India compared with only 8,500 in Britain. By the middle of the century Calcutta accounted for about 60 per cent of the world production of jute cloth; Dundee for only about 7 per cent.[25]

To fully appreciate the calculus which eventually tipped the relationship against Dundee and in favour of Calcutta, it is essential to understand the place of jute in world markets. Beginning in the 1830s when Dundee factories successfully developed techniques for the spinning and weaving of the raw material from Bengal, jute had become the single most important wrapping material in international commerce. As a Bengal government report, in its retrospective view of the industry, summed up in 1934, 'jute became supreme . . . and jute cloth took its place as the world's packing medium'.[26] One dramatic example of the significance of jute's reach was that the entire cotton crop in the southern states of the USA was wrapped in jute. Each bale of cotton required about six yards of jute cloth, which meant that the American cotton crop alone required about one million yards of jute every year. When cotton became an important commercial crop in Russian Turkestan in the last decades of the nineteenth century, the entire crop, amounting to 2 million bales each year, was 'baled in jute to be sent to the mills in Moscow'.[27] Once jute manufacturing began in Calcutta it had obvious advantages over Dundee. The factories there were closer to the raw jute crop; they were well positioned for Asian, South American and western US markets. As early as 1878 a small news item in the Calcutta *Statesman* was a harbinger of future developments. There was report from the British Consul in San Francisco noting that 'hardly anything of importance was brought here from Great Britain. Calcutta supplied the market with grain bags last year almost altogether, the import of new bags from Britain being only 398,000 only against 6,692,947 in 1876. The imports from Calcutta were 6,900,000. Unless we have very large crops of wheat Dundee in the future will not have much to do with this market.'[28]

The Calcutta mills were closer to the raw jute, they had cheaper labour costs, and they had shipping lanes leading to all world markets. Another advantage held by the Calcutta mills is that in some respects they were more efficient than their Dundee counterparts. During his 1896 trip Leng, for example, was struck by how many of the Calcutta mills were laid out on one level across several acres, in contrast to the multi-level Dundee factories squeezed into awkward hillside locations. He noted that railroads and river boats came right to the mill loading docks in Calcutta, whereas in Dundee the raw jute bales had to be transported laboriously by horse-drawn wagons from the city docks to the spinning and weaving sites.[29] As late as the 1950s, it was still possible to see these jute carts, pulled by one plodding horse, slowly moving bales of raw jute from the landing quays up the hill into the Dundee factories.

A simple listing of some of the trade names for the products sold by the Calcutta mills gives a vivid sense of their ability to reach markets round the world. The Calcutta factories made Australian corn sacks, Egyptian grain sacks, Cuban sugar bags, Brazil salt nitrate bags, Buenos Aires grain bags, Levant sugar bags, Java sugar twills, Australian wool packs, Cape wool packs, San Francisco wheat bags.[30] A writer in the *Statesman*, exuding Calcutta confidence and pride, noted that 'no crop of grains or cereals, no wool, no foodstuffs of any description right down to fodder and even chicken feed, to say nothing of various ores, nitrates, salts and so forth – in fact, we may say none of the necessities of life – can be lifted without the most essential of all commodities, the gunny [jute] bag'.[31] D.P. McKenzie, the chairman of the Indian Jute Mills Association, put it simply in 1921 when he declared that 'the world is our customer'.[32]

Calcutta's attitudes towards Dundee reflected the primacy of its industry. In one of the earliest books on jute, *The Romance of Jute* (1909), a British jute wallah in Calcutta dismissed Dundee complaints about Calcutta competition as 'harmless wails from their small competitor on the Tay'.[33] When Dundee criticism intensified in the 1920s and 1930s the Calcutta jute men, Indian and British alike, responded by claiming that Calcutta was actually helping the smaller industry in Scotland. Their argument was that the Indian Jute Mills Association had organised an ongoing series of short-time working agreements ever since the 1880s, which had kept a floor under world jute prices. The Indian delegates to the Round Table Conference in 1937 summed up this view in a way that conveyed the impression that Calcutta understood more about the world jute scene than Dundee:

> The situation whereby the Dundee Jute Mills are now claiming protection is brought about by the present uneconomic working conditions which are common alike both to Calcutta and Dundee. In the past, the policy of restricted production by the Indian mills resulted in profitable working by the Dundee mills – in fact, it has been said that the Indian mills have held an umbrella over the heads of the mills in Dundee.[34]

H.H. Burn, the chairman of the Indian Jute Mills Association, made the same case in 1936 when he argued that efforts to curtail expansion of production in Calcutta were beneficial for Dundee: 'For many years past the policy of the Association has benefitted our Dundee friends; and in bringing matters to a head, and endeavouring to secure a stable basis for working for the Indian industry we are fighting the cause of the Jute industry in general – not only our own.'[35]

Such arguments reveal the extent to which Calcutta viewed itself rather than Dundee as the leading player in the world of jute. A vivid sense of this perception came in a letter written from the Calcutta offices of Thomas Duff & Company when C.M. Laurie thanked the Secretary of the company in Dundee for sending out newspaper clippings containing examples of Dundee grievances: 'The opinion here is frequently expressed that, generally speaking, the Dundee manufacturer is a pretty good grumbler.'[36] This dismissive comment in a private letter from someone employed by a Dundee company in Calcutta is a telling insight into Calcutta views of the relationship with Dundee.

The formidable quantity and variety of Calcutta jute products, the reach of the Calcutta mills in international markets, and the attitude of superiority assumed by the Calcutta industry, put Dundee on the defensive for much of the twentieth century. The Dundee firms survived by turning to higher-quality jute products for Western markets – such as carpet backings and linoleum, and jute cloth for tailoring needs, furniture fabrics and other more specialised and finer lines than the jute bags and wrapping cloth typical of Calcutta's output. Dundee also tried to fight back on two related fronts. They tried to persuade the British government to impose some restraints on Calcutta, and they raised frequent complaints about working conditions in the Calcutta mills.

On working conditions in the Calcutta jute mills the case was much less clear-cut than many Dundonians assumed. The ethos of cheapness dominated the jute industry wherever it appeared. Since the primary use of jute round the world was to carry raw materials and basic agricultural products, manufacturers were convinced they had to keep their prices as low as possible. As the Chairman of the Indian Jute Mills Association declared in 1915, jute was a product 'whose principal claim to popularity was its cheapness'.[37] This led to an obsession that labour costs had to be kept as low as possible. All businesses in modern economies are concerned about keeping the costs of production as low as possible, but pursuit of this goal was particularly intense in the case of jute. In Dundee this meant extensive use of female workers (and even part-time child workers in the early decades of the century). Labour was also recruited from the Angus countryside and, as in the Cox mills in Lochee, from Irish immigrants. It was a similar story round the world wherever jute was produced. In the New England jute mills cheap labour from French Canada played a key role. In Germany workers were brought in from Poland and Portugal. In Calcutta labour was recruited from the villages of Bihar and Orissa.[38] In all these settings the wages of vulnerable immigrant and female workers hovered at a precarious point around the level necessary for bare subsistence.

The predicaments of the Calcutta workers have attracted the attention of well-known international scholars such as Dipesh Chakrabarty, who have deployed concepts from the subaltern school of history to open up the lives of thousands of poor and often illiterate workers.[39] Chakrabarty's main point is that the Calcutta mill workers relied on their religious, family and communal cultural resources to resist the dehumanising impact of life in the mills and the bustee shanty towns that were built up round the factories. The workers were able to create some cultural space for themselves, and strove to retain their humanity, in the face of low wages, racist supervisors, split families, and relentlessly demanding working conditions. They did not have the material or intel-lectual resources, or the time, to develop a modern politicised trade union consciousness. These features of the Calcutta workers bear remarkable resemblance to their counterparts in Dundee as captured by William Walker in his nuanced and sympathetic account of jute workers.[40] Walker draws attention to the anarchic ways of the Dundee mill workers, their reluctance to become enlisted in political campaigns of unions, and their penchant for using work stoppages and demonstra-tions as occasions for asserting their cultural presence in the city.

Walker also notes the political antinomianism of the women workers in the Dundee mills. Their demonstrations often mocked the bourgeois world of their employers and their 'betters'. Their world was marked off from the masculine world of mainstream trade union activity. 'The mill girl was different,' Walker observes, 'in that for her a strike or a Prohibitionist street meeting could function very well as entertainment.' Walker argues that 'the reckless spontaneity with which mill workers would commence a strike threatened in the twentieth century to imperil textile trade unionism.' Rather than being precursors to a progressive

PLATE 1 (*Above*) A polish ex-serviceman who remained in Dundee after the War, pictured in the 1950s. Dundee also saw substantial immigration from Poland at the end of the century after Poland joined the European Union. (Michael Peto Collection, University of Dundee Archives)

PLATE 2 (*Left*) Woman photographed by Michael Peto in the back streets of Dundee in the 1950s. This is a characteristic shot by Peto, who in the 1950s and 1960s captured the people of what was still a traditional industrial city. (Michael Peto Collection, University of Dundee Archives)

PLATE 3 Horse and cart at work in Dundee. This form of transport was still quite common in the city into the 1960s. (Michael Peto Collection, University of Dundee Archives)

PLATE 4 Labour Exchange, Gellatly Street. In the 1950s and 1960s Dundee enjoyed much lower levels of unemployment than in any other peacetime years in the twentieth century. (Michael Peto Collection, University of Dundee Archives)

PLATE 5 The back streets of Dundee in the 1950s or 1960s. Despite comprehensive redevelopment, much of the City remained untouched. (Michael Peto Collection, University of Dundee Archives)

ᴛᴇ 6 Bernard Street, Coronation Celebration, 1937. (Turner–McKinlay Photographic Collection, iversity of Dundee Archives)

PLATE 7 Princess Cinema, Hawkhill. It was demolished in 1959. (Turner–McKinlay Photographic Collection, University of Dundee Archives)

PLATE 8 Potter at work at the College of Commerce in the 1970s. Founded in 1970, the College merged with the Kingsway Technical College in 1985 to form Dundee College. (Michael Peto Collection, University of Dundee Archives)

PLATE 9 Potter at work at the College of Commerce in the 1970s. The College site on Constitution Road was put up for sale in 2010. (Michael Peto Collection, University of Dundee Archives)

PLATE 10 A carefully posed photograph brings together jute and journalism in a mill owned by Malcolm Ogilvie & Co: the *People's Friend* has been published by D.C. Thomson since 1869. (Malcolm Ogilvie Collection, University of Dundee Archives)

ATE 11 An accident involving a tram on the Perth Road in the 1950s. Trams disappeared from the y's streets in 1956. (Malcolm Ogilvie Collection, University of Dundee Archives)

PLATE 12 (*Right*) A portrait of
Florence Horsburgh, MP for Dundee
1931–1945: Dundee's only woman, and
only Conservative MP, in the twentieth
century. (Dundee Conservative and
Unionist Association, University of
Dundee Archives)

PLATE 13 (*Below*) Florence Horsburgh
addressing an open air meeting. c. 1935.
By the 1930s open air political meetings
were supplemented by radio broadcasts. (Dundee Conservative and
Unionist Association, University of
Dundee Archives)

ATE 14 (*Above*) View north along the east side of the Tay Road Bridge to Dundee showing one of
last periods of substantial ice floe activity on the Tay Estuary, 12 January 1982. (Photo copyright
W. Duck)

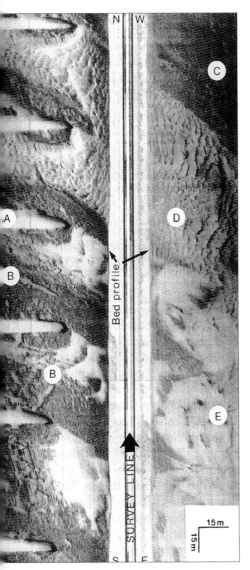

PLATE 15 (*Left*) Sonograph from part of a traverse parallel with the seaward side of the Tay Road Bridge. The strong reflections from the cutwaters of the bridge piers are striking with pronounced acoustic shadows behind (A). Minimal scour is present around the bases of the piers shown, as indicated by only small variations in the bed profile. Anthropogenic debris (B), associated with the building of the bridge and its subsequent maintenance programme, is detected on the bed. The darker tones (C), close to the northern margin of the estuary, are characteristic of silts and fine sands which are colonised by mussel beds and are generally stable. The lighter tones (D) are typical of mobile, medium grained sands characterised by small to medium dune bedforms with crest-to-crest spacing in the range 2–5 metres and heights of up to 0.5 metre (D). To the south and eastern part of the area, medium to large dunes, with crest-to-crest spacing of about 10 metres and heights of 0.5–2 metres, are the dominant bedforms (E). Bedform asymmetry in this zone of the estuary is, at all states of the tide, characteristic of the dominance of flood currents, indicative of the marine derivation of sands.

This figure was originally published in the article 'Side-scan sonograph from the middle reaches of the Tay Estuary, Scotland' in the *International Journal of Remote Sensing*, vol. 17, 1996, pp. 3539–3540. The article and the *International Journal of Remote Sensing* are copyright of Taylor & Francis, with whose permission the figure is re-published here.

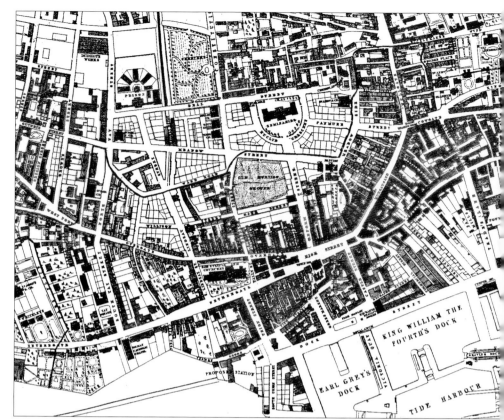

PLATE 16 (*Above*) The central section of Charles Edward's plan of current and intended improvements to Dundee in 1846. This section focuses upon the as yet unbuilt-upon Meadows, showing the new High School environed in gracious terraces with end pavilions rather in the manner of Edinburgh's fifth new town. It was never realised. (Thornton Collection of Manuscripts and Plans, University of Dundee Archives)

PLATE 17 (*Right*) The first phase of Dundee City Improvement took place in the mid 1870s, when Commercial Street was driven north through the densest of the city's mediaeval fabric – taking out the 'narrows' of both Seagate and Murraygate, widening Gellatly Street and removing Fenton Street altogether. The elegant replacement four storeyed offices and shops appear to have been modelled on Paris's boulevards Haussman. Taken from Lamb's *Dundee*. (Copyright Charles McKean)

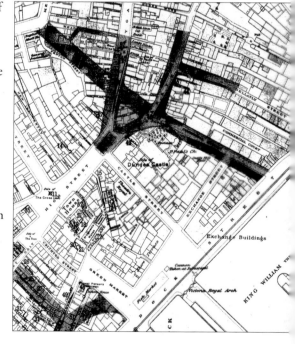

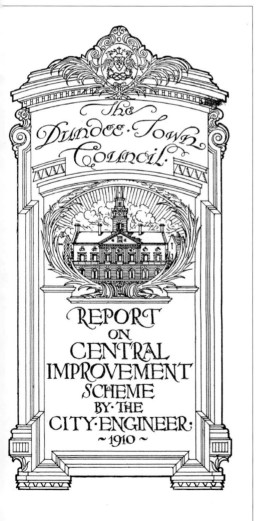

PLATE 18 (*Above*) Provost Longair's 1907 proposal for a new civic centre realised by James Thomson: the vertically proportioned Town House would have been inflated horizontally in neo-Baroque, and capped by an ill-proportioned dome. From the *Dundee Yearbook*. (Kinnear Local Book Collection, University of Dundee Archives)

PLATE 19 (*Left*) Cover of James Thomson's *Report on the Central Improvement Scheme* in 1910. Curiously, in the light of what was to follow, the Town House was the key image set within a typically Thomson baroque frame. (James Thomson Collection, University of Dundee Archives)

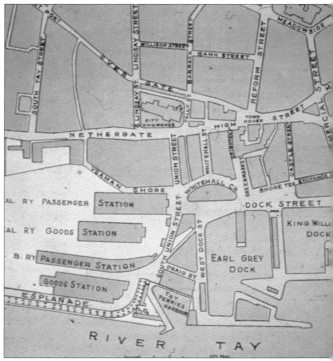

PLATE 20 The existing Town Centre plan from James Thomson's Report – exemplifying Thomson's criticism of a jumbled centre and a wasted waterfront: the whole entirely lacking in either grandeur or a suitable exploitation of a tremendous site. (James Thomson Collection, University of Dundee Archives)

PLATE 21 The Town House and expectant urchins viewed from the Overgate c. 1890. The entrance the Vault was beside the Town House gable straight ahead. No matter how redolent of an old Scots burgh centre, Dundee's market place now lacked the grandeur and dignity sought by the *city beauti* devotees. (Copyright D.C. Thomson)

ATE 22 The new Caird Hall rises high above the Strathmartine Lodging during the demolition of
Vault in the 1930s (its archway down to the Shore still visible on the left). It can just be made out
t the building shored upon the right was sitting upon arcades. (Copyright D.C. Thomson)

PLATE 23 Demolition of the buildings to the rear of the Town House c. 1928 in preparation for the new City Square. They included later administrative offices and prisons, but the buildings under demolition were probably sixteenth century – including the 1560 grammar school. (Copyright D.C Thomson)

PLATE 24 The wide roads and smooth low buildings of Thomas Adam's proposal to rebuild the Overgate district in 1937. The architecture closely presages that of the post-war rebuilding of England particularly central Bristol and Coventry. (Copyright Dundee City Council)

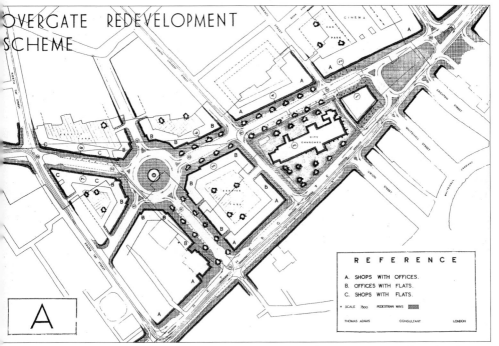

OVERGATE REDEVELOPMENT SCHEME

REFERENCE

A. SHOPS WITH OFFICES.
B. OFFICES WITH FLATS.
C. SHOPS WITH FLATS.

SCALE ⅟₅₀₀ PEDESTRIAN WAYS

THOMAS ADAMS   CONSULTANT   LONDON

A

PLATE 25 Adam's plan for the Overgate shows a widespread use of urban trees not reflected in his perspective. In neither case does he try to empathise with the strong character of the city's ancient core. (University of Dundee Archives)

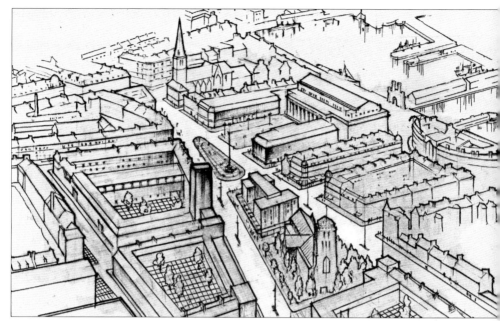

PLATE 26 A rather stronger (but undated) proposal for the same Overgate area as in Plate 25, with larger chunky architecture and a cinema tower. (Copyright D.C. Thomson)

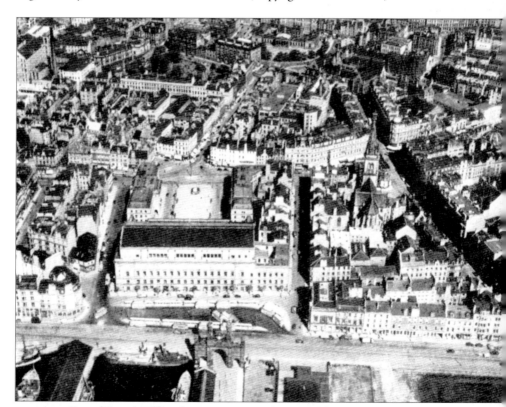

PLATE 27 Central Dundee from the air c. 1960. In the central foreground is the Royal Arch, with t Caird Hall and City Square behind. The sweep of the 1871 Commercial Street improvement is evident on the right. The Luckenbooths, Tally Street and Overgate are centre left. (Copyright D.C. Thomson)

PLATE 28 (*Left*) Sketch from the Advisory Plan by the architect Ian Burke for the total rebuilding of the Hilltown: a vision of windy plazas, multi-storey flats in an architecture fashionably Scandinavian. (Image from the Charles McKean library)

PLATE 29 (*Below*) Burke's vision for the Shore. It is lined with new public buildings (like Thomson's), and provides a small wet dock for the *Unicorn*. The traffic roundabout is similar to the one that was built, but the King William IV Dock was not filled in. The multi-storeyed Tayside House would arrive with the creation of the Regional Council in the 1970s. (Image from the Charles McKean library)

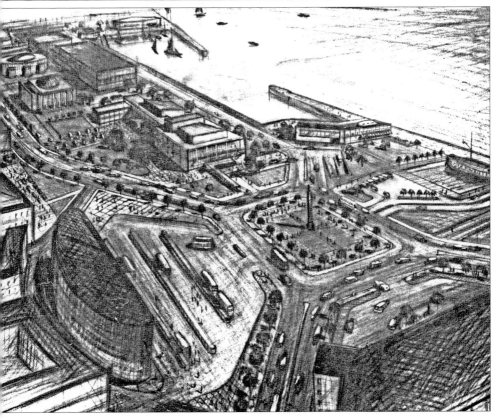

PLATE 30 Burke's original vision for St Mary's and the Overgate. As draconian but more imaginative than Adams', and now a pedestrian precinct rather than a wide straight traffic avenue. (Image from the Charles McKean library)

PLATE 31 The Overgate – looking toward the High Street from the Narrows c. 1900. This late mediaeval landscape of dense buildings facing the street concealed closes behind. (Copyright D.C. Thomson)

trade union movement seeking to transform the working of the macro-economy, the jute workers were concerned with basic survival and cultural assertion. 'The psychological extravagance of the mill girls was channelled into a fairly coherent and aggrieved self-consciousness.' In this reading, the Dundee workers could well be viewed as non-modern in much the same way that Chakrabarty described the Calcutta workers. 'To deny the heroism of the Dundee workers', concludes Walker, 'is merely to insist upon their humanity, or to understand how much heroism was needed in the business of dignified survival. Overall, the impression . . . is of a class which normally was too burdened by present anxieties to pursue politics, or accept responsibilities beyond their own domestic situation.'[41] Both Walker and Chakrabarty are describing a working-class culture that was shaped by religious, community, regional and kinship values rather than by a modern politicised trade union mentality.

Outside groups that studied working conditions were appalled by what they saw in Dundee. A report in 1911 from the Warden of the Dundee Women's Settlement, an organisation dedicated to helping poor women in the city, noted that 'wages that seemed the lowest possible have been reduced by one-fifth . . . Large numbers were on the verge of starvation.'[42] During a Commons debate in 1927 Tom Johnston, the Labour MP for Dundee, declared that 'the workers in the jute industry never have a living wage and live in the most incredible misery'.[43] As late as 1945, knowledgeable observers were struck by the backwardness of conditions in Dundee. A memorandum prepared in 1945 by H.V. Bonar, the wartime Jute Controller, made some telling comparisons between Dundee and Calcutta on these matters. He noted that the Dundee Association of Jute Spinners and Manufacturers 'has not been in the past highly progressive'. There was no standard system for wages as there was in Calcutta because each mill or company kept its rates for tenters, batchers, spinners and weavers a trade secret. 'The general atmosphere both of mills and factories is one of dinginess . . . and not enough attention was given to keeping paintwork clean, up-to-date, bright and cheerful.' Providing improved facilities in terms of cloakrooms and toilets was viewed as rather a waste of money because employers thought their workers were too lazy or ignorant to take advantage of such improvements. Bonar noted that in Dundee 'there are many mills and weaving sheds that had no facilities for workers at all'.[44] When challenged about such conditions, Dundee employers would often use Calcutta as an excuse, claiming that they were forced to cut things to the bone in Dundee because they were up against cheap labour in Calcutta. A common refrain was that 'the industry has done all it can and needs some assurance of protection against India'.[45]

This was the second Dundee strategy in the twentieth century – to push the British government into legislating protective measures against the Calcutta industry. The opening battle in the war of words between the two cities began in the last decade of the nineteenth century, when the Dundee *Advertiser* wrote an editorial drawing attention to the multiple shift system and use of electric lighting in the Calcutta factories which kept the machines working for more hours than the Dundee mills. The editorial demanded an investigation into working conditions in Calcutta to bring the Indian industry into line with the Factory Acts in the United Kingdom.[46] The Calcutta jute wallahs immediately accused their Dundee counterparts of hypocrisy in claiming to be concerned about the plight of the Indian workers. In a long speech at the Indian Jute Mills Association's annual meeting in 1895, George Lyall declared that 'the Dundee Chamber of Commerce has told us quite frankly that their object is to put a stop to a competition which threatens serious danger to them, and that to effect their purpose they will go direct to the British Government and demand that we shall be under the same Factory Act as they have in Dundee'.[47]

This initial salvo from Dundee failed in ways that foreshadowed all the failures in the twentieth century. Dundee's case ran into two immovable objects. The most obdurate of these was the prevailing free trade orthodoxy which made it anathema to attempt to shape and regulate trade through targeted tariffs and other protective mechanisms. The second obstacle was imperial politics. Any policy by the British government to rein in Calcutta would be viewed as an attempt to stifle economic growth in India. This was a particularly sensitive political and ideological matter as the campaign for Indian independence heated up in the 1920s, 1930s and 1940s under the leadership of Mohandas Gandhi and Jawaharlal Nehru. Curtailing growth in Calcutta would undermine British claims that they were ruling India for the benefit of Indians. These two views were made abundantly evident when Dundee tried to enlist the help of the Associated Chambers of Commerce of the United Kingdom in their cause. The British Chamber replied that they would not join Dundee's protest against Calcutta, and went on to warn Dundee of 'the dangers of inter meddling with the interests of the largest population subject to the British Crown'. They added for good measure that 'the policy which inspired the Dundee resolutions was the same policy that lost England the North American colonies'.[48]

This unpromising dynamic from Dundee's viewpoint was again demonstrated in 1919 when the newly formed Dundee Association of Jute Spinners and Manufacturers, in one of it first actions, made a plea to the British government. Ernest Cox, the first Chairman of the new Association, feared that rising wages and other production costs in Dundee had now raised 'the probability of the home market being swamped by cheap Calcutta made goods'.[49] The only option left was to appeal to London for quotas, or import duties, or even outright prohibition of the importation of certain classes of jute goods. To forward the attack on Calcutta a deputation was despatched to London. The India Office rebuffed the Dundee jute delegation in no uncertain terms. The Dundee delegates were informed that the prohibition of Indian imports was inconceivable 'on the grounds that India had put all her strength behind Great Britain and her allies during the war, and that such an act against her biggest industry would be a peculiar way of repaying India for her services'.[50] The Dundee delegates had no more luck with Winston Churchill, the city's Liberal MP since 1908. Churchill met the Dundee jute men in his rooms at the War Office on 15 April 1919. His reply was as comprehensively dismissive as that of the India Office. 'It was a problem of extreme difficulty,' Churchill explained to his Dundee constituents, 'as any prohibition in this case would be against one of the Dependencies of the Empire, and further, any form of protection would be against the Free Trade principles of the Government.'[51]

Dundee returned to the fray in the desperate years of the 1930s when the worldwide Depression reduced the demand for jute products. By this time new developments in Calcutta were putting additional pressure on Dundee. The new Calcutta companies, financed largely by Marwari entrepreneurs, were adding to Calcutta's productive capacity. These new firms needed quick returns to satisfy their investors. Since they had not had time to build up cash reserves in the way the older Calcutta companies had done in the decades since the 1880s, these new Indian companies had only one solution to their business predicament. They were determined to produce more goods and earn some money no matter the cost, in the hope that they could secure a big enough market share to keep them afloat. Simply keeping a cash flow going became a necessity. This in turn pushed down the price of jute goods, which made the established firms in the Indian Jute Mills Association consider ways they could protect their position. One solution for the older companies was to end their short-time working agreements and push so many of their goods on to the market at cheap prices that the new firms would be denied sales. In the face of the refusal of the Bengal government to intervene and force shorter hours on all the Calcutta mills, this is what happened during the 1930s.[52] So, in addition to the general ill effects of the Depression, the Dundee jute companies were faced with expanded competition from Calcutta. On 30 August 1935, H.A.F. Lindsay, Director of the Imperial Institute and former Indian Trade Commissioner in Britain, met with James Robertson, Chairman of the Dundee Chamber of Commerce, and Ernest Cox, at that time chairman of the Fiscal Committee of the Association of Jute Spinners and Manufacturers, to discuss the intensifying crisis. 'Dundee mill owners fear that if this policy [ending the short-time agreements in Calcutta] is adopted,' Lindsay explained in a letter to the Department of Overseas Trade, 'the Calcutta manufacturers will be able to undersell Dundee in the U.K. market even more effectively than they do at present.'[53]

Robertson organised discussions at the Dundee Chamber of Commerce to review the options. He reminded the meeting of the historical pattern of the relationship between the two jute cities: 'the reduced working hours in India had allowed the industry in the United Kingdom and other countries to manufacture at a reasonable profit'. The breakdown of that system in Calcutta meant that 'the United Kingdom was to be badly hit, and in his opinion the Home Trade's only chance was through the Board of Trade and the Department of Overseas Trade'. The figures produced at these Chamber of Commerce meetings were stark. George Donald, who had led a delegation to London, presented figures on world consumption which showed the imminent danger. With the Indian Jute Mills Association factories working at fifty-four hours per week, and the five new mills working at seventy hours, Calcutta would produce 1,223,500 tons of jute goods at a time when total world consumption stood only at 851,750 tons. Even if all the Calcutta mills reduced their working hours to forty per week, there would still be an output of goods 60,000 tons beyond current world demand. 'If we go to the Board of Trade,' Robertson told the meeting rather forlornly, 'they will have to do something.'[54]

In search of help from the British government, the Dundee Chamber of Commerce wrote a memorandum to the Board of Trade in January 1936 and followed up by sending a delegation to London in March of that year. They employed a London barrister, Archibald Crawford, who specialised in lobbying government departments, to assist them in making their case. Crawford sought some guidance on the gravity of the crisis. 'Had the trade made up its mind', he asked Cox, 'that the case was a grave one? If nothing was done, would the Trade go to the wall? Was the Indian position a real threat? Was it a fight for life or was it not?' Cox replied with appropriate gravity to this series of questions on Dundee's plight that 'the outlook at the present time appeared to be more serious than anything the Trade had ever had to face before'.[55]

This time Dundee had energetic help from one of its MPs. Back in the 1890s the Liberal MP John Leng saw no prospect of addressing the concerns of the Dundee industry because of the dominant hold of free trade doctrines in Britain at the time. He too was a believer in the free trade orthodoxy of the era, and his sympathetic report on Calcutta had undermined claims that workers there were being exploited. In 1919 Winston Churchill's position as a defender of the Empire and as a free-trader ensured that he also declined to take up the issue of Calcutta competition. By the 1930s Dundee's jute industry finally had a champion in Parliament. Florence Horsbrugh, the Conservative MP, encouraged by the turn to tariffs in the 1930s and by the efforts to organise intra-empire trade, threw her weight behind Dundee's complaints. Her persistent efforts led to the Dundee–Calcutta matter being aired in a full parliamentary debate for the first time. She made no bones about it during the jute debate in the Commons in July 1936 – Dundee's dire condition was due to unfair Calcutta competition. The expanded production in Calcutta, following the decision of the Calcutta mills to end their short-time agreements and open sealed looms, was the root problem: 'During the last few years we have watched the great increase in the imports of manufactured goods from India,' she explained to the House. 'The policy of restriction which was undertaken there has failed, and this year we have seen the last of the sealed looms unsealed, and the hours of work increased.' In dramatic language that reflected the position of Ernest Cox and other jute magnates, she declared that 'if something is not done, and done quickly, the jute trade of the United Kingdom will cease to exist'.[56]

But even at this critical juncture Dundee's case suffered from lack of support. The Labour Members who participated in the debate, such as Emmanuel Shinwell, found themselves in an awkward position. On the one hand, they were sympathetic to the terrible poverty of workers in Dundee. On the other hand, their Marxist orientation made them critics of imperialism and sympathetic to workers round the world. They could not argue in favour of placing any burdens on Calcutta because that policy would hurt Indian workers and could be viewed as an imperial imposition on Indian economic growth. All that Labour MPs could suggest was an international conference to set standards for wages and working conditions in the international arena.[57] Even if such a conference could have been mounted under the steadily weakening League of Nations, it would have taken years for such an approach to have any beneficial impact on Dundee and its jute workers. During the great jute debate in the Commons the city's second MP, the Liberal Dingle Foot, proved to be of no help. He declared his faith in the traditional free trade approaches that had stood Britain in such good stead over the past hundred years. He thought the Labour proposal for an international conference to be 'utterly fantastic'. The only solution he could suggest was for some kind of agreement between the two industries themselves, or for the British and Indian governments to agree that certain classes of goods would not be made in Calcutta. He concluded with the pious hope that in the ongoing trade negotiations between Britain and India, the British negotiators would 'consistently have regard to the peculiar position of the community of Dundee and the surrounding district, and their dependence in such a singular degree upon one industry'.[58]

A perceptive intervention in the debate was made by James Alexander Duncan, who sat as a Conservative and Unionist for North Kensington but had close ties with Dundee (he later represented South Angus from 1950 to 1964). Duncan, whose family estate was in Perthshire, was a founder and life Governor of the Dundee Institute of Arts and Technology, and had witnessed for himself the distress in Dundee caused by the dual impact of the Depression and Calcutta imports. He agreed with Foot that tariffs or quotas would not work because India could simply 'raise the existing tax on raw materials to a point at which it would meet any tariffs we put on'. Duncan reflected a common view in Dundee by speaking in somewhat bewildered language about the relationship with Calcutta. 'In a way, this is a new problem,' he told the House. 'Our old conception of the Dominions and Colonies was that they were mainly raw material producers, and that we, and other Continental countries, were the manufacturing nations. But this is one of the few cases where a Dominion product competes with European products.' The issue at stake, he continued, was 'the whole question of Asiatic competition with European standards'. He summed up the Dundee–Calcutta relationship with the perceptive insight that 'India holds all the cards'.[59]

War saved jute in 1939 as it had done in the past. Ever since jute products had been manufactured in Dundee, war had been kind to the industry. This was first evident by the demand for jute cloth and bags during the Crimean War (1854–6) and was demonstrated in spectacular fashion during the Great War (1914–18) as millions of sandbags were required for the trenches on the Western Front. The Second World War (1939–45) also led to huge demands for jute bags.[60] After the war had ended, however, the old economic threats to Dundee's jute industry reasserted themselves. Hope for intervention was revived in Dundee with the election of the Labour government in 1945. These hopes were raised when no less a figure than Sir Stafford Cripps came to Dundee to discuss the future of the jute industry. Cripps, serving as President of the Board of Trade in the new government, had been a significant figure in the war years – above all, when he was sent by Churchill to India in 1942 to discuss possible political solutions with Jawaharlal Nehru, Mohandas Gandhi, Mohammed Ali Jinnah and other leaders of India's campaign for independence. Now Cripps was on a mission to explore ways of saving Dundee. There was 'a very large attendance' at the meeting held in the Royal Exchange Building. The room was filled with representatives from sixty-eight firms involved in jute, along with the wartime Jute Controller, and delegates from the trade unions.[61]

This momentous meeting turned into a bleak reminder of how little Dundee could expect from any British government. The briefing papers prepared by the experts at the Board of Trade made it clear to Cripps that he should on no account promise any actions against Calcutta. 'There is no doubt that the Indian competition is a serious challenge to the Dundee industry,' the Board of Trade experts warned, but they pointed out that Bengal 'has the advantage of not only of growing the raw jute but also has cheap labour'. The intra-empire trade arrangements made at Ottawa in 1932 prohibited Britain from placing any discriminatory tariffs against other parts of the Empire. Cripps was advised to try and steer the Dundee negotiators away from discussion of measures against Calcutta. The Dundee representatives stubbornly refused to be brushed aside in that way. The Chairman of the Association of Jute Spinners and Manufacturers, P. Ewart Jack, welcomed Cripps with flattering remarks about his 1942 mission 'to settle the very difficult Indian problem' and proceeded to explain Dundee's own 'Indian problem'. Jack summarised Dundee petitioning in the 1930s, and reminded Cripps that a Post-War Planning Committee had warned of the need to protect the industry 'with regard to these abnormal importations [from India]'. Cripps declined to be drawn.[62] It was clear that the situation had not changed since the 1890s. No British government was prepared to act against India by restraining Calcutta jute imports. Such a policy could never work in economic terms, because the Indian government could respond by simply raising the excise on raw jute exports and so increase Dundee's costs. Moreover, any such action would undermine Britain's claim that it was in India to help Indians. Dundee could expect no action from London until the British Raj folded its tents and left India.

Once India did become an independent country, Dundee finally achieved some of the relief it had been seeking since the 1890s, with the Jute Control used to protect Dundee against the products of Calcutta. The partition of the subcontinent also helped Dundee a little in the late 1940s and 1950s by placing the best jute-growing regions in East Pakistan (now Bangladesh) rather than India. This meant that the Calcutta mills faced challenging conditions close to home. But it was too late to save the industry. By this time jute had lost its place as the world's cheapest and most widely used packaging to newer synthetic fabrics and paper products. Jute had finally succumbed to its old nemesis of cheaper substi-tutes. Dundee's jute industry gradually but inexorably wound down. In 1950 there were still 19,000 workers employed in jute; by the 1980s the number had dwindled to less than 1,000.[63]

The construction of the new Taybank Works between 1947 and 1949 seemed a sign that new life might be breathed into the industry. This was a forward-looking enterprise. Taybank New Works was the first plant to be commissioned after the war and was beautifully designed by Kenneth F. Mason. The mill was owned by the Scottish Cooperative Wholesale

Society and from the outset the conditions in which the workers operated were borne in mind. As the Scottish Architecture website explains, 'the Co-op's credo meant that its building derived from a vein of paternal socialism – an almost Fabian attitude to care of its employees – which stretches back to the example of Robert Owen's mills at New Lanark. At Taybank, the workers were bathed in light which poured through both the glazed curtain walls, and great expanses of patent glazing on the north-facing parts of the sawtooth roofs.'[64] But even such thoughtful and creative factory design could not rescue the jute industry in Dundee. The optimism of the Taybank promoters was carried on into the 1950s as Dundee firms hoped that better protection from Indian competition and some collective action on increased variety of goods and better marketing would provide some stability and even prosperity for the industry. Any hopes of re-establishing the Dundee industry as a force in the British and world economies, however, were dashed in the 1970s and 1980s. On 19 October 1998 the MV *Banglar Urmi* from Chittagong docked in Dundee with the final shipment of 310 tons of raw jute. The last bale was processed in May 1999, and in August of that year a ship sailed back to Calcutta taking Taybank's power looms with it. All the power loom machinery had been sold to the jute magnate G.J. Wadwha.[65] The jute era in Dundee finally ended in the last year of the twentieth century.

This dismantling of Dundee's last jute mill marked the end of the jute era in Dundee, and reminds us of all the issues that made Dundee's struggle for survival as a jute city such a fruitless one. Wadwha's factory employed no fewer than 10,000 workers. The Calcutta and Dacca mills were still close to the jute-growing regions and close to the vast markets in India, Bangladesh, Pakistan, and elsewhere in Asia, that still used jute. In retrospect it was more remarkable that Dundee had such a long run of success with jute than that it failed to sustain an industry that depended on importing raw material from halfway round the world. Jute was an early example of the impact of globalisation on the world economy, as cheaper labour in Asian settings began sucking out manufacturing jobs from the older industrialised regions of North America and Western Europe. No ingenuity, or hard work, or abysmal wages in Dundee could have stood up against these relentless forces shaping the world economy of the twentieth century. It is worth pointing out too that those companies in the Dundee region – such as William

Low & Company of Monifieth – which manufactured jute mill machinery were also opposed to any checks on the expansion of the Indian industry. Back in 1896 Leng had noticed mill machinery and boilers in the Calcutta mills made by Pearce Brothers of Dundee, Beely of Manchester and Fairbairn of Leeds.[66] By the 1930s the Scottish companies which manufactured bobbins and shuttles for textile mills sold about 90 per cent of their output to India. The Dundee jute manufacturers themselves sometimes worked at cross-purposes with each other. In the same year as a Dundee delegation was complaining vociferously to the India Office about Calcutta competition, the owners of the Angus Jute Works sold their entire plant to Marwari businessmen.[67] It is hardly surprising that the Dundee jute manufacturers never managed to find any allies anywhere else in Scotland or England for the entire course of their twentieth-century battle against Calcutta.

Throughout most of the century there was a sense of impending doom surrounding Dundee's jute industry. Successive governments in London – whether Liberal, Conservative or Labour – did nothing to help, either because of their commitment to free trade, or because of their obligation to respond to Indian concerns. In contrast to the other textile industry regions of Britain, Dundee had only a puny political clout at Westminster. The cotton industry could count on from sixty to eighty MPs representing textile towns in Lancashire and Yorkshire, while Dundee could muster a mere two.[68] And the jute industry could not even count on those two. Dundee's MPs were always divided about what could be done. Even in the depths of the 1930s Depression, Horsbrugh and Foot could not mount a united campaign. And Winston Churchill, the most influential MP Dundee had in the twentieth century, explicitly declined to fight for the city's industry. In these circumstances the Dundee jute community often felt abandoned. At the large meeting of owners and workers held in 1945, they told Cripps that Dundee jute was 'the Cinderella of the Textile Industries'.[69]

In contrast to the fairy tale, no fairy godmother appeared to save Dundee against its Calcutta rival. If we take this fanciful metaphorical comparison to its conclusion, Cinderella Jute continued to toil for less and less until she died. But Cinderella is a good story that has enchanted readers for hundreds of years. The Dundee–Calcutta story, with its strange mixture of intimacy and competition, is a fascinating historical tale. It deserves to be remembered as an extraordinary episode in the history of the city. It is a unique story of two cities in Scotland and Bengal that has no parallel elsewhere in world history.

NOTES

1. Sir John Leng, MP, *Letters from India and Ceylon including the Manchester of India and the Indian Dundee and Calcutta Jute Mills* (Dundee, 1896).

2. DUA, MS 15/1: O. Graham, 'The jute industry of Dundee 1828–1928', p. 94.

3. DUA, MS 83/3/1(1), AJSM Minutes 1918–1928: Minutes of the Meeting of the Association of Jute Spinners and Manufacturers, 22 April 1919; Report of a Deputation to London in Regard to Importation of Indian Manufactured goods, 7 February 1919.

4. Hansard, HC (series 5) vol. 314, cols 2168–9 (15 July 1936), cols. 2168–2169.

5. *British Association Handbook and Guide* (London, British Association, 1912), pp. 118–19.

6. Leng, *Letters from India and Ceylon*, p. 28.

7. J.K. Hardie, *India: Impressions and Suggestions* (London, Independent Labour Party, 1909), p. 8.

8. T. Johnston and J.F. Sime, *Exploitation in India* (Dundee, UJFTW, 1926), p. 3.

9. *Report of the Indian Industrial Commission 1916–1918* (Calcutta, 1918), p. 10; J.G. Parker, 'Scottish enterprise in India 1750–1914' in R.A. Cage (ed.), *The Scots Abroad: Labour, Capital and Enterprise 1750–1914* (London, 1985), p. 210.

10. University of Cambridge South Asian Collections [hereafter CSAC], Benthall Papers, Box X: Benthall to J.A. McKerrow, London, 6 September 1935.

11. CSAC, Benthall Papers, Boxes X and XI: Benthall to G.B. Morton, London, 2 September 1935 and 7 September 1935; Benthall to McKerrow, 31 August 1935; Benthall to McKerrow, 18 October 1935. Dornford Yates (pen name of William Mercer) 'in company with John Buchan and "Sapper" [Cyril McNeil, author of the Bulldog Drummond series] dominated the market for adventure stories between the wars.' See A.J. Smithers, *Dornford Yates: A Biography* (London, 1982), pp. 3, 125.

12. Indian Jute Mills Association [hereafter IJMA], *Report of the Committee 1908* (Calcutta, 1909), p. 18.

13. Indian Central Jute Committee [hereafter ICJC], *Report on the Marketing of Jute and Jute Products* (Calcutta, 1941), p. 52.

14. CSAC, Benthall Papers, Box X: G.B. Morton to H.P. Bennett, Calcutta, 23 August 1935.

15. TNA: PRO ED 26/201, Department of Overseas Trade, Correspondence on Jute, 1935: H.A.F. Lindsay to F. Hollings, London, 9 September 1935.

16. CSAC, Benthall Papers, Box X: Benthall to G.B. Morton, Bishopsteignton, Devon, 31 August 1935.

17. Eugenie Fraser, *A Home by the Hooghly* (Edinburgh, 1989), pp. 16–20, 30, 33.

18. Ibid., pp. 202–3.

19. DUA, MS 86/V/7/33, Alexander Murray Correspondence, 1937–1938: Alexander Murray to C. Mason, 11 January 1938.

20. Fraser, *A Home by the Hooghly*, pp. 202–3.

21. DUA, MS 84/3/1(1), Minutes of the Association of Jute Spinners and Manufactures:

Report of the Delegation to London in Regard to the Importation of Indian manufactured Goods, 15 April 1919.

22. D.R. Wallace, *The Romance of Jute: A Short History of the Calcutta Jute Mill Industry* (London, Calcutta and Simla, 1909), pp. 96–7.

23. G.T. Stewart, *Jute and Empire: The Calcutta Jute Wallahs and the Landscapes of Empire* (Manchester, 1998), pp. 93–4, 110–13, 211–13.

24. TNA: PRO BT 64/3700: H.V. Bonar, Jute Controller, Board of Trade, Confidential Memorandum, 4 October 1945.

25. ICJC, *Report of the Marketing of Jute and Jute Products* (Calcutta, 1941), p. 17.

26. *Report of the Bengal Jute Enquiry Committee 1934*, Chairman R.S. Finlow (Alipore, 1934), pp. 5–6.

27. W.A. Graham Clark, *The Linen, Jute and Hemp Industries of the United Kingdom* (US Department of Commerce, Washington DC, 1913), p. 139; IJMA, *Report of the Half Year ended 31 December 1890* (Calcutta, 1891), p. 1; Baron A. Heyking, 'Potentialities of Russo-Indian trade relations', *Imperial & Asiatic Quarterly Review* 13–14 (January–October 1918), p. 13.

28. *The Statesman* (Calcutta), 12 November 1878.

29. Leng, *Letters from India and Ceylon*, p. 73.

30. ICJC, *Report on the Marketing of Jute and Jute Products*, p. 21; Clark, *Linen, Jute and Hemp Industries*, p. 140.

31. 'Hessians', *The Statesman*, 24 November 1917, p. 6.

32. Speech by D.P. McKenzie, IJMA, *Report of the Committee 1921* (Calcutta, 1922), p. iii.

33. Wallace, *The Romance of Jute*, p. 48.

34. CSAC, Benthall Papers, Box XIII: Statement on Jute Manufactures by Unofficial Delegation, India House, London, 14 September 1937.

35. Speech by H.H. Burn, IJMA, *Report of the Committee 1936*, pp. 2–3, 14.

36. DUA, MS 86/V/7/24, Private Letters from Calcutta 1936–40: C.M. Laurie to C. Mason, Calcutta, 8 July 1937.

37. Speech by F.R.S. Charles, Chairman IJMA, *The Statesman*, 29 January 1915, p. 5.

38. Stewart, *Jute and Empire*, pp. 48–9; E. Gauldie (ed.), *The Dundee Textile Industry 1790–1885: From the Papers of Peter Carmichael of Arthurstone* (Edinburgh, 1969), p. xxvii; Helmut Vogt, *Die Beueler Jutespinnerei und ihre Arbeiter 1868–1961* (Bonn, 1990), pp. 30, 88, 198.

39. D. Chakrabarty, *Rethinking Working Class History: Bengal 1890–1940* (Princeton, 1989).

40. W.M. Walker, *Juteopolis: Dundee and its Textile Workers, 1885–1923* (Edinburgh, 1979).

41. Stewart, *Jute and Empire*, pp. 45–9; Walker, *Juteopolis*, pp. 47–8, 149, 155–6; E. Gordon, *Women and the Labour Movement in Scotland 1850–1914* (Oxford, 1991).

42. *The Times*, 13 March 1911, quoted in Sir Roper Lethbridge, 'The Dundee and Calcutta jute industries', *Imperial and Asiatic Quarterly Review* (3rd series) 33 (January–April 1912), pp. 10–11.

43. Debate on Board of Trade Report: Hansard, HC (series 5) vol. 209, col. 936 (25 July 1927), col. 936.

44. TNA: PRO BT 64/3700: Confidential Memorandum by H.V. Bonar, Board of Trade, 4 October 1945.

45. Ibid.

46. Stewart, *Jute and Empire*, pp. 62–3; *Advertiser*, 28 January 1893; IJMA, *Report of the Committee 1893*, Appendix A, p. 22.

47. Speech by George Lyall, IJMA, *Proceedings of the Annual General Meeting held at the*

Bengal Chamber of Commerce, 4 March 1895, pp. 2–11.

48. S.E.J. Clarke, Secretary of the IJMA, to C.E. Buckland, Secretary to the Government of Bengal, General Department, Miscellaneous Branch, Calcutta, 28 June 1895, IJMA, *Report of the Committee 1895*, Appendix F, pp. 58–61.

49. DUA, MS 84/3/1(1), AJSM Minutes 1918–28: Report of a Deputation to London in Regard to Importation of Indian Manufactured Goods, 7 February 1919.

50. Ibid.

51. Ibid., Reply by Winston Churchill to William Henderson, James Prain, and R.B. Sharp.

52. Stewart, *Jute and Empire*, pp. 111–13.

53. TNA: PRO ED 26/201, Confidential, Department of Overseas Trade: H.A.F. Lindsay to F. Hollings, London, 9 September 1935.

54. DUA, MS 84/5/3/4, AJSM, Fiscal Sub-Committee: Meeting on Indian Imports with the President and Secretary of the Dundee Chamber of Commerce, 16 October 1935.

55. Ibid., 'Mr. Crawford's Publicity Memorandum', 27 February 1936.

56. Speech by Florence Horsbrugh: Hansard, HC (series 5) vol. 314, cols 2168–9 (15 July 1936).

57. Ibid., cols 2170–80.

58. Ibid., vol. 331, cols 278–80, 281–3.

59. Ibid., cols 285–7.

60. Stewart, *Jute and Empire*, pp. 1, 5, 54, 137.

61. TNA: PRO BT 64/3700: G.H. Carruthers, Board of Trade, Note for the President's Meeting with the Jute Industry.

62. DUA, MS 84/6/1, Post-War Planning Committee: Report of the Meeting of Producers, Merchants, Jute Brokers, and Trade Unions with the Rt. Hon. Sir Stafford Cripps, President of the Board of Trade, Dundee, 14 December 1945; TNA: PRO BT 64/3700, Board of Trade: Jute Working Party Minutes, 3 January 1946.

63. J. and J. Keay (eds), *Collins Encyclopaedia of Scotland* (London, 1994), p. 564.

64. Scottish Architecture website, http://www.scottisharchitecture.com/blog/read/442.

65. Ibid.

66. Leng, *Letters from India and Ceylon*, p. 77.

67. Stewart, *Jute and Empire*, p. 197.

68. Ibid., pp. 10–11.

69. DUA, MS 84/6/1, Post-War Planning Committee: Report of the Meeting of Producers, Merchants, Jute Brokers, and Trade Unions with the Rt. Hon. Sir Stafford Cripps, President of the Board of Trade, Dundee, 14 December 1945.

CHAPTER 3

The Physical Development of the Tay Estuary in the Twentieth Century and its Impact

Rob Duck

Sometime Rector of the University of Dundee, the actor, comedian and television presenter Stephen Fry has described Dundee's waterfront as 'ludicrously ideal'.[1] Scotland's fourth city has a truly dramatic location on the north bank of what has for many years been widely regarded as the cleanest major estuary in Europe. The cleanliness of the Tay Estuary is in no small measure due to the large freshwater discharge from the influent River Tay. Along with its many tributaries, it drains a catchment area of around 6,500 square kilometres.[2] This extends into the rain and snowmelt-fed Grampian Highlands as far westwards as The Hill of the Calf, Beinn Laoigh, in Argyllshire and the flows generated downstream below Perth give the estuary a high natural flushing capacity on the ebbing or outflowing tide. For centuries this, along with the large tidal exchange, has helped to keep the estuary relatively free of pollutants, transporting and dispersing these seawards into the North Sea. While it may be small in wider European terms, the River Tay is, in fact, the foremost British river in terms of freshwater discharge; together with the subordinate River Earn it delivers a long-term mean inflow of around 180 cubic metres of fresh water per second (cumecs) into the estuary.[3] In flood events, such as the notorious one in January 1993, the largest flood since 1814, which devastated large residential areas of Perth including the North Muirton housing estate, discharges of over twelve times the average value have been recorded. A peak discharge of 2,269 cumecs was recorded on the 17th of the month and the corresponding daily mean flow of 1,965 cumecs represents a UK record.[4] It is, however, thanks to the upstream hydroelectric dams constructed in the 1950s, which created new lochs like Loch Faskally and raised the water levels of pre-existing ones, that the magnitudes of the peak discharges were not even greater and the downstream consequences even more severe.

As local journalist Norman Watson so aptly put it in his history of the city, 'The god of geography smiled on Dundee's stunning location.'[5] The urban frontage is not, however, particularly extensive in relation to the overall length of the estuary; only around 13 kilometres along the north bank are developed compared with the tidal reach of 50 kilometres from the estuary mouth upstream to Scone. Moreover, with little or no significant development on its southern shores, the Tay retains a predominantly rural character. As such, it is a rarity, a gem amongst Britain's major estuarine embayments. Nevertheless, it has been progressively modified over the centuries, often imperceptibly, by human intervention.

The natural Dundee shoreline took the form of a series of wide beaches backed by a stepped rocky cliff. The lower part of this is preserved today as the cutting of the Perth to Dundee railway line, through Lower Devonian sandstones with igneous intrusions, along the north part of Riverside Drive beneath the University of Dundee Botanic Gardens near the airport. Elsewhere the former shoreline is discernible as a marked break in slope, typically built upon, built against, graded or landscaped, as on the south side of Perth Road along Seabraes and the Nethergate, beneath the Queen's Hotel and the Dundee Contemporary Arts Centre. Further east, the old, stepped cliff line can be readily seen to the north of Dock Street with, among others, the elevated thoroughfares of Victoria Road and Arbroath Road high above. The land to the south of the foot of this cliff line has all been claimed by man from the estuary progressively over the centuries to create space for docks, harbours, railways, marshalling yards, roads, housing, and industrial, retail and recreational uses. As such, almost 7 per cent of the city's compact area from Invergowrie Bay in the west to the foot of Margaret Crescent, Broughty Ferry, in the east is developed on land that has been won progressively from the estuary, thereby contributing to a reduction in the natural volume of the latter.

The nineteenth century, in particular, witnessed important changes to the physical environment of the Tay Estuary. These included extensive agricultural land claim and reed planting on the north side,[6] major dredging operations to improve the navigation channel to the harbour of

Perth, the construction and subsequent rebuilding of the present Tay Railway Bridge following the infamous collapse of the original, and the completion of extensive dock and harbour engineering works at Dundee. In the following century, however, a series of no less significant developments were planned, some to be shelved but others completed, and these, along with the earlier works, continue to help reshape the Tay, modify its form and its flow dynamics, and impact upon its natural capacity to accommodate the tidal influx of water.

The surprise vista, dominated by the spectacular ice-sculpted igneous intrusion that forms The Law, suddenly greets the motorist heading northwards to Dundee. This is thanks to part of one such development: a deep rock cutting, blasted in the early 1960s through the ridge of Lower Devonian age lava flows that form the North Fife Hills, to establish the connection from the newly constructed Tay Road Bridge to the road network of Fife and beyond. The opening of the multi-pier bridge in August 1966, the lowermost crossing of the Tay, was a major engineering achievement comparable with those of its railway predecessors. It was one of the most readily apparent, important events of the twentieth century in the region and it had multifarious consequences. The obvious economic benefits, including greatly improved commuter and other motor travel opportunities, overshadowed the immediate demise of the Tay Ferries to and from Newport-on-Tay, thus ending two and a half centuries of a traditional means of estuarial crossing, the closure of most of the cluster of small shops adjacent to the ferry's southern terminal, and the loss of the local railway branch through Wormit, West and East Newport to Tayport. The latter was a casualty, not of the infamously short-sighted Beeching Report of 1963 on 'The Reshaping of British Railways', but severed by the imperative to excavate the cutting for the dual carriageway to the bridge, the new Road to Dundee, that was to open up the stunning northward view across the Tay to Dundee Law.

The view would have been substantially different had the road bridge been built immediately to the west of the railway bridge, as was the recommendation of the 1950 'Tay Valley Plan'.[7] Such a bridge would have crossed the estuary at a considerably wider point and would therefore have been more expensive to construct. It would not, however, have necessitated the extensive obliteration and destruction of large tracts of the central part of the city, including the Royal Arch and Dundee West Railway Station, and its nearby docks, to make way for the present city centre landfall with its proliferation of access roads and curving ramps, which has clearly outraged, among others, the architectural historian Charles McKean.[8]

Less obvious, however, was the impact that the bridge would have below water, within the Tay Estuary itself. Its ultimate design was, to a large extent, constrained by expense; it was constructed at a cost of £4.8 million, whereas the nearby suspension bridge that spans the Firth of Forth, which opened two years earlier in 1964, cost around £11.5 million to build. Two and a quarter kilometres in length, the Tay Road Bridge comprises tubular steel box girders fixed above a series of forty-three twin concrete columns supported by concrete piers, of which thirty-nine are in the water. Unlike those of the railway bridge, the piers of the road bridge were placed about twenty degrees offset to the principal current direction, to bring about the sighting alignment onto Dundee Law. As a result, they affect the currents considerably, having a blocking influence; indeed, there can be as much as a half metre difference in tidal level on either side of the bridge. The wedge-shaped ends of the piers, known as cutwaters, are designed to divide both the flood and ebb currents and also to break up ice floes. In the nineteenth century such floes had been an annual winter occurrence in the estuary and the blockage by ice of the spans of Smeaton's Bridge in Perth in 1814 resulted in the partial damming of the Tay, which was the cause of the highest water level ever recorded in the city.[9] The last periods of winter weather sufficiently cold to promote substantial ice floe activity in the estuary were in January 1982 (Plate 14) and, to a lesser extent, in January 1987. The final two decades of the twentieth century and indeed to date, with the exception of a relatively minor event in December 2001, have been essentially ice-free in that respect, a local consequence of the general climatic amelioration that Scotland and the rest of the world is currently experiencing.

Collectively, the thirty-nine solid concrete piers of the Tay Road Bridge in the water, askew to the ebbing and flooding tidal currents, reduce the cross-sectional width of the estuary by around 10 per cent.[10] This has the not insignificant effect of locally speeding up the tidal flows in the vicinity of the bridge[11] and generating elliptically shaped scour hollows in the estuary bed around the bases of the piers. These are largest around those piers that experience the greatest flows in the navigation channel, which, above water, is demarked by four spans that are wider than those of the main body of the bridge. A similar scour phenomenon occurs at the railway bridge, compounded by the fact that the piers of the original structure still remain largely intact within the bed immediately to the east.

The underwater geophysical technique of side-scan sonar has been used extensively to map the nature of the estuary bed[12] and how it changes through time. The acoustic images produced, known as sonographs, which are rather like oblique underwater air photographs produced not from light but from sound, reveal not only the so-called bedforms, various types of underwater dunes developed in the bottom sediments, but also how these change in their geometry as the flows creating them are subdivided by the bridge piers. In addition, along the line of the road bridge the method reveals the large amounts of anthropogenic debris on the estuary bed, material that was presumably dumped – out of sight, out of mind – at the time of its construction or during one of its many subsequent phases of repair works (Plate 15).

Although the road bridge helps to locally accelerate the velocity of tidal currents and create bedforms up to 3 metres in height, it has not had any major detrimental impact on natural processes in the estuary; its associated scour and hydrodynamic impacts on the bed may be thought of today as being in dynamic equilibrium. It is suggested that more impact than the construction of the bridge has resulted from the cessation of the commercial exploitation of sand and gravel between the two bridges.[13] Until the late 1960s two boats operated during the falling and rising tide,[14] dredging sands from Middle Bank for mortar and plaster manufacture. One quarter of a million tons were extracted each year from this large sand bank, the dominant feature of this reach of the estuary when exposed at low water. Repeated surveys have shown that Middle Bank has, however, grown no more extensive since commercial extraction stopped.[15] This is because most (within the range of 68 to 88 per cent)[16] of the coarse sediment (sand and gravel) that enters the estuary as what is known as bedload, rolling along the bed, is of marine derivation and can be transported as far upstream as Newburgh by flood tidal flows. In consequence, quantities of sediment of the order of a quarter of a million tons per annum are negligible in comparison with the storage capacity of the estuary and the total quantity of contemporary deposits that it contains.

The latter decades of the twentieth century witnessed the installation of numerous coastal protections schemes in the Tay, as at Monifieth, often on a piecemeal basis with little or no consideration of their impacts on other areas. The largest and most influential was a 3-kilometre-long rock armour revetment built at a cost of £3 million by the Ministry of Defence[17] in 1992–3 to protect the east-facing side of the promontory of Buddon Ness on which the Barry Links military training area has long been located. This massive, visually intrusive structure (Colour Plate 1), a continuation southward of an earlier defence near Carnoustie, has served to protect the promontory from wave attack but in so doing has cut off what is a natural source of beach sand for the Tay. Longshore currents on the north side naturally transport sand from east to west around Buddon Ness and into the Tay, feeding the beaches downdrift at Monifieth and Broughty Ferry. These sites are now starved of their natural sediment supply, which has contributed to the necessity to install further defences since these sites have become more vulnerable to marine erosion.

The site investigation that preceded the construction of the road bridge incorporated some thirty-six boreholes along with one of the earliest recorded uses of the so-called 'sparker' seismic reflection method of geophysical exploration.[18] This technique records the time of travel of sound emitted vertically through the water column to and from the estuary bed and reflecting horizons in the substrata, as a means of determining the nature, stratigraphy and structure of the earth materials present below. As well as providing vital information on the materials beneath the bed and the stability of foundations, the data acquired added much to our understanding of the geological and geomorphological history of the estuary, augmenting similar borehole information obtained close on a century earlier for the ill-fated Tay Railway Bridge.[19] It is thanks to the site investigation for the road bridge that we now know that the depth to rock head below the estuary is substantial in the centre of the estuary, extending to over 70 metres below Ordnance Datum. At high water on a spring tide the maximum water depth in the navigation channel is, however, around one quarter of this figure. The rock head section across the estuary thus takes the form of a deep channel that was gouged out by glacier ice during the Pleistocene period. Subsequently this was largely infilled by a complex sequence of Late Glacial and Holocene deposits, into which the present-day estuarine channels are cut,[20] capped by a veneer of contemporary sands, largely of marine origin.[21] Such is the buried channel's great depth that the road bridge, like its railway counterpart, is founded on to bedrock at its northern and southern ends only. For the most part, the piers rest on piles that were driven into the estuary bed, attaining resistance to further penetration into thick layers of gravel deposits.[22]

The collapse of the first Tay Railway Bridge in 1879 was to provide a major stimulus towards greater understanding of the currents and circulation patterns within the Tay Estuary[23] and laid the foundations for much subsequent research for the then Dundee Harbour Trust in the twentieth century.[24] Principally concerned with the practicalities of larger ships entering and leaving Camperdown and Earl Grey Docks, the Trust far-sightedly commissioned the construction of a scaled physical model of the Tay in the early 1930s, one of few British estuaries to possess such a structure. This was a relatively small, so-called fixed bed model, as opposed to one containing mobile grains of sediment. Constructed from plaster of Paris,[25] it was developed by Angus Fulton, Professor of Engineering and Drawing in University College, Dundee, who was also, from 1939 to 1948, simultaneously the college's Principal. The original model had two successors,[26] the more recent of which, owned by the Dundee Port Authority (and its predecessor, the Dundee Harbour Trust) was purpose-built in the 1950s to determine the effects of bridging the Tay by road on water circulation and currents. It was still in active use for subsequent research purposes by civil engineers from the University of Dundee until the 1980s and it was a feature of the University's prospectus (Colour Plate 2) from 1984 to 1987.[27] Calibration of the model was achieved by the radar tracking of multiple floats which followed the estuarine current patterns.[28] It was also a fixed bed model, constructed of concrete, at a horizontal scale of 1:1,760 (one yard to one mile) and a vertical scale of 1:144, and covered the whole of the estuary from the west side of the Bell Rock upstream as far as Perth.[29] As such it was both a very large and heavy structure, since it required a holding reservoir or sump at one end (the North Sea) for the substantial volume of water required to run the various tidal current simulations (see Colour Plate 2). This inevitably placed an uneven weight loading on the floor of the building in which it was housed, located close to the site of the then Caledon Shipyard. The foundations were, of course, on made ground, claimed from the estuary, and through time the differential loading led to differential subsidence that, in turn, caused the heavy model to first deform and then fracture. There was a lack of funding and apparently enthusiasm at the time to make good the foundations, so the model became unserviceable, fell into disrepair and disuse, and was ultimately demolished. Today it is largely forgotten but had it been repaired, properly maintained and made an integral part of the redeveloped Dundee docks, the model could have been promoted and marketed imaginatively as a visitor attraction; not only a research facility but also simultaneously a unique educational and tourist resource. Although the very existence of the Tay tidal model was never widely known, permitting its demise was short-sighted and no less an act of civic vandalism than the demolition of the Royal Arch some twenty years previously.

A new wave of land claim schemes seemed poised to begin in Britain following the Second World War, as the post-war, victorious and euphoric 'anything is possible' spirit prevailed in the country, and the Tay Estuary was no exception. Nearly fifty sites were identified in Scotland that could potentially be won from the sea,[30] but with no consideration whatsoever of the impacts of loss of habitat or the consequences to natural coastal and estuarine processes. The largest single site proposed in the country was within the Tay Estuary at its widest point, where over 1,000 hectares of inter-tidal flats would have been lost, essentially north of a line from Port Allen near Errol to the northern landfall of the Tay Railway Bridge. Much of this area today is a Special Protection Area (SPA), as designated in accordance with the European Community Birds Directive (1979). Moreover, it is noted for hosting the largest continuous reed bed in Britain, which supports nationally important populations of reed bed birds. Furthermore, internationally important populations of wading birds, sea-ducks and geese are dependent on the extensive inter-tidal flats. Thankfully, the proposal, which would have been an ecological disaster that would also have had a major impact on the hydrodynamics of the Tay, by substantially reducing its capacity, was never carried out. However, a lesser scheme, which was to change the physical character of the western part of the Dundee waterfront throughout the latter half of the twentieth century, was poised to do so.

The waterfront to the west of Buckingham Point, the northern landfall of the sweeping curve of the Tay Railway Bridge, on which the University of Dundee sports fields and Dundee airport are developed today, began being claimed from the Tay Estuary immediately after the Second World War, to the seaward of what was locally known at the time as the 'Dream Road',[31] the forerunner to Riverside Drive. The city's post-war refuse dump, or 'coup', was thus developed immediately to the west of the railway bridge and was the receptor for all general and household wastes from the city. Land claim took place in sections divided by rubble walls projecting out from the shore but otherwise unprotected from the waters of the Tay, working from the east progressively westwards (Colour Plate 3), with each being eventually cut off from the estuary by the construction of a masonry retaining wall.[32] Through the dumping of refuse, sufficient land had been claimed, levelled and capped with soil by 1949 to provide the site for the Royal Highland Show, approximately where the University of Dundee sports fields are located today, an event which was to return to the same location in 1957. A small recreational airfield slightly further east was the precursor to the present commercial airport site, which began being developed from the early 1960s to the present day. Its first scheduled services were flown by Loganair in 1963, the founder of which airline, the contractor Willie Logan, had won the tender that same year to build the Tay Road Bridge.

Like most very old landfills, that at Riverside doubtless contains debris of great heterogeneity and there will be little certainty as to exactly what is buried beneath; again, out of sight, out of mind. Some of the more unusual debris within it comprises four railway coaches.[33] At around 10.56 a.m. on Monday 22 October 1979, the 9.35 a.m. Glasgow to Aberdeen express passenger train was involved in a crash on the stretch of the Perth to Dundee line immediately alongside the edge of Invergowrie Bay, close to the site of the advancing landfill. Five people died and fifty-one people were injured when it crashed at a speed estimated at about 60 miles per hour into the rear end of the disabled 8.44 a.m. Glasgow to Dundee local passenger train. The official Department of Transport Railway Inspectorate Report on the accident indicates that the force of the collision threw the rearmost two coaches of the five-coach front train onto the muddy foreshore of the bay and that the second and third coaches were projected onto the sea wall.[34] At the site of the crash, the sea wall abutted the railway formation, forming the seaward edge of the embankment, and was of a low angle masonry construction that sloped for the very short distance down to the estuary. In effect, as others have reported[35] and as confirmed in photographs of the accident, the four rear coaches of the 8.44 were thrown into the Tay; fortunately it was low tide at the time of the accident. Those four damaged coaches were subsequently observed,[36] having been moved and repositioned in a roughly north to south trending line within the

Riverside landfill to the west of where the present western end of the airport runway is today, later to be buried, thus disposed of and now long forgotten.

The final phase of land claim continued westwards until the landfill eventually stopped accepting wastes in 1996.[37] The area to the west of the airport was capped and landscaped into a rolling topography that involved the raising of the land level above that of the general low flat elevation of the claimed land on which the airport and playing fields are located. The intention is that this area between Dundee Airport and Invergowrie Bay (Colour Plate 4), which for the last decade of the twentieth century was, in effect, a prohibited zone, will eventually be transformed into a nature park with full public access. However, this will only be once a satisfactory solution to the management of landfill gases, principally methane, has been agreed with the Scottish Environment Protection Agency. While this is consistent with the aim of Dundee City Council's twenty-first-century, long-term vision to connect the city to the waterfront,[38] reclaiming it for communities, an unfortunate aspect of this part of the site is that the landscaping has created a visual barrier that has completely obscured the view of the Tay from the Riverside carriageway level.

Following the reorganisation of local government in Scotland in April 1996, Dundee City Council replaced the former City of Dundee District Council. As a consequence of this reorganisation, the city's boundaries contracted to align with the built up sector, with the loss of the Monifieth and Sidlaw areas, reducing its land area by just over 75 per cent to around 60 square kilometres. A consequence was the loss to the local authority of land that might potentially yield sites suitable for landfill purposes. Despite the pressures to dispose of demolition waste from the many redundant multi-storey blocks in Ardler and also incinerator ash, the Riverside landfill was fortunately not extended even further westwards into what still remains of Invergowrie Bay (Colour Plates 3 and 4). Had it done so, an important habitat for wading birds, part of the Inner Tay Estuary Local Nature Reserve, would have been completely destroyed.

During most of the twentieth century, Dundee, in common with other coastal cities in Britain, relied on sewerage infrastructure that dated back to the Victorian period. Even until the 1970s the entire waste products of the city were discharged in untreated form into the estuary by means of thirty-six short sewer outfalls located along the length of the waterfront from Broughty Ferry to the docks,[39] with a further longer outfall into Invergowrie Bay (Colour Plate 4) serving the western part of the city. A century earlier in 1870, a far-reaching, integrated system of wastewater management had been proposed for Dundee, in part because, off the waterfront, the 'accumulation of black, foul mud is very offensive'.[40] Its author's thesis was that 'the points on which my opinion is desired are not only whether the nuisance which is created by the present outlets can be obviated, but whether the sewage can be utilized at a reasonable cost, and in such a manner as to be beneficial and remunerative to the Town'.[41] In this scheme, a new interceptor sewer from the east end of the High Street would be built to carry all of Dundee's sewage for up to 13 kilometres eastwards to the point of 'embouchure' on the north side of Barry Links. It was proposed that the sewage, which was perceived as 'wasted by being discharged into the River' could be put to good use to irrigate and cultivate some 2,000 acres of dunes at Barry Links which were then 'little more than a sandy desert and used as a rabbit warren'. By interception at the chosen point, 'six-sevenths or seven-eighths of the whole of the produce of the Town might be carried away without its being permitted to enter the River near Dundee. The small remainder may be allowed to flow into the River, or may be pumped into the intercepting sewer at any convenient point near the Docks.' It was calculated that a 5-foot-diameter sewer would be capable of conveying all of the town's sewage, based on a population estimate of 200,000, and 'probably five-sevenths of the storm water' and that 'any excess beyond this quantity may be safely discharged over storm-water overflows, or side weirs into the River, without loss, inconvenience or nuisance'. Pumping engines would be required to prevent deposition of solids in the interceptor sewer where the gradient was slight, as at Monifieth, with flow by gravity elsewhere where the gradient was steeper. The total cost of this scheme was estimated to be £82,000.[42]

It was not, however, until over a century later in 1975 that the then Tayside Regional Council eventually proposed that some improvement should be made to the existing short outfalls. Several options were considered and it was finally proposed that a scheme comprising four separate screening plants each with a long sea outfall should be constructed; three within or close to the city, at Riverside, Stannergate and Monifieth, with the fourth located outside the estuary at Arbroath.[43]

The scheme would not, however, involve any form of secondary treatment; the waste water would receive primary treatment only (that is screening to remove the larger solids), prior to its discharge. The first outfall to be built was at Monifieth Bay, completed by the early 1990s, along with the Panmurefield screening plant at Balmossie Mill. Construction of the Riverside outfall and associated screening plant followed, being completed by 1995, resulting in the Invergowrie Bay outfall (Colour Plate 4) being used only for storm water overflows. However, owing to the transfer of responsibility for water and sewerage from the local authority to the then North of Scotland Water Authority (now Scottish Water), the central Stannergate outfall was never constructed and untreated flows continued to be discharged directly into the estuary via numerous short outfalls until beyond the close of the twentieth century.[44]

One of the most important pieces of European Union legislation to emerge in the final decade of the twentieth century, a cornerstone of policy on the water environment, was the Urban Waste Water Treatment Directive (1991), which was initially transposed into Scottish law through the Urban Waste Water Treatment (Scotland) Regulations (1994). Its laudable aim was to protect the environment from any adverse effects due to discharges of urban waste water and waste water from certain industrial sectors. To meet the requirements of the Directive as stipulated in the Regulations, a single wastewater treatment plant was identified as providing the best overall improvement to the receiving waters of the Tay Estuary and lower Angus coastline.[45] Extensive offshore data collection, analysis and modelling, on this occasion by numerical rather than physical means, established that the optimum location for the outfall was well outside the estuary mouth, close to the site of the former Hatton Airfield near East Haven, between Carnoustie and Arbroath. The £100 million project, at the time the largest of its kind in Scotland, was to come to fruition at the start of the new century, with completion at the end of 2001. It involved the construction of a network of seven pumping stations and storm-water storage tanks, along with 35 kilometres of pipeline to intercept all of the pre-existing outfalls and move sewage from the entire length of the Dundee waterfront, Broughty Ferry, Monifieth, Carnoustie and Arbroath, to converge at the Hatton outfall.[46] Storm-water overflows occur when the storage tanks reach their capacity and these are discharged directly into the estuary via the existing Victorian short outfall pipes. An evaluation of the impact of this enterprise on improving the quality of the waters of the Tay is beyond the timeframe of this chapter, but it is anticipated to be profound. The similarities between the new 'Tay Wastewater Treatment Scheme', as it is known, and that proposed well over a century earlier in 1870 are, however, quite remarkable. Had the latter gone ahead and the irrigation of Barry Links proved both fruitful and remunerative, it is a matter for speculation as to whether the land would have been compulsorily purchased by the War Office from the 14th Earl of Dalhousie in 1893 as a military training area,[47] a purpose for which it has been used ever since. Moreover, the massive rock armour revetment that protects its eastern shores but has depleted other beaches of their sediment supply might, in that event, never have been built.

Serious pollution occurrences in the Tay were fortunately rare events during the twentieth century. The most notable was the *Tank Duchess* incident,[48] which took place on Leap Day, 29 February 1968. By means of a split in the hull, an estimated 87 tons of Venezuelan crude oil leaked from the tanks of the vessel, which had been moored between the road bridge and the Newcombe Shoal (to the west of Tayport). The spillage took place after low water and the oil was carried up estuary on the rising flood tide to beyond the railway bridge. On the succeeding ebb tide a north-westerly wind encouraged drifting towards the Fife shore, resulting in heavy pollution on the western side of most projecting headlands.[49] Speed is of the essence when dealing with an oil pollution incident like this in order to minimise loss of animal life, but the numerous author-ities involved were unprepared to deal with such an occurrence. Four days later, still no action had been taken and by that time substantial deposits of oil had been spread and transported by the tidal currents from close to Newburgh in the upstream direction downstream as far as Tentsmuir Point on the Fife shore. Pollution was particularly heavy at Balmerino and along the reach between Newport and Tayport. The Dundee side of the Tay was less affected, with the main concentrations of oil being at Stannergate, Broughty Ferry, Monifieth and to a lesser extent at Carnoustie. Overall, many kilometres of beaches in the lower part of the estuary were fouled. Furthermore, over 1,300 birds died as a result of the period of inaction following the incident, including between 5 and 25 per cent of the total British population of eider duck.[50] The necessity for a rapid, co-ordinated response was a hard lesson learned; the delay in cleaning up the pollution, during which period it spread so extensively, was the result of protracted discussion about whose responsibility it was to do so.[51] At the time, the Tay River Purification Board had no authority in the tidal waters; while above the tidal limit it had the power to prosecute for pollution, it had no authority to clean it up. The Dundee Harbour Trust was empowered to disperse an oil slick only if it was declared a hazard to navigation, which it was not. Furthermore, the various local authorities of Dundee, Angus and Fife, including county and burgh councils, were able to finance the cleaning of their own beaches but not of the waters lapping against them. It is of little surprise that this lack of a co-ordinated approach led to the organisation of a reflective conference of local authorities and other bodies in the Marryat Hall in April 1970 on a proposed 'Tay Estuary Oil Pollution Scheme'.[52] By the end of the twentieth century, however, no other significant oil spillages had occurred, though in December 1995 an oil tanker, bound for the Port of Dundee to discharge part of its cargo, touched gravel bottom near the entrance to the Tay.[53] Fortunately, no oil spillage took place, thanks to the double-hulled construction design of the vessel.

The twentieth century saw the last land claim in the Tay Estuary, the culmination of a centuries-old practice. The impacts of this human intervention are, however, unlikely to manifest themselves until well into the current century. The amount of water that flows into and out of an estuary with the flood and ebb tides, excluding any freshwater river discharges, is called the tidal prism. It has been calculated that, on an ordinary neap tide, some 213 million cubic metres of water enters and leaves the Tay. On an ordinary spring tide, however, this tidal exchange volume increases greatly to 380 million cubic metres of water.[54] It is also worth noting that a persistent 'high' or 'low' atmospheric pressure over the North Sea can alter the mean sea level. In the Tay, this can result in actual tidal heights being between 20 and 30 centimetres lower or higher, respectively, than predicted levels.[55] In addition, there is high confidence that mean sea level has risen both globally and around Britain during the twentieth century and that this trend has accelerated recently as a result of global warming. Global sea level rise through much of the twenty-first century is currently projected at around 4 millimetres per year.[56] In Scotland, however, mean sea level rise is to some extent moderated by isostatic uplift of the land following the melting of the last Scottish ice sheet some ten thousand years ago. This effect is, however, far from uniform owing to the wide regional variations in ice thickness and conse-quent depression of the crust. Owing to the land claim from the Tay, increasing quantities of water have to be accommodated by an estuary that is now smaller in its capacity than nature intended. Considered in isolation, the amount of land claim is unlikely to have any great impact on sea level rise in the area. However, when the most recent estimates for sea level rise in the Tay region are taken into account,[57] which indicate that the Dundee area could experience sea level rise of up to a maximum of 35 centimetres by 2080, the combined influence is likely to lead to future coastal flooding problems in the estuary. Low-lying, waterfront areas that are unprotected or poorly protected, such as parts of Broughty Ferry, are particularly vulnerable to wave run-up and potential flooding if storm waves are coincident with a high spring tide. Had the post-Second World War proposals to claim the extensive inter-tidal flats on the north side of the estuary gone ahead,[58] the impacts of sea level rise would, without doubt, have been far greater in the estuary. To accom-modate rising sea levels along the low-lying coasts of south-east England, a practice known as managed retreat began in Essex in 1991. This involves the breaching of old embankments originally built to claim agricultural land from the sea and allowing that land to re-flood. It is not incon-ceivable that this will take place in the upper Tay Estuary in the twenty-first century, breaching nineteenth-century embankments to provide accommodation space for sea level rise in downstream urban areas that require protection, many of which were, ironically, claimed from the estuary in the twentieth century.

ACKNOWLEDGEMENTS

I am greatly indebted to the collective encyclopaedic knowledge of William (Bill) Dow (formerly Dundee College of Education), Professor John McManus (formerly Department of Geology, University of Dundee and School of Geography and Geosciences St Andrews) and Professor Charles McKean (History, School of Humanities, University of Dundee) for their most helpful and thought-provoking discussions on Dundee and the Tay over more years than I prefer to recall and for allowing me to pick their brains on so many occasions. I would also like to record my gratitude to David Kett (Central Library, Dundee City Council), Caroline Brown and Jennifer Johnstone (Archive, Records

Management and Museum Services, University of Dundee) for their assistance in locating various manuscripts and reports.

NOTES

1. Dundee Waterfront: http://www.dundeewaterfront.com (accessed 27 December 2008).
2. R.W. Duck, 'Evolving understanding of the Tay Estuary, Scotland: exploring the linkages between frontal systems and bedforms' in D.M. Fitzgerald and J. Knight (eds), *High Resolution Morphodynamics and Sedimentary Evolution of Estuaries* (Berlin, 2005), pp. 299–314.
3. Duck, 'Evolving understanding of the Tay Estuary'.
4. A.R. Black and J.L. Anderson, 'The great Tay flood of January 1993' in *1993 Yearbook, Hydrological Data, UK Series* (Institute of Hydrology, 1994), pp. 25–34.
5. N. Watson, *Dundee: A Short History* (Edinburgh, 2006), p. 224.
6. A.N.L. Hodd, 'Agricultural Change in the Carse of Gowrie, 1750–1875' (unpublished PhD thesis, University of Dundee, 1974), p. 428.
7. G. Payne, 'The Tay Valley Plan: a physical, social and economic survey and plan for the future development of East Central Scotland' (East Central Scotland Regional Planning Advisory Committee, 1950), p. 433; A. Scarth, 'The physical setting of the Tay Road Bridge', *Scottish Geographical Magazine* 82 (1966), pp. 104–9.
8. C. McKean and P. Whatley with K. Baxter, *Lost Dundee: Dundee's Lost Architectural Heritage* (Edinburgh, 2008), p. 244.
9. D.J. Gilvear and A.R. Black, 'Flood-induced embankment failures on the River Tay: implications of climatically induced hydrological change in Scotland', *Hydrological Sciences Journal* 44 (1999), pp. 345–62.
10. J. McManus, 'The geological setting of the bridges of the Lower Tay Estuary with particular reference to the fill of the buried channel', *Quarterly Journal of Engineering Geology* 3 (1971), pp. 197–205.
11. J. McManus, 'Bottom structures of the Tay and other estuaries', *Scottish Geographical Magazine* 82 (1966), pp. 192–7.
12. S.F.K. Wewetzer and R.W. Duck, 'Side-scan sonograph from the middle reaches of the Tay Estuary, Scotland', *International Journal of Remote Sensing* 17 (1996), pp. 3539–40; S.F.K. Wewetzer, R.W. Duck and J. McManus, 'Side-scan sonar mapping of bedforms in the middle Tay Estuary, Scotland', *International Journal of Remote Sensing* 20 (1999), pp. 511–22; R.W. Duck and S.F.K. Wewetzer, 'Relationship between current measurements and sonographs of subtidal bedforms in the macrotidal Tay Estuary, Scotland', *Geological Society of London Special Publications* 175 (2000), pp. 31–41.
13. J. McManus, personal communications (2009).
14. J. McManus, 'Applied sedimentology in a non-tidal dock: a study of population addition', *Engineering Geology* 1 (1966), pp. 373–9.
15. J. McManus, personal communications (2009).
16. P.A. Jenkins, R.W. Duck and J.S. Rowan, 'Fluvial contribution to the sediment budget of the Tay Estuary, Scotland, assessed using mineral magnetic fingerprinting', *International Association of Hydrological Sciences Publication* 291 (2005), pp. 134–40.
17. J.D. Hansom, 'The coastal geomorphology of Scotland: understanding sediment

budgets for effective coastal management' in J.M. Baxter, K. Duncan, S. Atkins and G. Lees (eds), *Scotland's Living Coastline* (London, The Stationery Office, 1999), pp. 34–44.

18. W.T. McGuinness, W.C. Beckmann and C.B. Officer, 'The application of various geophysical techniques to specialised engineering projects', *Geophysics* 27 (1962), pp. 221–36.

19. McManus, 'The geological setting of the bridges of the Lower Tay Estuary'.

20. A.T. Buller and J. McManus, 'Channel stability in the Tay Estuary: controls by bedrock and unconsolidated post-glacial sediment', *Engineering Geology* 5 (1971), pp. 227–37.

21. Jenkins et al., 'Fluvial contribution to the sediment budget of the Tay Estuary'.

22. McManus, 'The geological setting of the bridges of the Lower Tay Estuary'; Buller and McManus, 'Channel stability in the Tay Estuary'.

23. D. Cunningham, 'The River Tay report', Report to the Honorable (*sic*) the Trustees of the harbour of Dundee (unpublished, 1887); D. Cunningham, 'The Estuary of the Tay', *Proceedings of the Institution of Civil Engineers* 120 (1895), pp. 229–322.

24. J. Allen, 'Firth of Tay scale model investigation', Report to the Engineer and Manager, Dundee Harbour Trust (unpublished, 1948).

25. W.M. Dow, personal communications (2009).

26. J. McManus, personal communications (2009).

27. University of Dundee University prospectus: undergraduate entry (1984, 1985, 1986 and 1987).

28. J.A. Charlton, 'The tidal circulation and flushing capability of the outer Tay Estuary', *Proceedings of the Royal Society of Edinburgh* 78B (1980), pp. s33–s46.

29. Ibid.

30. A.G. Ogilvie, 'Land reclamation in Scotland', *Scottish Geographical Magazine* 61 (1945), pp. 77–84.

31. W.M. Dow, personal communications (2009).

32. Ibid.; DUA, MS 205/2, p. 3: D. McMurchie, 'From Invergowrie to Stannergate', transcript, recorded at Roxburgh House, Dundee, 1986.

33. W.M. Dow, personal communications (2009).

34. Major C.F. Rose, *Department of Transport Railway Accident Report on the Collision that Occurred on 22 October 1979 at Invergowrie in the Scottish Region British Railways* (London, HMSO, 1981), p. 22.

35. Invergowrie rail crash: http://www.nationmaster.com/encyclopedia/Invergowrie-rail-crash (accessed 8 January 2009).

36. W.M. Dow, personal communications (2009).

37. J.C. Akunna, K. Hasan and K. Kerr, 'Methodology for estimating the methane potential of a closed landfill', http://www.uwtc.tay.ac.uk/Site/documents/Akunnaetal_FullPaper__ICSW2008.pdf (2008).

38. Dundee Waterfront: http://www.dundeewaterfront.com (accessed 27 December 2008).

39. A.T. Buller, J. McManus, J. Williams and D.J.A. Williams, 'Investigations in the estuarine environments of the Tay. Physical aspects: an interim report', *University of Dundee Tay Estuary Research Centre Research Reports* 1 (1971), p. 62.

40. J.F. Bateman, *Report by Mr Bateman, C.E. on, 'Drainage of Dundee and Lochee'*, Report to the Police Commissioners of the Burgh of Dundee (1870), p. 5.

41. Bateman, *'Drainage'*.
42. Ibid.
43. Halcrow Fox, Tay Wastewater Project, *Assessment of Best Environmental Solution*, Report for Catchment Tay Ltd and North of Scotland Water Authority (1998).
44. Ibid.
45. Scottish Water and Catchment Tay Ltd, *Discover a Cleaner Tay: A Guide to the Tay Wastewater System* (information leaflet, 2001).
46. Ibid.
47. C.R. McLeod, *Barry Buddon* (unpublished report, 2004), p. 67.
48. Dundee Corporation, *Oil Pollution in the Tay Estuary, 1968, Following the Tank Duchess Incident. Report of the Technical Advisory Committee on Oil Pollution in the Tay*, City of Dundee (1968), p. 28.
49. Ibid.
50. Ibid.
51. Ibid.; A. Nelson-Smith, 'Effects of the oil industry on shore life in estuaries', *Proceedings of the Royal Society of London* B180 (1972), pp. 487–96.
52. Tay Estuary Oil Pollution Scheme, 1970: Conference of Local Authorities and Other Bodies in Marryat Hall, Dundee on 15 and 16 April (1970). Papers presented by speakers.
53. J. McManus, 'Ballast and the Tay eider duck populations', *Environment and History* 5 (1999), pp. 237–44.
54. J.A. Charlton, W. McNicoll and J.R. West, 'Tidal and freshwater induced circulation in the Tay Estuary', *Proceedings of the Royal Society of Edinburgh* 75B (1974), pp. 11–27.
55. Ibid.
56. IPCC: Intergovernmental Panel on Climate Change (2008).
57. T. Ball, A. Werritty, R.W. Duck, A. Edwards, L. Booth and A.R. Black, *Coastal Flooding in Scotland: A Scoping Study*, Report for Scotland and Northern Ireland Forum for Environmental Research (SNIFFER, 2008), p. 86.
58. Ogilvie, 'Land reclamation in Scotland'.

CHAPTER 4

'Beautifying and Improving the City':
The pursuit of a Monumental Dundee during the Twentieth Century

Charles McKean

INTRODUCTION

Two novel approaches to 'the historic city problem' emerged in the United Kingdom in the late nineteenth century. The first was that of Ebenezer Howard who, in *Tomorrow: A Peaceful Path to Real Reform*, published in 1898, advocated a new type of urban settlement – a garden city – in which all the supposed ills of the large old cities would be eradicated. It was a counsel of beginning again. The other was that of Patrick Geddes, now regarded as the founder of modern town planning who, from his biological perspective, considered that cities were redeemable provided that the necessary actions were applied with sensitivity. In his *Survey of Edinburgh* in 1910, Geddes emphasised the importance of understanding the role the past played in the creation of the present:

> This enquiry requires, first, a survey of our geographical environment in its fullest and deepest aspects; secondly, a survey of the history of the city and region . . . We are thus learning to view history not as mere archaeology, not as mere annals, but as the study of social filiation. *That is, the determination of the present by the past* [my italics] . . . Retrospect, rightly interpreted, not only illuminates the present but sweeps through this and forward into intelligent foresight.[1]

Geddes's approach to historic urban areas was called 'conservative surgery' – effectively meaning doing only what was necessary, and doing it with empathy.[2] His broader vision has since been interpreted as believing that 'any redemption from the plight of the industrial city is achievable only if the historic city . . . becomes recognised as *the* place to achieve any improvement of city, society and life'.[3] However, renewal had to be undertaken both to the appropriate quality and with the necessary respect accorded to the historic fabric. Geddes's approach will be used as a constant reference in this analysis.

The Edwardian *Zeitgeist*, however, was entirely otherwise. The vast majority of case studies presented to the 1910 Town Planning Conference in London were neither as apocalyptic as Howard nor as subtle as Geddes. They were, by contrast, much more triumphalist. Sufficient wealth existed to transform historic cities according to the new theories of 'the city beautiful', which implied a grandeur of conception, fine axial avenues and majestic public buildings: sometimes reshaping what existed, and sometimes – as in Cardiff – creating something entirely new.

In July of that same year, 1910, the City Engineer of Dundee, James Thomson, presented a new vision of the city to the city council. His *Report on the Central Area Improvement Scheme* and its two successors recommended a new municipal centre and other civic buildings on the shore 'worthy of a city of the size and importance of Dundee',[4] grouped rather like Cardiff's, with realigned streets widened into avenues, a by-pass encircling the outer city, and peripheral housing estates. This vision, combined with his pioneering construction of the United Kingdom's first council estate in Logie in 1919, have earned him the reputation of a visionary – 'perhaps the most under-rated figure in the history of Scottish town planning',[5] and Dundee that of being 'close to the forefront of planning activity in Britain prior to 1914'.[6] However, a unique feature of his approach – in extreme contrast to Geddes's – was that Thomson based his vision upon the worthlessness of Dundee's inherited building stock and its impossible transport situation. The city's magnificent setting deserved something very much more imposing.

Thomson's principal legacy was a continuing taste for grand planning and monumentalism in the city over the following century – a constant demand that its commercial and industrial importance be matched by its architecture. In the pursuit of this goal, the city's pre-Victorian urban fabric was considered dispensable, so that, by the later part of the twentieth century, Dundee had been left with a negligible historic identity by comparison with any other non-war-damaged town of comparable antiquity and importance. From this had developed an identity problem – an indication of which emerged from sparse public comment at the public exhibition for the proposed Dundee Contemporary Arts held in the Central Library in 1996. The largest set of replies focused – not on the value of a new arts centre, nor indeed on the need to attract tourism, important though they both were – but on the necessity to restore the city's reputation and self-esteem.[7] Was this simply the typical introspection suffered by most post-industrial communities, or was there a specific Dundee dimension? This chapter suggests that there was indeed a particular Dundee dimension to this: namely that since the city's 'anchors of memory' had been cleared away, it could conceive of itself only as a failed jute town.

VICTORIAN DUNDEE

Dundee was untypical of Scots towns in that, although the second city of Scotland during the Renaissance, its plan and its buildings were predominantly the consequence of its being a major working port[8] – closer parallels being port towns such as Lubeck or Gothenburg rather than the other Scottish burghs. Its architectural quality was comparably high. There was only a single major public place – the High Street – from which a myriad of tight, tall and narrow closes led down through the maritime quarter to the harbour. Rather than by fine individual houses or civic buildings, its character was made up, instead, by the totality of its urban experience. By the mid-eighteenth century, visitors like Alexander Carlyle were already regarding it as old-fashioned, and since this very businesslike place still lacked the set pieces in the grand manner to be found in other towns, that had turned to embarrassment by the mid-nineteenth century.[9] The *Dundee Advertiser* expressed the general perception when it editorialised: 'We believe there is no town in the kingdom so awkwardly built . . . If a flight of gigantic crows had dropt our houses from the air, they could not have arranged themselves with a more admired confusion.'[10]

As the town industrialised in the first half of the nineteenth century, Dundee became the linen centre of the United Kingdom, and then, when jute become the dominant import, 'Juteopolis'. It was also a centre of railways, engineering and their associated industries.[11] Its expanding docks coped not just with the whaling fleet, the later herring fleet, and with an enormous increase in shipbuilding, but also with the gigantic clippers that travelled directly from Dundee to Calcutta. Its factory smokestacks represented business and progress to the Victorians, and those arriving by sea would have seen ancient Dundee fringed by some two hundred of them. Small-scale industry and warehousing filled up the gardens of the old port, whereas larger mills and engineering workshops lay in a thick swathe around the perimeter. From a combination of the steep slopes on which they were built, and the lack of any strategic planning, they were characterised by dense clumps of workers' housing in short streets blocked by industry. The resulting impenetrable industrial zone became the primary physical characteristic of Juteopolis.

The question is why Dundee's politicians had allowed this to happen. Other towns and cities – notably Glasgow, where regulations prohibited constructing buildings higher than the width of the street[12] – managed to regulate even the fiercest of nineteenth-century industrial growth quite satisfactorily. Part of the answer may well lie in the relationship between merchants and the council, which had been deteriorating since the end of the eighteenth century. When asked by a Parliamentary Committee in 1817 about the composition of Dundee's council under Provost Alexander Riddoch, 'Riga Bob' Jobson, a Baltic flax merchant, had replied that 'nobody respectable' was on the council.[13] Since they believed that the council did not comprehend the necessities of international trade and commerce, the merchants had removed harbour powers away from the council into a Trust. They then ruinously opposed the council's first attempt to introduce a municipal water supply to the town in 1833. Perhaps the council's reputation for business had been so damaged in the eyes of the town's businessmen that the latter would not trust the former with any but the most basic powers – albeit the Baxters in the Dens and the Coxes in Lochee to some extent looked after their own in what were virtual textile principalities. In striking contrast to Glasgow, however, Dundee's entrepreneurs and leaders of the town's industries remained aloof from urban politics.[14]

Before the 1871 Improvement Act, therefore, the planning of Dundee was a litany of half-completed concepts and unfulfilled ideas. Unaccustomed to undertaking development outside its medieval bounds, the council failed to implement any of the series of comprehensive plans for laying out the town's Ward and Meadow lands prepared in 1825, 1832, 1834 or 1846.[15] Moreover, despite the fact that the land was all council-owned, nothing – no overall plan, no feuing conditions, not even a modern road system by-passing the medieval centre – was ever imposed upon developers. Industrialists large and small occupied and developed whatever parcel they could purchase, in whatever form and to whatever orientation they chose.[16] Worse, that laissez-faire attitude spelt trouble from the very start of the industrial encirclement of Dundee. Back in 1793, the Rev. Robert Small had lamented how the 'late additional suburbs [had] been built without any general plan, and without the least regard to health, elegance or cleanliness'.[17] When cholera struck in 1832, Dundee's medieval centre suffered less than other comparable towns; the disease was at its most virulent, however, in the new industrial suburb of the Hawkhill.[18]

Even the proposal to develop the Meadows as a Victorian business centre to supersede the old-fashioned High Street (probably the original agenda behind moving the Royal Exchange there in 1851), was never fully realised. Instead, with the arrival of the Albert Institute and its later conversion into the art galleries, Albert Square was transformed from the commercial hub into one of commemoration and education. So the district that should have been the showcase of the modern city was developed in a confusing and embarrassing hodgepodge. Dundee's population grew by 500 per cent between 1820 and 1890, but for the first forty years of that period, the council had behaved like a rabbit in headlights, leaving the infrastructure of the town essentially that of the 1780s. Something would have to give.

In the 1860s, the business acumen of Dundee's entrepreneurs finally arrived in the council to leaven the small shopkeepers, and in 1868 James Cox, chairman both of Cox Brothers of the Camperdown works and of the Tay Railway Bridge undertaking, was persuaded to become involved in politics by his own workforce.[19] That year Dundee appointed William Mackison to the new post of Burgh Engineer, and two years later, Cox was elected provost. Once the 1871 Police and Improvement Act provided the necessary powers, small-trader indecision finally ceded to industrialist managerialism. By then, much of the atmosphere of the seaport had already been lost. The shore lands to the west were now occupied by railway sidings, marshalling yards and coal depots, and the Seagate, whose gardens had once dusted the water's edge, was now over half a mile inland. The shipmasters had quit the maritime quarter, and Kay's, Key's, Scott's and countless other closes were now packed with the poor and, as the drawings by Charles Lawson illustrate so vividly, often in a state of advanced decay.[20]

In 1871, furthermore, the fundamentally unmodernised town centre was also swarming with incomers. Given that the poor always seek the cheapest lodgings and that, generally, the cheapest lodgings were to be found in the oldest dwellings, it was axiomatic that Dundee's oldest districts at the heart of the town were also those that had become most overcrowded and insanitary. But although the Improvement Act tackled traffic efficiency, health, sewers, trams and civic imagery, it stopped short of rehousing the poor.[21] The consequence was that those displaced for reasons of improvement simply moved to the next cheapest location, making the latter even more overcrowded and susceptible to demolition; and so forth, seriatim. It became a self-fulfilling prophecy. By comparison with Glasgow, which lined its Improvement Act streets with working-class tenement buildings, Dundee lined its new streets with commercial premises with smart apartments above. That reflected their location. The centre of commerce had long since quit Glasgow's High Street, whereas Dundee's improvement streets were being driven through its very heart. It is notable, however, that although Dundee's principal problems were acknowledged as being primarily in the encircling industrial zone, city improvement was focused upon the city centre itself. So, behind the mask of water supply, sewage and traffic efficiency, lay the deeper agenda of civic aggrandisement.

The 'narrows' of the Murraygate, Seagate and Overgate (which had originally prevented the tempest from making the marketplace unuseable[22]) impeded trams and caused traffic jams. Those of the Murraygate and Seagate were obliterated by driving Commercial Street through Dundee's densest medieval closes in the 1870s. The second phase addressed the city's western maritime quarter, a warren of steep narrow curving closes punctuated by tight sheltered courts, lying between the High Street/Nethergate, bounded at their foot by Butcher Row. As was typical of maritime quarters, it had become offensive to the new morality, being a locality well represented in police files. There was much local satisfaction when it was targeted for demolition, as J.M. Beatts wrote in 1882: 'Every citizen must feel pleasure in seeing the commencement of the demolition of the nest of pestilence and crime situated between the Nethergate and Fish Street.'[23] Its removal was almost complete when Patrick Geddes arrived to take up a new part-time chair in botany at Dundee College in 1888.[24]

To late Victorians, Dundee appeared squalid, hopelessly old-fashioned and insufficiently monumental (of interest really only to antiquarians like Alexander Lamb[25]). Its (wealthier) peers could boast of Glasgow's George Square and Buchanan Street, Edinburgh's New Town and Princes Street, and Aberdeen's King and Union Streets, with civic buildings of a grandeur to match. Despite their great pride in its industrial success and in its culture (as represented by its art patronage), Dundonians had therefore developed a profound architectural inferiority complex: their town's workaday port architecture was insufficient to represent the city's achievements. So Mackison's new boulevards represented the first step in bringing Dundee into line with other British cities.

JAMES THOMSON

In 1904, James Thomson, Mackison's chief assistant, was appointed City Architect, and in 1906 City Engineer as well. The dominant post was that of engineer, for which he was paid £600, whereas the post of City Architect – evidently a contentious one – was worth only £200.[26] Indeed, to judge from the council minutes, most of Thomson's projects were proposed in his capacity as City Engineer, restricting his architectural role to buildings such as the new city libraries. Thomson was most at home as an engineer, and his architecture was unsubtle and largely derivative, as first became apparent in 1907 when he was asked to realise Lord Provost Longair's pet scheme for a new public hall and municipal buildings.[27] Thomson's plan extruded William Adam's Town House east and west to form an entire square extending down a greatly widened Crichton Street south to Shore Terrace. Vaguely baroque in manner, its corners were graced with cupola'd corner towers, and Adam's elegant steeple was replaced by a squat baroque dome. Interest on capital would be paid for through shop rentals.

Although the council desperately needed more space and more efficient accommodation, the plan was opposed by the Rev. Walter Walsh, Thomson's natural supporter,[28] who thought the money would be better spent on housing the poor. The influential Prohibitionist councillor and later MP, Edwin 'Neddy' Scrymgeour, suggested the project be funded instead by public appeal – that is, it should proceed, but not be a charge on the public purse. Longair's scheme was nonetheless approved; but to appease Walsh, Thomson was also instructed to examine model lodging houses in Aberdeen, Edinburgh, Glasgow and Perth (only Perth's washed its face),[29] in order to work up an experimental scheme of twenty-four houses for Blackscroft – allowing one bathroom, one washing house and two WCs for every six tenants.[30] He was also asked to draw up plans for unbuilt areas (such as the Craigie estate), since that is what, at that time, they all conceived planning to mean.

On 23 November 1909, following the passing of the Housing and Town Planning Act, the council launched a 'crusade against slum property', and over the following weeks condemned as unfit for human habitation six properties in the Vault, one in Crichton Street, and fifteen in the Overgate. Some of the reasons were standard – absence of ashbin, open space, sinks and water supply – but others, such as low ceiling heights and poor ventilation, were typical problems of historic buildings. When converting comparable historic properties into modernised working-class apartments in Edinburgh's Lawnmarket in the 1880s, Patrick Geddes had had little difficulty in resolving such matters.[31] Indeed, the minimum ceiling height regulation had been introduced to govern new building, not as a tool to remove the old. Given the housing and planning problems in industrial Dundee (the council went on to condemn forty-two further properties in industrial Hawkhill), this initial selection of properties in central Dundee again implied an agenda other than merely improving the conditions of the working class. That agenda was made patent in January 1910 when the council approved Thomson's proposals to widen the Overgate significantly and make it into the city's principal broad avenue – a plan that would be much cheaper now that many of its properties had been condemned.[32]

Provost Longair's scheme for municipal buildings, however, was delayed[33] – not by the fire in the Town House in 1909 (which destroyed so much of the city archive), nor even by the flood in February 1910. With a broader strategy in view, Thomson persuaded the Committee to defer any action on both municipal buildings and Overgate widening until he could present his Report on Central Improvement Scheme, which was placed before the council meeting of 4 August 1910.[34] Thomson and Walsh were duly authorised to attend what later became christened the 'great' National Town Planning Conference held by the Royal Institute of British Architects in London.

The Report recommended that Dundee's wonderful, south-facing sloping site merited a much better city, conceived along 'city beautiful' lines. In place of a historic port with a significant maritime identity, Thomson proposed structured vistas, wide straight avenues, parkland and a monumental civic centre. His underlying rationale was an engineering one: the central area was too dense, and had a 'clamant need' for 'opening up and improving the congested areas and narrow thoroughfares'. The main thoroughfares were in a 'contracted condition', there was an 'absence of symmetry' in some of the streets, and the view of the principal buildings was obstructed.[35] Moreover, the historic buildings of the centre were 'commonplace and unpretentious'; the Luckenbooths were a 'disfigurement', South Union Street buildings were 'not of a valuable kind'; Crichton Street buildings were 'of inferior class'; and the Vault was 'one of the worst blots' in the central district of the city.[36] Those arriving at the railway station received 'a far from favourable' first impression of the city – 'an inharmonious group of properties set down without any arrangement or design'.

The Central Improvement Scheme comprised five radical proposals: the straightening and widening of the Overgate into the principal axial street (and the removal of its 'narrows', which had remained at 13 feet wide); the widening and improvement of Crichton Street and Greenmarket; the creation of a new market, new riverside parkland, and the provision of a new city hall. Having worked on the Longair proposal for a civic square facing the High Street, Thomson had concluded that the historic location on the marketplace was insufficiently impressive: it was low, there was no axial vista to be had, and there would be no impact upon the crucially important waterfront. Thomson wanted monuments – what he called 'good architectural work', in which central Dundee was, by 'city beautiful' standards, sadly deficient. Influenced by other examples of 'the city beautiful' – particularly the 1909 proposals for Chicago's lakeside frontage by Daniel Burnham (whom he had met, and whose designs and approach appear to have influenced him very significantly[37]) – Thomson concluded that the *only* 'site for a City Hall and Municipal Buildings worthy of Dundee' was on the docks;[38] and most of his imagination was thenceforth devoted to that end. Indeed, that is what he is remembered for. Dundonians concurred with his analysis and were inspired by his proposition.

Of particular interest, however, is how Thomson had assessed and evaluated the historic fabric of the town in the terms of the emerging town planning philosophies. At this juncture, well over half of the pre-modern port's buildings still survived, concentrated in the Vault, Luckenbooths and the Overgate. But the man charged with responsi-bility for the city's fabric could find nothing in its inheritance of any value save the site itself; and there was none of the subtlety or holistic or historical understanding of Geddes in his report. Since the ancient buildings of the port generally lacked significant known historical or architectural associations – and there was no real successor to Geddes in his sympathetic approach to historic fabric – the argument for radical change fitted the epoch in that it addressed the city's architectural inferi-ority complex head-on. Thomson presented his improvements as essential equally for aesthetic as for practical reasons – at the opposite scale to Geddes's 'conservative surgery'. The 'only satisfactory method of treatment for the Overgate', for example, lay in its total demolition.[39] No one, at the time, would make the case for the retention of the tight, difficult and architecturally humdrum buildings of a port.

Thomson had undertaken none of the prior analysis that Geddes had recommended to the Town Planning conference – not even a cursory architectural evaluation to identify the extent to which the surviving fabric was medieval – as good new planning practice required. So, a year later, Walsh belatedly persuaded the council to approve a survey of the city seemingly upon Geddes's lines.[40] He informed the council that the desirability of such a survey – encompassing site, topog-raphy, communications, manufacturing and historical development – was supported by both the RIBA and the Sociological Society. Neither body, however, was likely to have supported Walsh's proposal that 'the City Survey could proceed collaterally with the consideration of the City Engineer's proposals'. Geddes's concept had been that the plan should *emerge from* the survey, not that the plan should be determined *a priori* and the survey be made to fit. Six weeks later, the council agreed to seek an Act of Parliament to deal with the Overgate, on the assumption that there was nothing that the survey might tell them that would incline them to change their minds.[41] The horse had bolted.

In December 1911, Thomson produced a supplementary report considering the implications of the proposal to build a road bridge across the Tay using the foundations of the demolished Tay Bridge.[42] He took this opportunity to develop plans for a magisterial 900-acre esplanade park focused upon the domed civic centre at its east end. He now produced the watercolours of his overall vision of riparian Dundee for which he remains famous. These encapsulated Thomson's vision of 'Dundee beautiful': an enclosed market with a roof garden and Edwardian flower-beds, widened and straightened streets and new avenues, axially placed statues and monuments, a new urban garden replacing the Luckenbooths, Dundee's stations unified into a *Hauptbanhof*, a monumental group of municipal buildings on the Earl Grey Dock and swathes of formally designed Edwardian parkland extending out into an estuary well known for its wind, whose wide tree-lined boulevards aligned south-west would have provided the prevailing south-westerlies with a suitable playground.

In 1912, however, the Harbour Trust refused to release the Earl Grey Dock for the civic building, so Thomson had to fall back on the original Longair footprint for his new city square. In 1914 Sir James Caird offered the city £100,000 for a new city hall and proceeded – as he had done when offering University College comparable largesse – to dictate terms relating to location and appearance.[43] University College rejected Caird's interference and his gift, whereas Thomson managed to satisfy both with the design of a mill-like hall as the rear wing of the 'Longair quadrangle'. It would thus take out the southern rim of the historic area known as the Vault.

Thomson's third report, the 1918 *Report on the Development of the City*, was intended to persuade the city of the value of adopting a long-term strategic plan so that Dundee's expansion might go forward 'advantageously, economically and scientifically'. Its rationale was based upon the dire consequences of the ad hoc industrial construction of the previous fifty years. 'Every citizen who takes a genuine interest in the City . . . must be conscious of the disfigurement and of the loss and damage which have resulted from the non-existence of a comprehensive plan of development . . . Traffic streets were made unduly narrow and residential streets unduly wide . . . Gradients were fixed excessively steep . . . Streets became monotonous and depressing . . . No regard was had to the proper separation of dwelling houses from industrial buildings . . . Railway companies totally disregarded the amenity of the city.'[44] Most fatal of all, he concluded, was that 'the citizens were mostly apathetic'.

The problem had been the lack of a strategic plan, 'and much of the work during the past half century would have been differently carried out had there existed such a plan'. The underlying structure of Thomson's new plan was a reorganised road system and a logical approach to the necessities of traffic (just as it was later to be in the Greater London Development Plan of 1969), from which would derive the elimination of congested areas, appropriate land allocation, and improved and new parks. He envisioned creating new and cleaner types of residential environments at a much lower density – as he was then exemplifying in Logie. The likely cost of all this would be offset by the gain to the economy of a lowered death rate.

In its broad strategy and in its identification of what would become significant problems in the twentieth century, Thomson's third plan was pioneering; its details, however, have a curiously mechanical feel. His proposed housing streets and boulevards conveyed a sense of neither identity, place nor enclosure – only purpose. In common with its predecessors, this new report lacked any consideration of Dundee's identity. The central main streets (the principal thoroughfares of old Dundee) featured only insofar as they required widening to permit increased traffic, and obstructive buildings in the Seagate and the Queen's Hotel in the Nethergate were earmarked for demolition with a white cross.

Since most discussion of Thomson's impact upon Dundee has focused upon his monumental municipal centre on the docks, he has been presented as a heroic if tragic figure whose unrealised vision was, over the following century, to provide the city with a sense of lost magnificence which fed a resurgent architectural inferiority complex. However, that perception is largely incorrect. Most of Thomson's vision for Dundee – the Kingsway, the suburban housing developments of north and east Dundee, and the closing of the upstream docks – was realised.

What distinguished Dundee's application of the 'city beautiful' concept was that it was predicated upon a total removal of the historic fabric, rather than simply being applied to one part of the city while leaving other parts intact. In this, it was more like Burnham's plan for Chicago than Cardiff's new civic centre, which had left its old town centre largely in place. Thomson's dismissal of the inherited character of the city had made a public policy of what had earlier been *sotto voce*: namely that the city was significantly architecturally inferior to its peers. Indeed, his lukewarm attitude even to the Town House would, as shall be seen, contribute to its demolition in 1932.[45]

DESCENDING INTO THE PIT

In the immediate post-war period, as the legacy of dense inner Victorian Dundee finally came home to roost, the city's priorities changed. In 1918, three-fifths of all dwellings in the city consisted of only one or two rooms, concentrated in the inner industrial rim, and they were overcrowded. There is some reason to believe that as the jute industry declined, families were driven to share accommodation, and flats that might have been perfectly adequate for a single family might now have to accommodate two or three. But much had also been very badly built. The City's Slum Visitation Committee[46] was instructed to identify any housing 'injurious or dangerous to the health of the inhabitants by reasons of disrepair, sanitary defects, overcrowding, narrowness or bad arrangement of streets'; and the slum visitors reported truly dreadful conditions to meeting after meeting. One example was the proposed clearance area at 94–106 Blackness Road (including Watson's and Wilkie's Lanes), where sixty-three households lived in dilapidated conditions in very poor repair, with only open insanitary ashpits. In one particular area, there were only eight WCs for thirty-five households and a clubroom.[47] Note that the worst slums lay in neither the town centre, nor in the Vault nor indeed in the Overgate – but in that impenetrable swathe of inner industrial Dundee.

Judging from the absence of any council discussion on anything other than implications of implementing Thomson's proposals, it would appear that his strategy had gone, as it were, onto auto-pilot. So, having finally obtained appropriate government grants in 1928, the council was ready to begin constructing its municipal buildings.[48] In their way lay a significant part of historic maritime Dundee – namely the eastern maritime quarter incorporating the partially arcaded Vault, the remains of St Clement's Church, the grammar school, the late seventeenth-century Strathmartine Lodging, Tyndall's Wynd, and William Adam's superb 1733 Town House itself. Although the Vault had been the primary urban space of Renaissance Dundee after the marketplace,[49] its proposed destruction aroused little comment save some sentimental views of Strathmartine's Lodging.

The Town House was a different matter. Considering it insufficiently grand, Thomson had made two unenthusiastic proposals to retain it – one clamping it within a barren new city square, and the other as a garden monument in the new municipal park proposed for the site of demolished Luckenbooths. In 1928, however, the council received notice from HM Office of Works that since the Town House was approaching its 200th birthday, the Office intended to schedule it as an ancient monument under Section 12 of the 1913 Ancient Monuments Act.[50] Since the Office of Works was thus according the Town House a value with which the city no longer agreed, the Town Clerk was instructed to protest. He pointed out that as the building was still three years short of being two hundred years old, it did not yet qualify for such protection and he repudiated the proposal. However, the demolition required for the construction of the east and west wings of the new city square released a watercourse running through the sandstone beneath the Town House itself, eroding its foundations. The council was already reluctant to spend much on the Town House, and the additional costs of £6,500 for underpinning it estimated by a consulting engineer, George Baxter, led to a council debate over whether it should be retained at all.[51] The decision was postponed until the west wing of City Square was complete so that the public would be able to see for themselves 'whether the old town house will interfere with the amenities of the City Square'[52] – which gave an unambiguous signal about the lack of value the ancient structure had for them.

The City Engineer, D.B. McLay, then claimed that the building's troubles were accelerating – its steeple tilting, riven and cracked to the extent that its dangerous upper portion should be dismantled without delay. This was just what the council wished to hear. However, the First Commissioner of Works, the Conservative MP William Ormsby-Gore, was displeased that the government's assessment of the quality of the building was being ignored. His department drew up a letter to the town council, which he ordered be reprinted in the press, making very clear his department's strong disapproval of any demolition of the Town House since, in its eyes, it enjoyed the protected status of an Ancient Monument already.[53] On 28 December 1931, unmoved by either press or the government, Dundee Corporation passed an emergency measure that 'the whole of the Old Town House buildings should be demolished at once'.[54] On 6 January 1931, scaffolding was put up around the spire prior to taking it down. Five days later, Sir John Stirling Maxwell wrote a letter on behalf of the Royal Commission on the Ancient and Historical Monuments of Scotland in protest at the haste with which the old building had been condemned – indeed, over the holiday period – which the council took (correctly) to be an accusation of sharp practice and bad faith. This the Town Clerk denied, pointing out that a contract for underpinning the Town House had been let on 7 December, with the intention of conserving the structure, and that it was only after work had begun that engineers had concluded that the extent of the work thus revealed would be far most costly than had been budgeted for.[55]

The Guildry, the Chamber of Commerce and the Dundee Institute of Architects all petitioned the council to save the building. At a special meeting held to consider the matter, the DIA voted that 'the Town House building is of outstanding architectural interest . . . and that the matter of its removal is . . . now a matter of national interest'.[56] One of its members, W.W. Friskin, invoked the Royal Incorporation of Architects in Scotland, which published this lament in its journal *The Quarterly*:

> The building never has been given any real place in the scheme of central reconstruction developed through so many years and in various forms all, however, with the constant idea of a recessed space open on one side only – the side occupied by the Town House. Let it be said that the only proper custodians of this building in the heart of the City were the Local Authority. They did not want to uphold it, and in the end it was swept away both unhonoured and unsung. This can be regretted for this notable work of William Adam was no common thing, and as the number of monuments of this standard in Scotland is now sadly diminished, the disappearance of this one, generally agreed to be the finest of its type and on the eve of becoming 200 years old when it would have been entitled to the full protection of the Ancient Monuments Act, seems worthy of a passing bell . . . This was a building of quietude and peace: skilfully composed: with distinction of design by proportion and dignity.[57]

What is striking, given these petitions, is the absence of cultural discussion within the council meeting itself. Unperturbed even by national outrage,[58] the council carried forward remorselessly, and only the ineffectual intervention of the government was recorded in its minute books. The final decision to demolish was taken on 20 January 1932. 'Impenetrable', Lord Cockburn had condemned Edinburgh's city council in 1828. Impenetrable Dundee's remained a century later, out of step with both the government and a number of its own significant citizens. It would be difficult, however, to use the Town House saga to suggest that Dundonians were beginning to value their historic town. It was an exceptional case. In architectural terms, the Vault and Strathmartine's Lodgings were probably of equal value, but they lacked any association with a celebrated architect.

Death by what, in the 1970s, would be termed 'planning blight' seemed to be the likely fate of the Overgate, Dundee's principal elite street during the Renaissance. The Overgate was now a term used to encapsulate Mid Kirk Style, Talley Street, Thorter Row, Lindsay Street, the Luckenbooths, and some twenty-five closes, vennels and entries – an area comprising probably the largest single concentration of pre-modern urban fabric then surviving in Scotland.[59] (Indeed, even when finally under demolition in the 1960s, Gothic doorways and relics of comparable age were found, implying that its antiquity and quality were not so difficult to discern.[60]) Thomson had originally planned to replace the Overgate with a wide straight avenue, and had obtained the requisite Act to purchase condemned properties compulsorily in 1913.[61] Anything that did not conform to contemporary building standards (particularly in relation to ceiling height) would be condemned. Once purchased by the council, and its residents exported, maintenance on that property would cease, thus compounding decay.

At about the same time, a different path was being taken in Edinburgh. Although it took the intervention of the Marquess of Bute to rescue significant buildings such as Lamb's House and Acheson House, both of which had been condemned as slum properties, and the Society for the Protection of Ancient Buildings failed to save William Adam's fine Gladney House in Kirkcaldy, which had suffered in the same way, the approach taken to less significant properties in Edinburgh's High Street and Grassmarket – of comparable age, scale and quality to those in Dundee's Overgate – was much more considered. Following Geddes's lead, the Edinburgh City Architect Ebenezer MacRae began a programme of conservative repair and replacement.[62] One of the pioneer conservationists, as he is described in the *Dictionary of Scottish Architects*, he restored buildings, inter alia, in the Grassmarket and Candlemaker

Row as early as 1929, and in Edinburgh's West Bow in 1930. Where the building had to be replaced, he ensured that careful measured drawings and photographs were taken of all interiors with quality. In the early 1940s, he produced a far-sighted report for the council, 'The Heritage of Greater Edinburgh'. Edinburgh, of course, had obvious historical associations, which MacRae used to justify the care he took. Since any such historical associations in Dundee had been long since forgotten, the Dundonian civic perception of the very similar Overgate buildings remained that they were worthless.

Although the death of the Overgate had been ordained, it took time, attitudes changed, and by 1936 Thomson's plans were no longer considered sufficiently modern. So, determined to tackle what he called 'one of the blackest spots of the city' (parroting Thomson of twenty-five years earlier), the Lord Provost persuaded the council to appoint the pioneer town planner Thomas Adams to prepare a new master plan for it. Having 'made a careful study of the Overgate area', Adams submitted four proposals in October 1937, recommending a preferred option. His objective was to double the size of the current business district to make the Overgate the 'most distinguished street in the city . . . The extended civic and business centre thus obtained would be in size, and could be in dignity, artistic quality and adaptation to modern needs, equal to that of any city.'[63]

He developed Thomson's concept of an arrow-straight Overgate as the spine of an entirely redeveloped area, in which only St Mary's Church itself was retained, but widened it to the scale of London's Kingsway. The monumental feature was an expansive roundabout approximately on the line of Long Wynd (the current Marketgait), whose function – given that three of the five streets emanating from it were but minor ones – was primarily visual.[64] The buildings replacing this dense, partially six-storeyed district, were (save for a proposed 'great new cinema' – a towered extravagance in Bank Street) uniform and architecturally bland. Its three storeyed terraces, with their shallow pitched roofs and flat façades enlivened only by piazzas, greatly resembled the rebuilding of bomb-damaged central Bristol and Coventry a decade later. Whereas the architecture was neutral, however, the planning and road layout had become monumental – with the requisite grandeur of concept needed to satisfy Dundonians. Only the war prevented the implementation of Adams's design.

BRAVE NEW WORLD

The 1947 Town and Country Planning Act required all local planning authorities to survey their area and prepare a development plan; and whereas the resulting plans all differed to some degree, common themes included efficiency, the need to avoid conflicting uses being adjacent to each other, industry and economic development, the ever expanding traffic, and the need to address the housing shortage as quickly as possible. Adopting Patrick Geddes's methodology of survey, analysis, plan, these development plans comprised two parts – a survey, one function of which was to establish the historic nature of the place, and an advisory plan. A good example of the genre is *Granite City: A Plan for Aberdeen*, written by W. Dobson Chapman and Charles F. Riley, which was published in London in 1952, in large lavish format with beautiful photographs. Its stance on heritage was explained in the opening paragraph:

> The historical heritage is, therefore, one to be cherished if the sense of community is to be vigorous and conscious of its enduring continuity. For this reason, the town planner attaches importance to the preservation of historic buildings and those parts of the town with historic associations which can be satisfactorily integrated with a plan designed to meet the needs of today and tomorrow. *But what is still more important is that no proper understanding of these modern needs can be attained without studying the growth and development of the community over the centuries* [my italics].[65]

Exactly Geddes's point of view.

With its Thomson legacy of the Kingsway, the reconfiguration of modern industries around it, and workers living in new housing projects just on the north side of it, Dundee was ahead in most respects. Indeed, developing and expanding its already thriving outer rim could have taken some of the pressure away from the city centre, providing the council with the leeway to reconsider how to approach its historic core, had it wanted to. In the same year as Aberdeen, and using the same planning consultant (now Dobson Chapman and Partners), Dundee published its development plan. Since Dundee did not have a formal town planning department in 1952, it being an adjunct of the Housing Department and responsible to the Housing and Town Planning Committee, Dobson Chapman effectively worked 'in-house'. That might explain why, by contrast with *Granite City*, their *City and Royal Burgh of Dundee Survey and Plan*, was not published in London in a glossy format with excellent photographs, but rather as a typed in-house report with few and indifferent illustrations.[66] Indeed, by contrast with most of the city development plans, it contained not a single illustration of Dundee's pre-Victorian streetscape – presumably because the consultants had absorbed the Dundonian perception of its worthlessness.

The absence of the required analysis of Dundee's historic character reinforces the impression that the Advisory Plan, far from being a fresh start, was built unquestioningly upon Thomson's and Adams's proposals. Having paid great homage to Geddes's influence, the *Survey* volume then proceeded to ignore it. Its starting point, like its predecessors', was that Dundee occupied 'one of the finest natural sites of any city in Scotland' but that there was 'general agreement that the least possible advantage' had been taken of it[67] – as though a significant Renaissance port should have been laid out along 'city beautiful lines'. Dundee was being held back by its dreadful legacy of 'unregulated and excessive concentration, over specialisation, and the evils arising from the indiscriminate inter-mingling of industry with residential and other forms of development'.[68] It proposed an entirely modern vision – not just for part of Dundee, as Thomson had, but for its entire territory – illuminated by apocalyptic and wintry black and white sketches by the architect Ian Burke.

The Advisory Plan proposed a town virtually without memory, ancestry or identity. Its historical survey had this to say: 'The process of adaptation to provide the facilities of a modern commercial city has left few buildings of architectural or historic importance', going on to name obvious isolated monuments such as the Steeple, the Howff and the Wishart Arch. It acknowledged the presence of seventy-nine buildings listed as being of either architectural or historic interest – including several in both the High Street and the Overgate, which it allowed dated back to at least the sixteenth century – but there were no photographs of them to allow the reader to challenge its judgement that 'most of the heritage from the past, insofar as buildings are concerned, is of a low standard'.[69] It came to this judgement without any analysis of historic character, and thus, in an echo of the Town House saga, contradicted the value that state officials had accorded those properties when they had listed them.

The Plan was organised around the creation of an inner ring road, with widened streets and avenues between, the creation of a new city centre, and the construction of modern neighbourhoods: it proposed, effectively, a new Dundee. Only eighteen historic buildings 'of importance' (nine churches, nine institutional buildings such as the city chambers and the art galleries, and a short section of South Tay Street) would make their way into new Dundee.[70] In its pursuit of monumentality, it accorded no value whatsoever to the townscape or urban grain of the Overgate,[71] and ignored the presence of ancient buildings both there and in the High Street. Given the progressive dereliction to which the Overgate had been subject now over four decades, perhaps *anything* would be better. The new Overgate, however, was now conceived in terms of a pedestrian precinct, which removed, at a stroke, the logic behind Thomson's original proposal to demolish it in the first place. This the Plan justified, wholly erroneously, by stating that since, by comparison with Aberdeen and Edinburgh, 'no major historic redevelopment of the Town Centre' had taken place, Dundee's centre was ripe for one.[72] That would have hit the right nerve: Dundee's architectural inferiority complex. Given its predecessors and its context, the report's myopia about Dundee's historic character was to be expected, albeit it revealed just how little original thinking the Plan contained. Thomson's legacy remained largely intact.

There was little contemporary public comment upon either the appointment of consultants or upon their recommendations. The *Courier* confined itself to the anodyne but not entirely correct observation that plans for the central area were under preparation:[73] it was in fact a blueprint for the entire city, whose impact upon communities like the Hilltown or Lochee would be just as drastic as upon the centre. Homer, sadly, was nodding. When the council's development plan was finally submitted to the government in June 1956, there was only scanty mention of central Dundee, presumably because it was expected that the investment would have to come from the private sector.[74] When scrutinising the proposal to designate the Overgate a Comprehensive Development Area, Department of Health officials noted that twelve listed buildings lay in its way – identifying particularly those on the corner of the Overgate/High Street known as Monk's Lodging;[75] but the

Secretary of State still approved the proposal in August 1958. The council leader announced that the council was finally implementing a scheme first planned forty-six years earlier – that is, Thomson's.[76] That, of course, was not entirely true. Thomson's monumentalism had been focused upon the Earl Grey Dock. Monumental modernity was now going to appear at the very heart of the city.

In the meantime, the Abertay Historical Society had written to the council seeking a meeting with its chief officers to express concern about historic buildings which were either under threat from the plan, or were being neglected. Buildings about which they were concerned included Dudhope, Mains and Broughty Castles, St Mary's Church, Camperdown House and the Royal Arch. It was particularly anxious about Gardyne's Land, a complex of ancient structures in the High Street dating back to the thirteenth century, which, at that time, was not yet listed. The letter stated:

> The local authority and citizens have certain responsibilities which cannot be shelved or ignored. True civic prestige is not built on temporary expediency or the kind of inverted economy that refuses expenditure on necessary repairs and then eventually has to spend more to off-set neglect.

The focus of the Society's concern was the monumental buildings of the city's heritage. When it came to the historic buildings about to be cleared for the Overgate, it judged that because the buildings had been so altered, 'we would not support any plea for their preservation'.[77] Had they been so devoid of historic interest, it is surprising that the government would have listed them. Once again, Dundonians remained unwilling to accept an outsider's perception of the value of their heritage.

While the council delayed to implement its Plan, two proposals for the Overgate were received – one from the Department of Health itself, the other from a local architect – probably Burke.[78] Eventually, it selected the Murrayfield Real Estate Co. as its development partner. It was the seventh proposal for the replacement of the Overgate[79] and was still not exactly as constructed. Murrayfield purred at the co-operation it was receiving from the council: 'The Dundee Corporation is well known for its forward-looking and enthusiastic attitude in the field of Urban Renewal. It is quite natural, therefore, that they should be among the first in Scotland to tackle the problem of the Redevelopment of their City Centre.'[80] A dense historic district on the western rim of the business district characterised by apartments and small shops was to be replaced by a much more monumental townscape. Designed by Ian Burke, Martin and Partners (who went on to design Edinburgh's St James's Centre on the strength of their Dundee success), it comprised ninety-three shops and four large department stores, framed between a six-storeyed slab of offices and hotel facing the inner ring road to the west, and an eleven-storey block of offices at the east end facing the High Street. Claiming that the Overgate would 'bring a new look to Dundee', the brochure, skilfully illustrated by Burke's pastel wash perspectives, emphasised the 'vastly superior conditions' to be provided in the 'most up-to-date shopping centre in Scotland', grouped 'round the major focus formed by the Old Steeple'. In reality, St Mary's Steeple was obscured and dwarfed.

In terms of its scale, and the extent to which it transformed Dundee's town centre, the pedestrianised Overgate scheme was indeed pioneering. Murrayfield's 'trophy' chairman, Field Marshal Sir Claude Auchinleck, told the *Courier*, 'What interests me is to see how modern buildings and modern ideas can improve and unify what has become out of date and ugly.'[81] Quality, and integration into the urban fabric were essential; yet difficult though it was to challenge a war hero, a few anonymous voices did so. 'A Dundonian' pleaded: 'A historic town such as Dundee with a tradition of its own deserves better designed buildings than those proposed.'[82] In his foreword to Murrayfield's brochure, Lord Provost Maurice McManus swept this aside, enthusing at the sheer extent of the project, which he justified on two grounds: first, 'the impetus to the trade of the city and to employment', and second, that it was the long-awaited realisation of 'an idea which the Civic Authority had been following for 50 years' – that is, Thomson again.[83] That could only be called correct if he had been referring, not to Thomson's actual designs, but to his understanding that what Dundonians craved was monumentality.

During the two years that it took to receive government approval, there was a dawning realisation of what was going to go. The predominantly small shopkeepers being displaced had agitated for a future for them in the new development; but despite the assurances given to them, 60 per cent of the shops trading in the area were to move or go out of business.[84] On 26 October, in a Cassandra-like warning of this likely result, the *Advertiser* ran a feature on 'nineteen well-known businesses that will close down for good' – predominantly restaurants, cafes, food and fish shops, and drapers.[85] At one point, the Chamber of Commerce seemed ready to take up cudgels on the behalf of them, but its *Journal* came out sternly in favour of redevelopment, the Dundee architect Tommy Thoms (then President of the Royal Incorporation of Architects in Scotland) stating, 'Fortunately no buildings of architectural merit have to be demolished.' When the new Provost, Sir Garnett Wilson, had come to sell the scheme to the Chamber he had founded his case, once again, on decisions made back in 1913 – that is, Thomson.[86] As if to underscore this, the *Evening Telegraph* celebrated the final decision to proceed with the Overgate redevelopment by publishing a lavishly illustrated six-page supplement of Thomson's baroque watercolours.[87]

When Forbes White commissioned the by now celebrated Dundee artist J. Macintosh Patrick to make a record painting of one of the old buildings – Thomson's Fish Shop on the corner of the doomed Nethergate and North Lindsay Street – the artist perceived value where the authorities saw none. Macintosh Patrick observed astutely that 'it had something of the effect of a French town'.[88] Farewell celebrations included a 'Last Dance' in Kidd's Rooms in South Lindsay Street on 3 March 1961. The continuing lack of sentimentality in council thinking was highlighted by the contemporary proposal – which not even the Abertay Historical Society had seen coming – namely to remove the Wishart Arch in the Cowgate (the city's sole surviving town gate, and only one of two surviving throughout Scotland) on grounds of traffic congestion.[89] The proposal remained abortive.

However, the demolition of the Overgate began only three years later, which implies further urban dereliction.[90] Indeed, the council policy of purchasing and emptying the inhabitants into Beechwood and Craigie, which had been continuing by now for half a century, meant that the west end of the Overgate area had become increasingly void and desolate, the partially blocked-off closes behind the street façade frightening and overrun by rats. Unsurprisingly, therefore, when the first phase of the new Overgate opened on 8 October 1963, it was greeted as 'Dundee's space-age shopping centre'.[91] The contrast between old and new was overwhelming.

Both council minutes and the newspapers give off a sense of not just the fragility of the town's economy which the new Overgate was intended to assuage, but of satisfaction that the city had finally achieved the urban trajectory set in 1910. Yet one has to be cautious, since Dundee's newspapers were not prone to publishing negative stories about the city; and the unassailability of the political caucus then in power meant that all writers of letters to the *Courier* on such subjects felt obliged to write under a pseudonym, to avoid any repercussions. Again, this was not unique to Dundee at that time.[92] So, when the threat to the Royal Arch caused by an approach road to the road bridge materialised in February 1964, opposition remained muted and ineffective, and the Arch was removed.

In 1964 the council identified a further fifteen areas comprising 508 acres of 'obsolete development' in inner Dundee which it wished to schedule for comprehensive redevelopment.[93] They included, inter alia, most of Perth Road, the neighbourhood of the Technical College and Victoria Road.[94] As before, the council gave no consideration of how that heritage might be used, confining its discussion of tourism to provision of bed spaces only. Conversely, however, the government's re-assessment of architectural quality in Dundee meant that there were now twenty-one Grade A and 222 other listed buildings; and the streetscape in places like Castle Street, Perth Road and Magdalen Yard was officially recognised as valuable for the first time. So 169 hardy souls dared challenge the council by lodging objections, mostly for personal or business interest, and when it came to the public hearing the council's QC, affronted at their temerity, alleged that they were all either politi-cally motivated or were too stupid to understand what was proposed. At this Inquiry, however, the gap between the government's and the council's assessment of historic value was exposed, since the proposed CDAs threatened some of the newly listed buildings. When the Planning Convenor, A.J. Thomson, was challenged about the proposal to demolish the perfectly satisfactory Airlie Place in the West End, given that its houses were 'in excellent condition, good stone built houses and so on', he replied, 'They may look like that, but I can assure you it is not the same inside. There are houses up there that are very very old.'[95] To a fixation with monumentality, Dundee appeared to have added a fixation with modernity.

Crucial to Dundee's development, however, was the road bridge across the Tay, first raised when Thomson had suggested using the foundations of the demolished Tay Railway Bridge with a landfall upstream to the west in 1911. A fully worked scheme for a road bridge which debouched into the Earl Grey Dock but left all the other docks intact, had been received enthusiastically by the council in 1930,[96] as was another by Maunsell and Partners in the late 1940s. The Advisory Plan had anticipated a bridge more or less where it is now, whereas a very elegant design by the engineer Ove Arup for a higher-level bridge, with a landfall tied logically into the regional road system downstream of the city centre at Stannergate, proved abortive. Indeed, the bridge's landfall on the north bank became a matter of such popular debate that the *Evening Telegraph* held a plebiscite upon it in 1965.[97] The chosen landfall site was on former dockland opposite the foot of Commercial Street, and when the Tay Road Bridge finally opened on 18 August 1966, the town centre was severed from the estuary by, effectively, a motorway. Dundee was not unique in this. At about the same time, its ancient trading partner, Gothenburg, did much the same with a comparable result.

To the *Courier*, the bridge was the keystone of the new Dundee:

> The new central shopping area, the fast growing expansion of the new university, the great new hospital at Ninewells, the multi-storey houses reaching upwards and creating a new skyline for Dundee, these and other things are signs of the big Dundee advance which started after the war.[98]

Using terms very similar to those used to justify the Tay Railway Bridge a century earlier, Lord Provost McManus welcomed the road bridge particularly because it would prevent Dundee from becoming isolated, as well as bringing countless industrial, commercial and tourist benefits. He also hoped that it would increase Dundee's 'status and importance'.[99] If the status of the new Dundee required bolstering by the new bridge, that implies he was not yet entirely convinced about the city's success. The opening of the bridge attracted commentators galore, one of whom – the architectural historian Colin McWilliam – welcomed the new Dundee in *The Scotsman*, praising particularly the four black and white slabs of flats in Derby Street. However, McWilliam also lamented the 'loss of old Dundee, with so much that was quaint and noble in the old Scots style'.[100] Noble? McWilliam was the first to put an aesthetic value on the buildings listed by the government but considered worthless by the citizens.

In 1968 the British Association made one of its periodic visits to Dundee, causing the production of the customary handbook.[101] Many of its authors did not quite know what to make of the changes within the city. Bruce Lenman ignored them, whereas the editor, in contemplating the historical geography of the town, sidestepped the issue: 'Thus the heart of the burgh changes in response to its growth . . . and the visitor to Dundee in 1968 will see a city, which has met the challenges of many centuries, being re-built to meet the opportunities which lie ahead.'[102] Although the Dundonian architectural historian David Walker, then working for the government, provided a deeply researched inventory of all the architectural quality that *survived* in the city, he contented himself with the following *sotto voce* message on the loss of its ancient, non-monumental character:

> It is to be hoped that such vast negations of architectural quality [the 'dismal aridity with which great areas of the city have been blighted following the post-war housing explosion'] will not be permitted to recur and that we will care for our modest legacy of fine architecture . . . better than we have done in the past.[103]

The scale of destruction caused by the inner ring road was such that the swathes of dereliction were nicknamed ironically the 'Trojan Ruins' after the principal demolition company, Trojan Demolitions. It may also have been a coded expression of a deep sense of lost antiquity.

THE RISE OF THE HERITAGE INTEREST

The sheer scale of urban reconstruction and destruction in post-war Britain, so manifest by the mid-1960s, stimulated a vehement reaction over the following decade. Lord Esher christened this breaking of the post-war rebuilding consensus as the 'Broken Wave'.[104] A pioneer in the rescue of old buildings had been the National Trust for Scotland which, in 1953, stepped in to rescue Provost Ross's House in Shiprow, Aberdeen, then threatened with demolition. When the Queen Mother opened the Renaissance Provost Skene's House in 1954 (saved from an earlier Aberdonian clearance in the 1930s), it was to tremendous public acclaim. Moreover, the Trust's Little Houses Scheme, which rescued lesser historic buildings in the Fife coastal burghs and, particularly, in Dunkeld, and converted them to modern dwellings, was immensely popular with its ever increasing membership.[105] So Dundee, which was set to become the only major town in Scotland lacking an NTS property, could not have been in any ignorance about the greater popular interest in heritage.

Concern about the retention of historic buildings had moved far beyond the confines of a stately waltz between a government listing buildings of historic value, and local authorities ignoring them. Keen to engage with the protection of architectural heritage, other conservation societies sprang up, an early one being the New Glasgow Society, which was bent on opposing Glasgow's twenty-nine proposed Comprehensive Development Areas (which encompassed virtually the entire inner area of the city) and its proposed network of motorways and expressways. When the Commonwealth Games took place in Glasgow in 1965, the Society greeted them with a slender, highly illustrated paperback called *Glasgow at a Glance*,[106] which, received with bemusement by Glaswegians and with fascination by the visitors, sold out rapidly. The following year David Walker and Andor Gomme produced their majestic tome *The Architecture of Glasgow*, with powerful muscle-bound photographs of architectural grandeur coated in thick black soot. The only other architectural volume of comparable ambition was devoted to the more obviously architectural city of Bristol some years later, at a time when that city was likewise threatened with wholesale redevelopment.[107] The two Glasgow volumes, however, had the result of changing Glaswegians' perceptions about themselves. The government response to popular disquiet at heritage loss was the 1967 Civic Amenities Act, which empowered local authorities to designate areas of particular architectural character as Conservation Areas. This Act stimulated the rise of bodies like the Civic Trust, the Scottish Civic Trust, the Civic Trust for the North-East, and many town civic trusts. Through their popular campaigns such as 'Pride of Place', they effectively democratised the subject.

In 1970, curious to find out which parts of their city impartial outsiders really thought should be protected by the new legislation, Glasgow Corporation invited a past president of the RIBA, Lord Esher, up to Glasgow to report on whether any part of the city should be 'preserved and enhanced'. After all, back in 1945 the City Engineer had proposed the destruction and redevelopment of the entire city based upon a new roads layout and large multi-storeyed living blocks.[108] Esher's evaluation of Glasgow was forthright: 'This remarkable and to many people surprising wealth of good architecture, very largely of the nineteenth century, instead of being peppered about the City's square miles, is mainly concentrated in the city's beautiful inner suburbs to the west and the south . . . As a result, Glasgow is now the finest surviving example of a Victorian City.'[109] Taken aback, Glasgow Corporation duly instituted Conservation Areas, and the city began its slow crawl back to self-respect.

Twentieth-century interest in Dundee's heritage had possibly begun with the foundation of the Abertay Historical Society at a meeting in the University back in May 1947 – although its focus was broader than Dundee, and wider than urban. Its publications, however, added substantially to the knowledge about the city – and David Walker's *Architects and Architecture in Dundee 1770–1914*, a pioneering production for its date in 1958,[110] evidently had a powerful influence on the Scottish Office's *List of Listed Buildings*. It has been suggested that the Society's successful 1958 campaign, led by Sir Francis Mudie, to save Dudhope Castle from demolition as a 'dilapidated old slum',[111] was the first signal of a change in attitude by Dundee's town council to its heritage,[112] but that seems improbable. Dundee had always given special consideration to those buildings deemed to be 'monuments', of which Dudhope was one. So a Dundee Civic Trust was founded in 1973, and a body called the Machar's Guild was formed to campaign to prevent Gardyne's Land from being moved, stone by stone, away from the High Street because it obstructed development potential.

But since Esher or his equivalent was never invited to Dundee, the city thereby deprived itself of the outsider's perception. There was no change in its attitude to lesser buildings, and Dundee's response to the Civic Amenities Act was the selection of the outlying textile village of Trottick on the Dighty Burn to the north, suburban terraces in the West End, and the fisher town of Broughty Ferry to the east. Despite the quality of Dundee's Improvement Act streets – never mind of its earlier fabric (whatever the 1952 *Survey* had said disparagingly[113]), the city centre was still accorded no value. One way of gauging whether or not civic attitudes were changing is to examine the city's response to the invitation issued to all local authorities throughout the United Kingdom in 1974 to devise appropriate activities and celebrations for European Architectural Heritage Year 1975. After some initial high-sounding supportive rhetoric in the council minutes, no action was recorded.[114]

In 1981 the *Dundee Project* was established jointly by the Scottish Development Agency, the city council and Tayside Regional Council with the objective of transforming Dundee into a leading location for investment and development. It was given the particular mission of transforming the city's image – but from what, was not made clear.[115] As so many of its industries declined or vanished, an increasingly negative view of Dundee as a depressed de-industrialised community had been growing. This was of a self-destructive and anti-cultural industrial city in terminal decay – first expressed by Hugh MacDiarmid, then in the autobiography of the journalist James Cameron, and finally – perhaps at its most extreme – by the writer Martin Horan in the diatribe 'Meh hame toon' in the *Scottish Review* in 1981. In trying to exorcise his experiences as the council's drama therapist in Dundee's deprived areas, Horan depicted Dundee as an 'industrial jungle . . . of unbelievable inverted snobbery'.[116] This perception – a world away from the bright new world of high-technology industries and new housing estates of outer Dundee – was compounded by the serial losses not merely of the jute industry as a whole, but of what were regarded as icons of the old town's identity – such as the Royal Arch, the harbour, Caledon shipbuilding, the Blackness Foundry and the Overgate.[117] Effectively, in a manner unparalleled in comparable cities, there had arisen two very different Dundees. Crucially, the new Overgate development had not brought the city centre the long-term advantages it had hoped for. It had cut through existing 'desire lines', effectively marooning the north-west city centre; commercially. It was only ever successful in those eastern parts nearest the High Street. Moreover, the architecture of its windy monumentalism proved indifferent, and quickly lost its gloss. Despite various refurbishments, the new centre never met its objectives and was demolished (save the eastern office block) in the late 1990s. Dundonians had exchanged their past for a better future, and the future had not delivered.

When cities go through post-industrial cycles such as these, however, the architectural heritage can provide *anchors of memory* as a balancing counterweight to the sense of collapse and loss, and thus become the springboard of regeneration. The Merchant City in Glasgow, effectively rediscovered in 1972 when under threat of total demolition, is an excellent example. Without such anchors, not only does the task become more difficult, but the interpretation of identity becomes that much more risky. In 1983 the city council jointly with the Dundee Project sponsored *Dundee: An Illustrated Introduction*[118] – effectively the first architectural guide to the city, published in 1984. In drawing attention to the regeneration of Blackness and the creation of Dundee Technology Park, the sponsors trod a fine (and not always comprehensible) line between praise for heritage and enthusiasm for the future:

> Victorian landmarks such as the Albert Institute and the Royal Arch, which stood at the entrance to Dundee harbour, are today counterpointed by developments with our contemporary and forward-looking relevance.[119]

The Guide's preface by the distinguished architect/playwright Sinclair Gauldie pithily presented a history of the town that entirely accorded with the then knowledge: namely a workaday town with little qualitative history dominated by coarse textiles, becoming a proletarian mill town in the nineteenth century. No concept, therefore, of the major seaport that had been Scotland's second city for over two centuries, with an architectural grandeur second only to the capital. Yet since the evidence of Dundee's earlier past had mostly vanished, Gauldie's was an entirely legitimate narrative to construct from what remained. It just happened to be skewed.[120]

There were three varying reactions to the publication of the architectural guide. The civic one, represented by the Lord Provost at the book's launch, was disbelief that sufficient had survived the 'Trojan Ruins' to merit a book; whereas the non-Dundee one, that 'a pamphlet had been inflated into a book' – that is, too much was being made of an insignificant location – indicated just how far Dundee had slipped from the national consciousness.[121] Dundonians themselves, however, quickly purchased so many copies to send to exiles abroad that it sold out in months – indicating an unexpected level of residual pride. Historic Scotland's subsequent commissioning of one of the earliest of the Scottish burgh surveys in recognition of the quality of Dundee's archaeology[122] consolidated the growing feeling that Dundee had perhaps been misjudged.

The heritage tourism that the Dundee Project had set about to increase was conceived solely in terms of either whaling heritage – underscored by the arrival of RRS *Discovery* in 1986 and its move into a new dock with visitor centre in 1992,[123] or of mill heritage, with the restoration of Verdant Works as a tourist attraction. Both related to the nineteenth century, and since neither was in the city centre, it was only too easy for visitors to go to either without engaging with the town centre, separated from it, as both were, by the inner ring motorway. The *Discovery* therefore failed in its intention to lead to 'the creation of a central Waterfront area that maximises its full potential or reflects the city's identity, both past and present'.[124] Nonetheless, with the founding of the Tayside Building Preservation Trust in 1991, designated Conservation Areas rising to twenty-three, the conversion of much of the substantial inheritance of mill buildings into flats, and the government's creation of the Dundee Historic Environment Trust in 2004, the feeling was that the conservation of the city's heritage was now in safer hands.[125]

A re-evaluation of Dundee's pre-nineteenth-century identity was catalysed in 2004 by a reinvigorated Dundee Civic Trust which, with new independence,[126] undertook a study of the thirty closes and lanes of ancient Dundee that had escaped the modernisation process.[127] Yet, whereas a study of Edinburgh's medieval closes in 1984 had led to the establishment of the Old Town Renewal Trust, which then set about transforming them into one of the principal tourist attractions of Edinburgh's Old Town (as they remain today), the Dundee Closes survey was officially ignored, and the closes mostly remained in a desperate state comparable to those of Edinburgh back in 1984. However, the 2008 award-winning restoration of Gardyne's Land, facing the High Street, into a backpackers' hostel, developed by the Building Preservation Trust over a long decade, at last provided Dundee with a tangible anchor of memory for the pre-Victorian seaport. Coincidentally, Dundee University's three-volume *History of Dundee* project, initiated in 1997 with the aim of understanding and interpreting the town beyond jute, jam and journalism, now provided such properties with their historical context by revealing the importance of Dundee in Renaissance Scotland.

A city with a new confidence in itself and its identity might have been able to bring its century of architectural inferiority complex to a close. However, in 2002 civic attitudes were revealed as fundamentally unchanged; for, almost a century after James Thomson proposed a new Dundee constructed down on the Earl Grey Dock, a monumental plan with neo-classical overtones was once again proposed for the windy waterfront, to replace the legacy of the 1952 Advisory Plan. It is in this that Patrick Geddes's advice was most sage. If you embed the history of the town in its redevelopment, it is more likely to survive. If you do not use the architectural anchors of memory to create an authentic identity in a new development, a city will face waves of successive redevelopment every time fashions change.

CONCLUSION

Central to this investigation has been Dundonians' perception of their own city. In what appears to have been an intense desire to become more like other cities, a deep architectural inferiority complex developed during the nineteenth century. Although the legacy of the industrial inner ring was shameful and certainly demanded radical action, the historic city centre was peripheral to it. So the steadfast determination of the city authorities over half a century to demolish the Overgate indicated a different explanation. Unable to appreciate just how 'quaint and noble' Dundee's medieval inheritance had been, James Thomson and his contemporaries persuaded Dundonians that its architecture and streetscape was unworthy of the new Dundee: other cities were doing better. Indeed, the belief that this was the case is recurrent throughout a century of town council minutes. Seduced by the opportunities offered by its magnificent setting, Dundonians initially sought an appropriate monumentality, which mutated in the mid-twentieth century to a desire for monumental modernity.

In time, the low esteem Dundee accorded its heritage led it to be out of step with other Scottish cities, not just in how it should value its own heritage, but also in how it should respond to the valuation placed upon it by outsiders – particularly by the government. No matter what the government might say about the quality of Dundee's buildings, Dundonians and their leaders, trapped within their inherited negative perspective of their city and fixated upon a monumental future, found themselves unable to understand. As each new scheme was advanced, they remained fixated by James Thomson's baroque municipal vision. Rather than using its past to build upon, as Geddes had urged, repeating concepts of modernity were therefore imposed upon the city. There is a strong link between urban self-esteem and an authentic civic identity. Without the one, the other can be damaged. The new Overgate, which had replaced buildings at least 400 years old, itself lasted barely thirty. That Dundee had lost something precious in order to end up with something worse might explain those negative responses about the city's image to the Dundee Contemporary Arts proposal in 1996.

If the University's *History of Dundee* gives Dundonians their memory back, those remaining physical anchors of memory of the seaport that survived the century of monumental modernisation process might yet prove significant to Dundee's future.

ACKNOWLEDGEMENTS

A number of people have assisted me, and I am particularly grateful to Neil Grieve, Stuart Walker, Innes Duffus, David McDougall, Chris Whatley, Jim Tomlinson, Adam Swan, and the extraordinarily helpful staff of Dundee University Archives, Dundee City Archives, and the Local History Section of the Central Library, Wellgate.

NOTES

1. P. Geddes, 'Beginnings of the Survey of Edinburgh' in RIBA, *Town Planning Conference 1910 Proceedings* (London, 1910), p. 292.
2. R. Haworth, 'Patrick Geddes' concept of conservative surgery', *Architectural Heritage* 11 (2000), pp. 37–42.
3. V. Welter, 'History, biology and city design', *Architectural Heritage* 6 (1996), pp. 61–82.
4. DUA, MS 112/1/2: Dundee Town Council, *Report on the Central Area Improvement Scheme by the City Engineer 1910* (Dundee, 1910).
5. B. Lenman and W.D. Carroll, 'Council housing in Dundee' in The British Association, *Dundee and District* (Dundee, 1968), p. 285.
6. B. Harris, '"City of the Future": James Thomson's vision of the city beautiful' in L. Miskell, C.A. Whatley and B. Harris (eds), *Victorian Dundee: Image and Realities* (East Linton, 2000), p. 182.
7. Dundee City Arts Centre Architecture Competition Comments Sheets. Analysis of the thirty-eight feedback forms received. 48 per cent referred to the city's reputation/self-esteem; 26 per cent to the value of an Arts Centre; and 26 per cent to the need to encourage tourism. Only a single reply mentioned the City of Discovery.
8. See C. McKean, 'What kind of Renaissance town was Dundee?' in C. McKean, B. Harris and C.A. Whatley (eds), *Dundee: Renaissance to Enlightenment* (Dundee, 2009).
9. C. McKean, 'Not even the trivial grace of a straight line' in Miskell et al. (eds), *Victorian Dundee*, pp. 15–37.
10. *Advertiser*, 6 May 1851.
11. See C. McKean, *Battle for the North* (London, 2006).
12. See particularly B. Edwards, 'Alexander Thomson and the Glasgow Improvement Scheme' in G. Stamp and S. McKinstry (eds), *'Greek' Thomson* (Edinburgh, 1994), p. 138.

COLOUR PLATE 1 Part of the largest extent of rock armour revetment in Scotland protecting the ~~ern~~ side of the promontory of Buddon Ness, looking towards Carnoustie. This has caused a ~~'etion~~ in the amount of sediment entering the Tay Estuary on the north side, starving Monifieth beaches further to the west of their natural sand supply. (Photo copyright R.W. Duck)

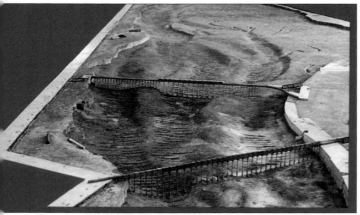

COLOUR PLATE 2
(a) Upper Tay. Part of the scale Tay Model empty of water (amended from the University of Dundee Prospectus, 1984) looking upstream towards Perth, showing the Railway and Road Bridges, channels and sand banks. Note the main navigation channel passes beneath the southern end of the Road Bridge (navigation spans marked in red) and the central part of the Railway Bridge (High Girders).
(b) Lower Tay: the model in use during a tidal simulation. (Lower image courtesy D.C. Thomson)

COLOUR PLATE 3 Vertical aerial photographs of the western end of Dundee and Riverside taken 1948 (a – top) and 2001 (b – above). The expansion of the city onto what was previously agricultu land is striking as is the extent of land claim from the Tay creating the site for the runway of Dun Airport. Two rubble walls projecting into the Tay are visible in the south east corner of the 1948 photograph, built in preparation for the next phase of refuse dumping as much of Invergowrie B was to become progressively claimed from the Tay working from east to west. (Image (a) referenc 540_A_0385_5108. Reproduced under licence from RCAHMS: National Collection of Aerial Photography; image (b) unknown source)

COLOUR PLATE 4 (*Above*) Detail of the extent of land claim at the western end of the Riverside Landfill, Dundee, in this oblique aerial photograph looking over Invergowrie, what remains of Invergowrie Bay and Dundee Airport towards the Railway Bridge at low tide. The Perth to Dundee railway line approximately follows the foot of the cliff marking the natural shoreline. The sewer pipe extending into the bay is now used to carry storm water overflows. (Photo courtesy of the late Andy McKinlay, Central Media Services, University of Dundee)

COLOUR PLATE 5 (*Left*) James Thomson, city engineer and architect, at his desk. (Copyright Dundee City Council)

COLOUR PLATE 6 Thomson's 1911 perspective of a new civic centre on Earl Grey Dock looking d[...] a widened and mutilated Crichton Street. The building on the left was to be a multi-storeyed mar[...] with a roof garden; and the possibility of the Caird Hall had not yet emerged. Of all Thomson's visions, this was the one that most resembled Daniel Burnham's proposals for Chicago. (Copyright Dundee City Council)

COLOUR PLATE 7 Thomson's (reluctant) proposal to save the Town House by relocating it to Tall[...] Street, on the site of the demolished Luckenbooths. The somewhat blank architecture of his prop[...] rebuilding of the Overgate in the right foreground resembles Burnham's contemporary suggested rebuilding of Chicago's Magnificent Mile. (Image hangs in City Development offices, Tayside Ho[...]

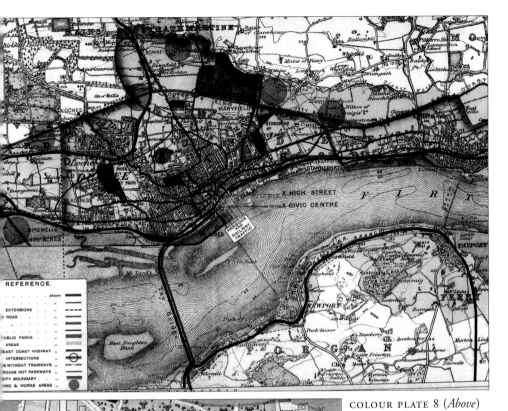

COLOUR PLATE 8 (*Above*) Thomson's 1918 Strategic Plan for Dundee. It shows the piers of the fallen Tay Bridge used for a road bridge, the Kingsway by-pass, and large circles of new housing for people relocated from the centre lining the north and west of the city. (Copyright Charles McKean)

COLOUR PLATE 9 (*Left*) The central area plan from the 1952 Advisory Plan for Dundee. The driving force was the inner ring road, which was used to shape the central area. Fewer than 20 buildings in the entire city centre were highlighted as worth retaining. (Image from the Charles McKean library)

COLOUR PLATE 10 The 2002 plan for the waterfront. Big city planning, with a new 'triumphal arc' over the bridge, and a token leisure harbour. In the Thomson tradition, it proposed a significant sl of the city towards the water. Plan for the Shore, drawn in 2000 by Mike Galloway. (Image courtes of Mike Galloway)

COLOUR PLATE 11 View from the Shore to St Mary's up St David's Close. The largest complex of buildings surviving from pre-modern Dundee, it is still largely neglected. Its restoration could make an inspiring entrance to central Dundee for visitors. (Copyright Charles McKean)

COLOUR PLATE 12 Dundee's Docks from the east in the 1990s, before dockside regeneration had begun. The spires of the city loom over a deserted port. (Copyright Charles McKean)

COLOUR PLATE 13 Demolition of the barely 30-years-old Overgate in 1998, providing new views of the west front of St Mary's steeple. (Copyright Charles McKean)

COLOUR PLATE 14 James McIntosh Patrick, *The Tay Bridge from my Studio Window* 1948, oil on canvas – probably Dundee's most iconic artwork. (Copyright Dundee Art Galleries & Museums)

COLOUR PLATE 15 (*Above*) The competition-winning Dundee Contemporary Arts opened in 1999, which transformed perceptions about the city. It was a collaborative project that brought together the Dundee Printmakers Workshop, the Steps Cinema, Dundee University's Visual Research Centre, and the City's arts administration. (University of Dundee Archive Services)

COLOUR PLATE 16 (*Right*) Public art in Dundee – one of Keith Donnelly's Saltire Award-winning ceramic panels on Bellfield Street. (Photo by Matthew Jarron)

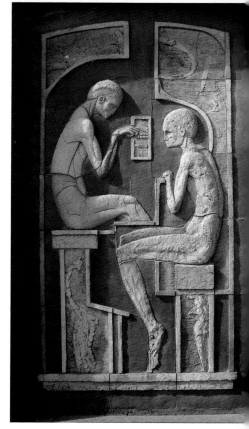

COLOUR PLATE 17 William Halley and Sons derelict mill in September 2010. Most jute mills have either been demolished or converted to other purposes, especially residential use. (Photo by Beth Lord)

COLOUR PLATE 18 The *Gorilla 7* oil rig in Dundee docks for maintenance, 2010. Dundee captured only a small proportion of the employment generated by the exploitation of North Sea oil. (Photo by Beth Lord)

COLOUR PLATE 19 The eastern approach to the centre of the city in 2010. The Nynas refinery uses oil imported through Dundee from South America for products such as bitumen, bunker fuel and diesel oil. (Photo by Beth Lord)

COLOUR PLATE 20 Visit of Margaret Thatcher to Canmore Works, Forfar (Don & Low), 2 September 1982. The economic policies of the Thatcher government greatly contributed to the sharp decline of the jute industry in the 1980s. (Don & Low (Holdings) Ltd Collection, University of Dundee Archives)

13. R. Jobson's evidence, *Report from the Select Committee* . . . [into] . . . *the Royal Burghs of Scotland* (Edinburgh, 1819), p. 28.

14. See R.H. Trainor, 'The elite' in W.H. Fraser and I. Maver (eds), *Glasgow*, vol. 2: *1830–1912* (Manchester, 1996), pp. 227–64; L. Miskell, 'Civic leadership and the manufacturing elite' in Miskell et al. (eds), *Victorian Dundee*, pp. 63–6.

15. Act of Parliament 1824 (William Burn), and plans by James Brewster 1832, George Matthewson 1834, Charles Edward 1846, all in either Dundee University Archives, the City Archives or the Central Library, Wellgate.

16. See McKean, 'Not even the trivial grace of a straight line'.

17. R. Small, *The Statistical Account of Dundee* (Dundee, 1793), p. 54.

18. D. Barrie, *City of Dundee Illustrated* (Dundee, 1890), p. 16.

19. DUA, MS 6/2/78/74: J. Cox, Autobiography.

20. 684 pencil sketches made by Charles Lawson, possibly at the behest of Alexander Lamb. Now in the Wellgate Library.

21. Clause 12 of the Act stated that the 'Commissioners shall not eject or displace within any period of six months any number of persons of the labouring classes exceeding 500 without a certificate from the Sheriff that other and suitable accommodation for them exists within the burgh or its immediate neighbourhood, or has been provided by the Commissioners in manner hereafter mentioned or otherwise.' But they did not. There was no rehousing as was the case in Glasgow.

22. For an explanation of the historic urban form of Dundee, see McKean, 'What kind of Renaissance town?'

23. J.M. Beatts, *Reminiscences of a Dundonian* (Dundee, 1882), p. 31.

24. M. Macdonald, 'The patron, the professor and the painter' in Miskell et al. (eds), *Victorian Dundee*, pp. 135–50.

25. See Alexander Lamb, *Dundee: Its Quaint and Historic Buildings* (Dundee, 1895).

26. DCA, TCM 13 January 1908. For more on Thomson, see Harris, '"City of the Future"' in Miskell et al. (eds), *Victorian Dundee*, pp. 169–84.

27. *Dundee Year Book* (1907), pp. 102–3.

28. Harris, '"City of the Future"', pp. 174–5.

29. DCA, TCM 19 August 1907, p. 244.

30. DCA, TCM 13 February 1907/4 March 1907.

31. DCA, TCM 26 October 1909.

32. DCA, TCM 1 January 1910.

33. The RCAHMS has a partial set of drawings for a new civic centre with magistrate's court on the site of the Luckenbooths in a refined baroque from the hand of Sir Robert Lorimer. No trace can be found in the council minutes of who commissioned them.

34. DCA, TCM 4 August 1910. DUA, MS 112/1/2: The Dundee Town Council, *Report on Central Improvement Scheme by the City Engineer 1910*. Even the title is odd: Dundee had had a *City* Council for twenty years.

35. Ibid., p. 4.

36. Ibid., p. 11.

37. D.H. Burnham and E.H. Bennett, *Plan of Chicago* (Chicago, 1909). It was a paean of praise for grand-scale planning on the Haussman or Vienna models. Burnham, whose deep influence is apparent in almost all Thomson's post-1909 proposals, began with traffic and an outer by-pass, and proposed a long-term plan, the rebuilding of central streets in large blank blocks, and buildings 'monumental in character and classical in style of architecture' (p. 110).

38. The Dundee Town Council, *Report on Central Improvement Scheme*, p. 15.
39. Ibid., p. 6.
40. DCA, TCM 1911–12, 2 August 1912: Sub Committee of the Improvement Committee, pp. 1338–9.
41. DCA, TCM 20 September 1912.
42. *Supplementary Report* to Dundee Town Council, 21 December 1911.
43. For more, see Harris, "'City of the Future'", pp. 180–1.
44. J. Thomson, *Report on the Development of the City* (Dundee, 1918), p. 2.
45. *Report on Central Improvement Scheme*, p. 21.
46. In the implementation of the 1930 Housing Scotland Act.
47. DCA, TCM Medical Officer of Health's report, 15 May 1931, pp. 905–7.
48. *The Scotsman*, 29 January 1932.
49. See McKean, 'What kind of Renaissance town?'
50. DCA, TCM Works Committee 21 February 1928, p. 389.
51. DCA, TCM 24 December 1931, p. 255.
52. DCA, TCM Works Committee 4 December 1931, p. 148.
53. *The Scotsman*, 22 January 1932.
54. *Courier*, 29 January 1932.
55. *Courier*, 6 January 1932.
56. DUA, MS 14/2/3: Dundee Institute of Architects, Minutes 27 January 1932. I am grateful to Kenneth Baxter for this reference.
57. *Quarterly of the Royal Incorporation of Architects in Scotland* (1932), pp. 110–16.
58. *The Scotsman*, 9 January 1932.
59. For more on this, see C. McKean and P. Whatley with K. Baxter, *Lost Dundee: Dundee's Lost Architectural Heritage* (Edinburgh, 2008).
60. I am grateful to Dr Bruce Walker for this information.
61. The Dundee Corporation (Improvements and Tramways) Act (1913).
62. Ebenezer MacRae became Edinburgh City Architect in July 1925: D.M. Walker, *Dictionary of Scottish Architects*: www.scottisharchitects.org.uk.
63. DCA, TCM 22 October 1937, pp. 1627–30. Also cited in J. Braithwaite, 'The Overgate, Dundee', *Scottish Geographical Journal* 105:2 (1989), pp. 85–93, at p. 87.
64. *Courier*, 26 March 1938.
65. W. Dobson Chapman and C.F. Riley, *Granite City* (London, 1952), p. 1.
66. Personal comment, David MacDougall, City Planning Department.
67. Dobson Chapman and Partners, *City and Royal Burgh of Dundee Survey and Plan*, Folio One: Civic Survey Report (Dundee, 1952), p. 58.
68. Dobson Chapman and Partners, *City and Royal Burgh of Dundee Survey and Plan*, Folio Two: Advisory Plan (Dundee, 1952), p. 2.
69. Dobson Chapman and Partners, *Survey and Plan*: Civic Survey Report, Appendix 1.
70. Dobson Chapman and Partners, *Survey and Plan*: Advisory Plan, Redevelopment Plan – the Central Area, p. 104.
71. Burke had arrived in Dundee during the war from Manchester, and there is little in his career to show an empathy with the concept of historic identity.
72. Dobson Chapman and Partners, *Survey and Plan*: Advisory Plan, p. 9.
73. *Courier*, 19 May 1952.
74. TNA: PRO MT 81/159: City and Royal Burgh of Dundee, Development Plan 1956, Written Statement. I am grateful to Jim Tomlinson for this.
75. TNA: PRO DE 16692/2: Department of Health for Scotland, Note on the City of

Dundee Development Plan, February 1957. I am grateful to Jim Tomlinson for this.

76. *Courier*, 14 August 1958.

77. DUA, MS 21/12/1: Letter from James D. Boyd to Robert Lyle, Town Clerk, 10 July 1957. I am greatly indebted to Kenneth Baxter for this source.

78. DCA, TCM 8 April 1958.

79. The first being Thomson's, two between the Wars, the one in the Advisory Plan and the two commercial schemes of the 1950s.

80. DCA, TCM 8 April 1958.

81. *Courier*, 30 December 1958.

82. *Courier*, 4 July 1958.

83. *The Overgate, Dundee: Scotland's First Shopping Precinct* (London, n.d.).

84. A. Hart, 'Redevelopment and the Small Retailer' (unpublished Dip.T.P. thesis, Duncan of Jordanstone College of Art, 1972), cited in Braithwaite, 'The Overgate'.

85. *Courier*, 26 October 1969, contained in DCA, HH 1992 337: Ian Burke, Martin and Partners, *Cuttings Book*.

86. *Dundee Chamber of Commerce Journal* (December 1961), p. 981; (March 1960), p. 528.

87. *Evening Telegraph*, 29 June 1963; *Courier*, 25 February 1964.

88. *Courier*, 3 April 1961.

89. Ibid.

90. LHC, *Dundee Newspaper Cuttings Books*, 23 Oct 1958/3 Mar 1961/25 Feb 1964. A number of newspaper stories covered the difficulties of inhabitants trying to survive in increasingly derelict areas.

91. *Courier*, 8 Oct 1963.

92. *Courier*, 11 February 1964, 27 February 1964. While the author was campaigning around that time against the inner ring road in Glasgow, he was warned that his father would be blacklisted from any future contracts if he continued. He did, and he was.

93. Comprehensive Development Areas or CDAs.

94. *1964 Quinquennial Review of the Development Plan* (Dundee). Although not intended as such, in some places – such as, say, Glasgow – CDAs earned the nickname 'comprehensive demolition areas'.

95. *City of Dundee Development Plan, First Quinquennial Review: Report of Proceedings*, 30 August 1965, p. 25.

96. DCA, TCM, 4 December 1930 and 4 June 1931. *City of Dundee Development Plan, First Quinquennial Review: Report of Proceedings*, pp. 959–61.

97. *Evening Telegraph*, 14 May 1965.

98. *Courier*, 18 September 1966.

99. I. Nimmo, *Crossing the Tay* (Edinburgh, 1966), foreword.

100. *The Scotsman*, 17 January 1966.

101. S.J. Jones (ed.), *Dundee and District* (Dundee, British Association, 1968).

102. S.J. Jones, 'Historical geography of Dundee' in Jones (ed.), *Dundee and District*, p. 277.

103. D. Walker, 'The architecture of Dundee' in Jones (ed.), *Dundee and District*, p. 300.

104. L. Esher, *A Broken Wave* (London, 1981).

105. D. Watters and M. Glendinning, *Little Houses: The National Trust for Scotland's Improvement Scheme for Small Historic Homes* (Edinburgh, 2006).

106. For more on this, see C. McKean, 'From castles to Calvinists: Scottish architectural publishing since 1960', *Architectural Heritage* 17 (Edinburgh, 2006).

107. M. Jenner and A. Gomme, *The Architecture of Bristol* (London, 1979).

108. R. Bruce, *First Planning report to the Highways and Planning Committee of Glasgow* (Glasgow, 1945).

109. Lord Esher, *Conservation in Glasgow: A Preliminary Report* (Glasgow, 1971), p. 1.

110. David Walker, *Architects and Architecture in Dundee 1770–1914* (Dundee, Abertay Historical Society, 1958; reprinted 1977).

111. This is virtually the same language that Burntisland Town Council was using at the same time to justify the demolition of Rossend Castle, again unsuccessfully.

112. Royal Commission for the Ancient and Historical Monuments of Scotland, *Dundee on Record* (Edinburgh, 1992), p. 56.

113. Dobson Chapman and Partners, *City and Royal Burgh of Dundee Survey and Plan*, Folio One: Civic Survey Report, p. 55.

114. DCC, Planning and Development Committee Minutes, 24 June 1974.

115. C. Di Domenico and M. Di Domenico, 'Heritage and urban renewal in Dundee', *Journal of Retail and Leisure Property* 6 (2007), p. 333. Braithwaite, 'The Overgate', p. 91.

116. M. Horan, 'Meh hame toon', *Scottish Review* 21 (1981).

117. Even though workers from the old industries provided the key skills for the new ones.

118. C. McKean and D. Walker, *Dundee: An Illustrated Introduction* (Edinburgh, 1984).

119. Ibid., p. 153.

120. That same year, when Gauldie collaborated with Bruce Walker on *Architects and Architecture on Tayside*, they stopped the story just at the point that James Thomson was beginning.

121. Personal comment to the author from the Lord Provost and certain Edinburgh architects.

122. S. Stevenson and E.P.D. Torrie, *Dundee Burgh Survey* (Edinburgh, 1988).

123. See Di Domenico and Di Domenico, 'Heritage and urban renewal in Dundee', pp. 317–39.

124. Ibid., p. 336.

125. N. Grieve, 'Conservation in Dundee' in H. Begg (ed.), *100 Years of Planning in Dundee* (Dundee, 1992).

126. For its first two decades, membership of the Civic Trust's ruling council was so dominated by present or past employees of the city or regional council that expectations of its taking an independent line were low.

127. Dundee Civic Trust, Dundee Closes Study (unpublished report, 2004).

CHAPTER 5

A Women's Town?
Dundee Women on the Public Stage

Sarah Browne and Jim Tomlinson

The epithet 'women's town' has long been applied to Dundee. Norman Watson's detailed study notes how frequently and enthusiastically this designation has been used, perhaps most colourfully by *Scotland on Sunday* in 1994: 'Dundee women are strong, gallus and an inspiration to their sex. Today, as in the past, Dundee women are different.'[1] As Valerie Wright shows in 'Juteopolis and After: Women and Work in Twentieth-Century Dundee', Chapter 6 below, such views have an obvious material base in the peculiarities of the city at the beginning of the twentieth century. 'Dundee is pre-eminently a city of women and of women workers', wrote Mary Walker in 1912, and contemporary data supports this.[2] In 1901 there were 127 women for every 100 men in the city, and the employment figures show almost 28,000 women in textiles (overwhelmingly in jute) out of a total of 40,000 operatives.[3] Dundee *circa* 1900 was unusual in this numerical predominance of women and the prevalence of married women's employment. Though there were more men than women in the total labour force,[4] employment openings for men were limited by the small number of male job openings in jute, and many men joined the forces,[5] emigrated,[6] or worked away from the city. The employment opportunities available to women meant that they also played a prominent role in many household economies (Table 5.1), data which provides a nice counterpoint to any simple notions about male breadwinner households predominating in Britain before the First World War.[7]

Over the century both the overall numerical predominance and the significance of women's employment in jute diminished. By 1951 the

TABLE 5.1
Dundee households in 1905

Status of household	Number	Percentage
Dependent on one male wage-earner	769	25
Dependent on one female wage-earner	684	23
Dependent on husband and wife's joint earnings	433	14
Other two-wage households	656	22
Three-wage households	487	16
Total sample	3,029	

Source: Dundee Social Union, Report on Housing and Industrial Conditions and Medical Inspection of School Children (Dundee, 1905), pp. 24–7.

ratio of women to men in the total population was down to 119:100, and by 2001 to 111:100.[8] Jute employment disappeared finally in the 1990s, but during the long decline of the industry the *share* of women in its employment also diminished.[9] The rise of alternative employments in Dundee was paralleled by women's increased participation in paid employment throughout Britain, so that by the end of the century Dundee was much less distinctive in this regard than at its beginning.

WOMEN'S PUBLIC ROLE

Against this background, this chapter focuses on women's changing public role in the city: how far did the demographic and employment patterns translate into a major role in the city's public activities? There already exists detailed work on women's role in electoral politics. This shows how slowly women were to develop any substantial place on elected bodies, even in comparison with Scotland's other major cities. Local government was hugely important before 1914, spending over 50 per cent of all government expenditure, and in some parts of Britain women played a significant role in local bodies.[10] However, in Dundee, while women were elected to the parish council from 1901, they only gained places on the Education Authority in the 1920s, and the first woman on the Corporation was not elected until 1935. The proportion of women on that body and its successors was generally less than 10 per cent of total membership until the 1970s, and the first female Lord Provost was not appointed until 1999.[11] At the parliamentary level, Dundee was more 'advanced', having Florence Horsbrugh as its first female MP from 1931 until 1945, but she remained a singular case until the end of the century. It is doubtful if her election in 1931 owed much to her gender, as this victory was part of a countrywide electoral triumph for the Conservative Party.

Behind the scenes women played a substantial part in all the political parties, though as we largely lack archives for both the Labour and Unionist Parties, we can not say much on how that worked. In the Liberal Party women were numerically significant, but did not gain many of the key posts in the organisation.[12] There is also a lack of good evidence on women's role in trade unions in the city, though a persistent suggestion is that while men dominated in leadership roles, women acted as a powerful force where they had numerical strength, whether it be in jute before 1914, or at Timex in the 1980s.[13]

Some important women operated on the borderlands of electoral politics, and this would be the case for Mary Brooksbank, who stood as a Communist Party candidate, but who was more prominent as an agitator and fermenter of discontent not focused on elections and formal politics. Such activities are not to be dismissed, and at certain points secured considerable support from women in the city, especially during the agitation for the vote before the First World War, the battle against mass unemployment in the inter-war years, or at the time of resistance to redundancies and factory closures in the 1980s and 1990s.[14] But for most of the city's women, most of the time, public activity was in neither the political parties nor in street protests, but in other, diverse organisations which allowed them to articulate distinct views on issues of the day they deemed important.

The existing literature on women in the city is richest for the pre-1914 period, notably on suffragettes/suffragists and trade unionists, so these years will receive less prominence than later periods, about which much less has been written.[15] Our discussion is empirical and very much based on the available archival evidence. But in looking at this evidence we have necessarily to engage with the enormous literature that exists on women's role in twentieth-century Britain.

First, our work supports recent literature in this field which rejects an older narrative of 'two waves' of feminism, the one at the time of the pre-1914 suffrage battle, the second at the time of the rise of the Women's Liberation Movement in the 1960s and 1970s. Such a narrative was based on a very narrow, contingent view of what was to count as feminism, and had the effect of disregarding the evidence of much more sustained activity by women's organisations throughout the century. We now have a very large literature exploring the nature and significance of that activity, at UK, Scottish and local levels.[16] It should be stressed that the interpretation of this women's activity remains very much a matter of controversy. The issues addressed by women in these organisations were highly diverse, and much has been written about how far those issues are to be regarded as genuinely 'feminist'. Thus a common correlate of the 'two waves' story was a view that, for example, after the First World War women's organisations fell back on a conservative agenda concerned with childcare and motherhood, belying any claims to feminism, and parallel arguments can be found about the years after 1945.[17] Against this view we assert two points. First, that the public agendas pursued by women throughout the century were always diverse, even sometimes contradictory, and cannot be neatly divided up chronologically into 'radical' and 'conservative'. Second, that what is to count as feminism is historically contingent, and not something to be decided by a fiat which necessarily reflects the views of one generation of historians. Hence, our emphasis is on the issues that contemporary women themselves have defined as their concerns, how and why these changed over the century, and, as far as it is possible to discern, how successful women were in achieving their aims. We focus attention on women's organisations, while Valerie Wright in Chapter 6 deals with women's activities in other organisations, especially trade unions.

Alongside the well-known suffragette and trade union activity of Dundee women before 1914 was the role they played in other organisations. One such was the Dundee Social Union, founded in 1888, to 'promote the well-being of the inhabitants of the town'.[18] The DSU's minute books, available from 1906, show an organisation in which women were the majority of the membership and of its General Committee.[19] There seems little doubt that the majority of the DSU's membership was middle class, but that, of course, is no reason to dismiss the organisation as insignificant. It articulated the widespread concerns of the Edwardian middle classes with housing, children's welfare and 'sweating' (low wages), which were also major issues for the emergent working-class movement. Within the DSU there were divergent views on the way to address these 'social problems', especially on the relative responsibility of individuals, the state and voluntary bodies. But it is unhelpful to historical understanding to dismiss the DSU as simply the home of middle-class do-gooders. Not only was it representative of a hugely important trend in British society – widespread concern with the 'social question', and philanthropic action, much of it by women, to address that 'question' – but it also played a pioneering role in social investigation with its Report of 1905, focusing on housing and the health of children.[20] This investigation, it should be noted, was carried out by two women, led by Mary Walker, a pioneer woman member of the Parish Council.

The DSU, like almost all 'informed opinion' before 1914, was hostile to married women being employed, certainly while their children were young.[21] This opposition was particularly grounded in the alleged link between such employment and infant mortality – a theme of almost all discussions of the 'social question' in Dundee in the early 1900s, but also reflecting a wider national debate.[22] Undoubtedly infant mortality was high in Dundee, even by contemporary British standards, but how far this was directly related to the city's employment pattern is unclear.[23]

The DSU had its heyday before the First World War, partly because of that war's impetus to the expansion of the state's role in welfare provision (especially at the local level), which tended, albeit gradually, to displace the contribution of philanthropic bodies.[24] The 1920s saw more divided political attitudes on welfare provision, especially with the drive for economies at both local and national level. The DSU seemingly did not fit very well into these arguments. On the one hand in 1923 the (conservative) *Dundee Advertiser* was praising the Union for 'doing good cheaply'; on the other, in 1925 the Women's Section of the local Labour Party donated £158 raised from a flag day.[25]

DUNDEE WOMEN CITIZENS' ASSOCIATION

The biggest women's organisation in inter-war Dundee was the Women Citizens' Association, an organisation whose nationwide importance is now coming to be recognised.[26] This was founded in anticipation of the extension of the franchise in 1918:

> To bring together on non-party, non sectarian, and democratic lines all women's Societies and individual women in order to: a) foster a sense of citizenship in women; b) encourage the study of political, social and economic questions; c) secure the adequate representation of the interests and experience of women in the affairs of the community.[27]

The DWCA had a membership of 800 in 1918, growing to a peak of 1,235 in 1931, then falling inexorably to 172 in 1966.[28] The first meeting of the Association appropriately focused attention on the Representation of the People Act, and was accompanied by a local press notice urging women to register for the vote. Both the second and third meetings addressed the issue of housing, for the first of which 20,000 handbills were printed and distributed to organisations such as the Mill and Factory Co-operative Union and the Women's Labour League. In discussing this issue three categories of concern were identified: the single woman earning 23–25 shillings per week, a family of parents and four children earning 35 shillings, and the same family earning 45 shillings. In this categorisation we may see a combination of the continuation of the pre-war extremely pressing concern with the 'social problem' of housing, and a more specifically women's concern with the plight of the wage-earning single woman.

In the run up to the December 1918 general election (the first one in which women would be able to vote) the DWCA proposed to organise a mass meeting of women to press the issues deemed crucial; these were six-fold:

1. Housing reform
2. Rescindment of section 40 of the Defence of the Realm Act (concerning the treatment of prostitutes)
3. Recognition of the dual parenthood of every child
4. Temperance
5. Equality of pay for equal work
6. 'Further legislation with regard to education'.[29]

This list indicates the breadth and diversity of the WCA's interests in Dundee at this time. In order to pursue these issues, the Association pressed for women to play a larger role in public bodies. It rejected the idea of putting up a woman candidate for Parliament in 1918 as 'not advisable at the present time' but focused attention on local elected bodies, including the School Board, which until 1930 was separate from the town council.[30] This was to be a persistent feature of the Association's activities, including canvassing its membership for women candidates for all local elected bodies, and for selection as Justices of the Peace, encouraging women to pay the subscription necessary to be eligible for election as a governor of the Dundee Royal Infirmary, and setting up a local government sub-committee.[31]

Temperance was of course a major issue in Dundee in the 1920s, marked in 1922 by the election of Edwin Scrymgeour as Britain's only Prohibitionist MP.[32] The DWCA was an enthusiastic supporter of the temperance movement, and there seems little doubt that in this they were articulating the views of a significant proportion of Dundee's women, who seem to have been vital in securing Scrymgeour's election.[33] In June 1920 the Association passed a resolution deeply regretting that 'a representative of the liquor trade in Dundee should have been singled out for the honour of a baronetcy, and this, at the moment, when the 1920 Temperance Scotland Act has just come into force . . .'.[34] This Act allowed for local ballots on licensing, and the DWCA supported the 'no licence' position in the three ballots held in 1920, 1923 and 1926, each of which saw the defeat of the temperance position, though with a margin of only around 3 to 2 on 60–70 per cent turnouts.[35]

Allied to the temperance campaign, in what may be called a continuing concern with 'rational recreation', were worries about the social consequences of the cinema, which led to a survey by Association members to assess the moral tone of the films shown in the city.[36] Perhaps more surprising was a concern with late-opening ice cream shops, because of the 'undesirable influence which it is felt such places exercise upon the habits of children and young people'.[37] Concern with moral matters was also expressed by support for raising the age of consent for sex from sixteen to eighteen.[38] As the post-war boom evaporated after 1920, the rise in local unemployment led to a concern with the welfare of the unemployed which was to persist through the inter-war years.[39]

There is not much evidence in the DWCA minutes on attitudes to married women's employment, a controversial issue among women before 1914. In 1922 the Association was reported to be divided on whether it should support a protest against Glasgow Corporation dismissing married women employees.[40] On the other hand, support for access for women in general to employment opportunities, and concern at women's low wages, were persistent.[41] An important issue for the DWCA was the employment of women police, but this seems to have been motivated more by a concern that such women would deal better with young miscreants, than any notion of employment rights.[42] Accommodation for single women was also a concern, though the focus of the early years on housing in general later faded.[43]

To very briefly summarise Dundee women's inter-war concerns from the DWCA perspective, we may say that there is no evidence of a simple focus on issues relating to wives and mothers at the expense of other matters. Certainly domestic skills were seen as important, and the welfare of children a perennial focus.[44] But alongside these the Association was continuously active in pressing for women to receive equal access to public bodies, and was very much concerned to express views on the great national crises of these years – in the 1930s, for example, voicing strong responses to the financial crisis of 1931, the Peace Ballot in 1935, and the Munich Agreement of 1938.[45]

As membership fell away in the 1930s there is an impression of slackening activity in the Association, but the coming of the Second World War seems to have provided a renewed impetus, with new issues coming to the fore. Unemployment among women in 1941 was especially high as jute was compulsorily contracted, and as yet few new munitions jobs were established, and in September of that year the Association was writing to the Minister of Labour 'expressing dissatisfaction with the conditions obtaining among the working women of in Dundee, and pointing out that there are in Dundee over 4,000 unemployed women, all skilled operatives, and all drawing unemployment benefit and begging him to use his good offices to remedy this state of affairs'.[46] Thereafter an influx of munitions jobs tightened the labour market for women, and this may have been one impetus for the focus on nursery school provision in the city, though this was a complex issue because it could derive both from a desire to facilitate women's employment or from concern with child welfare. In Dundee as elsewhere in Britain, such provision grew during the war, and neither before 1945 nor in the immediate post-war period is there any evidence of local voicing of the view that such provision should be discouraged because of alleged detrimental effects on the children concerned.[47]

Better wartime prospects for their employment may have encouraged women to participate more actively in public affairs; certainly the DWCA was very much involved in both the war effort and the great debates on social reconstruction after the war. On the former, activity ranged from supporting the conscription of women through to weekly 'work parties' to knit hospital comforts for the Red Cross, money-raising for a 'City of Dundee' ward in a Stalingrad hospital, plus reasserting support for temperance as a way of increasing wartime productive efficiency.[48] On social reform, the Association held discussions on the Beveridge Report, and participated in drawing up a report on *Social Conditions in Dundee*.[49] This latter was drawn up as part of the activity of a newly formed 'Standing Conference of Dundee Women's Associations', which held its first meeting in June 1944. The other participants in this body included the Business and Commercial Women's Club, and possibly the Soroptimists, but the others are unknown.[50] However, its foundation seems to reflect a new-found confidence in women in their public role.

This Standing Conference survived until at least 1955, but for the Association the post-war years were ones of uninterrupted decline in membership and activity.[51] Women's protests against rationing in the late 1940s were heard in Dundee as elsewhere in Britain.[52] The DWCA visited the new NCR factory in 1949, but seven years later were impressed by the new machinery seen on a visit to a jute factory, and were able to admire 'the accommodation provided for the children of the women who were at work, secure in the knowledge that their children were well looked after'.[53] In such ways perhaps the Association sought to reflect the sentiments of the speaker at the 1944 AGM, who stressed that women's future was as both workers and mothers, but it is evident that whatever its efforts the post-war Association was never able to return to its inter-war role as the pre-eminent public body for women.[54]

THE SOROPTIMISTS

Another organisation emerging as women achieved voting equality with men was the Soroptimist International. Derived from the Latin *soror*, sister, with 'optimist', roughly meaning 'best for women', this group had its beginnings in the United States, and in 1927 branches were established in Edinburgh and Glasgow.[55] Five years later a branch of the Soroptimist

International was formed in Dundee. Unlike other women's organisations of the time, the Soroptimist movement did not have an open membership; instead, the 'Rotarian' method was preferred, in which only one person from a particular occupation could join any one branch. This, it was argued, would fairly represent the local business community.[56] Indeed, the membership within the Dundee group was extremely varied, with early members including Miss Carlton, a local chemist, Edith Luke, the Superintendent of the nursery school, and Dr E. Philip Smith, a lecturer at Queen's College, Dundee. Their work was guided by the motto 'Looking further', and in many ways they looked beyond not only the boundaries of Dundee but also to issues that were not yet on the policy agenda of government.[57]

One of the first actions they undertook was to honour recently elected Florence Horsbrugh MP, commenting that she was a 'visible symbol of something . . . which had always stood as a shining example, the work of women, for women and, through women, for humanity'.[58] This emphasis on working for women became an important strand to their campaigning work in Dundee. This included, as early as 1933, discussing the topic of nursery schools and how best Soroptimists could support their work. It was decided that representatives should visit local nursery schools in order to see the work being done.[59] They also held fund-raising events in order to provide new toys and equipment.[60] However, the reasons why Soroptimists in Dundee supported nursery schools is unclear and caution has to be exercised over claiming too much. Unlike discussions of the late 1960s, many women's groups in the inter-war period supported nursery schools as a strategy to overcome neglect in the home, rather than a desire to assist in the employment of women.

Nevertheless, the Soroptimists did consider the role of women beyond matters to do with the home and children, and this is perhaps because their membership was drawn from the business and professional classes. This sentiment is made clear during meetings: for example, in 1934 the minutes recorded a discussion in which it was observed that 'the more individual women join together to be of service to their fellows, the more they realise how many are their opportunities'.[61] Furthermore, the Soroptimists prided themselves in being part of a 'women's town'. Speakers to the group frequently emphasised this point, with the Rev. D. Duncan in 1948 stating that 'Dundee was one of the first cities in the emancipation of women', citing evidence, such as Dundee having the first woman town clerk and professor in Scotland.[62] Again, there are limits to how much can be claimed. Although references are made to the burgeoning role of women in society, it is evident that they failed to support important equality campaigns of the inter-war period, including protests against attempts to limit the working hours of women and young people. As one member, Miss Johnson, argued, 'However desirable it might be to be associated with movements pressing for equal opportunities for women . . . the time was not opportune.'[63]

As the twentieth century progressed, however, the agenda of women's issues expanded. The economic situation and the need for more workers heavily influenced discussions on the widening role of women in society during the 1950s.[64] Important publications, such as Myrdal and Klein's *Women's Two Roles*, argued that it was now economically expedient for women to re-enter the labour market once they had raised a family.[65] It now became culturally acceptable for women to have children and a career and the Soroptimists in Dundee reflected these developing discussions, considering topics such as equal pay and fairer income tax.[66]

Rather than equality for women being the guiding principle of Soroptimist work, it was actually service to the community. For Dundee Soroptimists this service was epitomised by a campaign in the 1950s and beyond to establish a Soroptimist House for elderly, single women. This campaign was similar to that of the British Business and Professional Women's Federation, who had argued there was a need for accommodation for single women who had little chance of securing housing by any other means.[67] Over the next two decades the Soroptimists fund-raised to buy a house and they were also assisted by local charitable organisations. By 1962 they had raised £1,900 and held a special business meeting to discuss with their membership what kind of house they wished to establish. In 1969 a Soroptimist Housing (Dundee) Ltd was formed and a house at Magdalen Yard Road purchased and officially opened on 26 September 1971.[68] This was a long-running campaign for the Soroptimists in Dundee and one they were extremely passionate about, taking almost two decades to come to fruition.

It is clear, however, that although the Soroptimists were civic-minded they also at all times, and especially from the 1950s onwards, considered the myriad of roles women held in society. They did not limit discussions to women who were wives and mothers but also supported campaigns for fairer pay and tax practices. Their campaigning culminated in the establishment of a house for elderly women, leaving a legacy to the city that elderly single women should not be overlooked in the allocation of housing. This idea of serving your community continues to be popular, as out of those women's organisations that emerged during the 1920s and 1930s in Dundee the Soroptimists are the last surviving group.

A WIDENING AGENDA

The Soroptimists were not the only group to represent the interests of the female business community, as there was also an active branch of the Business and Professional Women's Federation (BPW) in Dundee. Like the Soroptimists, the BPW had been founded in the United States during the 1920s, eventually emerging in Britain during the late 1930s. Where the BPW and Soroptimists differed was in membership procedures. The BPW was open to any woman from any occupation, abandoning the Soroptimists' favoured 'Rotarian' method. The BPW aimed to 'awaken and encourage in business and professional women a realisation of their responsibilities in their own country', echoing the idea of 'service' so central to Soroptimism.[69] This message proved popular, as during 1947 a separate Scottish federation was established with eighteen branches, and by 1962 this had increased to forty-four.[70]

The group in Dundee was formed in 1940 but unfortunately records only exist for the period from 1965 onwards. Indeed, little has been recorded of the work of the BPW across Britain, and this is surprising given the progressive nature of their agenda in terms of being openly supportive of equality for women in many areas of society.[71] At a British level, for example, the BPW supported the equal pay campaign that gathered momentum during the 1950s. They argued at all times that 'one of the future tasks of the Federation was to lead its members into the full freedom of economic and social equality with men', yet due to a lack of records it remains unclear where the Dundee branch stood on this issue.[72]

From the mid-1960s onwards Dundee BPW considered a whole gamut of issues related to the status of women. It has now been recognised by a number of historians that even before the arrival of the Women's Liberation Movement (WLM) in the late 1960s, the women's movement was experiencing something of a revival, widening its agenda to consider issues which were deemed more personal and private. Issues such as sexual health and family planning began to emerge in the discussions of various women's groups.[73] Locally, Dundee BPW was important in this regard, openly supporting the cervical cancer campaign. Medical research in the 1960s revealed alarming statistics that during 1963 alone there had been a British total of 2,511 deaths from the disease. Researchers recommended that women over thirty should be screened at five-yearly intervals and many women's groups, from various political traditions, took up the issue and began fund-raising for mobile cervical cytology units. Groups like the Co-operative Women's Guild and women's sections of the Communist Party, Labour Party and TUC publicised this campaign, with N. Rafeek arguing that the campaign's broad-based nature led to its ultimate effectiveness.[74] The BPW in Dundee also took an active interest in the issue, raising money and taking a delegation to visit the new cervical cytology clinic in order to educate their membership about the disease and its effects.[75] This was a pioneering move and indicated an interest in an issue long before women's health became a major priority for government.

This did not mean that the BPW abandoned the old stalwart issues like equal pay. During 1966 they wrote to both MPs for Dundee, George Thomson and Peter Doig, hoping to secure their support on the matter of equal pay.[76] This was a full four years before the passing of the Equal Pay Act in 1970 and clearly indicates how Dundee BPW were able to anticipate issues which would remain important concerns for women during the 1970s and beyond. Indeed, this recognition of women's role outside the home was happening in wider society. By the mid-1960s the idea of women taking an active part in the labour market had largely been accepted.[77]

The expansion of the agenda of women's issues gathered apace in the 1970s, ushering in an era where women's issues featured more prominently in the discussions of both the media and government. The Women's Liberation Movement became the focus of this renewed vigour around women's issues, campaigning on a variety of topics, including equal pay, sex discrimination, equal education and twenty-four-hour childcare.[78] These topics were similar to many of those that had been quietly campaigned on by other groups before the 1960s and 1970s, but where the WLM was radically different was in their campaigning techniques. Based on the popular WLM slogan 'The personal is political', the movement in Scotland attempted to reinvigorate politics by placing women's personal experiences centre stage. Instead of letter-writing and lobbying, the WLM, more reminiscent of the New Left and campaigns of the Labour and student movements, took to the streets favouring marches and direct protests, proving to be more provocative in their political message and subsequently gaining wider media coverage than the women's movement had received since the days of the Suffragettes.[79] While the women's groups of the inter-war period prided themselves on organisational procedures, the WLM abandoned minute-taking in favour of a non-hierarchical movement, which attempted to be as structure-less as possible.

Women's liberation groups were formed in Scotland during the 1970s in Edinburgh, Glasgow, St Andrews, Dundee, Aberdeen and the Shetland Islands. The women's liberation group in Dundee was formed in 1972 and drew a mix of members, including single and married women, but like other women's liberation groups with a propensity for young, middle-class students to dominate.[80] The *Courier* reported on their first open meeting in 6 Allan Street on 17 April 1973, where twenty-one women had attended.[81] The premises at Allan Street were an early base for the women's liberation group with later meetings held at Beano's Health Food Store on the Perth Road and the Trade Union Council Hall.

There appeared to be a sense of flux in the Dundee group, with frequent rumours that they had disbanded.[82] This was probably due to the short-term nature of the student population. But it is also clear that the group experienced a lull during the mid-1970s, only to reinvent itself as a Women's Action Group in the later half of the period, but still holding true to the first principles of women's liberation.[83] Despite this, the Dundee group campaigned on a variety of issues including an early focus on the topic of pornography. This included protesting outside a sex shop in the Hilltown, and threatening to photograph their customers and have it published in the evening newspaper, the *Evening Telegraph*.[84] In direct contrast to the campaigning tactics of the previous generation of women's groups, the WLM in Dundee would also resort to defacing billboards. Margaret Adams recalled one such instance:

At that time it was quite acceptable to have billboards up with – half naked women . . . reclining on the bonnets of cars, and stuff like that . . . one incident was quite funny, one of the women was quite small, quite dumpy and she was quite sort of butch looking and she put on painter's overalls and she got a ladder and a tin of white paint and she went to cover over this offensive billboard and somebody stopped her and said what – are you doing? And she said well I'm a council – worker and I'm putting this stuff on over this billboard and when it dries, it dries clear, you know. Which it wasn't at all it was white paint, you know. Because she looked like she knew what she was doing – nobody sort of challenged it.[85]

This theme of the use of women in advertisements was also raised at the University of Dundee's Students' Union (DUSA) in 1978. At their dance event, 'Rave up Against Racialism' the DUSA executive had booked a male and a female stripper. The women's liberation group picketed the event with about twenty people turning up to protest. As Nina Woodcock, member of Dundee women's liberation group, noted, the only protest occurring inside was when the male stripper appeared, with no one objecting to the female act.[86] While the women's groups of the inter-war period would have objected to this act with moralising tones, the WLM rather argued that to be objectified by men was an infringement of women's rights.

The WLM was most effective in gaining momentum for issues that had been quietly campaigned on for many years, including most notably domestic violence. One part of the wide coalition on this issue was the DWCA, which helped to introduce a resolution at the Scottish Council of WCAs, urging the Lord Advocate to amend the law of evidence in cases of domestic violence so that corroborative evidence was no longer needed.[87] This would be an important development if more cases of domestic violence were to be proved in court, since in many instances a woman was unable to provide witnesses or evidence of injuries to support her case.

The WLM gave this topic fresh impetus, arguing that the problem of domestic violence had now reached epidemic proportions, creeping into many women's lives no matter what class or background. The WLM was important in conceptualising the issue, making clear that every woman had the potential to experience domestic violence and that they had more to fear from the man they lived with than the stranger on the street. They argued that for all women to be liberated no woman could live in fear in her own home.[88] Women's Aid (WA), a direct offshoot of the WLM, therefore, sought to break this cycle of violence by providing refuges and also by educating the wider public on the issue.[89] Women's Aid established its first refuges in Scotland in Edinburgh and Glasgow during 1972.[90]

Inspired by these examples, the Dundee women's liberation group formed a WA branch in 1974.[91] With an extremely limited budget, the first refuge in the city was set up using donations from local people. The volunteers of the WA branch then painted and decorated the refuge.[92] Volunteering for WA was a large commitment, with weekly house meetings, administration to complete and answering the phone. In addition to providing a refuge, the local branch attempted to educate the public on their work. On many occasions they opened up the refuge for journalists, only to be left disappointed by the coverage they received, as one volunteer at Dundee WA discovered:

> We had a whole spate of press reports . . . culminated in the autumn with a *News of the World* reporter coming round to the refuge. Our first instinct was to send the guy away but we thought if we did that he'll just speak to the neighbours and . . . so we spoke to him . . . [T]hat Sunday what should appear in the *News of the World* but a photograph of me that I didn't know they had taken under the banner headline which read – 'Saucy frolics rumpus at battered wives hostel!'[93]

They also raised awareness about the issue of violence against women through participation in Reclaim the Night marches. These were held in many cities throughout the UK during the 1970s, as women followed a route, normally one renowned for high incidences of sexual assault, to highlight how unsafe the streets were. They argued against the containment of women, believing that they should be free to walk the streets without fear of sexual assault.[94] During 1979 a Reclaim the Night march was held in the centre of Dundee, with one hundred women gathering.[95] By holding events like these to publicise the issue and by providing practical solutions like refuges, the WLM and WA began to generate discussion on a topic which many women had tirelessly worked hard on for many years but on which they had failed to engage the wider public.

The major issue to unite all women's groups in Dundee was childcare, from the DSU's concern for children of working mothers right through to the WLM's argument that women had the right both to work and to have access to childcare during working hours. The WLM in Dundee adopted this issue and campaigned on it particularly strongly, perhaps due to the presence of mothers in their membership. During 1973 they distributed 3,000 leaflets on the 'Hands off our Family Allowance' issue and collected signatures for a petition.[96]

With more women working nationally during the 1970s than ever before, the provision of adequate childcare became a pressing matter for all local authorities.[97] Indeed, the provision of childcare in Dundee looked very different from that of local neighbours Perth and Angus. Although all three areas had more pre-school playgroup places than other types of childcare, Dundee combined this with a heavy reliance on day nursery and nursery school places, as Table 5.2 makes clear.

The ethos of nurseries and playgroups differed quite significantly; for example, day nurseries opened during working hours, concentrated on the physical care of children, and were run by specialists with nursery nurse training. In contrast, playgroups were only open part-time, recognised play as a major part of a child's learning, focused on the role and development of the mother, and were run by committees of parents.[98] Much like the women's groups of the inter-war period, playgroups provided an important space for women to meet, socialise and grow in confidence.[99] Playgroups had first been formed in Scotland in Milngavie

TABLE 5.2
Provision of childcare in 1977 for the under-fives in Tayside by region

Area	Day nursery places	Nursery school/class places	Pre-school playgroup places	Childminding places	Total pre-school
Angus	–	144	981	2	1,127
Dundee	713	1,347	1,178	32	3,270
Perth & Kinross	76	128	1152	44	1,400
Tayside Region	789	1,619	3,311	78	5,797

Source: Tayside Regional Council, Joint Report by the Directors of Social Work and Education, no. 293/77 (1977), p. 9.

during 1960 and proved so popular that by 1967 there was an identifiable pre-school playgroup movement in Scotland with thousands of playgroups set up.[100] Originating in London during the early 1960s, playgroups had been the idea of a mother, Belle Tutaev, who had been unable to find a nursery place for her daughter and began her own playgroup.[101] Women in Dundee began to form playgroups from the late 1960s, with the first being established in Camperdown and Menzieshill in 1967. A Dundee District branch brought together all playgroups into one forum during the late 1960s.[102] Providing training in childcare and giving women the responsibility of running playgroups, they were important in increasing the confidence of women and in many cases breaking the isolation of being at home all day. In this regard they differed quite significantly from nurseries, in that they supported the growth not only of the child but also of the parents.

Playgroups in Dundee during the early 1970s gained widespread support from prominent members of the local community, including George Thomson, MP, who was so impressed by their work that he became an associated member of the Dundee and District branch during 1971.[103] By the mid to late 1970s, however, playgroups in Dundee had fallen out of favour, with greater emphasis placed on nursery education. Women's groups, such as the Dundee BPW, also refused to support playgroups in the area, arguing that there were already too many.[104] The WLM seemed more supportive. They held an open meeting on the topic with Dr T.E. Faulkner, Convener of Dundee Corporation Education Committee, in attendance. He made clear, much to the opposition of the audience, that from the mid-1970s onwards nurseries would be expanded into areas where playgroups were already established.[105] The opposition of the Dundee women's liberation group to the growth of nurseries in Dundee is surprising, given that many in the wider WLM in Scotland held a deep disquiet about the role of playgroups and the issue of childcare more generally. Believing they placed too much emphasis on the mother, the women of the WLM often found childcare a problematic issue.[106]

By 1977 Tayside Regional Council, in a desire to clarify the state of childcare in the region, commissioned a joint report of the Directors of Social Work and Education to look into the issue. The report's recommendation was that, in the short term, they wished to sustain nursery schools and day nurseries to at least their current level but significantly made no mention of the role of playgroups.[107] Over the next twenty years, the number of playgroups dwindled as the emphasis on nursery education increased.[108]

The issue of childcare did not prove problematic just for Tayside Regional Council but also for the women's movement in Dundee throughout the twentieth century. Due to the peculiar nature of the workforce in Dundee, this became a campaigning issue that was an important strand of the work of the DSU right through to the WLM, with no clear strategy on how to reconcile what were viewed as women's competing roles of mothering and work. The arguments made by women's groups in Dundee as to why childcare needed to be provided changed during the twentieth century; from the DSU's belief in it being an essential part of social care to the WLM's desire to give all women the right to work. Irrespective of the shifting discourse surrounding the issue, however, it is clear that the importance of childcare to the women's movement in Dundee remained a constant theme in campaigns and discussions throughout the twentieth century.

Around the end of the twentieth century women began to play a larger role in the formal, electoral politics of the city, where previously men's numerical predominance was striking. Shona Robison (SNP) became an MSP for Dundee East in 2003, having previously been a member for North East Scotland; Marlyn Glen (Labour) became an MSP for North East Scotland in the same election. The success of these women is significant, but, as this chapter has argued, throughout the whole century, Dundee women have persistently organised themselves to pursue their own agendas, and in doing so have had a major impact on what has counted as a 'public' issue. Allied to largely 'backroom' work in political parties and trade unions, these women's organisations may not have made Dundee a 'women's town', in the sense of a town where women's interests have been predominant over those of men. But they have made it a town where women's concerns, diverse and sometimes even contradictory, have found powerful and effective expression.

NOTES

1. Cited in Norman Watson, 'Daughters of Dundee. Gender and Politics in Dundee:
    The Representation of Women 1870–1997' (unpublished PhD thesis, Open University,
    2000), p. 1. See also K.J.W. Baxter, '"Estimable and Gifted"? Women in Party Politics
    in Scotland c.1918–1955' (unpublished PhD thesis, University of Dundee, 2008); E.
    Wainwright, 'Gender, Space and Power: Discourses on Working Women in Dundee's
    Jute Industry, c.1870–1930' (unpublished PhD thesis, University of St Andrews, 2002);
    E.M. Wainwright, 'Constructing gendered workplace "types": the weaver-millworker
    distinction in Dundee's jute industry, c. 1880–1910', *Gender, Place and Culture* 14
    (2007), pp. 467–82.
2. M. Walker, 'Work among women' in A. Paton and A. Millar (eds), *Handbook and
    Guide to Dundee and District* (Dundee, 1912), p. 69.
3. General Register Office, Scotland , *Census of Population*, vol. 3: *Occupations of the
    People of Scotland in 1901* (1901).
4. Ibid., pp. 680–1. There were 46,504 occupied males and 37,567 occupied females.
5. ' Female labour is the best recruiting sergeant in Dundee. It prevents the employment
    of men in civil life. In fact half of the men who join the army are forced to enlist by
    the successful competition of their mothers and sisters', DUA, MS 134: D. Lennox,
    'Working Class Life in Dundee for 25 Years: 1878 to 1903' (unpublished manuscript,
    1928), p. 71.
6. Emigration of single men from Dundee was estimated at 7,000 for the five years to
    1912: H. Templeton, 'What Dundee contributes to the Empire' in Paton and Millar
    (eds), *Handbook*, p. 120.
7. The notion, however, that there were large numbers of households where men
    normally took childcare and household responsibilities, so-called 'kettle boilers', is
    surely a myth, though it may have occurred periodically is some households where
    men's work was particularly subject to periodic unemployment, such as shipbuilding:
    H. Morton, *In Search of Scotland* (6th edn, Edinburgh, 1929), p. 327; E. Gordon,
    Women and the Labour Movement in Scotland 1850–1914 (Oxford, 1991), pp. 164–5.
8. D. Riddell, 'Social structure and relations' in J.M. Jackson (ed.), *The Third Statistical
    Account of Scotland*, vol. 25: *The City of Dundee* (Arbroath, 1979), p. 474; *Scotland
    Census Results On Line* (SCROL): www.scrol.gov.uk.
9. C. Morelli and J. Tomlinson, 'Women and work after the Second World War: a case
    study of the jute industry, circa 1945–1954', *Twentieth Century British History* 19
    (2008), pp. 61–82.
10. S. Szreter, *Health and Wealth: Studies in History and Policy* (Rochester, NY, 2005), ch. 9.
11. Baxter, '"Estimable and Gifted"?'; compare Watson, 'Daughters of Dundee', chs 2 and
    3. The first parish councillors were Agnes Husband and Mary Walker: see E. Ewan, S.
    Innes and S. Reynolds (eds), *Biographical Dictionary of Scottish Women* (Edinburgh,
    2006).
12. Baxter, '"Estimable and Gifted"?', ch. 1.
13. Gordon, *Women and the Labour Movement*, though note in particular the leading role
    played by Mary MacArthur; in the battles at Timex, while women were numerically
    predominant, men seem to have dominated in the decision making: N. Watson,
    'Emerging from obscurity: how Dundee women made their mark' in G. Ogilvy (ed.),
    Dundee: A Voyage of Discovery (Edinburgh, 1999), p. 212. Some idea of women's role in
    the unions in the intervening years is given in the Scottish Trades Union Congress

archives, where the 'Organisation of Women Committee' reported persistent if small-scale activity in Dundee, and the formation of a Women's Group in 1929, with, however, limited success: Minutes of 13 January 1930, 21 November 1932.

14. Graham Smith, 'Protest is better for infants: motherhood, health and welfare in a women's town, c. 1911–1931', *Oral History* 23 (1995), pp. 63–70.

15. L. Leneman, *A Guid Cause: The Women's Suffrage Movement in Scotland* (2nd edn, Edinburgh, 1995); Gordon, *Women and the Labour Movement.* Watson, 'Daughters of Dundee', pp. 62–9, 90–1 argues that while there were very active middle-class activists in the city, the suffrage movement in Dundee found little significant support among working-class women.

16. S. Pedersen, *Family, Dependence, and the Origins of the Welfare State: Britain and France, 1914–1945* (Cambridge, 1993); A. Hughes, 'Fragmented feminists? The influence of class and identity in relations between the Glasgow and West of Scotland Suffrage Society and the Independent Labour Party in the West of Scotland, c.1919–1932', *Women's History Review* 14 (2005), pp. 7–32; S. Innes, 'Constructing women's citizenship in the interwar period: the Edinburgh Women Citizens' Association', *Women's History Review* 13 (2004), pp. 621–47.

17. For example, Olive Banks, *The Politics of British Feminism, 1918–1970* (Aldershot, 1993).

18. Miss M.O. Valentine, *Dundee Social Union and Grey Lodge Settlement* (Dundee, 1920), p. 1; M. Baillie, 'The Grey Lady: Mary Lily Walker of Dundee' in L. Miskell, C.A. Whatley and B. Harris (eds), *Victorian Dundee: Image and Realities* (East Linton, 2000), pp. 122–34; Watson, 'Daughters of Dundee', pp. 180–91.

19. DCA, DSU Minute Books, vol. 1: 1906–1920; vol. 2: 1920–1936. For a Foucauldian account of the DSU see Wainwright, 'Gender, Space and Power', ch. 6.

20. DSU, *Report on Housing and Industrial Conditions and Medical Inspection of School Children* (Dundee, 1905).

21. Ibid.

22. Lennox, 'Working Class Life', ch. 6.

23. Gordon, *Women and the Labour Movement,* pp. 165–6; on the general problems of this link, E. Garrett, A. Reid, K. Schire and S. Szreter, *Changing Family Size in England and Wales: Place, Class and Demography, 1891–1911* (Cambridge, 2001), pp. 128–33, 299–315.

24. The DSU merged with the Grey Lodge Settlement in 1936 to become the Grey Lodge Settlement Association: D'Arcy Wentworth Thompson, *Fifty Years Ago and Now* (Dundee, Grey Lodge, 1938).

25. *Advertiser,* 3 May 1923; DSU Minutes, vol. 2, 3 July 1925.

26. Innes, 'Constructing women's citizenship'; V. Wright, 'Women's Organisations and Feminism in Interwar Scotland' (unpublished PhD thesis, University of Glasgow, 2008). There was no separate branch of the National Union of Societies for Equal Citizenship in Dundee (the successor body to the pre-war suffrage societies): DCA, DWCA Minutes, vol. 2, 5 December 1921. Watson, 'Daughters of Dundee', pp. 197–222 discusses the DWCA, largely drawing on the Executive Minutes for the inter-war period.

27. DCA, DWCA Minutes, vol. 1, 6 May 1918. Lady Baxter, wife of a prominent jute baron, was elected the first President.

28. DCA, DWCA Minutes, vol. 6, 45th anniversary meeting 2 October 1963, AGM 28 March 1966. (The Minute Books end with the 1966 AGM.)

29. DCA, DWCA Minutes, vol. 1, 4 November 1918. In the event, the meeting did not happen, but election candidates were sent this list of issues: ibid., 2 December 1918.

30. Ibid., 18 November 1918; 16 December 1918; 3 February 1919.

31. Ibid., 15 September 1919; 2 February 1920; 29 March 1920; 6 October 1919.

32. Watson, 'Daughters of Dundee', pp. 92–102.

33. The DWCA ruled out party political activity, but temperance was deemed a non-party issue: Minutes, vol. 2, 5 February 1923.

34. Ibid., 7 June 1920.

35. People's Journal, 27 November 1926, cited in K. McGregor, 'A Question of Choice: The Leisure Activities of Dundee Women in the 1920s' (unpublished MA Honours dissertation, University of Dundee, Department of History, 2003), p. 52.

36. DCA, DWCA Minutes, vol. 2, 20 June and 19 December 1921.

37. DCA, DWCA Minutes, vol. 3, 23 June 1924.

38. Ibid., 2 December 1929.

39. e.g. DCA, DWCA Minutes, vol. 2, 7 March 1921, 6 February 1922; vol. 4, 20 January 1936 and 16 May 1938.

40. DCA, DWCA Minutes, vol. 2, 6 March 1922.

41. e.g. ibid., 2 July 1927, 4 February 1929.

42. DCA, DWCA Minutes, vol. 2, 22 May 1922; vol. 4, 14 May 1934; also vol. 5, 1 December 1941.

43. DCA, DWCA Minutes, vol. 3, 3 November 1930; vol. 2, 5 February 1923; vol. 4, 16 May 1938.

44. On the former, support for the teaching of domestic science at the new Dundee Institute: DCA, DWCA Minutes, vol. 4, 10 September 1934, 14 January 1935; on children there were, for example, protests about child labour in potato picking, and about proposed increases in the hours of under-16s working in jute: Minutes, vol. 2, 21 February 1927; vol. 4, 19 May 1939.

45. DCA, DWCA Minutes, vol. 3, 21 September 1931; vol. 4, 14 January 1935, 4 October 1938.

46. DCA, DWCA Minutes, vol. 5, 15 September 1941.

47. The DWCA Minutes show only support for such provision, and this seems to be in line with local attitudes: see Morelli and Tomlinson, 'Women and work after the Second World War', pp. 69–70.

48. DCA, DWCA Minutes, vol. 5, 1 December 1941, 18 September 1939, 6 December 1943, 11 September 1944.

49. Ibid., 30 August 1943, 5 March 1945.

50. Ibid., 4 June 1944, 6 November 1944.

51. DCA, DWCA Minutes, vol. 6, 10 October 1955; membership decline is a perennial issue at Association AGMs from the early 1950s.

52. DCA, DWCA Minutes, vol. 5, 3 February 1947; I. Zweiniger-Bargielowska, Austerity in Britain: Rationing, Controls and Consumption 1939–1955 (Oxford, 2000), ch. 3.

53. DCA, DWCA Minutes, vol. 5, 10 January 1949, 28 May 1956.

54. Ibid., 24 April 1944.

55. Soroptimist International, Soroptimist International of Dundee: The First Sixty Years 1932–1992, p. 6.

56. Watson, 'Daughters of Dundee', p. 224.

57. DCA, GD/S1/1/1: Soroptimist Club of Dundee, Minute Book, 26 May 1932.

58. Ibid., 2 February 1933.

59. Ibid., 20 September 1933.

60. See, for example, ibid., 1 May 1934.

61. Ibid., 31 January 1934.

62. DCA, GD/S1/1/2: Soroptimist Club of Dundee, Minute Book, Report of dinner held on 18 February 1948.

63. DCA, GD/S1/1/1: Soroptimist Club of Dundee, Minute Book, 23 November 1937.

64. For example, M. Pugh, *Women and the Women's Movement 1914–1990* (London, 2000), pp. 286–7; J. Lewis, 'From equality to liberation: contextualizing the emergence of the women's liberation movement' in B. Moore-Gilbert and J. Seed (eds), *Cultural Revolution? The Challenge of the Arts in the 1960s* (London, 1992), p. 98.

65. Many historians attribute importance to the publication of Myrdal and Klein's book, with Lewis indicating that by the 1970s it was still selling 1,500 copies a year. Ibid., p. 99.

66. See, for example, GD/S1, 1/2: Soroptimist Club of Dundee, Minute Book, 10 October 1951.

67. D.V. Hall, *Making Things Happen: History of the National Federation of Business and Professional Women's Clubs of Great Britain and Northern Ireland* (London, 1963), p. 182.

68. DCA, GD/S1/1/4: Soroptimist Club of Dundee, Minute Book, 12 March 1963; Soroptimist International, *Dundee: The First Sixty Years*, pp. 10, 29.

69. Hall, *Making Things Happen*, p. 82.

70. Ibid., p. 129.

71. The only publications are D.V. Hall's account charting the first twenty-five years of the Federation and more recently, L. Perriton, 'Forgotten feminists: the Federation of British Professional and Business Women, 1933–1969', *Women's History Review* 16 (2007).

72. Hall, *Making Things Happen*, p. 170.

73. This has been argued by H.L. Smith, 'The women's movement, politics and citizenship, 1960s–2000' in I. Zweiniger-Bargielowska (ed.), *Women in Twentieth-Century Britain* (Harlow, 2001), who said that any revival was 'already underway when the first WLM groups were formed in 1968' (p. 278). Furthermore, Caine has identified that a key question still to be answered is what the relationship was between feminist discussions of the 1960s and those of the WLM in the 1970s: B. Caine, *English Feminism 1780–1980* (Oxford, 1997), p. 224. Some work has been completed in this area including Lewis, 'From equality to liberation' and S.F. Browne, '"Dreary Committee Work"? The Work of Established Women's Groups in the North East of Scotland during the 1960s and 1970s' (unpublished M.Litt. dissertation, University of Dundee, 2006).

74. N. Rafeek, 'Women in the Communist Party in Scotland: An Oral History' (unpublished PhD thesis, University of Strathclyde, 1996), pp. 169–72. See also N.C. Rafeek, *Communist Women in Scotland: Red Clydeside from the Russian Revolution to the £end of the Soviet Union* (London, 2008).

75. DCA, GD X210 DBPWC: Dundee Business and Professional Women's Club Committee Minutes, 1 February 1966; 17 May 1966.

76. Ibid., 30 June 1966.

77. See, for example, Lewis, 'From equality to liberation', p. 102, who has argued that by the mid-1960s working women and their place in the labour market had been largely legitimised.

78. WLM, a movement originating in America, spread throughout Western Europe. The British WLM focused its work on a list of seven demands that were devised during the 1970s. These were: equal pay, equal education and opportunity, twenty-four-hour nurseries, free contraception and abortion on demand, financial and legal independence, an end to all discrimination against lesbians, and freedom from intimidation by threat or use of violence.

79. This media attention has been widely noted by historians, who are now beginning to realise that one of the major reasons why the Suffragettes and WLM have dominated the historiography is the contemporary media attention they received. For example, Harrison argued that 'historians, like journalists, relish the dramatic, the flamboyant, the outrageous': B. Harrison, *Prudent Revolutionaries: Portraits of British Feminists During the Wars* (Oxford, 1987), p. 1. Furthermore, Olive Banks has suggested that because the campaigns the inter-war women's movement undertook were perceived to be less epic, they have subsequently been overlooked: Banks, *Politics of British Feminism*, pp. 1–2.

80. While the historiography of the women's movement in Scotland is structured around the 'two waves' concept, there is actually very little written on the impact of the WLM itself. The only scholarly publication directly related to the topic is E. Breitenbach, '"Sisters are doing it for themselves": the Women's Movement in Scotland' in A. Brown and R. Parry (eds), *The Scottish Government Yearbook 1990* (Edinburgh, 1990); and, on the impact of the movement in the 1980s, Shirley Henderson and Alison Mackay (eds), *Grit and Diamonds: Women in Scotland Making History 1980–1990* (Edinburgh, 1990).

81. *Courier*, 18 April 1973.

82. For example, *Annasach: University of Dundee Student Newspaper*, 24 January 1975.

83. The Women's Action Group declared that they were abandoning the term 'liberation', rejected as unsuitable. The Women's Action Group carried on the work of women's liberation but added three further principles for their work, including to represent the interests of women in the University and other colleges; to provide an environment in which women can meet to discuss issues which concern them; to support and work in conjunction with the NUS Women's Campaign. *Annasach*, 24 January 1975.

84. Transcript of interview with Margaret Adams* [* denotes that the interviewee has been anonymised and a pseudonym has been used], 3 May 2007, p. 4. Oral history interviews referred to in this chapter were collected as part of Sarah Browne's doctoral research on the Women's Liberation Movement in Scotland c.1968–c.1979. Future plans for these interviews are that they will be deposited in Glasgow Women's Library and will be available to the public.

85. Ibid., p. 5.

86. *MsPrint* 2 (1978), p. 23.

87. This resolution was seconded by Dundee WCA, as found in Arbroath WCA Minute Book, 2 November 1976.

88. For example, Ann Oakley argued in *Subject Women: A Powerful Analysis of Women's Experience in Society Today* (London, 1981) that 'it is ironically true that they have more to fear from men they "love" than from the strangers in dark alleys' (p. 257). As Dobash and Dobash have succinctly argued, 'it is within marriage that a woman is most likely to be slapped and shoved about, severely assaulted, killed or raped': R. Emerson Dobash and R. Dobash, *Violence Against Wives: A Case Against the Patriarchy* (New York, 1979), p. 75.

89. *The Scotsman*, 19 October 1974, said of Dundee Women's Aid, that it was 'an offshoot of a women's liberation group in the city'.

90. Scottish Women's Aid, *The Herstory of Women's Aid: Scotland* (Edinburgh, 1984), pp. 3, 8.

91. *Courier*, 8 May 1975.

92. Transcript of interview with Mary Henderson, 14 June 2007, p. 3.

93. Scottish Women's Aid, *Herstory*, p. 7.

94. E. Hunter, *Scottish Woman's Place: A Practical Guide and Critical Comment on Women's Rights in Scotland* (Edinburgh, 1978), p. 106.

95. *MsPrint 3* (1979), p. 11. Transcript MA*, 3 May 2007, pp. 11–12.

96. *Courier*, 18 April 1973.

97. E. Breitenbach, *Women Workers in Scotland: A Study of Women's Employment and Trade Unionism* (Glasgow, 1982), pp. 42, 78.

98. Tayside Regional Council, *Joint Report by the Directors of Social Work and Education*, no. 293/77, 1977, pp. 9–10; F. Gordon and M. Henderson, *Mummy, Where Do Playgroups Come From? Playgroups in Tayside 1966–1979* (Perth, 1979), p. 22.

99. Gordon and Henderson, *Mummy*, p. 22.

100. The Scottish Pre-School Playgroups Association Annual Report 1972–73, pp. 2–3.

101. Pre-School Playgroups Association, *PPA and its Past: Pre-school Playgroups Association* (London, 1979), p. 1.

102. Gordon and Henderson, *Mummy*, p. 21.

103. Letter from Mary Henderson, Tayside Playgroups Area Organiser, to George Thomson on 12 November 1970, from which it is evident that he had visited playgroups in the area and donated money. In his reply on 27 January 1971 Thomson argued that he saw playgroups as 'a contribution to education and as an experiment in democratic self-help'.

104. DCA, GD X210 DBPWC: Dundee Business and Professional Women's Club Committee Minute Book, 7 November 1972. Indeed there was widespread opposition, with the readers' page of the *Courier* printing disgruntled letters from local residents who were unsure what role playgroups had in the care of children; see, for example, *Courier*, 20 April 1974.

105. Report of meeting held by Dundee Women's Liberation Group on 18 September 1973.

106. Transcript of interview with Ellen Galford, 2 April 2007, p. 16; transcript of interview with Fran Wasoff, 20 February 2007, p. 6.

107. Tayside Regional Council, *Joint Report*, p. 15.

108. By the late 1970s it is clear that many playgroups in Dundee were having to close their doors, including, from 1975 onwards, Charleston, Dawson Park, Happyhillock, Kindergarden, St Leonard's and Stobswell: Gordon and Henderson, *Mummy*, p. 27.

CHAPTER 6

Juteopolis and After:
Women and Work in
Twentieth-Century Dundee

Valerie Wright

> In Juteopolis, a breed of strong, independent-minded women
> was forged and more than any other place in Scotland certainly,
> possibly in Europe, Dundee is very much a matriarchal society.[1]

In the popular history of Dundee, the city is commonly characterised as
a 'women's town'. The participation of women in the city's workforce,
especially the jute industry, has been largely influential in this characterisation. Yet Dundee remained an overwhelmingly patriarchal society
throughout the twentieth century, which reflects the national picture at
a Scottish and British level.[2] This was evidenced in the largely inequitable
employment opportunities available to the women of Dundee.[3] This
chapter will consider the ways in which Dundonian women were
affected by their involvement in the workforce, and how far they were
able to take advantage of the economic and cultural circumstances of the
city.[4]

JUTE AND DUNDEE BEFORE THE FIRST WORLD WAR

The roots of the characterisation of Dundee as a 'women's town' can be
found in the imbalance of the city's population structure in the late
nineteenth and early twentieth century, with there being three women
for every two men in 1911.[5] In the same year women formed 43 per cent
of the labour force, and 54.3 per cent of women aged over fifteen were in
employment.[6] The jute industry dominated Dundee's economy,
employing 34,000 people, and women accounted for 75 per cent of the

workforce.[7] Conversely, the percentage of married women employed in domestic service was unusually low in Dundee, partly as a result of the opportunities offered by the jute industry. The Scottish average in 1911 was 21 per cent, while in Dundee only 3.4 per cent of women worked in this sector.[8] Women's role in jute in the first half of the twentieth century was significant for two reasons. First, Dundee had a comparatively high percentage of married working women.[9] In 1911 85.8 per cent of Dundee's employed married women worked in the jute industry.[10] Dundee also had a comparatively high proportion of female-headed households as a result of the disproportionate number of female 'breadwinners'. The notion of a 'women's town' can largely be traced to the dominant role that women played in the workforce of the jute industry, and the economic and social consequences of this.

As Eleanor Gordon has shown, despite their numerical predominance, women in jute occupied jobs deemed 'unskilled', and this was reflected in their much lower wages than men's.[11] There were few possibilities of vertical mobility for women, while men could progress through the ranks of authority, largely due to the fact that male workers served apprenticeships recognised by their employers. 'Skilled' work remained the preserve of men. The absence of formal apprenticeships for women was not unique to jute. In many industries girls were positioned as 'learners'; they were 'not really acquiring a skill' but 'just "learning" on the job'.[12]

There was also little option of horizontal mobility for female workers, with the boundaries between the weaving factory and spinning mill being clearly drawn. As Margaret Fenwick, former general secretary of the Dundee Union of Jute, Flax and Kindred Textile Workers, suggested, 'A weaver widnae, a weaver couldnae go across the mill and work.'[13] Physically the weavers and spinners were separated in two different workplaces – the factory and the mill, which aided the development of the stereotypes which were perpetuated by both groups of female workers. Weavers were better paid than spinners and were piece-workers, which theoretically gave them a degree of control over their job, while the spinners were paid a set hourly wage.[14] As a result weavers were 'often accused of regarding themselves as a "cut above" the spinners' and were described as 'toffs'.[15] Oral history evidence confirms this with one respondent stating that 'the weavers aye said they were better than the spinners . . . 'cause they made their ane pey, but we only had a set pey'.[16]

Such attitudes were not surprising given that the local press bluntly distinguished the weavers and the mill girls, stating, 'Below the surf of industrious, respectable and respected factory workers ebb and surge the flotsam and jetsam of the stream – the millworkers.'[17] Thus the industry was characterised by a 'caste system' in which weavers were considered 'a class . . . superior'.[18] This caused a certain amount of animosity between the two groups of female workers, which was further exacerbated by the fact that most commentators acknowledged that spinning was more skilled than weaving.[19] As Walker argues, 'spinners had reason to feel aggrieved at a privilege of the weavers which no one could or even tried to defend'.[20] Weavers themselves contested this, arguing that 'the weaver must turn out the very best cloth, and she has spinners' bad work, winders' knots on the yarn, bad cops, and big bobbins. Everything must be put right on the loom, and no extra wage given.'[21] Similarly Bella Keizer, a former weaver, stated that

> Eh think Eh wis round every jute factory in Dundee tae see if any looms wis better thin the last ain, because it the weaving' ye seemed tae get everybody's bad work, it wis, it, it, if the cops wirnae bad it wis the weft wisnae, wisnae good, 'nd if the weft wis good the bloody dressin' wis rang, ye got everybody's trouble, cause it wis piece work, and if ye didn't make a penny ye didn't get a penny.[22]

However, another oral history respondent, a former spinner, stated that 'we used tae say we were better workers than them'.[23] Similarly Margaret Fenwick stated that:

> Eh'll never forget how hard these people had tae work. The Mill workers were really the hardest workers Eh've ever seen. Oh eh, the old cop machines Eh dinna ken how the women could stop moving when they got hame cause they were going tae that mill nine, ten hours a day, when Eh started first it wis twelve hours a day.[24]

Nevertheless, weaving was seen as a more 'respectable' occupation for women. This was due to the fact that the mill gained a reputation for attracting 'the poorer class of worker'.[25] No previous experience was required for work in the preparing sections in the mill, and it therefore attracted women from the poorest sections of the community as well as widowed and deserted women, many of whom were migrants to Dundee. Similarly girls could only enter the informal apprenticeship in weaving after leaving school. Yet many girls were forced through poverty to leave school early, and at the equivalent school-leaving age a girl could have her own spinning frame in the mill and be earning a higher wage.[26] Thus to move into the better-paid weaving after beginning in spinning, girls would need to take a reduction in earnings to train as an 'ingiver' in the weaving factory. Not only would girls and their families be reluctant to give up much-needed money, but socially it was difficult to make the move from spinning to weaving, given the cultural identities surrounding both occupations. Thus the 'respectability' associated with weaving was derived from the fact that its workforce was drawn from families who could afford for their daughters to finish their schooling and serve the informal apprenticeship, rather than enter work as soon as possible.

The classification of weaving as 'cleaner' work was also significant, with weavers wearing hats and gloves to work 'as if they were going to a party', to highlight the fact that their clothes did not get as dirty in their work as that of the spinners, who would come from the mills 'covered in stoor' or 'jist hanging wi' the dust'.[27] Although oral history evidence suggests that while in the preparing departments of the mill, where the female workers were paid less than the spinners, 'it wis jist stoor flying bak and forit oot the jute', in the 'spinning flet' 'ye got some stoor on ye but nothing tae talk aboot'.[28] This serves to emphasise the fact that dirt, while having some practical meaning, was also a marker of social difference. The cleanliness of conditions in the factory therefore enabled weavers to sustain their perceived superiority.[29] The weavers were distinguished from mill girls by the wearing of hats and gloves, which conformed to notions of respectable femininity and gentility. Such dress could be described as a reflection of the 'discipline implicit in wider discourses of Victorian femininity'.[30] Indeed, a former manager suggested that 'weavers were the "aristocrats" of the workplace' and were 'not only well conducted, but well dressed'.[31] Such differences in dress were internalised by the women workers, as the following oral testimony illustrates:

They were different from us altogether, they never looked at us, see we were low mill hands and we used to just run, we' just our jackets on, nae hats nor gloves. And they thought they were something special because they did the finishing off the jute. An' they used tae walk pass you as if you were something low. An' they were it. An' if you said tae them, 'An' what is your occupation?' – 'Oh, I'm a weaver.' You see that distinction was there.[32]

In addition, married women may not have been such a permanent part of the labour force in weaving as was the case in spinning, where the workforce was characterised by casual female labour and 'married women in necessitous circumstance'.[33] Weavers often had aspirations of marrying men 'with a trade' and becoming non-working wives, also a symbol of working-class respectability.[34] This was closely tied to the pursuit of the ideal of the male breadwinner, a key aspect of working-class masculinity. Indeed, the skilled men and supervisors in jute tended to have non-working wives, while the majority of unskilled men had working wives.[35] Therefore the weavers and their husbands were able to conform more closely to ideals of respectable working-class masculinity and femininity than those working in the mill.

The divisions between mill girls and weavers were not confined to the workplace, but were also present in other of aspects of life in Dundee. In reality the leisure activities of weavers and mill girls were not that different. Both groups enjoyed promenading around the town, meeting friends and 'ha'in a gossip', going to dances, concerts and picnics. However the two groups socialised separately and rarely mixed. This was due to the fact that in spite of the similarities, mill girls were perceived to be the 'rougher element of jute workers'. Spinners and other mill workers were characterised in the memories of weavers by the singing of bawdy songs and the drinking of alcohol, both of which challenged notions of respectable femininity. Walker suggests that the Dundee mill girl 'was the major anarchic influence in a city bent on respectability'.[36] Such was the threat of the activities of the female jute workers, especially the mill girls, that Dundee's Committee on Public Morals tried to prevent women 'promenading' in the town in 1913, as this was an 'unsuitable and unseemly activity'.[37] Thus the independence shown by the mill girl, and female jute worker more generally, through her pursuit of leisure activities on her own terms was seen as threatening the moral order of Dundee. Yet the efforts of philanthropic reformers in the city, such as the Band of

Hope, to encourage the mill girl to become 'respectable' were futile, as they 'were paid enough to resist the authority of husband or father' and were able to 'over-rule the male element at home'.[38]

How far women's role in jute shaped domestic life is unclear. There is a persistent story of women workers being married to 'kettle-bilers', men who allegedly stayed at home looking after the children while their wives went to work. Thus Walker suggests that Dundee's character reflected 'the substantial reversal of male and female economic functions', where 'men were frequently dependent upon the earnings of mothers, sisters or daughters'.[39] In reality, the extent and influence of this 'role reversal' was limited. Undoubtedly, women worked in comparatively higher numbers than in other cities in Scotland, and 'took pride in the fact that they worked hard for their money', but 'the association of women with the domestic sphere and men with the world of work was not undermined'.[40] The Dundee Social Union found in its investigations many homes where women were at work, men were at home, and the children were being looked after by neighbours.[41] Similarly oral history evidence suggests that girls were trained by their mothers to perform a range of domestic tasks but boys were not. When asked what chores she had as a child, one respondent replied:

> Oh God hunders' everybody took thir week o' the dishes, an' then everybody took thir week o' the scrubbin' the kitchen or scrubbing the lobby or, daein' the room or polishin' the flair an' that, everybody hid joabs, an' never the laddies.[42]

It would therefore be surprising if men took on the responsibility of housework when it was so firmly associated with women. Another respondent, when asked whether her father had done any jobs about the house, had stated simply 'Meh father did nothing.'[43] In addition Riddell suggested that in the post-war years in Dundee 'more often than not the high rate of female employment merely increased the burden on the shoulders of the housewife, whose household work and cooking were transferred to the evening'.[44] Thus women continued to perform household tasks, as housework and childcare remained 'a woman's job' even when she was in paid employment.

The provision of classes by philanthropic organisations and employers for married and single women in the pre-war years in domestic skills such as cooking and sewing support this assertion. Mill girls were a particular focus of such classes, as they were perceived to be unable to 'make or mend, wash or clean, bake or cook a dinner'.[45] Women remained very much associated with the domestic sphere in spite of their prevalence in the workforce in Dundee. There was much contemporary concern relating to the number of young single girls in Dundee who 'leave home when they begin to earn good money, simply from the love of independence'.[46] Such women were able to share lodgings with other single women workers and enjoyed 'comfortable circumstances'. This was often considered 'desertion' of family responsibilities. Lennox even suggested that women were 'independent of marriage as a means of livelihood'.[47] Similarly he also argued that in Dundee 'the burden of motherhood is often to be avoided for financial, social and personal reasons' and 'an average of 3,000 child bearing women in Dundee tax their energies in the toil of mill and factory life to the detriment of their maternal duties'.[48] Whether women actively chose work over marriage and motherhood, or this was simply a result of the fact that women outnumbered men in Dundee is debatable. Nevertheless, Dundee's women challenged their association with the domestic sphere through the independence afforded them by participation in the workforce. As Gordon argues, their public role 'arguably undermined the material basis of this ideology of gender divisions'.[49] The employment of married women in particular challenged the 'unrealistic expectations' of separate spheres of activity for men and women and highlighted the tensions inherent in the pursuit of this ideal.[50] Dundee's middle classes and working-class men may have been uncomfortable with women's participation in the workplace and the independence this gave them; however, Dundee's women workers 'took pride in their skill and their labour'.[51]

Thus while men continued to hold the authority in both the mill and the factory, women had the numerical advantage in both weaving and spinning.[52] Perhaps as a result, shopfloor life could have a 'rich and robust' character, which was 'barely stifled by the level of supervision' and the pace of work.[53] This enabled 'networks of solidarity and mutual assistance' to be established among women in the mill and factory. The weavers even developed lip-reading skills and a sign language to overcome the noise of machines and allow them to communicate without detection by supervisors.[54] As Bella Keizer stated:

Ye couldnae carry on a conversation, it had tae be all done beh signs in mouth and even it times the shakin' o' the hands as tae what time it was, 'n' three fingers up, two fingers up half past two, two pinkies crossed, two, two thumbs fir twelve o'clock ye know.[55]

This work culture enabled the weavers and spinners to form close bonds in opposition to the male supervisors, and also owners, which was evidenced in frequent 'unofficial' industrial action. Women are often portrayed in the historiography as a docile workforce. As a result, in some popular histories of Dundee it has been argued that women workers did not organise, through lack of assertiveness, and were therefore poorly paid. Yet Walker argues that the explanations given in the historiography relating to the weakness of female trade unionism have 'only a limited applicability to Dundee'.[56] Thus this characterisation fails to recognise the ways in which women resisted the control of employers and supervisors in the workplace in their attempts to improve working conditions and wages. The actions of Dundee's female jute workers were often 'unorganised' in the sense that it had not been sanctioned by trade unions. In the early twentieth century trade unions in the jute industry were mainly the preserve of skilled men. In spite of the fact that the majority of its workforce was female, workplace relations in the jute industry therefore favoured male skilled workers. Women were subordinated within this labour process, which Gordon argues had important implications for the ways in which women organised, as well as the issues that they prioritised.[57]

Sectionalism was a common feature on strike committees, with conflicts arising as a result of the differing priorities of the higher-paid skilled male workers and the women workers, which often were connected to the sexual division of labour in the home and family. In this sense women's identities as wives and mothers again played a role in their work lives. Women experienced a gendered workplace and a gendered home, which was 'complementary and mutually reinforcing'.[58] Women therefore found it difficult to make their voices heard on strike committees, as the male-dominated nature of trade union politics survived in early twentieth-century Dundee.

The way in which women chose to spend their free time in Dundee was also influential in the characterisation of Dundee as a 'women's town'. In the early years of the twentieth century Dundee women were portrayed as being 'out of control'. As the Rev. Williamson stated in 1922, 'the Dundee millgirl' was 'the most serious of Dundee's social problems'; 'fifty years ago she was a problem, and she is a problem still'.[59] Yet in spite of his efforts in forming the Dundee and District Mill and Factory Operatives' Union, as well as those of the Dundee and District Union of Jute and Flax Workers (DDUJFW), the majority of the female jute workforce did not join trade unions. Their militancy was unrestricted by attempts to establish collective bargaining and strike committees. Women chose spontaneous, self-organised strike action to address their grievances.

In the community more generally attempts were also made to control the actions of working women. Particularly important here was the linking of high female labour participation to Dundee's high level of infant mortality.[60] In particular, the Dundee Social Union (DSU) blamed the 'over-exertion on the part of the mother at too late a period during pregnancy' for causing 'congenital weakness' which led to death.[61] This led to a scheme of house visitations to instruct 'ignorant and careless mothers on the subject of infant hygiene', which focused especially on breastfeeding.[62] This was accompanied by a milk depot, the aims of which were to solve the problems of 'improper feeding', to increase the number of women breastfeeding and prevent women returning to work too early.[63] In addition the DSU established the first of its restaurants for nursing mothers in 1906 and a maternal and child welfare scheme grew out of this, eventually being taken over by the city council in 1917.[64] Arguably, in this case Dundonian femininity was not celebrated, but instead women were positioned as the cause of infant mortality and the solution was to try and control their behaviour.

While economic conditions ensured that there was a high demand for female labour, the authorities and middle-class philanthropic organisations, concerned with morality and child welfare, struggled to prevent women, and especially married women, from working in the jute industry. In this context women were able to resist attempts to restrict their freedom to spend their leisure time how they liked, go on strike and conduct their families and the care of their children in the manner they wanted. Before the First World War labour turnover in the jute industry was high, especially in the spinning and preparing departments. The lack of uniform wage rates as well as 'the erratic trade cycle of the jute trade' meant that if women were unhappy with their wages or conditions in one company they would simply leave and seek work at another.[65] This was a common way of dealing with grievances and highlights the agency of the female workforce as a result of the high demand for its labour.

ECONOMIC UPHEAVAL AND UNEMPLOYMENT
IN INTER-WAR DUNDEE

The impact of the First World War on women, especially in their stereotypical role as munitions workers, has become, as Braybon argues, a 'key part of the greater war story'.[66] It has become a common view that the war led to 'progress' for women, such as the expansion in women's employment opportunities, higher wages, work for married women, availability of birth control and childcare, and improved diet and health. However, Braybon suggests that such approaches, which present the war as a 'watershed' in gender relations where 'women's status was raised by their war work, their higher wages, greater independence and so on', are superficial at best.[67] The case of Dundee certainly seems to support this assertion, especially with regard to women's involvement in the labour force. The First World War undoubtedly affected the lives of many Dundonians, and indeed women in Dundee did work in war-related industries. However, women in Dundee worked before the war and continued to do so after, with this also being the case for married women. Whether the war afforded the women of Dundee greater independence in respect of the availability of paid work is questionable. Perhaps in relation to participation in the labour force, Dundee's women are best characterised as experiencing continuity rather than change during the period of the war.

Women in Dundee were more substantially affected by the contraction of the jute industry in the inter-war years, and the mass unemployment that followed. Approximately 8,000 people left the industry by the late 1930s, leading to a reduction in the numbers of female workers in the jute industry, but also the displacement of female workers by men. This was driven by the fact that many jute firms moved to a double shift system. 'Protective' legislation prevented women from working at night; therefore increasing numbers of men were hired to work nightshifts.[68] Employers hoped that men would be a more stable workforce, as women were seen as being particularly strike-prone when compared with men in the industry, with managers also arguing that women were more likely to be absent or late.[69] Despite this trend in jute, the high levels of male unemployment ensured that the overall percentage of married women working in Dundee increased during the inter-war years, from 24 per cent in 1921 to 33 per cent in 1931.[70]

The female workforce in the jute industry continued to participate in strike action in the early 1920s, and it is notable that in an important continuity with the pre-war period, this was largely 'unorganised' and spontaneous. Even where there was evidence of trade union involvement in particular strikes, not all of the women were members, which confirms that women were capable of successful independent action. Of sixty-nine strikes involving women in Scotland in the inter-war years, twenty-seven were in the jute industry in Dundee.[71] Strike action was taken to prevent wage reductions or secure wage increases, and very few attempts were made to gain wage increases, which highlights the contraction of the jute industry. Other causes included attempts to improve working conditions or a rejection of changed working conditions, such as employers' imposition of efficiency measures, which resulted in women having to work more weaving looms or spinning frames, or bigger looms, or having to learn to use more complicated machinery. Women also went on solidarity strikes with dismissed colleagues.

Such strikes were often confined to the workers directly affected, weavers or spinners, and were localised, confined to a small number of firms, and relatively short.[72] There was one widespread strike in 1923, which began at Jute Industries' Camperdown works and concerned proposals to move to double spinning.[73] The strike resulted in 30,000 workers throughout the city being locked out from June to August. Widespread civil unrest and violence involving 50,000 people followed at a demonstration in Albert Square. Ultimately the workers were defeated. An important consequence of this was that there were very few strikes in the jute industry in the remainder of the 1920s and, crucially, there is no evidence that jute workers were involved in strike action during the General Strike in 1926.[74] After 1923 employer programmes of rationalisation and modernisation continued in the jute industry, largely without complaint from John Sime, the leader of the DDUJFW.[75] While other methods of workplace resistance may have been employed by women workers in Dundee, the absence of collective action in the late 1920s was significant and highlights the limited power of women in economically depressed Dundee.

High unemployment continued to be predominant in Dundee in the 1930s, with the jute industry undergoing a greater contraction in this decade, and the workforce and trade union membership both declined as a consequence. It was not uncommon in the inter-war years for women seeking work to have to queue to be chosen by the supervisors at the factory gates. As Margaret Fenwick suggested,

> The more they'd on the market, they could pick and choose, An they were good at that in those days, pickin' and choosin'. They were like a lot a bloody cattle standin' at the door wonderin' if ye were goin ti be picked.[76]

In addition, the failure of strike action in the early 1920s set a precedent. In the 1930s the nature of strikes was different in that large numbers of workers were involved across a number of works with activity spreading quickly. Alterations in work practices were the main cause of strike action among female workers. The introduction of modern spinning frames was a particular focus of opposition, as this resulted in a fall in wage rates. Men were also employed in increasing numbers to work on this new machinery, especially on night-shift working.[77] In 1933 a six-day strike to prevent wage reductions at Low & Bonar's Eagle Works was unsuccessful with the exception of male night-shift workers.[78] This distinction in the treatment of male and female workers was significant and again highlights the weakening position of women in the jute industry. A year later spinners at Jute Industries' Walton, Caldrum and Camperdown works went on strike following the introduction of high-speed spinning frames. The month-long strike for higher wage rates was unsuccessful, with the 600 workers involved returning to work with no alteration in their conditions.[79] The failure of strike action was influential on the actions of workers at other jute works. An oral history respondent who worked at Cox's suggested that in the 1930s 'naebody stiked'.[80]

The DDUJFW encouraged strike action and often expressed its dissatisfaction that workers, especially weavers, were not more militant and instead accepted more work for the same wages. However, the union simultaneously failed to support strike action taken by women workers. Weavers organised two one-day 'stay in' strikes in Caldrum works in late 1937 and early 1938, neither of which was supported by the DDUJFW.[81] This lack of support for female industrial action, as well as the failure of strike action, resulted overall in less militancy in the inter-war years than in the period before. In a continuation with the pre-war period, female spinners were more likely to go on strike than weavers. Arguably mill girls continued to be 'a problem' in the inter-war years, while weavers were more 'respectable' in their actions. However, in a departure from tradition, all female-led strikes in the inter-war years were less lively than had been the case before the First World War and instead were subdued and restrained. Female strikers were no longer challenging male authority in the same manner as before; in addition, strike action was not characterised by the carnival atmosphere of the pre-war period. This was undoubtedly due to the prevailing economic conditions in inter-war Dundee. As noted above, strikes in the inter-war years were largely defensive, with attempts being made to prevent further degradation of their work conditions and wages. It would follow that strike action in this context was a desperate measure, and the women strikers had little bargaining power; in the eyes of their employers the women were lucky to have jobs at all.

POST-WAR DUNDEE AND THE DECLINING INFLUENCE OF JUTE

The Second World War brought increasing employment opportunities for Dundee's women, as the reserved occupation list issued by the Ministry of Labour resulted in diversification. As a result of the war Dundee became a centre for munitions production and marine engineering, with women working in both areas. Women were also drafted in as tram conductors and worked in the construction industry in the city. Yet 1,300 young women were also sent by the government to work in munitions factories in England. Fewer than half were volunteers and some women never returned to Dundee. As Scott argues, 'the social cost of this for the women concerned or the community was barely considered'.[82] The president of the Dundee Chamber of Commerce suggested that 'it would appear to be the policy of the government to drain Scotland of all its best labour to the advantage of English manufacturers and affecting the output of munitions in Scotland'.[83] Nevertheless, in Dundee jute remained the largest employer of women, as jute products such as sandbags were very much in demand during the Second World War, as had been the case during the First World War.

High demand for jute products continued in the immediate post-war period as the market returned to peacetime conditions. However, the jute industry experienced a labour shortage as it struggled to attract women back into the industry. In the immediate post-war years efforts were made to reclaim jute workers through the introduction of a registration system to track individuals who had worked in jute before the war. Attempts were also made to prevent such individuals working in other industries through the Control of Engagement Orders, which were reintroduced in 1947.[84] Men were not expected to return from war and replace women in the jute industry as was the case in other industries, as jute continued to be seen as 'women's work' in the post-war years, although some companies provided training for ex-servicemen who wished to train as rove spinners.[85]

After 1945 the economic situation differed from that in 1918 in that there were more opportunities for women workers as a result of new industries locating in Dundee. The relative economic prosperity following the Second World War made all the difference to the employment prospects of the women of Dundee. Female participation in the labour market declined following the war, as was the case at a national level, which was largely attributable to a rise in fertility rates, with marriage and birth rates both increasing in Dundee in the immediate post-war years. Perhaps economic circumstances in Dundee, in which male unemployment was substantially reduced in comparison with the inter-war years, enabled women to make the choice to fulfil the roles of wife and mother without the double burden of working outside the home. Yet many married women chose to continue to engage in paid employment following the war, with participation of women in the labour force being comparably high. In 1951 33,127 women were recorded as being in employment or 39.5 per cent of the workforce, married women accounting for 30.6 per cent of women employed.

Married women were therefore an important source of labour in post-war Dundee. As a result Dundee City Council, in an attempt to facilitate the return to work of married women, continued public provision of nurseries in the post-war years, which was in contrast to the policy of many other British local authorities.[86] In 1947 there were eleven day nurseries operated by the city council; interestingly, these nurseries kept the same hours as the jute works.[87] The council also subsidised workplace nurseries. This policy was in contrast to the patriarchal attitudes of local politicians, who opposed married women working. Such individuals argued that the council should be concentrating on improving male employment prospects while women should be in the home caring for their children and homes. At a national level the Ministry of Health also did not support the council's nursery building programme in the early 1950s, although the council continued to lobby for nursery expansion to enable married women to work, in jute as well as in the new industries locating in the city.[88]

Such new industries were located in Dundee as a result of the city's 'Development Area' status, provided by the Distribution of Industry Act of 1945. This measure was welcomed by Dundee City Council as well as by the Board of Trade. Dundee's 'cheap' female labour force was positioned as a prominent selling point to industries considering locating in the area. As the council's policy of diversifying the industrial base of Dundee became increasingly successful, women in Dundee chose to work in many of the new industries.[89] The jute industry experienced difficulty in competing with the conditions and, most importantly, the higher wages offered in such establishments. Rather than offering comparable rates of pay, the jute companies instead established 'welfare facilities' such as canteens, lockers, washing facilities, improved toilets and heating, as well as the provision of drinking fountains and 'forenoon tea' for workers.[90] Several companies also opened their own nurseries. Low & Bonar were the first to do so, in 1947, with Jute Industries following a year later, and with a second following in 1950.[91] Jute Industries gave three reasons for the establishment of nurseries: the recruitment and retention of working mothers, to prevent absenteeism among working mothers, and the fact that public provision was full and had long waiting lists.[92] Indeed, Jute Industries felt that the provision of day nurseries would be 'the main factor likely to help recruitment of women workers, particularly the type of productive workers likely to be in demand and in short supply'.[93]

However, the private company nurseries were rarely full to capacity. As early as 1905 Dundee employers helped to fund four crèches in the city, and these were also underused by the women they were aimed at. Women may have preferred to use the 'child-minding services of neighbours', thereby resisting philanthropic provision characterised by 'regulation and social control'.[94] After 1945 this may also have been true, many women not wishing to use the facilities offered by their employers, although they were willing to use Corporation nurseries. No doubt some women did not want to use nurseries at all if avoidable, and would rather exploit opportunities available to work part-time. But the jute industry did not offer part-time work, which was in contrast to the rising availability of flexible hours and part-time work in a range of industries in the post-war years at a national level.[95]

The welfare measures offered by the jute companies were therefore not sufficient to attract women back into the industry. The new industries locating in Dundee also provided such facilities as well as paying relatively higher wages. Another significant reason for women taking jobs in the new industries was that such work was viewed as 'cleaner' than jute. The novelty of learning a new skill and working in a clean, new factory arguably provided workers in the new industries with an enhanced social status when compared to those women who remained in jute. The practical considerations of a cleaner work environment may have continued to be accompanied in the post-war period by the association of cleanliness with moral purity and respectability.[96] The jute industry simply could not compete in these terms. Young women in particular were attracted to the new industries. Women aged between fourteen and seventeen comprised almost 9 per cent of the jute workforce in 1939 but only 6 per cent in 1947.[97] In 1944 a civil servant stated that Dundee was 'outstandingly a women's work town' and he predicted that 'Postwar, that is still likely to be the case for some time at any rate.' He was right. In the immediate post-war years, and arguably for the duration of the 1950s, women in Dundee could choose where to work, although such jobs in the new industries were, like those in the jute industry, largely unskilled in character. Nevertheless, women took full advantage of the options available to them. Unfortunately for the jute industry, it was not a popular choice.[98]

A MORE DIVERSE ECONOMY IN POST-WAR DUNDEE

Statistically jute remained Dundee's largest employer until 1966. The industry experienced full employment during the 1950s, and although the labour shortage persisted throughout this decade, in the 1960s it would appear that the jute industry ceased its efforts to attract women workers. Instead, jute companies focused on lowering their reliance on labour through capital expenditure on more efficient machinery. This strategy was dependent on the further extension of double shift working to ensure that the machinery was running for as many hours in the day as possible, which resulted in further employment of men to work night shifts. The ratio of female to male employees therefore declined dramatically from 1.6:1 in 1948 to 0.5:1 in 1977.[99] Between 1960 and 1977 the number of women working in the industry fell by 68 per cent; the equivalent figure for men was 40 per cent, and consequently men accounted for two-thirds of the workforce by the end of this period.[100]

Margaret Fenwick also stated that women left the jute industry as the machinery became 'more difficult for the women to handle' and the 'machine charges got greater'.[101] She suggested that as the companies made attempts to increase labour productivity in weaving, the number of looms each woman had to operate increased, and while automation was introduced to make the job easier, 'it never ever really wis successful'. In addition as wider looms were introduced to produce the wide cloth required for carpet backing, Fenwick argued that the stretching involved for women resulted in 'miscarriages . . . cervical cancer, this sort o' thing'. Thus 'women werenae able tae cope, ye know, so more and more men were trained intae the industry'. As she stated, 'the heavier the machine wis eh it wisnae a woman's job anymore, ye know, . . . It wis a man's job.' Fenwick suggested that 5-yard loom weaving and above should be 'a male responsibility' as it was 'outwith the capabilities of a woman'.[102]

Arguably, as the machinery installed became more sophisticated and demanding, and eventually jute companies began to specialise in woven plastics, some jobs in the jute industry were designated as requiring greater skill and men were employed. Such a 'reworking of the gendered division of labour' enabled men to gain higher-status 'skilled' positions.[103] The extension of the double shift system throughout the industry was also instrumental in the expansion of men's employment in jute, as was the hiring of men to work night shifts perceived to be unsuitable for married mothers. The differential in wage rates between male night-shift workers and the female day shift was attributed to the fact that men on average operated more machinery and were therefore more productive. As Fenwick stated in relation to male weavers, 'it wis amazing once they did get used tae it they made damn good weavers, they made good weavers, Eh, Eh must say that'. Whether such marginalisation of women was a purely economic concern relating to the relative productivity of men and women is open for debate, and may have been a product of patriarchal attitudes relating to measurements of skill. Indeed, the majority of organised training offered to jute workers in the post-war years was aimed at the male occupation of tenter, a type of mechanic who oversaw the operation of the machinery, which was seen as a 'skilled' occupation.[104] Such classes were held at the technical college in Dundee with apprenticeship schemes of three years being essential. This training undoubtedly elevated the status of this occupation within the industry.

McCloskey suggests that across the industrialised world paid work became the norm for women following the 'social earthquake' of the 1960s and 1970s.[105] Yet in Dundee female participation in the labour market had been consistently high throughout the first half of the twentieth century, and this remained the case. In 1971 the number of women working in Dundee reached a post-war height of 34,807 with numbers declining thereafter.[106] In contrast, female participation in the workforce as a percentage of the total workforce continued to increase from 42.7 per cent in 1971 to 45.8 per cent in 1991.[107] Thus in Dundee women continued to work and exploited the opportunities available to them in these and subsequent decades. As the number of women employed in the jute industry declined, women contined to find alternative employment. A significant opportunity was in the incoming multinationals, the biggest of which, National Cash Register (NCR) and Timex, both employed large numbers of women workers.

In the case of Timex, women were predominant, and their position within it provides a good comparison to the role women played in the jute industry. Women occupied the 'unskilled' positions, in this case as assemblers, while men were employed in the 'skilled' machine room or as supervisors of the female workforce.[108] As was the case in jute, this led to a certain amount of antagonism between the sexes, with this being most pronounced during the industrial action which ultimately led to the demise of Timex in Dundee. Although women were the numerical majority in the workforce, men dominated official trade union organisation in Timex, which marks another parallel with jute.

The division of labour in such assembly industries was also similar to that in jute, in that work was vertically and horizontally segregated, and this was the case in Timex. Men and women did not perform the same jobs and tasks in such industries: women were occupied in 'unskilled' assembly line work and men worked in 'skilled' areas of production. In addition, men and women did not often work on the same shop floor in such industries, thus there was also a demarcation of space. The only men visible in the same spaces as the women were the supervisors. Management in such industries was also male-dominated. In such environments women's work was 'segregated, repetitious, monotonous, unthinking' and 'required rapid detailed work at high speed'.[109] Assembly line work was seen as particularly suited to women's abilities, as women were 'unaffected by the monotony of the work'.[110] Simonton suggests that such segregation allowed 'men to claim their special position and wages', which was certainly the case in both jute and in Timex.[111]

More broadly, the workforce employed in instrument making and electrical engineering, the type of work carried out in NCR and Timex, was transformed following the Second World War. In the early 1930s women accounted for 20 per cent of this workforce, by the 1970s this had increased to 50 per cent.[112] Yet women's participation in this workforce was governed by gender stereotypes. Women were largely employed in mechanised assembly line work as this required less strength and skill, which ensured that they could be paid a lower wage. Simonton argues that in the post-war years women were 'increasingly associated with non-qualified jobs using a machine'.[113] For Dundonian women who had worked in jute, the character of assembly line work was very similar. The material conditions of the workplace may have changed in that the new factories may have been brighter and cleaner; however, the type of work and most importantly the level of skill expected of women by the management was largely the same. Women continued to be subordinated in the labour process.

In addition, women were constrained in taking up the shift-work opportunities in these new employments by childcare responsibilities. In such circumstances the division of labour in the home shaped women's work life. Arguably such women workers were viewed as expendable; women were seen as a flexible workforce or 'a reserve army of labour', to 'be drawn on when needed and released when not needed'.[114] In Timex the part-time female workers were also the first to go in times of economic necessity.

WOMEN AND NON-INDUSTRIAL EMPLOYMENT IN TWENTIETH-CENTURY DUNDEE

The working women of Dundee were largely occupied in manufacturing industries throughout the best part of the twentieth century. Given Dundee's comparatively small middle-class population in the first half of the twentieth century, the dominance of manufacturing industries was not surprising. Yet there were increasing opportunities for women to work in other sectors. The growth of the tertiary sector became particularly important, especially in the post-war years.

Shop work was popular among 'respectable' working-class girls in the early twentieth century. The wages and conditions were often more favourable than those of mills and factories and it was cleaner work, but the working hours were also very long. More importantly, 'a young appearance was essential to remaining in work' and 'youthfulness was often the determining factor in securing shop work'.[115] As a result shop work may have been seen as the type of job a girl would do before marriage, whereupon she would give up work in favour of becoming a full-time housewife. Clerical and typing work fulfilled a similar role for young girls from 'respectable' working-class and also middle-class homes, as the operation of marriage bars in many offices ensured that women could only work when single, with such practices being further entrenched during the inter-war years. The growth of the 'feminisation' of clerical work began in the 1880s, when women were for the first time recruited in 'significant numbers'.[116] Thus by 1941, 46 per cent of Britain's clerks were female, with such employment being focused in commerce and the civil service. In Scotland female clerical employment grew steadily from 77,451 women in 1931 to 138,699 in 1951.[117] The two world wars undoubtedly accelerated the process of the feminisation of the clerical workforce, with women retaining their position in this workforce in the post-war years. Yet, in the first half of the twentieth century there were few opportunities for this type of work in Dundee as a result of the small professional and white-collar sectors.[118]

In both shops and offices the employment of young women was strategic, as their wages were lower. In the case of clerical or typing work, employers justified this by giving such young women the most routine and monotonous tasks.[119] In the early years of the twentieth century, shorthand typists earned approximately the same wage as domestic servants or employees in a low-paid manufacturing industry. Yet Anderson argues that clerical work 'compared favourably' with the narrow range of alternative white-collar occupations such as nursing, although schoolteachers earned more than female clerks.[120] Arguably it was the 'respectability' of such clerical jobs that was attractive to young women.[121] As was the case in jute and in the new post-war industries in Dundee such as Timex, women occupied subordinate positions in shops and offices. In addition there was little opportunity for promotion, thanks to the operation of official or unofficial marriage bars. This led to the expectation that in the clerical sector men had careers while women were concentrated in low-paid and low-status jobs.[122] Thus clerical employment operated within a patriarchal system in which work was gendered.

Nevertheless, such work was attractive to middle-class women and was an aspirational choice for many 'respectable' working-class girls. Oral history evidence suggests that parents encouraged girls to take night classes and train as shorthand typists.[123] Such classes had been offered in Dundee since the early twentieth century, with Dundee Commercial College offering 'expert tuition in shorthand, typewriting, bookkeeping and all commercial subjects' and Skerry's College providing 'training for women clerks'.[124] This became a fairly popular choice during the inter-war years, and one respondent, who described herself as middle-class, suggested the queues of shorthand typists at 'the unemployment place' meant that she had to drop her salary 'from a princely two pounds a week to twenty-five shillings, to get into Low and Bonar's'. She worked for this company until she married a widower when she was forty, with her husband stating that she should go 'into the kitchen now, it's your job'. Working-class parents could be equally aspirational for their daughters. A working-class respondent suggested that 'meh mother kept on saying, she didn't want any of us tae go into the factories'.[125] This was because 'she worked in the factory herself, she wis a weaver, an' she didn't want any of us have to do what she did'. As a result this woman's first job was working in an office 'ledgering', which she left after two and a half years as the 'money wisn't very good'. She later worked in a jute factory, which she felt 'wis a lot more fun'.

Women's participation in clerical work further increased in the years after 1950, with the growth of part-time employment, which became a feature of women's work in the post-war years in all sectors.[126] This facilitated married women's work and enabled women to combine motherhood and paid work as marriage bars were dismantled. By the late 1980s women dominated office work and it represented the 'largest single category of female employment', with this being focused in the then developing areas of public administration, finance, banking and insurance.[127] In 1981 74 per cent of 'clerical and related workers' were women.[128] In the more limited category of women working as typists, shorthand writers and secretaries, female predominance was even higher, at around 98 per cent, a figure which showed little change between 1951 and 1981. However, as Crompton argues, clerical work remained gendered in the 1980s, with women concentrated in poorly paid work with comparatively less opportunity of promotion or career development. Thus, while equal pay legislation was successful in ensuring that women were not paid less than men in the same jobs, crucially women and men largely worked in different jobs. Such occupational segregation in the clerical and other sectors remains an issue in the present day.

The growth of Dundee City Council throughout the twentieth century and the range of services provided for Dundee's population also provided increased numbers of clerical and other jobs for women. By 1961 the council was the city's largest employer and 38 per cent of its 7,800 workers were women, although this was less than the proportion of women working in Dundee overall.[129] However, half of all female employment in workplaces employing over 1,000 employees was in the public sector. Dundee's hospitals and educational services were among the main contributors to women's employment in the 1970s.[130] Women had been employed as doctors in Dundee from the early years of the twentieth century, often in relation to the treatment of children. Indeed the Dundee Women Citizens' Association protested against the exclusion of women doctors from Dundee Infant Hospital in 1919, which had been founded by two female doctors, a campaign which resulted in the reinstatement of women.[131] The construction of Ninewells Hospital in 1974 was also significant in the employment of women, both as medical and administrative staff. Similarly Dundee's further and higher educational sector has flourished in the second half of the twentieth century, with the establishment of the University of Dundee in 1966 and its subsequent expansion, including the merger with Duncan of Jordanstone College of Art & Design, as well as the formation of Abertay University and Dundee College. All of these provided employment opportunities for women, again in the clerical sector, and as teaching and research staff, and continue to do so today.

By 1971 the service sector in Dundee had overtaken manufacturing, and a decade later accounted for two-thirds of the city's workforce, in which women played a significant role.[132] This trend was not unique to

Dundee. In the post-war years increasing consumption has resulted in the appearance of purpose-built shopping centres throughout Britain. In Dundee the construction of the first Overgate shopping centre in the 1960s was undoubtedly instrumental in the increase of the number of people working in distributive trades in the city, with 11.2 per cent being employed in this sector in 1953, which rose to 14.6 per cent in 1962.[133] The addition of the Wellgate shopping centre and the rebuilding of the Overgate in the 1990s ensured that this trend continued, with family retailers such as William Low being replaced by familiar British high street shops. In the post-war years such expansion of shopping facilities was crucial in the availability of part-time and flexible working and played an important role in enabling working mothers to enter the formal labour market. Indeed, in 2009, 60.8 per cent of Dundee's jobs were full-time and 33.6 per cent were part-time. Unsurprisingly, women held 74.7 per cent of the latter and 43 per cent of the full-time jobs.[134] The changing economy of post-war Dundee has resulted in the growth of sectors in which women are represented in significant numbers, most obviously the public sector and private services such as retailing.

CONCLUSION

While this chapter is not representative of all occupations and women's work lives in Dundee, it has illustrated the agency and economic power that women held in the labour market of the city throughout the twentieth century.[135] Case studies of women's role in jute as well as in the new industries locating in Dundee following the Second World War have shown the ways in which women were able to negotiate their position in the gendered hierarchy. Yet Dundee remained a largely patri-archal society in which women occupied subordinate roles in the workplace. Throughout the twentieth century, generally men were the owners, managers and supervisors in Dundee's manufacturing industries. Gendered occupational segregation in clerical and administrative work and in the service sector have also ensured that women often occupy subordinate roles. Evidence of a gender pay gap regardless of equal pay legislation supports this assertion. Although this is not restricted to Dundee and is a nationwide problem, in May 2008 median gross weekly earnings of full-time employees in the city highlight that while men earned £502.90 women earned £391.70.[136]

In this context the characterisation of Dundee as a 'women's town' is problematic. Dundee can be accurately described as a women's town in relation to the comparatively high participation of women and especially married women in the local labour market. Women were dominant in the jute industry, which in turn looms large in the historiography of the city. In addition, women remained dominant in the labour force of the new industries locating in Dundee in the post-war years. Consequently the way in which Dundee presents itself to the outside world is inextricably linked with its female population. As Wainwright suggests, the notion of Dundee as a 'women's town' has 'reverberated through Dundee's own sense of heritage'.[137] Local histories celebrate Dundee's women as being unique to the city, which enables Dundonians to set their city apart from the others in Scotland. Dundee women are presented as going against the prevailing gender ideologies in the early twentieth century and the inter-war years by being independent and strong working women. Yet from the early 1970s the proportion of women working in Dundee has been closely comparable with the other cities in Scotland, as Figure 6.1 illustrates. Moreover, the types of jobs

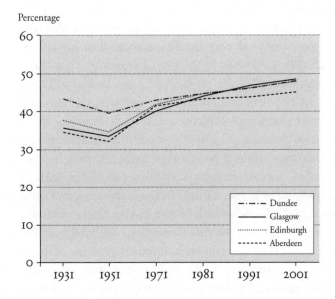

FIGURE 6.1
Number of women in employment as a proportion of total employment in major Scottish cities.

available to women in Dundee bear close resemblance to those on offer elsewhere in urban Scotland and Britain. Dundee's distinctiveness in the 'post-industrial' late twentieth and early twenty-first century is in its reliance on public administration, health and education, in which women play a significant role, as they do in other urban centres.

Thus the narrative relating to Dundee as a 'women's town' is overly simplistic, as this chapter has illustrated. While women in Dundee chose to work, and they chose where they worked, the decisions that women could make at any time throughout the twentieth century were limited by circumstances such as the availability of employment and the prevalent gender ideologies. The same was true of women throughout Scotland and indeed Britain. In the twentieth century women were subject to patriarchal authority in society. This was particularly influential in the workplace, where gender stereotypes helped to create occupational segregation in manufacturing as well as in clerical and service occupations. Moreover, the gendered division of labour in the home was undoubtedly influential in the choices that women could make regarding paid employment. The pattern of women's work in Dundee increasingly conformed to the national model as its economy became more like the rest of post-industrial Scotland. For example, women in Dundee were able to take advantage of the increasing opportunity of part-time work and therefore manage their unpaid work in the home with their paid work in the formal economy. Thus the role of the female 'breadwinner' of the pre-war years was eroded in Dundee as the employment opportunities for women followed the national pattern. The patriarchal attitudes evident in the jute companies in Dundee as well as those locating in Dundee in the immediate post-war years ensured that men retained positions of authority while women worked in 'low-skilled', monotonous and repetitive jobs. Even during the more recent expansion of public administration, education and health sectors in Dundee, and also the growth of distribution, there remained a gender pay gap, with this being the case throughout Scotland and Britain.

Yet in spite of the generally male-dominated nature of the workplace, and society more broadly, Dundonian women were in specific circumstances able to illustrate their strength and independence by subverting and challenging this authority in a range of ways. A vision of working-class femininity based on such actions, while not unique to Dundee and with similar stereotypes being found throughout Britain, has nonetheless culminated in the enduring celebration of Dundee as a women's town. It is significant that Dundee celebrates its industrial heritage and the role women played in this so prominently. The high participation of Dundee's women in the workforce throughout the first half of the twentieth century was unique to the city. Such experience has endured in popular memory and has been influential in the way women are positioned in the history of Dundee. However, Dundee became less distinctive in the latter half of the twentieth century in terms of its economy and in the participation of women in the labour force. Perhaps this explains why women's role in jute and in the manufacturing industries locating in Dundee during the post-war boom is celebrated.

NOTES

1. B. Kay (ed.), *The Dundee Book: An Anthology of Living in the City* (Edinburgh, 1990), p. 10.
2. Patriarchy is a complex concept; however, in this context 'patriarchal' is used to describe the largely male-dominated nature of Dundee society in the twentieth century. Men were in the numerical minority in Dundee, yet men were dominant in the political and economic leadership of the city. This dominance was also reflected in the social and cultural norms that governed familial relations and women's place therein. For further discussion of definitions of patriarchy, see L. Segal, *Is the Future Female? Troubled Thoughts on Contemporary Feminism* (London, 1987), p. 49.
3. Women played an important role in the labour market in Dundee, yet they largely worked in unskilled occupations. In contrast, men were more prominent in skilled occupations.
4. Women's role in the formal economy of paid employment will be the main focus, although it is not the intention of this chapter to distinguish between paid and unpaid work and 'simply perpetuate gendered ideologies that have valued work in business or industry over "free" work in the home': K. Cowman and L.A. Jackson, 'Introduction. Women's work: a cultural history' in K. Cowman and L.A. Jackson (eds), *Women and Work Culture: Britain c. 1850–1950* (Aldershot, 2005), p. 2.
5. E. Gordon, *Women and the Labour Movement in Scotland, 1850–1914* (Oxford, 1991), p. 142; W.M. Walker, *Juteopolis: Dundee and its Textile Workers, 1885–1923* (Edinburgh, 1979), p. 39.
6. Ibid.
7. Gordon, *Women and the Labour Movement*, p. 141.
8. In Glasgow 25.8 per cent of married women worked in domestic service; in Aberdeen 28.2 per cent; in Edinburgh 46.8 per cent: Census of Scotland, 1911.
9. The percentage of married women in employment in Dundee was 23.4 in 1911, 24 in 1921, 33 in 1931 and 30.6 in 1951. The corresponding figures for Glasgow, which were also higher than the Scottish national average, and were the second highest after Dundee, were 5.5 in 1911, 6.1 in 1921, 7.3 in 1931 and 18.5 in 1951: Census of Scotland, 1911–1951.

10. Walker, *Juteopolis*, p. 86. By 1921 the number of married women working in jute had risen to 6,080 from 5,639 in 1911.
11. Gordon, *Women and the Labour Movement*, pp. 147–51.
12. D. Simonton, *A History of European Women's Work, 1700 to the Present* (London, 1998), p. 266.
13. DOHP, Transcript 040/A/1, Dundee Local Studies Library, interview dated 1985.
14. Walker, *Juteopolis*, p. 44.
15. Gordon, *Women and the Labour Movement*, p. 156. Also see DOHP, Transcript 021/A/2 and 040/A/1.
16. DOHP, Transcript 003/A/1.
17. E.M. Wainwright, 'Constructing gendered workplace "types": the weaver-millworker distinction in Dundee's jute industry, c. 1880–1910', *Gender, Place and Culture* 14 (2007), p. 473. Also see *Dundee Year Book* (1893), p. 176.
18. Walker, *Juteopolis*, p. 43. Also see DSU, *Report on Housing and Industrial Conditions and Medical Inspection of School Children* (Dundee, 1905), p. 49.
19. Gordon, *Women and the Labour Movement*, p. 158.
20. Walker, *Juteopolis*, p. 44.
21. Wainwright, 'Constructing gendered workplace "types"', p. 476.
22. DOHP, Transcript 022.
23. DOHP, Transcript 003/A/1.
24. DOHP, Transcript 040/A/1.
25. Gordon, *Women and the Labour Movement*, p. 159.
26. Spinning and preparing in the mill also absorbed half-time child labour, while weaving did not: Walker, *Juteopolis*, p. 45.
27. DOHP, Transcript 040/A/1.
28. DOHP, Transcript 003/A/1.
29. Walker, *Juteopolis*, p. 44.
30. Wainwright, 'Constructing gendered workplace "types"', p. 473.
31. Ibid., p. 474.
32. Interview with Sarah Craig, in B. Kay (ed.), *The Complete Odyssey: Voices from Scotland's Recent Past* (Edinburgh, 1980), p. 40.
33. Gordon, *Women and the Labour Movement*, pp. 160–1, 150.
34. DOHP, Transcript 016.
35. Gordon, *Women and the Labour Movement*, pp. 153–4.
36. Walker, *Juteopolis*, p. 45.
37. Gordon, *Women and the Labour Movement*, p. 163.
38. Walker, *Juteopolis*, p. 46.
39. Ibid., p. 40
40. Gordon, *Women and the Labour Movement*, pp. 163–4.
41. Ibid., pp. 164–5.
42. DOHP, Transcript 013. Also see Transcript 044/A.
43. DOHP, Transcript 011/A/1.
44. D.S. Riddell, 'Leisure' in J.M. Jackson (ed.), *The Third Statistical Account of Scotland*, vol. 25: *The City of Dundee* (Arbroath, 1979), p. 526.
45. Walker, *Juteopolis*, p. 45.
46. M.L. Walker, *Work Among Women* (1912), p. 74, quoted in N. Watson, 'Daughters of Dundee. Gender and Politics in Dundee: The Representation of Women 1870–1997' (unpublished PhD thesis, Open University, 2000), p. 165.

47. DUA, MS 134: D. Lennox, 'Working Class Life in Dundee for 25 years: 1878 to 1903' (unpublished manuscript, 1928), p. 132, quoted in Watson, 'Daughters of Dundee', p. 166.

48. Lennox, 'Working Class Life', p. 131 and 171 as quoted in Watson, 'Daughters of Dundee', p. 167.

49. Gordon, *Women and the Labour Movement*, p. 168.

50. K. Honeyman, *Women, Gender and Industrialisation in England, 1700–1870* (London, 2000), p. 142.

51. Gordon, *Women and the Labour Movement*, p. 168.

52. Men were outnumbered two to one in the weaving factory and ten to one in the spinning mill. Ibid., pp. 149–50.

53. Ibid., pp. 154–5.

54. E.M. Wainwright, 'Dundee's jute mills and factories: spaces of production, surveillance and discipline', *Scottish Geographical Journal* 121 (2005), p. 136.

55. DOHP, Transcript 022.

56. Walker also argues that the poor level of trade unionism in Dundee's textile industry in the late nineteenth century cannot be attributed to the high number of females in the jute industry, as men may also have had problems unionising and also 'the reversal of male and female economic roles was complete enough to promote a mode of masculinity among females', which may have 'encouraged a propensity to organise': Walker, *Juteopolis*, pp. 39 and 36.

57. Gordon, *Women and the Labour Movement*, p. 172.

58. Honeyman, *Women, Gender and Industrialisation*, p. 142.

59. Wainwright, 'Constructing gendered workplace "types"', pp. 473–4.

60. Gordon, *Women and the Labour Movement*, p. 166. Also see E.M. Wainwright, '"Constant medical supervision": locating reproductive bodies in Victorian and Edwardian Dundee', *Health and Place* 9 (2003), p. 168.

61. DSU, *Report*, p. 68.

62. Wainwright, 'Constructing gendered workplace "types"', p. 168.

63. The law stated that women were not able to return to work before their child was a month old, yet 'Dundee women broke the law with impunity': Walker, *Juteopolis*, p. 106.

64. R. Morrison, 'Poverty, distress and social agencies' in Jackson (ed.), *Third Statistical Account: Dundee*, p. 612.

65. Gordon, *Women and the Labour Movement*, p. 152.

66. G. Braybon (ed.), *Evidence, History and the Great War: Historians and the Impact of 1914–18* (Oxford, 2003), p. 13.

67. Ibid.; P. Summerfield, 'Women and war in the twentieth century' in J. Purvis (ed.), *Women's History: Britain, 1850–1945* (London, UCL Press, 1995), pp. 307–32 and G. Braybon and P. Summerfield, *Out of the Cage: Women's Experiences in Two World Wars* (London, 1987).

68. The government later revised such legislation to allow women to work until 11 p.m. in order that industries could fully implement double day shifts 'to meet production needs'. TNA: PRO CAB 129/19: Ministry of Labour and National Service, *Report of Committee on Double Day Shift Working* (1947).

69. J. Arnott, 'Women Workers and Trade Union Participation in Scotland 1919–1939' (unpublished PhD thesis, University of Glasgow, 1999), p. 305.

70. The Scottish average was 4.8 per cent in 1921 and 6.4 per cent in 1931: Census of Scotland.

71. Arnott, 'Women Workers', pp. 295, 255.

72. Ibid., p. 301.

73. See Walker, *Juteopolis*, ch. 11.

74. Arnott, 'Women Workers', pp. 311–12.

75. Walker, *Juteopolis*, p. 529.

76. DOHP, Transcript 044.

77. Walker, *Juteopolis*, p. 529.

78. Arnott, 'Women Workers', p. 315.

79. Ibid., p. 316.

80. DOHP, Transcript 003/A/1.

81. Arnott, 'Women Workers', p. 319. The first strike was called to voice dissatisfaction with supervision methods and the second strike was to protest against the inferior quality of yarn supplied to the weavers.

82. A.M. Scott, *Modern Dundee: Life in the City since World War Two* (Derby, 2002), p. 22.

83. Ibid.

84. C. Morelli and J. Tomlinson, 'Women and work after the Second World War: a case study of the jute industry, circa 1945–1954', *Twentieth Century British History* 19 (2008), p. 64.

85. DUA, MS 66/10/1/4/5: Jute Industries, General Committee Minute Book, 9 May 1946.

86. Braybon and Summerfield, *Out of the Cage*, p. 263.

87. Morelli and Tomlinson, 'Women and work after the Second World War', pp. 69–70; Jackson (ed.), *Third Statistical Account: Dundee*, p. 414.

88. Morelli and Tomlinson, 'Women and work after the Second World War', p. 70.

89. In 1947 1,600 men and 1,344 women were employed in new industries recently located in Dundee; by 1949 the total was 4,000. Morelli and Tomlinson, 'Women and work after the Second World War', p. 76. Mr McHugh of Dundee Corporation argued that this was a record 'which could not be equalled anywhere else in Britain' with Dundee 'bidding fair' to become 'the Birmingham of Scotland': *The Scotsman*, 25 September 1947.

90. DUA, MS 66/10/1/4/4: Jute Industries, General Committee Minute Book, 27 February 1942, 19 November 1943, 15 September 1944, 1 December 1944, 14 September 1945, 3 January 1946.

91. DUA, MS 66/10/1/4/5: Jute Industries, General Committee Minute Book, 27 November 1947, 8 January 1948, 5 February 1948, 1 July 1948, 19 May 1949, 29 September 1949.

92. DUA, MS 66/10/1/4/5: Jute Industries, General Committee Minute Book, 1 July 1948.

93. DUA, MS 66/10/1/4/5: Jute Industries, General Committee Minute Book, 19 May 1949.

94. Gordon, *Women and the Labour Movement*, pp. 166–7.

95. For example, the Lancashire cotton industry, which was also keen to attract more women, offered part-time work and was therefore more flexible in terms of taking into account the 'double burden' of women's work in the home and workplace.

96. Cowman and Jackson, 'Introduction' in *Women and Work Culture*, p. 7.

97. Morelli and Tomlinson, 'Women and work after the Second World War', p. 71.

98. As its attempts to entice female workers back into jute failed, the industry simultaneously opposed further expansion of the Corporation's policy of attracting new industry.

99. Morelli and Tomlinson, 'Women and work after the Second World War', p. 71.

100. W. Stewart Howe, *The Dundee Textiles Industry, 1960–1977: Decline and Diversification* (Aberdeen, 1982), p. 145.

101. DOHP, Transcript 044/A/1, Dundee Local Studies Library, interview dated 1985.

102. DUA, MS 84/7/1: Association of Jute Spinners and Manufacturers (AJSM), Minutes of Joint Meetings with workers' representatives, 11 May 1961.

103. Simonton, *History of European Women's Work*, p. 263.

104. DUA, MS 84/7/1: AJSM, Minutes of Joint Meetings with workers' representatives, 4 March 1952, 28 April 1952, 25 August 1952, 8 December 1952, 22 December 1952, 30 January 1952, 23 April 1953, 14 April 1954, 21 February 1955, 5 May 1955, 27 February 1956, 13 May 1959.

105. Quoted in Cowman and Jackson, 'Introduction' in *Women and Work Culture*, p. 2.

106. In 1981 31,163 women were in employment in Dundee, declining to 29,376 in 1991 and 26,002 in 2001. Census of Population, 1971–2001.

107. Women accounted for 44.6 per cent of the workforce in 1981 and 48.2 per cent in 2001. Census of Population, 1971–2001.

108. See Bill Knox and A. McKinlay, 'The Union Makes us Strong? Work and Trade Unionism in Timex, 1946–83', Chapter 11 in this volume, for further details.

109. Simonton, *History of European Women's Work*, p. 230.

110. Ibid., p. 231.

111. Knox and McKinlay, Chapter 11 in this volume.

112. Simonton, *History of European Women's Work*, p. 228.

113. Ibid., p. 229.

114. Ibid., p. 263.

115. Arnott, 'Women Workers', p. 84.

116. G. Anderson (ed.), *The White Blouse Revolution: Female Office Workers since 1870* (Manchester, 1988), p. 2.

117. Ibid., p. 11.

118. Arnott, 'Women Workers', p. 85.

119. For the conditions of women's clerical employment following the First and Second World Wars see Braybon and Summerfield, *Out of the Cage*, pp. 127, 181 and 261.

120. Anderson (ed.), *White Blouse Revolution*, p. 9.

121. Honeyman, *Women, Gender and Industrialisation*, p. 145.

122. Anderson (ed.), *White Blouse Revolution*, p. 15.

123. DOHP, Transcript 044.

124. *The Piper O' Dundee*, 5 January 1906 and 12 January 1906. Advertisements repeated in weekly issues.

125. DOHP, Testimony 011/A/1.

126. Anderson (ed.), *White Blouse Revolution*, p. 14.

127. Ibid., p. 15.

128. R. Crompton, 'Feminisation and the clerical labour force' in Anderson (ed.), *White Blouse Revolution*, p. 122.

129. Riddell, 'Leisure' in Jackson (ed.), *Third Statistical Account: Dundee*, p. 477.

130. Ibid., p. 478.

131. Women have also been represented in a range of professions in Dundee, as was and is illustrated by the presence of a branch of the Soroptimists in Dundee from 1932 to the present day. Only one woman is admitted from each profession or career to the organisation. By 1938 there were fifty-six members: Watson, 'Daughters of Dundee',

pp. 214 and 224. Also see S. Browne and J. Tomlinson, 'A Women's Town? Dundee Women on the Public Stage', Chapter 5 in this volume.

132. C. Whatley, C.B. Swinfen and A.M. Smith, *The Life and Times of Dundee* (Edinburgh, 1993), p. 185.

133. Jackson (ed.), *Third Statistical Account: Dundee*, p. 193.

134. DCC, City Development Department, *Dundee Economic Profile*, December 2009.

135. Due to the restrictions of space, omissions include Valentines card factory and Keiller's confectioners, both of which employed large numbers of women, as well as D.C. Thomson, the infamously secretive publisher of newspapers, magazines and comics.

136. DCC, City Development Department, *Dundee Economic Profile*, December 2009.

137. Wainwright, 'Constructing gendered workplace "types"', p. 470.

CHAPTER 7

Dundee:
Art, Artists and their Public from 1900

Matthew Jarron

Well-nigh a generation ago there began to arise a not inconsiderable art movement in Dundee. To a Public Library and Museum was added a Picture Gallery, which by and by had to be enlarged; and their capable and enthusiastic organiser . . . greatly daring, began a series of picture exhibitions. This was the golden age; with new factories and new big houses going up everywhere, and more space and ease even in a good many older ones; so the pictures sold well; new ones came in accordingly, and went off in their turn, till the sales and shows were second to none out of London itself.[1]

Writing in 1907, Patrick Geddes was here describing the extraordinary artistic renaissance that Dundee had undergone in the late nineteenth century. Geddes had come to the city in 1888 to take up the chair of botany at the new University College, but quickly extended his interests into helping to foster Dundee's burgeoning art culture. His chief artistic protégé was the painter John Duncan, who also wrote about this artistic development in the city. At an address given in 1911, he claimed that by the last decade of the previous century, 'Dundee had had a run of fine Exhibitions that were equal to anything outside London. The most distinguished works by the most distinguished artists had been ours to love and live with. The best artists of the country were coming and going amongst us, the guests of our merchant princes; and the fame of Dundee as an art centre was spread far and wide.'[2]

This fame was certainly apparent in the art world. In 1890, when the

163

Dundee Graphic Arts Association was founded, many artists wrote to express their opinions in the most enthusiastic terms. John Pettie claimed that 'Dundee has been and is one of the art centres of the North.' John MacWhirter wrote: 'The men of Dundee are an example to other towns in their love of art, and the vigorous way in which they show it.' William Hole described the 'energy, enterprise and artistic appreciation of Dundee', and William Darling McKay concluded that Dundee was 'perhaps the most vital centre of art appreciation in Scotland'.[3]

A century later, Dundee has once again established a reputation for the vibrancy of its art culture, with Dundee Contemporary Arts chosen to curate Scotland's entry in the 2009 Venice Biennale; the city's permanent art collections awarded Recognised status by the Scottish Government; and the leading contemporary art magazine *MAP* relocating to Duncan of Jordanstone College of Art & Design, now one of the largest and most prestigious art colleges in the UK.[4]

But what happened in between? Robert McGilvray, who played a crucial role in the city's artistic revival in the 1970s and 1980s, states that Dundee was 'considered more of a cultural backwater than a City of Discovery'.[5] John Kirkwood, who studied at Duncan of Jordanstone in the 1960s, asks, 'What was the visual arts [in Dundee]? There was nothing, nothing at all.'[6] And as early as 1934, one of the city's leading painters, Stewart Carmichael, had declared, 'Art appreciation in Dundee is dead.'[7]

This chapter will examine the changing fortunes of art culture in Dundee, attempting to explain its apparent decline and subsequent renewal, and arguing that while artistic activity in the city continued unabated, the changing economic climate had a considerable impact on the nature of that activity. It will also point out that the increasing polarity of fine art and commercial art has led Dundee's success in the latter to be overlooked.

By 1900, art had become a significant part of the cultural life of Dundee. The huge success of the flax and jute industries led to a massive population increase, which in turn created a demand for cultural and social activities and civic amenities. Wealthy businessmen built up large art collections of their own but also came together to organise block-buster exhibitions that are thought to have been the largest outside London.[8] The success of these led to major extensions of the city's museum, the Albert Institute, the most significant being the addition of the Victoria Art Galleries in 1889.[9]

An important development of art education was also under way at this time. Since 1856 Dundee had had a small art school operating out of the High School. By the 1870s it was booming, thanks to a talented and influential teacher, William Grubb. Enrolments increased, as did the school's success in examinations: in 1880 it was claimed that only two other schools in Britain had achieved such good results.[10] Grubb would soon have competition, however, as several other art schools began to appear around Dundee, including publicly funded classes run by the Young Men's Christian Association (YMCA), the Central School of Art in the Nethergate, and the Lochee Science & Art School. By far the most successful, however, was the Dundee Technical Institute, which opened in Small's Wynd in 1888. Art classes were taught there from the start by YMCA teacher George Malcolm, but it was the appointment of Thomas Delgaty Dunn (a former assistant of Grubb's at the High School) in 1892 that saw the first provision of day classes as well as evening, and of more advanced study than had previously been offered elsewhere.

Three factors thus combined to provide a unique stimulus to the city's own artistic creativity. Firstly, a growing middle class eager to express its cultural awareness through the appreciation of art (along with a sizeable artisan class inspired by the contemporary Arts and Crafts ideals of art and decoration for all). Secondly, an impressive new museum and art gallery building up a significant permanent collection and also hosting major exhibitions featuring some of the finest art to be seen anywhere in Britain. And thirdly, the ready availability of art education for students of all classes, with various bursaries available for those who had hitherto been unable to afford such education.

It should be no surprise then, that the number of professional artists working in the city rocketed, from four in 1875 to twenty-three by 1895.[11] For the first time artists were able to organise themselves collectively, the Dundee Art Cub being formed in 1880, replaced a decade later by the more professional Dundee Graphic Arts Association. This gave artists the clout to organise their own exhibitions, life classes and fund-raising events, set up an Art Union and even create shared studio facilities of the sort that would seem revolutionary when reinvented in Dundee eight decades later.[12] Many of these artists were unexceptional, but some were outstanding. David Foggie painted portraits of working men and women with unrivalled clarity and humanity; W.B. Lamond made vigorous landscapes and seascapes that beautifully captured the blustery Angus coastline; Frank Laing was an etcher of great sensitivity and Whistlerian freedom of line.

In particular, Dundee established for the first time an artistic style of its own thanks to the influence of Patrick Geddes on a number of artists who embraced his ideas of a Celtic revival in art and design. John Duncan, Stewart Carmichael and George Dutch Davidson were the leaders of this movement, creating richly decorated historical and mythical scenes, while Celtic motifs quickly found their way into the rapidly growing field of applied art. Sadly, much of the impetus behind the movement was lost with the premature death of Davidson at the age of only twenty-one.

Contemporary reviews indicate that the Celtic style was recognised if not necessarily appreciated. Referring in 1901 to a painting by Charles Mills (who also died at an early age, just a short time after Davidson), the art critic of the magazine *The Piper o' Dundee* said: 'This little picture, so beautifully drawn and coloured, was in itself a sufficient justification for the existence of the harshly derided Dundee Celtic School.'[13]

A greater problem was the general lack of interest Dundonians showed in their own local talent. Writing in 1907, Patrick Geddes complained:

> Glasgow has learned to respect the 'Glasgow School' now that it has 'arrived', and its members are scattered and mostly out of Scotland – but in this city [i.e. Dundee] how many yet know, care for, or even notice the steady development, these ten years past and more, of an art movement also significant, and even more genuinely of local growth? The Graphic Arts Society, and now, more lately, the Tayport Artists' Circle, have not only worked for, but fairly earned, a far wider and warmer recognition from their fellow citizens than they have yet received.[14]

This was certainly not due to a lack of interest in art. The local population came in their thousands to attend major loan exhibitions, but stayed away when the city's own artists put on their shows. And while Dundee was home to several wealthy collectors looking to acquire Scottish contemporary art to decorate their walls, it was established Edinburgh or London-based artists that they bought from rather than supporting the talent on their doorstep.

These collectors were the same people who organised the Dundee Fine Art Exhibitions and supported the Albert Institute and the development of its permanent collections. James Guthrie Orchar (whose firm manufactured textile machinery) took the lead by donating the first painting to enter the city's collection, *Old Letters* by G.P. Chalmers. He would later bequeath his entire art collection (over 300 works) to the neighbouring burgh of Broughty Ferry, where he had served as Provost for many years. Many other private collections came to less fortunate ends – business partners William Ritchie and G.B. Simpson (whose firm owned several jute works) were each forced to sell off their sizeable collections as a series of failed investments (particularly in America) left them close to bankruptcy.

For many of these collectors, art was not just a way of expressing their social status. Orchar's business partner William Robertson stated:

In a purely manufacturing town like Dundee it is of vital importance that love for and a knowledge of Art should be widely diffused, especially among the working classes . . . it is mainly on account of the want of this that foreign competition has been felt so keenly in recent years.[15]

The rapid growth of art education at the end of the nineteenth century was a partial answer to this, and the success of Delgaty Dunn's classes at the Technical Institute showed a substantial demand for art instruction among the working class. In 1895–6, 125 fees were paid by students, rising to 265 by 1901–2.[16] Although still restricted by the South Kensington system, Delgaty Dunn tried where possible to include subjects that would be of particular relevance in Dundee. One of these was 'Drawing in "Black and White" for process reproduction', reflecting the fact that the city was already becoming an important breeding ground for successful newspaper illustrators and cartoonists.[17]

Two large companies dominated the newspaper business in Dundee at the time – D.C. Thomson (originally W. & D.C. Thomson) and John Leng. In 1880 Leng had broken new ground by including regular illustrations in his daily paper, the *Dundee Advertiser*, something never successfully achieved in Britain before.[18] Fife-born illustrator Martin Anderson was employed as the company's first full-time staff artist, and he was soon introducing humorous cartoons into the papers and (from

1885) short comic strips, an extraordinary innovation.[19]

Dundee was soon producing successful cartoonists at an astonishing rate, and a small but flourishing magazine industry started to showcase their work, the most successful titles being *The Piper o' Dundee* (several runs in 1878, 1886–1901, 1905–6 and 1912–13) and *The Wizard of the North* (continuously from 1879 to 1912). At that time, however, Dundee could not compete with London. Following Anderson's success there under the pseudonym Cynicus, many other Dundee cartoonists would follow: Max Cowper, Alick P.F. Ritchie, David Burns Gray and Howard Somerville were among those finding success on *Punch*, *Illustrated London News* and other magazines, while Somerville's brothers Sydney Adamson and Penrhyn Stanlaws would enjoy notable success in America.

At that time there was little distinction made between fine art and commercial art. The very name of the Graphic Arts Association showed that its members (including Dundee's leading painters) regarded illustration as being on equal terms with painting, and many artists (such as John Duncan) worked in both fields. The steady increase in student numbers at the city's art schools was largely caused by the demand for newspaper artists.

In 1901 the Scotch Education Department commenced a major reorganisation of technical and art education – in Dundee this meant closing down the School of Art at the High School and amalgamating the YMCA classes in with the Technical Institute's. Delgaty Dunn's classes became increasingly overcrowded, and in 1907 work began on a larger building in Bell Street, to be renamed Dundee Technical College & School of Art. This coincided with a major campaign by the city's professional artists to found a proper advanced-level art school in the city. Stewart Carmichael and Frank Laing wrote eloquently in the local papers about the need for such a school, both choosing to stress its influence on the quality of manufacturing and design. Laing wrote:

[S]ome imagine fine art to be a luxury, a thing that is not utilitarian and practical. This is a mistake. Fine art is utilitarian in the highest sense. A touch of art redeems the meanest thing. The art in a thing lengthens its chances of life and extends its influence; and the principles of fine art are beneficial and helpful to all the activities of such a city as Dundee from the simple laying out of a street to that of a public park or the building of a new Town House.[20]

Two years later came what seemed to be the answer to their prayers, with the death in 1909 of local businessman James Duncan, who lived at Jordanstone House near Alyth. In his will, Duncan bequeathed part of the residue of his estate (amounting to some £60,000) to 'be applied by my trustees in founding in Dundee a School of Industrial Art, to be named and known in all time to come as the "Duncan of Jordanstone Art School"'.[21] He specified that the school should be run in conjunction with the Technical Institute, but should be separate from it. The problems with this were quickly apparent. Duncan had made his will in 1899, but by the time of his death most of the subjects he expected it to teach were already well catered for by the Technical College. The College's trustees therefore made a swift bid for the money, drawing up a plan to site the school on Ireland's Lane, immediately adjacent to the new College on Bell Street.

It soon became clear, however, that the Technical College and the Duncan trustees were unable to come to an agreement, and for the next twenty-five years the bequest would remain in dispute. At the time of his retirement in 1927, Delgaty Dunn was still hoping for increased accommodation for the School 'as a result of the Duncan of Jordanstone Bequest'.[22] In the meantime, the city's aspiring artists had to be content with the new Bell Street College, which was able to offer accommodation six times the size of that of its predecessor. Several new staff were employed, most notably John Milne Purvis as Head of Drawing & Painting. But despite its impressive facilities, the new School of Art was still only able to offer the first two years of the Diploma course – students would have to go to Edinburgh or Glasgow to complete their training.

During the 1910s the School of Art began to establish itself as a major centre for the city's art culture. Regular social events such as fancy-dress balls or dramatic performances were widely reported in the press, making Dundee publicly aware of its art students in a way that had never happened before. The Graphic Arts Association had been renamed Dundee Art Society in 1904, and its membership now came to be dominated by staff and former students of the School of Art. A significant change was under way in the type of student attending the school. Back in 1904–5, Principal Lumsden had written that 'fine art is of very secondary importance with us. Most of our students are artisans in the engineering, building and textile trades . . . there are practically no purely art students.'[23] Sixteen years later, however, the College syllabus would claim that 'Many of the art students attend for the love of making artistic things, and what they do has no relation to their daily employment.'[24]

In 1915 the school was given permission to teach the full four-year Diploma course in Design, but it would be another fourteen years before Dundee could offer the equivalent in Painting. The most promising of the new generation of artists (like James McIntosh Patrick) were still forced to study elsewhere. Patrick returned to the city, but other notable artists (like the sculptor William Turnbull) did not.

In 1927 Delgaty Dunn retired and Francis Cooper took his place as head of the School of Art. Extremely conservative when it came to the rules and regulations of the school (he deplored the bohemian style and dress of his students and staff), he nevertheless had the vision and political astuteness necessary to take the school to the next level. His first mission was to expand the Drawing & Painting department so that from 1929 the school could finally offer a Diploma in Painting. Recognising that this put Dundee in competition with the other Scottish art schools, he chose a number of highly talented young painters to ensure a high standard of teaching – these included Dundonians James McIntosh Patrick and Talbert McLean (a former student at the school) and Montrose-born Edward Baird. All of these embraced modernism in art in a way that Cooper himself could never have done.

Cooper did follow Delgaty Dunn's lead in placing the school at the heart of the city's artistic life. Many of the staff (particularly John Milne Purvis, Alex Russell and William Armstrong Davidson) became actively involved in public and private commissions for the city. These included stained glass for churches and the new City Chambers, murals for Dundee Rep Theatre, and portraits of provosts and other local worthies. All of this was work that thirty years previously would almost certainly have gone to artists from Edinburgh or further afield.

Cooper's most significant achievement, however, was to win the battle over the Duncan of Jordanstone Bequest. The Education Endowments Act (1928) allowed for a fresh assault, and following lengthy discussions from 1931 to 1934 the Technical College was eventually reorganised as Dundee Institute of Art & Technology, with Dundee

College of Art (as it was now known) having enough autonomy within that to meet the demands of the Duncan trustees. In 1935 the Belmont site on Perth Road was acquired and two years later a nationwide competition was held to find the best design for the new building. The winner (from more than seventy submissions) was Glamorgan-based architect James Wallace, whose plans were approved in 1938. By this time the costs had risen to over £110,000, and it was only when the Scottish Education Department came up with an additional grant of £35,000 that the plans could go ahead. Just as everything was ready to go, the war intervened and the whole scheme was mothballed.

The late 1930s saw an artistic landmark of another kind – the birth of the *Dandy* and the *Beano*. By that time the major publishing empires of Thomson and Leng had merged and, using the combined talents of their art departments, had built up an impressive list of successful children's magazines dating back to the launch of *Adventure* in 1921. Joined by the *Rover* (1922), the *Wizard* (1922), the *Skipper* (1930) and the *Hotspur* (1933), Thomson's so-called 'Big Five' established them as a major rival to the biggest children's publishers elsewhere. Previously Dundee had lost most of its best cartoonists to London – now artists were coming to Dundee from throughout the country. The most famous of these was Dudley D. Watkins, born and educated in Nottingham. At the age of eighteen he was spotted by one of Thomson's talent scouts and signed up for a six-month trial, which would turn into a forty-four-year career.[25]

It was the popularity of Watkins's weekly comic strips 'The Broons' and 'Oor Wullie' in the *Sunday Post* that convinced Thomson's head of children's publications, Robert D. Low, to launch *The Dandy* in 1937 – the first publication to make humorous cartoon strips the main feature, rather than the text-based adventure stories that dominated the Big Five. Its instant success led to the *Beano* (1938) and the *Magic* (1939), and while the latter became a victim of wartime cutbacks, its two predecessors have gone on to become the world's longest-running comics. Although their full cultural influence in Britain has yet to be examined in detail, they have certainly helped to give Dundee international status as one of the world's five leading centres of the comics industry.[26]

The city had another major employer of artists in Valentines, who in 1937 opened a new expanded factory on the Kingsway. Founded in Dundee as a printing business by John Valentine in 1825, it was transformed by his brother James into a leading photographic company. By the start of the twentieth century Valentines was Britain's foremost producer of picture postcards, and soon began to branch out into Christmas and greetings cards. As well as commissioning designs from well-known illustrators around the country (most notably Mabel Lucie Atwell), the company employed dozens of artists in its Dundee headquarters to mass-produce original images on an assembly-line scale.

By the 1930s Valentines and D.C. Thomson were two of the largest employers in the city, the jute industry desperately struggling against competition from India and a fall in demand. Unemployment reached an all-time high (over 37,000 in 1932) as the Depression hit Dundee hard.[27] But the effect of this in the art world was not immediately apparent. The number of professional artists listed in the Dundee Directories remained at around twenty-five throughout the decade. Crowds continued to flock to exhibitions at Dundee Art Galleries & Museum (which the Albert Institute and Victoria Galleries were now called).[28] The difference was that they were no longer spending money. Over 2,500 people visited the museum for free on Sunday 8 April 1934, of which a mere seven were willing to pay the 7d charged to see the Dundee Art Society's biennial exhibition. 'I don't like to think that Dundee is so unfortunately below the standard of other towns in art culture', Stewart Carmichael commented, 'But it really does seem as if appreciation of the creative spirit is absent in Dundee.'[29]

Certainly Dundee was no longer producing the same number of wealthy art patrons who had once done so much to stimulate art culture in the city. Among the last was William Boyd, managing director of the famous marmalade manufacturers James Keiller & Son.[30] During the 1910s he had followed the tastes of earlier Dundee collectors in mainly buying work by Scottish artists, but after retiring in 1920 he began to set his sights altogether higher. Modern French painting became a particular passion and over the next ten years he bought works by (among others) Monet, Vuillard, Bonnard and Matisse. His collection of Van Goghs was unrivalled in Scotland and he sold one of them in order to endow a Chair of Dental Surgery at University College, Dundee in 1936.[31]

Dentistry was where the most influential patron of art in 1930s Dundee had made his money. John Robertson had run the successful Dundee Teeth Depot in Victoria Road where he liked to decorate the waiting room with highlights from his collection (which was particularly strong in works by the Carnoustie painter Robert Gemmel Hutchison). After handing the business over to his son, Robertson began to indulge his passion for art full-time. In 1927 he became a professional art dealer, running the Panmure Art Salon in Commercial Street. It was home to an extraordinary variety of exhibitions, from Corot to Peploe. Perhaps most unusual was a 1938 exhibition of original celluloid paintings from Disney's *Snow White and the Seven Dwarfs*, which must have been a particular thrill for the cartoonists working at D.C. Thomson. Robertson was also actively involved in the Dundee Fine Art Association, which acquired work for the permanent collections of Dundee Art Galleries & Museum, and he organised major exhibitions there by some of Britain's leading painters, including Philip de Laszlo (1932), Sir John Lavery (1936) and W. Russell Flint (1938), all of whom were personal friends. In 1934 he organised a major loan exhibition from private collections around the country as a fundraiser for Dundee Royal Infirmary. Comprising 186 works, it was a deliberate attempt to emulate the blockbuster shows of the previous generation.

Robertson and Boyd both died in the early 1940s at a time when one might have expected the war to preclude much in the way of artistic activity. In fact, the opposite seems to have been the case. The Dundee Art Society reported record membership numbers (well over 300) and although several of their leading members were absent (in 1940 McIntosh Patrick served just six months as president of the society before joining the army), their social activities continued as successfully as ever.[32] One obvious result of the fear of bombing was that the most valuable treasures from the city's art collection were removed to the country for safety. Instead, the museum showed touring exhibitions organised by the Ministry of Information or the Council for the Encouragement of Music and the Arts. Many of these were on topical themes such as methods of camouflage, and occasionally they had local relevance – in 1944 they showed paintings by Dundee College of Art graduate Ian Eadie, who was with the 51st Highland Division at El Alamein.

The decade following the end of the war was one of change and expansion in Dundee's art world. In 1949 the museum gained its first professional curator (having previously been run by the city librarian) – thirty-one-year-old James D. Boyd was an artist himself (a graduate of Glasgow School of Art) and encouraged more contemporary art collecting. Over the next few years, works by Joan Eardley, William

Gillies, Anne Redpath, Dame Laura Knight and Stanley Spencer were among those purchased for the city's collection.

At D.C. Thomson, the end of rationing and the post-war baby boom combined to see sales of the *Dandy* and the *Beano* reach an all-time high in the early 1950s.[33] This success led to the introduction of new titles such as the *Topper* (1953) and the *Beezer* (1956). Meanwhile a new generation of artists was responsible for transforming the *Beano* into the most radical comic in Britain – David Law's 'Dennis the Menace', Ken Reid's 'Roger the Dodger' and Leo Baxendale's 'Minnie the Minx' and 'The Bash Street Kids' were surreal and chaotic and changed the style of comic art irrevocably. It is no coincidence that all these characters are still popular favourites today.

At the Art College, construction finally got under way on the new Perth Road building in 1953, with Francis Cooper retiring as Principal a few months after the foundation stone was laid. In his last few years, Cooper had recruited a number of highly talented new tutors including painter Alberto Morrocco, sculptor Scott Sutherland and silversmith Bernard Harrington. Under the dynamic leadership of Cooper's successor, Hugh Adam Crawford, the new College (which would soon be renamed Duncan of Jordanstone College) opened in 1955 and quickly built up a reputation far exceeding anything that had been possible before. At a time when the other Scottish colleges were regarded as closed shops, employing only their own graduates to teach there, Dundee cast a wider net for the best talent, bringing David McClure from Edinburgh, Gordon Cameron from Aberdeen and many others.

The Art College increasingly came to be seen as the centre of Dundee's artistic and cultural life. In the 1960s, regular social activities such as the Revels or the Jazz Band Ball drew huge audiences, and attracted considerable musical talent to perform at them, from Pink Floyd to Sonny Boy Williamson. A film society thrived and students were able to make use of the Tivoli Theatre on Bonnybank Road, guaranteeing the owners an audience for foreign and arthouse films that might otherwise never have been shown in the city.

Ironically, all this activity came at a time when opportunities for graduating art students were shrinking rapidly. The commercial galleries that had once been numerous in Dundee had mostly closed – there had been eleven before the war but this gradually dwindled until 1965 when just one remained, Fraser & Sons in Commercial Street. It continued to show some new work but, as painter Joe McIntyre recalled, 'they never actually engaged with the artists'.[34] The new industries that came to Dundee after the war offered occasional commissions (for example NCR's new factory opened in 1949 with an impressive mural designed by Gertrude Scales), but these were few and far between. As Peter Lloyd (who graduated from the Art College in 1957) recalled, 'At that time probably 90 per cent of graduates were destined to be art teachers. Most ended up in secondary schools, the best were taken on as part time Lecturers in the Colleges.'[35] Lloyd opted instead for a career as a commercial artist, working for the George Outram Group (printers and publishers) at £7 per week. He claims that the Art College still made little distinction then between fine art and commercial art, employing D.C. Thomson artists to run evening classes teaching Illustration.[36] This did not include cartoon art, and as Lloyd recalled: 'We did tend to look down on the people who worked on the *Dandy* and *Beano* cartoons although one of the people in my year ended up doing just that.'[37] Another example of this can be seen in the *Courier Artists' Exhibition* held at Dundee Art Galleries & Museum in November 1957 – it featured work by thirteen D.C. Thomson illustrators but cartoons were notably absent.[38]

The lack of commercial galleries was not a problem unique to Dundee – across Scotland there were only a handful, and those in Edinburgh and Glasgow were largely booked up by staff from their respective colleges and the established elite of the Royal Scottish Academy. Dundee Art Galleries & Museum continued to be the prime opportunity for the city's artists to show their work to a wider public. In 1968 the museum employed its first Keeper of Art, twenty-six-year-old William Hardie, who took an immediate interest in Dundee's contemporary art scene, staging exhibitions such as *Three Tayside Painters* (1964, featuring recent College graduates Alan Buick, John Johnstone and Elliot Rudie) and the influential Scottish Arts Council-funded touring show *Seven Painters in Dundee* (1970, featuring College tutors and graduates Neil Dallas Brown, Dennis Buchan, Peter Collins, Ian Fearn, James Howie, Jack Knox and James Morrison). Hardie purchased key works by many of these artists for the city collection, and also undertook significant research into Dundee's own art history, bringing back to prominence long-forgotten artists such as George Dutch Davidson with the exhibition *The Hills of Dream Revisited* (1974). At the same time the

University of Dundee began actively acquiring major works of Scottish art (though rarely by Dundee artists) thanks to a bequest from former student James Lamb.

Dundee artists were also now being represented to a far greater extent in national and international exhibitions, such as *Young Scottish Contemporaries* (Edinburgh 1963, including Brown, Buchan, Fearn, Howie and Lilian Neilson) or Neil Dallas Brown's inclusion in *Seven Scottish Painters* (New York 1965) alongside the likes of Joan Eardley and Robin Philipson. At a 1965 exhibition of work from the four Scottish art colleges for the Commonwealth Festival in Glasgow, *The Scotsman*'s art critic Emilio Coia claimed that 'the Dundee artists are by far the most impressive'.[39]

The Dundee Art Society continued to provide an important platform for the city's artists, their biennial exhibitions still being staged at Dundee Art Galleries & Museum. In 1964 *The Scotsman* described the society as 'one of the strongest in Scotland . . . among its own members Dundee Art Society have a roll-call that sounds like a miniature Establishment all on its own.'[40] These included Art College tutors such as Morrocco, McClure and Patrick as well as leading secondary school art teachers like Alexander Allan, Hamish Soutar and William Vannet.

By this time Dundee had built up a considerable reputation as the most exciting place in Scotland to study Drawing & Painting.[41] Despite fewer resources than the art schools in Edinburgh or Glasgow, Duncan of Jordanstone College boasted a teaching staff of rare quality and variety. Their own work was giving Dundee art a reputation it hadn't enjoyed for over half a century – from the bright colours and expressive brushwork of Alberto Morrocco and David McClure through the symbolic figurative and abstract work of Neil Dallas Brown and Jack Knox to the meticulous landscapes of McIntosh Patrick and James Morrison and the metaphysical realism of Peter Collins. The work of Design and Sculpture staff had also gained prominence, such as Joseph McKenzie's haunting photographs of the demolition of the old Hawkhill tenements (1964–6), or Scott Sutherland's major commissions to build the Commando Memorial at Spean Bridge (1952) and the Black Watch Memorial just outside Dundee (1959).

To make a living as an artist in Dundee without resorting to commercial work or substantial hours of teaching was almost impossible – James Howie perhaps came closest to it in the 1960s, and was looked on as something of a role model by the next generation of young artists. He had a significant reputation thanks to sell-out exhibitions at the Whitechapel Gallery in London and an appearance on the BBC's arts programme *Monitor*.[42] Howie was one of many established artists who regularly gathered in the back of Livingstone's art shop in Bell Street. Painter John Johnstone recalls: 'It was quite funny for young people like myself to see all these bearded beatniks in the back of this shop in Bell Street, talking to the lady Pat Holmes who ran it. And every now and then Pat would give them some money and they would go to the pub next door.'[43]

But for most Art College graduates, it was still standard practice to move away from Dundee – often to London, as even Edinburgh and Glasgow offered few opportunities for professional artists. In 1975 a small group of recent graduates led by Robert McGilvray decided they wanted to stay in Dundee, having been tipped off by staff at the College that the Scottish Arts Council was considering the idea of funding shared studio facilities for artists. McGilvray recalls:

> Gordon [Cameron] tipped us off about that, and Jack Knox was on the Arts Council panel at the time so I spoke to Jack about it . . . and he said 'if you find a property then they'll look at it' and of course we found the property which was easy in Dundee, I mean there were loads of empty buildings . . . So we got this school, St Mary's, Forebank, and went back to the Arts Council and [they] took a fright – 'Ahh, it's in Dundee, this shouldn't happen, this should only happen in Edinburgh or Glasgow.'[44]

McGilvray managed to convince the Arts Council that there would be suitable demand but faced a further hurdle when they insisted that someone from Edinburgh or Glasgow would have to be brought up to run the studio. Once again McGilvray had to persuade them that Dundee was capable of managing things on its own. Renamed the Forebank Studios, the building opened in late 1975 with McGilvray as administrator. The first independent, shared studio facility in Scotland, it would prove the model for WASPS (Workshop & Artists' Studio Provision Scotland), a nationwide charity supported by the Scottish Arts Council that now has seventeen studio spaces across Scotland.

With Forebank Studios up and running, the next step was to form the artists using it into a formal organisation, the Dundee Group (Artists) Ltd. In the catalogue for their first touring exhibition, McGilvray explained the logic behind this:

> The Dundee Group came about quite naturally as a result of the platform or 'Common Ground' provided by the studios. It had long been felt that little was known of the artistic activity (probably because of its sporadic nature) both in Dundee and throughout the country. Subsequently, the idea of an organisation that could facilitate the movement of artists and [their] work and thus create an interest both locally and elsewhere, seemed the natural course to take.[45]

Support came initially from the Scottish Arts Council and then Tayside Regional Council. The Forebank Gallery was set up at the studio and the first exhibition of the Group's work was held in February 1978, just three months after its formal constitution. Twelve artists were represented; by the time of the Group's first touring show the following year, this had risen to seventeen (fifteen of whom were Duncan of Jordanstone graduates). The Group was soon involved in exhibition exchanges with similar groups in Cardiff, Exeter, Belfast and even Canada; Sandra McNeilance, another Duncan of Jordanstone graduate, acted as gallery organiser. To encourage the public to visit, the gallery hosted occasional crowd-pleasing shows such as photographs of old Dundee from the Central Library's collection.

At the same time, the Dundee Printmakers Workshop (DPW) was being formed at the new Dudhope Arts Centre in St Mary Place, its inaugural exhibition being held there in November 1977. DPW followed the pattern of open-access print studios in the other Scottish cities in the facilities offered to artists, but also undertook substantial community outreach through adult classes, school projects and exhibitions in a range of venues. Run initially by Donald MacKenzie, the facility struggled to survive at first, but took off after a successful re-launch by new manager Norrie Colston in 1979.[46] His ambitious yet businesslike approach ensured commercial success for the Workshop, which was soon attracting financial support from (among others) the Royal Bank of Scotland, at a time when business sponsorship of the arts was a largely unrealised concept. DPW was soon getting involved in ambitious projects like the Tayside Print Loan Scheme. Launched in 1978 by the regional council, it circulated significant contemporary artists' prints around public buildings throughout Tayside.[47]

All this renewed artistic activity was taking place against a backdrop of increasing economic hardship and social deprivation in Dundee. Many of the new post-war industries that had come to the city were now cutting back on staff, and the end of import protection saw the jute industry go into terminal decline. Even the major commercial employers were suffering – Valentines had been taken over by Waddington in 1963 then Hallmark in 1980, the Dundee factory closing for good in 1994; D.C. Thomson also found their comic empire slowly contracting as TV and video games provided children with alternative forms of entertainment. But with considerable perspicacity, in the early 1980s the local and regional authorities recognised the potential of art to spearhead the city's economic revival.

In 1976 Robert McGilvray had been commissioned by the Dundee Housing Association (with financial support and some arm-twisting from the Scottish Arts Council) to create two gable-end murals for council houses in Wolsely Street and Court Street. This was at a time when the term 'public art' was only just beginning to be used, but community art schemes were increasingly getting Arts Council support, particularly in new towns such as Glenrothes. Liz Kemp, an artist and exhibitions assistant at Dundee Art Galleries & Museum, had been involved in one such scheme in the Craigmillar area of Edinburgh. In 1981 she began discussions with Alan Lodge of the town planning department concerning the potential role of artists in a new programme of environmental improvements that had just been approved for the Blackness area of Dundee. As one of the densest areas of industrial activity a century before, Blackness was now left with dozens of empty, derelict buildings. The Blackness Business Development Area scheme was initiated with more than £2 million to spend on the area. An integral part of this was the Blackness Public Art Programme, a three-year, £90,000 project funded by the District Council, the Scottish Development Agency and the Scottish Arts Council. The programme was revolutionary – artists, architects, planners and engineers worked together to create a unified approach to the visual transformation of the area. Robert McGilvray, the co-ordinator of the programme, described how this worked:

A pioneering, consultative design process was developed whereby artists weren't simply given a brief and sent away; on the contrary, each project was carefully monitored with several interim progress meetings attended by the management group and the client. The most important stage was the design period, which involved full consultation among all the parties at all meetings. Artists were seen as conduits to the community, public and private, ensuring their full consultation and inclusion in the design-making process, from concept to completion. This approach avoided the all-too-common practice of 'parachuting-in' [the artwork] to great fanfare and subsequent local derision and political panic. The artwork instead came in with the bricks and mortar, the trees, the shrubs, and the benches.[48]

The programme became a model of innovative practice that would be copied throughout Scotland and attracted considerable critical attention.[49] In total, sixteen separate projects were completed during the three-year period, including Keith Donnelly's Saltire Award-winning ceramic panels on Bellfield Street. More important than any architectural prize, however, was the success of the project in its original aim – to regenerate the area by attracting new businesses (though ironically this sometimes meant demol-ishing the buildings on which the artworks were sited to create purpose-built industrial units). This success encouraged the local authority to continue the project, expanding it to become the city-wide Dundee Public Art Programme, formally established as a limited company in 1988.

As public art was such a new field when the Blackness programme started, most of the artists involved were brought in from elsewhere, such as Stan Bonner and John Gray, both of whom had worked in Glenrothes. Recognising the potential for developing new talent in this field, the Head of Design at Duncan of Jordanstone College, Atholl Hill, initiated a postgraduate course in Public Art & Design. The first of its kind in Britain, it was run for many years by Ronald Forbes, who served along with Hill on the Dundee Public Art Programme management group. Another Art College tutor, sculptor Gareth Fisher, chaired the group during its initial period of city-wide expansion, and did much to foster its ambitions and win national recognition for its work.

By this time Forebank Studios had closed and its artists had moved to larger premises at Meadowmill, the Dundee Group becoming part of

WASPS. Dundee Printmakers Workshop was also expanding and in 1986 the two groups came together to found the Seagate Gallery in a derelict whisky bond close to the city centre, a major step forward in Dundee's cultural renaissance.[50] Its inaugural exhibition was staged by Duncan of Jordanstone graduate David Mach, who was already building an international reputation for his audacious sculptural works. Over the next twelve years the Seagate would host an ambitious programme of exhibitions (organised originally by Robert McGilvray then Dave Jackson) which showcased the work of local artists but also brought in high-quality contemporary art from elsewhere. An innovative education and events programme helped the gallery to engage with a far wider audience than had hitherto been possible.

The Seagate not only brought the work of Dundee artists to greater prominence but also encouraged the city museum (now renamed McManus Galleries) to purchase more contemporary artworks. Under new art curator Clara Young, the McManus Galleries' exhibition programme was then at its liveliest, and included major retrospectives of McIntosh Patrick (1987) and Alberto Morrocco (1993).[51] As well as showing a wide range of modern art, the galleries undertook a major re-hang of their nineteenth and early twentieth-century art to mark the centenary of the Victoria Galleries. The new display incorporated highlights from J.G. Orchar's collection, which was transferred to the McManus in 1987 after its previous home, the Orchar Gallery in Broughty Ferry, was forced to close.

At the same time, a programme for contemporary art exhibitions was also being developed at Duncan of Jordanstone College. Based in the Francis Cooper Gallery, it was spearheaded by Myer Lacome, who had become principal of the College in 1977. Lacome's first plan was to get the local and regional authorities to support his dream to establish a major contemporary design museum on the city's waterfront:

> I believed that Dundee had a unique opportunity to have a great architectural landmark on Riverside Drive which could take the form of a museum/gallery housing a collection of internationally acclaimed twentieth-century masterpieces of design and craft . . . In my view the Tay estuary needed – and still needs – a major architectural landmark at the entrance to the city, one comparable to the Sydney Opera House, for example.[52]

Lacome had little success in getting his ideas off the ground, though they sound remarkably similar to the proposals currently being discussed for a Dundee branch of the V&A.[53] Instead, he appointed Peter Esgate, formerly a tutor in the printing department, to run an exhibitions service within the College. Starting in 1978, a regular series of exhibitions showcased the output of College staff and also brought the work of internationally renowned artists and designers to Dundee. Under Deirdre Mackenna in the 1990s and Jenny Brownrigg in the 2000s, the Exhibitions department continued to expand, attracting widespread critical attention for ambitious shows featuring leading contemporary artists such as Simon Starling and Nathan Coley, as well as helping to develop students' own experience of curatorial practice.

With so much activity, the idea of a major contemporary arts centre for Dundee had inevitably remained on the agenda; indeed, one reason that the whisky bond building had been chosen as the location for the Seagate Gallery was the idea that the rest of the building could potentially be developed into such a venue. Two feasibility studies were commissioned in the late 1980s to explore this and other options, followed by a succession of consultation documents and meetings in the early 1990s.[54] One result of these was the publication of the city's first Arts Strategy in 1994, recognising that 'arts and cultural activities can make a major contribution to "putting the heart back into the City"', a key component of this being 'the development of a City Arts Centre, primarily for the contemporary visual Arts'.[55]

Steve Grimmond, Corporate Planning Officer with the District Council (also an artist and musician) was put in charge of the arts centre project. For many, the Seagate building remained the favoured option, but the advent of the National Lottery encouraged a far more ambitious, purpose-built project on the site of the Nethergate Garage, which was purchased in 1995.[56] A limited company, Dundee City Arts Centre Ltd, was formed to bring together the key stakeholders, chiefly the local authority (now Dundee City Council), the Art College (who planned to use part of the building as a research centre) and Scottish Enterprise Tayside. Although it was clear that the Seagate Gallery would have to close when the centre opened, and the Printmakers Workshop would transfer to the new location, the gallery's board (who represented many of the practising artists of Dundee) seem to have been kept at arm's length throughout the process. On threatening to pull out from backing the project they quickly found their financial support withdrawn by both the city council and the Scottish Arts Council.

In 1996 the National Lottery Fund awarded a record sum of £5,380,756 to Dundee City Arts Centre Ltd, and a competition was held to design the building, won by Richard Murphy Architects from Edinburgh. The result was estimated to be the largest contemporary art space after the Saatchi Gallery in London. Named Dundee Contemporary Arts, it opened in 1999 and has since brought an extraordinary range of international art to the city. Only occasionally, however, has the work of Dundee artists been featured, leaving the local art community once again without a high-profile venue for its endeavours (though the Gallery's tenth anniversary saw an attampt to redress this with *The Associates* and a show by the artist collective Ganghut).[57]

To counter this, the last ten years have seen an increase in the number of commercial galleries attempting to operate in Dundee, with established operations like the Queen's Gallery on Nethergate joined, albeit briefly, by newcomers such as Nael Hanna's Gallery on South Tay Street. Both the University of Dundee and the University of Abertay have also developed regular public exhibition programmes, the art collections of the former now totalling almost 4,000 pieces. Meanwhile the Dundee Art Society have continued to exhibit members' work regularly from their own gallery in Roseangle, but have increasingly become dominated by amateur painters working in traditional styles.

More experimental work has been produced through Generator Projects, a non-commercial artist-run organisation founded in 1996 in order to establish 'a platform for new, innovative and mixed artforms'. Its founding chair, Duncan of Jordanstone graduate Caz McIntee, explained:

There is a terrific art college in Dundee . . . but, as yet, there aren't that many opportunities for many of its graduates to stay in the area and set up here. As a group, we think it's important to harness the interest and talent that's coming out of the city, . . . so that all Dundee's people can benefit from having a vibrant artistic scene on the doorstep.[58]

Initially based at the Old Bakery in Nethergate, Generator held its first exhibition in a warehouse in Douglas Street in 1998, and currently runs a lively programme of events and exhibitions from a unit in the Mid Wynd Industrial Estate.

Most of the artists who have served on Generator's committee have been graduates of Duncan of Jordanstone College, which has continued to play a crucial role in the Dundee art scene. In 1994 the College became part of the University of Dundee and since then academic research has played an increasingly important role in its activities. The College's Visual Research Centre, based at Dundee Contemporary Arts, has helped Duncan of Jordanstone to be recognised as the leading art school in Scotland (and one of the top five in the UK) for its research work.[59] Among the internationally renowned artists currently working at the College are painters and Royal Scottish Academicians Calum Colvin, Edward Summerton and innovative artistic partnerships Dalziel + Scullion and Tracy Mackenna and Edwin Janssen.

It has not been all good news for Dundee's artistic renaissance. In 2003 the Dundee Public Art Programme came to an end after its core funding was withdrawn. In its twenty-one years of existence it had created well over 100 works of public art, including David Wilson's street furniture in the city centre and a set of twenty-five bronzes on the walls of the Overgate; Alastair Smart and Tony Morrow's *Dundee Dragon* on Murraygate; Alastair White's kinetic sculpture *Strange Attractor II* near the railway station on Marketgait South; and Diane Maclean's *On the Wing* outside Dundee Airport. Less successful was the programme's last major project, a scheme known as Ambassador Routes to redesign the four main road routes into the city, creating landmark visual art features that could define the city culturally. As Robert McGilvray recalled, 'the public art element of the project was never to be realised, foundering in a welter of confused thinking and a crisis of confidence on the part of the client group, just prior to the Dundee Public Art Programme closing down, having insufficient guaranteed work to cover an increasing debt'.[60]

This was not, however, the end of public art for the city. John Gray, a key member of the programme's management group, was by now working for the city council as Public Art Officer, and in 2004 the council officially adopted a Percent for Art Policy, whereby at least 1 per cent of the construction costs of any new building over £1 million will be spent on public art.

Two of the most iconic pieces of art to have appeared recently in the city centre are the sculptures of Desperate Dan and Minnie the Minx by Tony Morrow, finally giving public recognition to the immense cultural contribution made by D.C. Thomson. Although the *Dandy* and the *Beano* have continued, most of the firm's other comics have not, and only a few Dundee-based artists are still employed, most working freelance from London or elsewhere.[61]

As one form of commercial art has declined, another has emerged, and Dundee is now establishing itself as a leader in the computer games industry. Graduates from both Duncan of Jordanstone College and the University of Abertay have found employment as artists and designers on some of the best-selling computer games in the country.

The first few years of the twenty-first century have seen significant developments in the artistic life of the city, and it seems that William Darling McKay's description of Dundee in 1890 as 'perhaps the most vital centre of art appreciation in Scotland' may well be coming true once again.[62] At the beginning of the twentieth century, art in Dundee was almost entirely reliant on private investment from some of the city's wealthiest individuals. By the end of the century, public funding had taken over private and much of the city's success was in making the most of the opportunities available. There may be far greater variety to the kinds of art being produced in the city, but there has also been a greater attempt to co-ordinate artistic activity as part of a wider cultural planning in the city, through organisations like the Dundee Cultural Agencies Network and government-funded projects such as the Cultural Pathfinders scheme.[63]

ACKNOWLEDGEMENTS

Numerous individuals have provided me with information and assistance for this essay. I would particularly like to thank Julie Brown, Jenny Brownrigg, Norrie Colston, Peter Esgate, Douglas Gray, Morris Heggie, John Johnstone, Susan Keracher, John Kirkwood, Peter Lloyd, Deirdre Mackenna, Eric Marwick, Bob McGilvray, Joe McIntyre, Anna Robertson, Elliot Rudie and Clara Young for their kind support.

NOTES

1. 'Recent art movements in Dundee', *Advertiser*, 18 January 1907.
2. LHC, Dundee Art Society, Annual Report, 1911.
3. LHC, Dundee Graphic Arts Association, Annual Report, 1890.
4. This is just a snapshot of events from 2008, when the bulk of this chapter was written. Recognition is a scheme administered by Museums Galleries Scotland on behalf of the Scottish Government to reward museum collections deemed to be nationally significant.
5. R. McGilvray, 'From industrial wasteland to cultural quarter: the importance of partnership in the integration of art into the built environment', *Arras* 18 (2007), p. 28.
6. Interview by the author and Julie Brown, 21 February 2008.
7. *Courier*, 13 April 1934.
8. For more on these, see C. Young, 'Dundee's earliest fine art exhibitions', *Journal of the Scottish Society for Art History* 11 (2006), pp. 10–17.
9. For a history of the building, see D. Scruton, *The Victoria Galleries: Art and Education in Late Nineteenth Century Dundee* (Dundee, Dundee Art Gallery and Museums, 1989).
10. From an account of the prize-giving reported in *Wizard of the North*, 25 December 1880.
11. According to names listed in the annual Dundee Directories (held in LHC).
12. Nine artists shared studios in the former Theatre Royal building at 15 Castle Street in the 1890s, anticipating the much larger Forebank Studios founded in 1975.
13. *The Piper o' Dundee*, 16 January 1901.
14. 'Recent art movements in Dundee', *Advertiser*, 18 January 1907.
15. LHC, Dundee Art Union, Annual Report, 1882.
16. Dundee Technical Institute, Statement of Accounts 1888–1909 (held by University of Abertay Library).
17. Dundee Technical Institute syllabus 1893–4 (held by University of Abertay Library).
18. For more on this innovation, see M. Jarron, 'Before the Beano: the prehistory of Dundee comics', *International Journal of Comic Art* 10 (2008), pp. 9–17.
19. Although comic strips had appeared in illustrated magazines for some time, these seem to have been among the first in the world to appear in newspapers, thus introducing the form to a far wider audience.
20. *Advertiser*, 30 January 1907.
21. The full details of this part of the will are quoted in the *Dundee Year Book* (1909).
22. *Evening Telegraph*, 18 April 1927.
23. Technical Institute Letter Book, vol. 2, 22 November 1904 and 1 January 1905 (held at University of Abertay Library).
24. Technical College & School of Art Syllabus 1921–2.
25. The most detailed account of Watkins's career can currently be found on www.thatsbraw.co.uk (written by Gavin Brightwell).
26. Dr Chris Murray ranks it alongside London, Paris, New York and Tokyo in C. Murray, 'Thur's a man wi a big chin an' a dug in thon City Centre: uncovering the importance of Dundee comics', *Journal of the Scottish Society for Art History* 11 (2006), pp. 75–81.
27. S.J. Jones (ed.), *Dundee and District* (Dundee, British Association, 1968).

28. In fact, over the next four decades the building was also known as Dundee Corporation Art Galleries, Dundee Art Gallery, Dundee Art Galleries and Dundee Central Museum & Art Gallery, while still being popularly known as the Albert Institute and/or Victoria Galleries! For the sake of consistency I shall use the name Dundee Art Galleries & Museum until 1984 when it was renamed McManus Galleries. Following its triumphant re-opening in 2010 after a £12 million redevelopment, the building is now called The McManus: Dundee's Art Gallery and Museum.

29. *Courier*, 13 April 1934.

30. For more on Boyd, see Frances Fowle, 'Pioneers of taste: collecting in Dundee in the 1920s', *Journal of the Scottish Society for Art History* 11 (2006), pp. 59–65.

31. He also left a McTaggart and other artworks to the Dundee Dental School (now part of the University of Dundee).

32. Dundee Art Society Annual Reports (held in LHC).

33. The pinnacle of their success came in the week of April 1950 when the *Dandy* sold 2,300,111 copies and the *Beano* sold 1,974,072 (information extracted from sales ledgers by Morris Heggie, D.C. Thomson).

34. Interview by the author and Julie Brown, 7 March 2008.

35. Email from Peter Lloyd to the author, 22 January 2008.

36. Staff lists from the Dundee College of Art prospectuses do not give names of the tutors on these courses, but we do know that Dudley D. Watkins was employed to teach Illustration during the 1930s.

37. This was Bob McGrath, who drew 'The Three Bears' for the *Beano* for twenty-four years.

38. Dudley D. Watkins was finally honoured with an exhibition of his work in 1979, ten years after his death.

39. *The Scotsman*, 22 September 1965.

40. *The Scotsman*, undated 1964 article from Neil Dallas Brown press cuttings book owned by the artist's family.

41. As well as Duncan of Jordanstone College, art was also now being taught in Dundee College of Commerce and Dundee College of Education, allowing every level of study to be undertaken in Dundee.

42. In the 1960 episode 'Private View', directed by John Schlesinger.

43. Interview by the author and Julie Brown, 7 March 2008.

44. Interview by the author, 7 February 2008.

45. R. McGilvray, *Dundee Group (Artists) Ltd Travelling Exhibition*, catalogue (Dundee, 1979), p. 1.

46. A graduate of Duncan of Jordanstone College (as was MacKenzie), Colston would later join the District Council and become Arts & Heritage Manager for the city.

47. The collection is now held by The McManus: Dundee's Art Gallery and Museum.

48. McGilvray, 'From industrial wasteland to cultural quarter', *Areas* 18 (2007).

49. See, for example, its citations in M. Miles, *Art for Public Places* (Winchester, 1989) and M. Fisher and U. Owen (eds), *Whose Cities?* (London, 1991).

50. The two groups had previously joined forces at a different venue, Meadowplace Gallery, but sufficient funding was not then available to keep it running.

51. The sheer volume of exhibitions at this time is astonishing, with a new show opening almost every week in any of the five temporary exhibition spaces in the McManus or the new Art and Nature gallery in the Barrack Street natural history museum.

52. Quoted in Richard Carr's unpublished history of Duncan of Jordanstone College 1993 (draft MS held in the Art College Library), p. 72.

53. First announced in 2007, the proposals were the subject of a feasibility study and business plan funded by Scottish Enterprise Tayside and carried out by Whetstone Group Ltd and Conran & Partners, completed in December 2008. A company, Design Dundee Ltd, has been formed to take forward the project, holding an architectural competition for the design of the building in 2010.

54. The somewhat tortuous and often acrimonious series of events that led to the creation of Dundee Contemporary Arts are related with exceptional frankness by Marshall Anderson in 'A story of art development', an article written 1999 and published online at www.stirmargrev.demon.co.uk/dundee.htm (accessed 1 December 2008).

55. Quoted in Anderson, 'A story of art development'.

56. The garage had actually been considered as a possibility by DPW and the Dundee Group before they settled on the site of the Seagate Gallery.

57. The McManus Galleries continued to show the work of Dundee artists (and also acquired new pieces that had been commissioned by Dundee Contemporary Arts), but suffered a notable drop in visitor numbers after Dundee Contemporary Arts opened. However, the DCA has provided useful employment opportunities (not to mention significant artistic inspiration) for Duncan of Jordonstone students and graduates.

58. *Courier*, 4 July 1997.

59. This is according to the results of the last Research Assessment Exercise published in December 2008 at www.rae.ac.uk.

60. R. McGilvray, *Dundee Public Art Programme 1982–2003* (Dundee, Duncan of Jordanstone, 2004), p. 32. For more on this scheme, see R. McGilvray, *Ambassador Routes: Four Gateways for Dundee* (Dundee, Dundee Public Art Programme, 2001).

61. Those still based locally include some of the firm's longest-serving artists, notably David Sutherland, who has drawn 'The Bash Street Kids' since 1963, and Duncan of Jordanstone graduate Jim Glen, who drew 'Lord Snooty' for most of the 1970s and 1980s.

62. See n. 3 above.

63. The Cultural Pathways project ran throughout 2007 with funding from the Scottish Executive. Its main aim was to increase cultural opportunities for people living in parts of the city designated as community regeneration areas.

PART 2
Key Episodes

CHAPTER 8

Labour Politics and the Dundee Working Class c.1895–1936

Kenneth Baxter and William Kenefick

The general election of November 1922 is considered the breakthrough for the Labour Party in Scotland. In capturing almost a third of the Scottish vote, Labour bettered the performance of the party south of the border, setting a pattern that would prevail until 1935.[1] Labour had the wide support of the Scottish trade union movement, but its political success was largely due to the intense local activism of the members of the Independent Labour Party (ILP) and the financial backing that the ILP provided. Indeed, for many Scots the ILP *was* the Labour Party.[2] Glasgow and west Scotland accounted for around half of the twenty-nine seats the party won in 1922, and Labour made a clean sweep of all eleven coalfield constituencies. But there were equally impressive socialist successes elsewhere. In Dundee, Labour's E.D. Morel, and Scottish Prohibitionist leader Edwin Scrymgeour beat the National Liberals Winston Churchill and D.J. MacDonald,[3] and as almost half of the Dundee electorate voted Labour, Prohibitionist or Communist the city could legitimately regard itself as more red than Clydeside.[4] For almost a decade thereafter Labour advanced significantly on all fronts in Scotland until the collapse of the second Labour government in 1931 left the party with only seven seats. At Dundee Labour lost the seat it first won in 1906 and Scrymgeour lost the seat he had held since 1922. Labour recovered to win twenty Scottish seats in 1935 (although Dundee was not among them) and in local elections captured Glasgow Council in 1933 and Dundee Council in 1936, paving the way for its long period of dominance in Scottish politics after the Second World War.[5]

Iain Hutchison contends that Labour's electoral breakthrough in

1922 was sudden and that its political success lay in the upsurge in trade unionism experienced between 1914 and 1920. For him Labour's political advance was a relatively recent phenomenon, and was not rooted in the pre-1914 era when Scottish Labour lagged behind the political advances taking place south of the border.[6] Labour in Dundee likewise shared in the party's changing fortunes during the war and inter-war years, but as Labour experienced electoral success in the city before 1914 would this not tend to undermine Hutchison's argument? William Walker would agree with Hutchison that it was the trade unions' rapid advancement during the Great War that transformed the Dundee working class politically. Indeed, he suggests that despite Alex Wilkie's success in 1906 and 1910 – which was in any case 'more a confirmation of Dundee's liberalism than a challenge to it' – Labour made no significant advance in the city before 1914.[7]

This chapter presents a somewhat different picture, suggesting that increasing concerns over poverty, housing and worsening economic conditions combined with the aspirations and political demands of a Labour movement – buoyed by Wilkie's electoral success at Dundee in 1906 – laid the solid foundations for Labour's further advance during the early twentieth century. In examining the activities of Dundee's early Labour radicals and socialists this chapter reveals how Labour's slow-but-steady progress from the late 1880s contributed to the important developments that were to take place in Dundee between 1905 and 1910; how the period of labour unrest from 1910 further advanced the Labour cause before 1914; and how with the ever present support of the ILP Dundee became a leading centre of the anti-war movement in Scotland during the Great War. The final section focuses on post-war developments within the Labour movement and the growing 'Moderate' anti-socialist alliance which politically polarised Dundee during the inter-war years. Press coverage is important to our understanding of the changing nature of class politics in Scotland. As the press in Dundee was the leading critic of the radical Left in the city, it was intimately involved in this political discourse. An examination of its role is therefore essential to our understanding of the political developments taking place in Dundee between the late nineteenth century and the 1930s.

RELATIVE QUIESCENCE IN DUNDEE'S
WORKING-CLASS POLITICS *c*.1893 TO 1905?

For much of the second half of the nineteenth century, class relations in Dundee were relatively peaceful. While many deplored 'the unevenness of capitalist society', most were disinclined to advocate any form of 'class war'.[8] This was to change by the late 1880s as across Britain Labour radicals and early socialist pioneers began to challenge the existing political order and further the cause of independent labour. Dundee shared in these national developments and by 1888 had two branches of the Social Democratic Federation (No. 1 and Central), a Labour Church (probably the only one in Scotland) and a branch of the Scottish Labour Party.[9] In 1890 two 'Labour candidates' were elected to the town council (R.D.B. Ritchie and Robert Bruce) and Dundee also established a branch of the ILP shortly after its inception in 1893 – and with Dundee Trades Council (DTC) organised the first May Day Demonstration in the city in 1893.[10] Walker argues that because the ILP and the other 'early pioneers' of socialism 'sought not to identify with jute workers' they had a limited influence on how Labour politics developed at Dundee before 1915.[11] Indeed, he argues that the period between the 1890s and 1905 'was one of relative quiescence in Dundee working class politics'.[12] John Kemp would tend to agree, noting that 'the lateness in recognising the importance of independent labour representation' at Dundee can more or less be dated to 1905 and the election of ILP-er John Carnegie as a councillor.[13]

By examining evidence from reports in the ILP's *Labour Leader* – published weekly in Glasgow between 1893 and 1904, and which does not figure in either Walker's or Kemp's work – it is clear that this view (at least from an ILP perspective) greatly underestimates the progress that was being made in Dundee before 1905. There is no doubt that Walker's *Juteopolis* is wide-ranging, rigorously researched and quite breath-taking in its sheer breadth and scope, but despite its comprehensive coverage much of his political analysis is predicated largely on evidence gleaned from the columns of the Dundee press. He is clearly aware of some of the problems this might cause:

For the historian of the local world of labour the problem is not one of a paucity of information, but of discovering the reality underlying journalistic pieces designed in the first instance to serve the purposes of political editors.

Indeed, Walker notes that the Liberal *Dundee Advertiser* and the steadfastly Tory *Courier* portrayed the city's 'socialists and advanced radicals' as either 'lunatic and amusing' or more alarmingly 'dangerous and disreputable'.[14] In his observations of the activities of the SDF he claimed that they 'may have survived the 1890s but, if so, ceased to make copy in the Dundee papers'. It is not clear whether he is suggesting that they simply faded out of existence, but he certainly did not believe that the SDF was so dangerous 'that editors thought it best to ignore it'.[15] Walker's analysis nevertheless strongly suggests that this might well have happened, or that Labour activities were largely disregarded in the local newspapers.

Walker makes no reference to non-Dundee newspapers, and while asserting the claim that the early pioneers of socialism had little influence in Dundee, and that this accounted for the relative lack of political progress made by the Labour movement before 1915, he never at any time consulted the Labour press. As Ann Petrie recently asserted, 'despite Walker's valuable contribution to our understanding of the jute industry his thesis lends credence to the one-dimensional view of Dundee as a single-industry city based on jute production', and, more importantly, that this approach detracts 'from a deeper examination of general class issues' in the city.[16] Considered from this perspective, Walker fails to place the 'local world of labour' at Dundee in the wider context of Labour movement developments taking place across Scotland and largely disregards the wider world of Labour view of what was happening in Dundee.

A cursory examination of the *Labour Leader* reveals the Scottish ILP's great suspicion of the Dundee press. At the time of the 1895 election, for example, they 'did their best to ignore' James MacDonald (ILP parliamentary candidate) and what did make copy was 'garbled and unfair'.[17] In 1902 they opined that 'the meetings of the Dundee ILP [were] not reported in the local newspapers'[18] and later chronicled 'the scurrilous abuse' received by Wilkie at the time the 1906 election.[19] Indeed, even *The Scotsman* felt the need to report that Wilkie's victory was secured 'in the face of the strenuous hostility of the whole political and newspapers organisations that the Radicals (Liberals) could command'.[20]

The *Labour Leader* (hereafter the *Leader*) regularly reported on the activities of Labour at Dundee and placed these events in a broader national perspective. By July 1895 the ILP was the leading socialist group in Dundee, and their main focus was securing an election victory for the ILP's parliamentary candidate MacDonald. On the eve of the 1895 general election, 'Red Lichtie' – an Arbroath ILP-er and a regular contributor to the *Leader* – reported glowingly that the ILP 'deserved success' at Dundee 'for they were working like Trojans'.[21] MacDonald nonetheless came last of the five candidates, polling only 1,313 votes. However, the *Leader* noted that out of the twenty-eight candidates only Keir Hardie found success, at West Ham, and that MacDonald polled the highest of the seven candidates contesting Scottish seats. Indeed, MacDonald's vote in Dundee accounted for 30 per cent of the total vote polled for ILP candidates across Scotland. The *Leader* seemed fairly happy with this result and reported rather optimistically:

> We have simply plodded on in an intensely Liberal town . . . we shall plod some more, buoyed up by the hope that we shall yet capture Dundee for Socialism.[22]

Walker notes that MacDonald drew large and enthusiastic audiences, and that emerging from the 1890s were men who would assume great importance in Dundee politics. He also notes that the ILP ran nine candidates for the parish council in 1895 and that two were successful (one included Scrymgeour).[23] However, there is no sense of how these Dundee ILP-ers and early socialists were viewed beyond Tayside. Lochee-born George Barnes came to prominence at this time as an influential trade unionist and ILP-er and would have been MacDonald's election organiser had he not accepted the invitation to contest Rochdale for the ILP.[24] Barnes later sought nomination as the prospective parliamentary Labour candidate (with Liberal support) in 1902, but the Dundee Liberal Association vetoed this idea because Barnes wished to stand exclusively as a Labour candidate. This earned him the approbation of James Keir Hardie who, when visiting Dundee in October 1902, stressed that it was not for other parties to say which candidate the workers should select, and added that Barnes was 'without exception . . . the most outstanding figure, so far as ability and strength are concerned, in the trade union movement'.[25] Barnes had been a prominent figure in Dundee since the late 1880s, yet Walker makes only one mention of him in *Juteopolis* (but much later and specifically in relation to the question of Indian competition and the jute industry after the Great War in 1919).[26]

Walker makes no reference either to ILP member and staunch socialist William F. Black, who was selected to contest Dundee in 1902 or that his resignation in June 1904 cleared the way for Alex Wilkie's selection the following year.[27] Black was a native of Dundee, worked as a compositor for the *Courier*, and a journalist for the *Advertiser* and later the *People's Journal*, where he became sub-editor. He left Dundee to join the staff of the *Labour Leader* when its operations moved from Glasgow to London in 1904, where he was a sub-editor. Black died suddenly aged fifty-one just days after Wilkie's victory at Dundee. His obituary stated that he was one of Keir Hardie's closest friends, having joined the SLP at its formation in 1888, and that he worked tirelessly to gain justice for the poor and the unemployed. Black was therefore probably involved in the early unemployed movement formed by the ILP in Dundee in January 1895, which set up a rudimentary unemployment exchange to find work for 200 unemployed men seeking alternative employment. The ILP also supported the city's unemployed tailors and painters, who pooled their labour under the 'co-operative principal of production' to spread more evenly any work available. On this the *Leader* reported: 'This looks like Socialism. May it go and Prosper, "and we shall arrive".'[28] Such initiatives were praised by the Labour press and it seemed entirely appropriate that a delegation of the unemployed assembled outside Black's home to pay their respects on the day of his burial. At his graveside the mourners included Keir Hardie, J. Bruce Glasier, Mrs Pankhurst, John Hodge, MP and R.J. Clynes, MP. The *Labour Leader* concluded that 'his death takes away one of the sincerest and most earnest Socialists in the land'.[29]

The *Leader* praised the ILP and the DTC in their decision to jointly run future parliamentary candidates in 1899. The ILP and DTC jointly organised a local Scottish Workers' Parliamentary Election Committee (SWPEC), and along with Aberdeen, Edinburgh, Glasgow, Paisley and West Fife were among the first to form such a committee in Scotland.[30] In 1902 the *Leader* reported on Black's first address as Dundee parliamentary candidate to a packed meeting in November, speaking on 'Home Rule, Land Nationalisation, the eight-hour day, manhood suffrage, and nationalisation of the railways and other great monopolies'.[31] Kemp suggests that Black was considered 'a poor platform speaker' and because he lacked the financial sponsorship of a trade union failed to win the support of the DTC. Indeed, he suggests that some on the trade union wing felt that Black was 'killing' the Labour movement in Dundee and that was probably why he resigned in 1904.[32] Yet the *Leader* stated that Black resigned because he took up the position as their sub-editor in 1904, and the 1906 *Dundee Year Book* appears to confirm this. Certainly neither mention any lack of support by the local Labour movement.[33] Kemp might be correct in his assessment of Black's platform skills, but he was a very popular ILP speaker who addressed many meetings across Scotland.

As parliamentary candidate for Dundee, Black was intimately involved in 'one of the most successful propaganda efforts' in the ILP's history. In October 1903 the National Administrative Council (NAC) of the ILP formulated a plan to organise a country-wide series of 'Tariff Demonstrations' in seven locations across England and Scotland. The NAC settled on Birmingham, Darlington, Dundee, Glasgow, Manchester, Oldham and Sheffield. The NAC campaign was launched at Dundee, where the first meeting of its type in Britain opened at the Gilfillan Hall on the evening of 2 December 1903.[34] Black chaired the meeting and opened proceedings by asking, 'Why, with the enormous increase in wealth, poverty still kept more than pace with it?' Other speakers included George Barnes, Ramsay MacDonald and J. Bruce Glasier as well as local ILP-ers John Carnegie and James Reid. Indeed, the matter was perhaps best addressed by Carnegie, who proposed the following motion:

> That this meeting protests strongly, on national and international ground, against all proposals for placing tariff restrictions upon imports, and especially against any tariff scheme calculated to increase the cost of food; and no less strongly against the existing extraction on rents, royalties, and railway rates, which seriously handicap British industry . . . and further, recognising that in this country under free trade, as in other countries under protection, the bulk of the population remains in a shameful condition of poverty, bad housing and uncertainty in employment.

In supporting the motion George Barnes stated that the purpose of the meeting was twofold. First, to make a constructive reply to Joseph Chamberlain's tariff reform proposals and to give Labour's remedies for the 'disease of fiscalitis'; and second, 'to promote the principle of labour representation in general, and the candidature of Mr Black in particular'. Ramsay MacDonald and others also addressed the gathering, which closed with Black putting the resolution to the meeting, which 'was carried unanimously, amid great enthusiasm'.[35] *The Scotsman* reported that some 1,000 people were in attendance at the ILP meeting in Dundee.[36]

After William Black's departure in June 1904 the ILP branch in Dundee became more or less moribund and perhaps for the first time since the *Leader* went weekly in 1893, Dundee did not feature in any of the paper's reports. By January 1905, when the *Leader* reported the establishment of thirteen new branches, it was noted that a new Central Branch of the ILP had been formed in the city with John Carnegie, Agnes Husband and James Reid acting respectively as President, Vice-President and Secretary.[37] Membership was also on the increase and over the summer, working closely with the DTC, the ILP were organising 'large and enthusiastic' propaganda meetings.[38] By September the ILP in Scotland was 'stronger than it has ever been at any period in its history'.[39] ILP membership in Scotland soon expanded from 1,250 to over 5,000 and by 1910 the number of branches had increased from 22 to 125. Chris Harvie attributes this growth in part to the 'plausibility [of] socialist principles' and the remedies advanced by the ILP to tackle 'unemployment and poverty' and Scotland's appalling housing problem.[40]

By campaigning on the issue of poverty, unemployment and poor housing socialists, including Labour and Scottish Prohibition Party supporters, were elected to Dundee town council in 1905, 1906, 1907, 1908, 1911, 1912, 1913 and 1914. The ILP also had members elected to Dundee Parish Council and the School Board, demonstrating a definite shift to Labour at the municipal level.[41] The *Leader* stressed that the ILP was now a force to be reckoned with in Scotland. Indeed, events taking place at Dundee were providing hope and inspiration for its editors, who sensed that Dundee 'was going to make history':

It will be an eye-opener for the men of the West if Dundee should lead the way with the first Labour member for Scotland.

That seems not unlikely, for all reports agree that Alex Wilkie's chances are excellently hopeful.[42]

The members of the Scottish ILP would clearly have disagreed with those who would later dismiss Wilkie's election victory in 1906 'as an aberration or a fluke'.[43]

Kemp rightly argues that Wilkie's success must be viewed as part of a broader process of political change taking place at Dundee.[44] Bob Stewart suggested that Wilkie's victory 'started a final break with Liberal–Labour unity' in Dundee and marked 'the birth of organised independent working-class political action'.[45] And there is much truth in this. Unlike most Labour candidates across Britain – who gained seats from Unionists with Liberal collusion and agreement – Wilkie pushed a second Liberal candidate into third place (and against the widely reported opposition of the Liberal *Dundee Advertiser*) to capture his seat in what was otherwise a landslide victory for the Liberal Party across Scotland. It is a testament to the growing confidence of the ILP at Dundee that they ran G.H. Stuart as a candidate against Winston Churchill in the famous by-election of 1908. The ILP did so against the wishes of Alex Wilkie and senior elements of the Labour Party in London because this strategy risked splitting the anti-Unionist vote.[46] Churchill won easily with Liberal Unionist Sir George Baxter second and ILP candidate Stuart third. Had the Scottish Prohibition Party decided not to run Edwin Scrymgeour – who was last, polling 655 votes – Stuart might well have finished second, as he was only 367 votes short of Baxter.[47]

Kemp speculates that had Labour (and Wilkie in particular) backed the campaign against Churchill in 1908, and selected a second candidate in 1910, Liberal representation in Dundee could have ceased before the war.[48] Indeed, Stuart believed that a great opportunity had been missed 'to make Dundee the first place in Great Britain' to have two Labour MPs.[49] While the elections of 1910 saw the Scots returning to Liberalism in great numbers, Dundee had become one of the least Liberal cities in Scotland.[50] During the January election in 1910 the *Glasgow Herald's* political correspondent reported that the Labour Party in Dundee was working with 'great confidence' and was certain that Wilkie would be re-elected.[51] Thus the political shift signalled in 1906 was confirmed in 1910 just as workers entered into a prolonged period of industrial unrest that would significantly alter labour relations at Dundee.

'WORRYING AND PUZZLING':
SOCIAL AND INDUSTRIAL UNREST IN DUNDEE, 1910 TO 1914

Dundee experienced several major industrial disputes from the 1890s onward. A textile dispute in early May 1893 saw 24,000 workers on strike, halting production at forty-five factories across this city,[52] and strikes of similar intensity among female workers took place in 1895 and 1899.[53] In the early 1900s a major dispute affected much of the engineering sector across Dundee, when 600 engineers and apprentices went on strike between November 1903 and February 1904. During the dispute the employers brought in imported labour from beyond Dundee to replace striking workers and resorted to selective re-employment when the strike ended.[54] In February 1906 there was another major dispute among female textile workers, and although the strike ultimately failed it prompted the formation of the Dundee and District Union of Jute and Flax Workers in March with around 4,252 workers.[55] In terms of industrial unrest 1907 was 'crowded with incident', but the most serious dispute took place over July and September when bleachworkers went on strike for a 5 per cent increase in wages. In this dispute workers were evicted from their homes and the police had to intervene to quell the violence that erupted during the strike.[56]

Relations between capital and labour in Dundee were clearly strained as employers became increasingly more autocratic in their response to workers' grievances. When economic conditions improved it therefore came as no great surprise that Dundee workers were to play a full and active part in labour unrest experienced between 1910 and 1914. This began in earnest when the engineering employers declared a lockout across Scotland in response to a strike ballot called by the boilermakers' union in September 1910. The boilermakers' officials requested a second ballot to allow them to end the strike and start talks with the employers, but this was overwhelmingly rejected by the rank-and-file. A third ballot was finally agreed in mid-December and the boilermakers' dispute was officially over. But Dundee boilermakers voted against their union's executive in the final ballot.[57] The engineering employers' federation's decision to call a lockout, when Dundee boilermakers had initially voted against strike action, had moved them to a more militant position because they 'refused to place their union at the mercy of the [employers'] federation'. The *Advertiser* concluded that this 'worrying and puzzling' development formed part of the 'crest of a deep wave of social and industrial unrest' affecting labour across the country.[58]

During February 1911 a dispute involving 5,000 workers, mainly female spinners and members of the Dundee Jute and Flax Workers' Union, shut down the Cox Brothers' Camperdown Works complex in Lochee after squad sizes were cut from ten to eight persons. Unusually, the Dundee press was critical of the mill owners for their heavy-handed attitude, and the company was forced to make concessions in an attempt to resume normal relations. The strikers returned to work three weeks later on condition that all the discharged workers were found alternative employment.[59]

The key industrial dispute in 1911, however, was the carters' and dockers' strike in December. This strike was of some considerable scope and consequence, involving 700 dockers and 600 carters, and 30,000 textile workers who took to the streets in support of the strikers. The strike was organised by Peter Gillespie (Dundee ILP-er and syndicalist sympathiser) with the support of the Jute and Flax Workers (Dundee's biggest union) and the DTC, which held street collections 'to give all classes an opportunity of assisting the men on strike'.[60] The dispute brought Dundee to a standstill. Cargoes of materials bound for Dundee were blocked at Leith, and the Scottish Union of Dock Labourers (SUDL) ensured that no blacklegs would leave Glasgow bound for Dundee. The dispute was resolved in favour of the workers and *Forward* proclaimed the outcome as 'a glorious lesson in the usefulness of solidarity'.[61]

The role of the SUDL was central to the success of the strike. They transformed Dundee from a free labour port that from 1904 had been under the control of the Shipping Federation and its Free Labour Bureau. Indeed, in June 1911, the Bureau confidently reported that 1,235 dockers and carters had 'signed the free labour pledge'. Within six months, however, Dundee's free labourers had become determined trade unionists with a growing, and 'regrettable', reputation for 'disorderliness'.[62] The press was convinced that unrest was due to the 'vague Syndicalism of the French Socialists' and an ideology that proposed 'the universal strike [as] the best means of bringing "capitalism" to its knees'. It would seem that *The Scotsman* in particular, and the Scottish press in general, considered the dockers' and carters' strike at Dundee to be a potent example of syndicalism at work.[63] Perhaps the local magistrates at Dundee held similar fears, for they drafted in 167 extra police and three hundred troops of the 4th Battalion Black Watch ('Dundee's Own').[64]

Between January and March 1912 Dundee workers became involved in Rent Strike Action in a campaign which involved the British Socialist Party, the ILP, the Scottish Prohibition Party and the DTC.[65] The rent strike activity was somewhat eclipsed when in early February 1912 a small strike began in Lochee, which between then and April escalated into a General Strike and lockout involving more than 30,000 textile workers. For the fourteen-year-old Mary Brooksbank (Dundee radical, socialist and later communist) the textile strike 'was her first lesson in class warfare in Dundee' and as for many others it raised her political awareness:

Private property [took] paramount place over ordinary people. Blacklegs were often escorted to work by the police, but strikers were not considered to require protection from the bosses.[66]

There were further industrial disputes throughout the year and in June 300 mill workers at Dens Works went on strike, followed in July by 150 ship painters and carpenters at the Caledon shipyard, and by the end of the month even Dundee's doctors were on strike. In August 250 apprentices at Caledon shipyard went on strike and precipitated a national dispute that spread from Dundee across Scotland and within a week involved 5,000 apprentices. The Dundee apprentices were the last to return to work after nearly four weeks on strike.[67]

The apprentice boys' strike was one of twenty-five to take place in Dundee and one of sixty-five disputes across the east of Scotland in that year. Dundee thus accounted for over 38 per cent of all strikes which took place in the region during 1912. The strike wave continued throughout 1913 and 1914, although perhaps not at the same level of intensity. Yet with over one million working days lost, the Dundee textile workers' dispute of 1912 was one of the most significant of all the disputes to take place across Scotland during the unrest.[68] In the meantime membership of the Jute and Flax Workers' Union had increased from 4,250 to over 9,250 between 1910 and 1913.[69] These strikes also produced a new generation of labour leaders including Peter Gillespie, Nicholas Marra and Patrick Fletcher (all well-known ILP-ers). Gillespie and Fletcher were both elected to the town council in November 1913 and within a month Dundee's carters were again on strike. This would lend credence to Brooksbank's view that what occurred in the years before the war brought about an 'upsurge of political awareness amongst the mass of the people' of Dundee.[70]

The labour unrest had been viewed with a mixture of mild unease and outright fear, but at Dundee the local press generally subscribed to the alarmist view. Between January and February 1914 the *Courier* alone printed no fewer than thirteen separate articles on the threat of socialism and syndicalism.[71] Nonetheless, when Britain went to war with Germany on 4 August 1914 an industrial peace was declared, and the great labour unrest 'slipped away into the limbo of unfinished argument'.[72] Yet this was an uneasy peace, and the experience of total war would reawaken in many workers a rebelliousness that had been so prevalent in the days before the war.[73]

THE FIRST WORLD WAR:
DUNDEE AND THE ANTI-WAR MOVEMENT

When war broke out internationalist socialist unity quickly dissolved and in Scotland 'red flags turned to tartan' as Scots enthusiastically volunteered for service.[74] With its association with Dundee's Own, the 4th Battalion of the Black Watch, the city had a proud military tradition and expected – and demanded – a high level of voluntary recruitment. Scotland generally responded to the call and in November the *Advertiser* proudly proclaimed:

> All honour to the lads who have put Scotland in the front this time . . . We must not let the sons of the Rose or the Leek or the Shamrock get in front of the proud Thistle.[75]

The Dundee press never wavered in its patriotic duty: men who would not volunteer were castigated as cowards; those unwilling to attest (under the Derby Scheme) were reviled as shirkers, and after conscription was introduced in January 1916 they quickly turned on those who claimed their conscientious right not to fight. Dundee was a bastion of 'Hun-hating super-patriotism' and in November 1915 the *People's Journal* openly advocated military and civil conscription:

The day is fast approaching when a girl who fiddles away at fancy work when she might be making shells . . . will as much be an object of public scorn and as much deserving of military treatment as the 'nut' who carries a golf club when he ought to be carrying a rifle.[76]

When conscription was introduced those who sought exemption on the ground of conscience were referred to the military tribunals. At Dundee this meant public ridicule and ritual humiliation before the local tribunal chairman Alexander Spence (a staunch Unionist and later Lord Provost).[77] Spence was one of the most pro-war public figures in Scotland and he actually suspended the Dundee tribunal when the War Office granted an exemption against the advice of Dundee's senior military officer, Major Cappon. On another occasion he refused to allow a solicitor to represent a client until he withdrew remarks made at a previous tribunal. When the solicitor again refused, Spence ordered him to 'clear out'. It would seem that by 1917 even the Ministry of National Service had concerns about Dundee and within a year Major Cappon was forced to retire, much to the chagrin of Spence.[78]

The plight of Dundee conscientious objectors (COs) has been well chronicled in more recent historical accounts of the war.[79] However, it must be stressed that Dundee was a leading centre of ILP anti-war activity in Scotland and that the branch of the No-Conscription Fellowship (NCF) was second only to Glasgow in its scope and activity. After conscription members of the Trades Council offered succour to both bodies and as a result Labour's opponents on the town council rebuked then for acting as a 'pro-German gang'.[80] Despite criticism and press ridicule, the editor of *Forward* proudly proclaimed in April 1917 that Dundee 'was fair hotchin wi conchies'[81] and later praised the city's anti-militarists for standing their ground well.[82] Indeed, in February 1918 the editor of *Forward*, Willie Stewart, made 'special mention' of Dundee noting that:

The ILP had stood its ground there through the war and the dark days of militaristic oppression. It has its sons in every prison and penal centre set apart for conscientious objectors to militarism. It has steadfastly and fearlessly fought for liberty and Socialism.

'In the great inevitable political uprising which is destined to place Labour permanently in power,' Stewart predicted, 'the working class of Dundee will demand foremost place.'[83]

THE RADICAL LEFT AND THE MODERATES:
THE DEATH OF LIBERAL DUNDEE, 1918–39

Despite Labour's success in Dundee the movement did not survive the war unscathed. Councillor Thomas B. Barnes, brother of George Barnes (now a staunchly pro-war MP) left the party and helped to form the Municipal Electors' Association (MEA) which ran 'Moderate' candidates against Labour.[84] The MEA (and its successor the Dundee Ratepayers' Association) provided the principal opposition to Labour in local elections in Dundee (up until the 1970s) and united local Liberals and Unionists into a solid conservative anti-Labour group. This was one of several signs that Dundee's Liberals were abandoning the remains of their radical past. During the 1918 general election their candidate Churchill (now closely associated with Lloyd George's Conservative-dominated coalition government) was also endorsed by the local Unionists. More surprisingly, the Unionists also backed Wilkie because of his 'past record' – a clear sign that he himself had moved to the right since 1914, which would be confirmed during the election campaign.[85] In a far cry from 1906, Wilkie called for the 'expulsion of all aliens from Britain', not to let shouts of the Red Flag carry them to bloody revolution, and – in a likely reference to the MacDonald pacifist wing of the Labour Party – criticised 'the pacifists who had done nothing to assist to win the war'.[86] Unsurprisingly, Wilkie's candidacy was not universally popular. At one 'lively meeting' – where he was critical of COs and 'Bolshevism' – an attempt to pass a vote of confidence in him was howled down while a section of the audience sang the Red Flag.[87] Nonetheless, post-war euphoria (and an inaccurate electoral register) meant that Churchill and Wilkie won easily, while James 'Sunny' Brown (the other, more radical, Labour candidate), finished bottom of the poll. For the first time since the Great Reform Act, Dundee's electors rejected liberal-radicalism in favour of political conservatism.

This shift did not last. In the municipal election of November 1919 (the first for five years) Labour won eight seats and increased their representation on the council to nine (from three in 1914) along with

Independent Socialist James G. Fraser. Together the radical Left (Labour, Fraser and the Prohibitionists) captured 51.5 per cent of the total poll at Dundee and by November 1920, 33 per cent of Dundee's councillors represented Labour or belonged to another socialist group. This was more than Edinburgh, where fewer than 5 per cent of councillors were socialists in 1920, and only marginally behind 'Red' Glasgow, where 39 per cent of councillors were Labour members.[88]

Labour now looked to the next general election and selected the anti-conscription activist E.D. Morel and R.C. Wallhead as parliamentary candidates (Wilkie – it would seem – was not considered for nomination).[89] By the general election of 1922, however, Labour fielded only Morel.[90] The decision to field one candidate was almost certainly made to avoid splitting the socialist vote – given that the Unionists were likely to support the Liberals. It was also known that Scrymgeour (who in 1918 had out-polled Brown) and the Communist Party of Great Britain (CPGB) were to enter the contest. Indeed, the CPGB had high hopes for Dundee and selected its best-known Scottish member, Willie Gallacher, to fight the seat. *The Communist* propaganda publication gave much coverage to Gallacher's campaign and in one edition his address to 'the working men and women of Dundee' dominated the front page. By comparison, Walton Newbold – the only other Scottish CPGB candidate – received less attention until his surprise victory at Motherwell in 1922.[91]

When Labour made its historic electoral breakthrough in 1922, the 'great inevitable political uprising' that *Forward* predicted in 1918 came to pass.[92] Almost half of the Dundee electorate voted Labour, Prohibitionist or Communist and as a result Scrymgeour and Morel secured Dundee's two parliamentary seats.[93] Churchill came fourth and independent Liberal R.A. Pilkington (an old radical-style Liberal) finished a poor fifth. Gallacher was last, polling less than 6,000 votes (just under 5 per cent). This did not stop Tom Bell from claiming in a letter to the Moscow Politburo, however, 'that 75 per cent of the credit for Churchill's defeat' was due to the Communists and the good work done by Gallacher and a cadre of seventy active party members at Dundee.[94]

In truth the CPGB had achieved little in electoral terms in Dundee and would fail to greatly improve on that record in the future. Indeed, unlike Perth, Aberdeen or the mining areas of Fife, Dundee would never elect a Communist councillor. Perhaps the CPGB blundered in selecting Gallacher, who had no connection to the city, rather than Dundee-born Bob Stewart? Or perhaps their poor showing reflected that fact that in Scrymgeour and Morel, Dundee had two hard-working radical Left champions and therefore had no need for communism? Whatever the case, the result at Dundee was as significant as the great victories won by Red Clydeside ILP-ers such as Maxton, Kirkwood and Wheatley. Interestingly, when they and the other Red Clydeside MPs left Glasgow's St Enoch Station en route to Westminster in 1922, Dundee's Edwin Scrymgeour accompanied them and he addressed the cheering crowd who had gathered to wish them well.[95] This may help explain why Labour did not attempt to displace him at Dundee with an alternative official Labour candidate in 1922 or anytime thereafter. Indeed, Scrymgeour's presence at Glasgow not only proves his close connection to the ILP, but confirms his place in the pantheon of the radical Left Labour movement in Scotland in the 1920s.

THE 'PRESS MONOPOLY', LABOUR DISCORD AND DUNDEE WOMEN: THE INTER-WAR YEARS

Labour's achievements at Dundee were made in the face of the fierce opposition of the local press which, as Hugh MacDiarmid observed, fulminated against the activities of the socialists and the Labour movement more generally in the aftermath of the General Strike in 1926.[96] In truth, as shown early in this chapter, the Dundee press had long been decisively against the Labour movement and even before D.C. Thomson (a Unionist) had acquired control of John Leng's press holdings in 1905. Indeed, Leng's newspapers demonstrated a great hostility to the radical Left Labour movement that was taking shape in Dundee from the late nineteenth century. While the *Advertiser* retained a vaguely liberal quality up until the 1920s, it was never sympathetic to the Labour cause. Any lingering vestiges of liberalism, however, disappeared when the *Advertiser* merged with the pro-Unionist *Courier* after the 1926 General Strike.[97]

Other publications such as *The Tocsin* were sympathetic to the Labour movement in Dundee. Founded and edited by the talented Dundee journalist Joseph Johnston Lee in 1909 (a well-known Dundee artist, writer and poet), *The Tocsin* was held in high esteem by many leading luminaries in the Labour movement. Philip Snowdon declared the paper 'the smartest and best got-up all round' local Labour periodical he had seen and Keir Hardie proclaimed that 'We cannot have too much in the way of high-class journalism in connection with our Socialist and Labour Movement.' *The Tocsin* did not survive beyond 1909, but that it existed at all provides evidence of a strong and active Labour movement in Dundee – for apart from Glasgow no other area could boast its own independent socialist publication.[98]

A later paper sympathetic to Labour was the *Dundee Free Press*. It was established in the wake of the General Strike in 1926 and published weekly until it finally folded in 1933. It set up in opposition to the new *Courier and Advertiser* to counter the 'unsatisfactory and biased news service' that operated in Dundee, and its workforce was drawn from a pool of some 250 unemployed journalists and printers – the majority of whom had previously worked for D.C. Thomson before the strike.[99] On the eve of the local elections in 1935, however, when Thomson's *Evening Telegraph and Post* denounced all 'Socialists' (including Labour) as untrustworthy, there was no alterative or independent press voice to be heard in Dundee.[100]

The Labour Party's fortunes fluctuated in the local elections, and throughout the 1920s the party never took more than ten of the city's thirty-three council seats. In general elections, however, Labour fared well and more or less adopted a joint platform with Scrymgeour to avoid splitting the pro-socialist vote. Consequently, Dundee had socialist representation in Parliament until 1931. The Unionist and Liberal Parties responded by fielding one candidate each to unite the 'moderate' vote and this ensured some close elections. Indeed, in 1923 Gallacher's increased level of support cut into the Labour vote to such an extent that if every Unionist voter had given their second vote to the Liberal candidate, Morel would have been defeated. In 1924 and 1929, however, the result was more clear-cut and Dundee was regarded as safe territory for Labour.

However, there were serious internal divisions within the Labour movement in Dundee during late 1920s. After the General Strike the Dundee Trades and Labour Party (TLP) decreed that none of their members in the newspaper business were to sell newspapers produced by non-unionised publishers (such as the *Glasgow Herald* or *Evening Times*, produced by George Outram Ltd, or any Thomson-Leng publications produced in Dundee and Glasgow). However, in 1928 the wife of veteran ILP activist Ewan Carr ignored this edict and when the ILP refused to take any action against her husband the TLP disaffiliated from the ILP. Consequently Morel's successor as MP, Tom Johnston – a prominent ILP member – declined to contest Dundee again.[101] Labour managed to heal this rupture by the time of the 1929 election and Johnston's replacement, Michael Marcus, was easily elected alongside Scrymgeour. Ironically, this split arguably worked in the Labour Party's favour in Dundee, for it weakened the ILP as a force in the city and affirmed the TLP as Dundee's supreme Labour body. When the ILP finally disaffiliated from Labour in 1932, the Labour Party in Dundee emerged largely unscathed. In Glasgow and other parts of Scotland, where the ILP remained strong, they were able to run municipal (and parliamentary) candidates against official Labour nominees, which split the vote and cost Labour seats.[102]

The demise of the ILP in Dundee was probably hastened by the ageing and loss of some of its leaders, including the ex-ILP President Agnes Husband, who died in 1928. Interestingly, Husband was one of a relatively small number of prominent Labour women in Dundee, and female involvement in socialist politics was less obvious at Dundee than at Glasgow in the inter-war period. Aside from Lily Miller (a nationally well-known and respected figure in the 1930s, but now largely forgotten), few women made an impact on the leadership of the Labour and Communist Parties in inter-war Dundee, and the city did not elect a female councillor until 1935 (fifteen years after Glasgow and eleven after Edinburgh).[103] Moreover, Dundee was almost unique in Scotland in that it did not have a strong branch of the Scottish Co-operative Women's Guild (SCWG – an offshoot of the Co-operative Party established in the 1890s). In 1918 the SCWG had 201 branches across Scotland, but did not establish a branch in Dundee until the 1920s and its membership was never substantial. In 1935 the Dundee SCWG had fifty members when Ferryhill SCWG in Aberdeen (one of fifteen branches in that city) had over 150 members.[104] The weakness of the SCWG was undoubtedly in part due to the fact that the city's main co-operative society, the Dundee Eastern Co-operative Society, was a non-political body. Nonetheless, the failure of the SCWG in Dundee arguably limited women's political involvement and development and may be one reason why Dundee was the last city in Scotland to elect a female councillor. Also the high numbers of women in paid work in Dundee probably meant that many working-class women simply had no time for serious political activity.[105]

Dundee's lack of prominent socialist women may have played a part in the defeat of Marcus and Scrymgeour in 1931, and in the victory of the Unionist Florence Horsbrugh – as it has been contended that Horsbrugh's victories in 1931 and 1935 were due to her ability to attract women voters. However, she and Liberal Dingle Foot probably triumphed because of the spectacular collapse of the Labour government in 1931, and because of the economic crisis which hit the jute industry and which dramatically increased unemployment in the city in the 1930s.[106] Horsbrugh's and Foot's re-election against two Labour candidates in 1935 was made easier by the fact that both had performed well in Parliament, and by Labour's ill-conceived informal electoral pact with the Communists in Dundee (who claimed the pact's intention was to establish 'a great Soviet Republic' in Scotland), which is likely to have alienated undecided voters.[107]

At municipal level things were slightly better. Although the 1931 municipal elections left Labour with just four councillors, by 1935 the party had equalled the Moderate total on the council.[108] This was impressive since Labour's attempt to win control of Dundee had been made all the more difficult because of an electoral anomaly caused by Broughty Ferry, which consistently returned right-wing candidates who

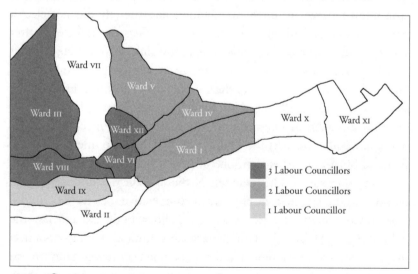

FIGURE 8.1
Spread of Labour councillors in Dundee, November 1936

allied themselves with the Moderates. This staunchly conservative suburb was guaranteed two wards (and thus six councillors) under the terms of its annexation in 1913 – despite the fact that these two wards had a much smaller electorate than any ward in the rest of Dundee. However, the creation of a new council ward in the solidly working-class Hilltown in 1935 partly redressed this democratic imbalance. Labour also developed a very efficient election campaign machine organised by talented local activists including Councillors William Hughes and Lily Miller, and in 1936 the party finally gained control of the council (Figure 8.1).[109]

CONCLUSIONS

Why did Labour succeed in Dundee given the city's reputation as a Liberal bastion before 1914? This is too complex a question to fully answer in a single chapter and there is undoubtedly scope for more research into this issue. However, it is clear that Wilkie's victory in 1906 was not the bolt from the blue it has sometimes been presented as. Unlike in England, where in many cases the Liberals actively assisted the rise of Labour before 1914, in Dundee the ILP and Labour Party became a significant political force despite the considerable opposition of the local Liberal Party and the Dundee press. Likewise, Alex Wilkie became an MP for Dundee in 1906 in the face of a determined campaign against both him and the Labour Party by Liberal politicians and in particular by Dundee's 'national Liberal daily', the *Dundee Advertiser*.

It is clear that Dundee Liberals viewed Labour and working-class politicians as more of a political threat than the Unionist Party. A year after the election of John Carnegie to the council in 1905, it was reported by James Reid in *Forward* that the *Advertiser* was openly hostile to working men running for the council. Indeed, by 1909 a body called the Citizens' Union – described by *The Tocsin* as an alliance of 'reactionary forces' in the Liberal and Conservative Parties who wished to prevent the return of Labour members to the council – was attempting to nominate middle-class candidates for municipal office.[110] This set the tone for future class relations in the city, and during the inter-war years this developed into a political standoff between two opposing factions – the Moderates (Unionist and Liberal) and the socialists (Labour and the Prohibitionists).

The Labour movement in Dundee was clearly growing in confidence and gaining in strength before 1914 and was able to expand trade union membership, mount successful strike action, elect Labour officials and front prominent national political campaigns between the 1890s and 1914. Walker, and to an extent Kemp, by focusing on local sources close to the Liberal Party including the Dundee press, have tended to under-estimate the full significance of Labour's advance in the city before 1922. Sources like the *Labour Leader, The Tocsin* and *Forward* present a very different picture, and while their reports undoubtedly contain some bias and embellishment, at least some of their claims are borne out in reports in newspapers such as *The Scotsman* and the *Glasgow Herald.*

Smyth notes that a significant part of Labour's and the ILP's electoral success was thanks to the efforts they made to tackle social issues and problems such as poor housing and unemployment and that in campaigning on these issues they won the wide support of working-class voters across Glasgow.[111] Rodger and Melling also assert that the main cause of class conflict in Scotland between 1890 and 1914 was over the issue of housing and the power of landlords. But these writers focus on Clydeside and west Scotland and, in the main, view the rent strike action of 1915 as the single most important event in transforming Labour politics in Scotland thereafter.[112] They entirely ignore the fact that the first rent strike action of this type took place in Dundee between January and March 1912, a full three years before, and was fully supported by the ILP, the Trades Council and the other socialist groups in the city.[113] This chapter has shown that clear parallels can be drawn between the rise of Labour in Dundee and in Glasgow, but would stress that this was more pronounced in Dundee in the period before 1914 than was hitherto thought to be the case.

This chapter demonstrates that Labour and other socialist groups in Dundee were able to use the city's social and economic problems to advance their political cause. Dundee had long been plagued by poor living conditions and high levels of poverty and this remained the case well into the twentieth century. D'Arcy Wentworth Thompson – on his appointment as professor at University College, Dundee in 1884 – recalled being 'shocked and saddened' by the poverty he saw around him, and argued that the slums of Dundee were even worse than those of London, Glasgow and Liverpool.[114] Along with the indomitable Mary Lily Walker and others associated with the fledgling University College,

Dundee, D'Arcy Thompson went on to become one of the founders of the Dundee Social Union in 1888, and in 1905 published their damming report into the social and industrial conditions of workers in the city.[115] Indeed, it is very tempting to speculate that this report may have had a direct impact on the success of Wilkie in the general election of 1906.

Upon the publication of the DSU Report in 1905, Mary Lily Walker asserted that she intended to shake middle-class complacency, but the report was largely met by apathy from the local press and an indifferent middle class. Further afield, Ramsay MacDonald – then secretary of the Labour Party – used evidence drawn from the DSU Report in support of a House of Commons bill 'permitting local authorities in Scotland to feed school children'.[116] But the report did shake local working-class organisations into action in Dundee, and in an attempt to help reduce city's alarmingly high child morality child rate, Labour members on the town council supported the Dundee Social Union in establishing restaurants for nursing working mothers in the city in 1909. Indeed, ILP Councillor John Reid in particular was praised for his part in promoting this scheme and in so doing established Dundee as the first municipality in Britain 'to have these [restaurants] as branches of civic work'.[117]

There were other advancements made in child healthcare in particular, and between 1911 and 1937, for example, child mortality rates fell from 156 deaths to 87 deaths per thousand.[118] But overcrowding remained a serious and recurring problem and in May 1936 *The Scotsman* reported that approximately 12,641 families in Dundee lived in overcrowded conditions. This prompted Dr Burgess, the Chief Medical Officer of Dundee, to demand the immediate construction of 10,000 new council houses in order to improve this situation.[119] It would seem, therefore, that by the mid-1930s Dundee was still struggling with many of the same social and welfare issues (amplified by mass unemployment) that the DSU had reported on a generation earlier. Indeed, in terms of overcrowding, the percentage of the population living in one-room and two-room houses had only dropped marginally, to 61.9 per cent in 1931 from 70.1 per cent in 1911.[120] Viewed from this perspective, it would be difficult to find fault with Hugh MacDiarmid's description of Dundee in the early 1930s as a 'grim monument to man's inhumanity to man'.[121]

The Dundee press had historically played an important role in helping to shape and influence political opinion in the city. But the press was never a friend of the trade union and Labour movement, and in the aftermath of the 1926 General Strike Thomson-Leng would only employ non-union labour. MacDiarmid argued that it was 'in perfect keeping' with their attitude that they chose continually to 'inveigh against socialism' and political extremism rather than deal directly with the plight of the unemployed and the social deprivation all too evident in their midst.[122] This was to an extent borne out in the aftermath of Labour's victory in 1936, when the *Courier and Advertiser* – rather than address the 'burning social and economic issues of the day' – issued a warning to the Dundee ratepayers that they now had an opportunity of experiencing at first hand 'a Socialist administration' and that this might well prove 'an instructive lesson'. As the press had done in the aftermath of Carnegie's election to the town council in 1905, they blamed Labour's rise to power in 1936 on the 'apathy and neglect' of the Moderates, and they clearly hoped that a taste of Labour in office might drive the voters back to the Moderate fold.[123] The *Courier and Advertiser* worked hard to discredit the Labour movement, characterising the Dundee Trades Council as the 'Wellgate Soviet', while reporting openly that this organisation was in fact the 'secret junta' that was really running the city (by influencing the Labour members controlling the council).[124] The *Courier and Advertiser* in the end got its wish when Labour lost control of the council in 1937. Notwithstanding the attitude of the press and the strength of the moderate political opinion in Dundee, Labour would recover after 1945 and with sweeping landslide victories take power in both local and national elections. Labour thereafter held both Dundee parliamentary seats and largely controlled Dundee city council for most of the twentieth century.[125] Perhaps the *Labour Leader* was not so overoptimistic in 1895 when it reported on the aftermath of the general election of that year that they hoped yet to capture Dundee for socialism.

NOTES

1. I.S. Wood, 'Hope deferred: Labour in Scotland in the 1920s' in I. Donnachie, C. Harvie and I.S. Wood (eds), *Forward! Labour Politics in Scotland 1888–1988* (Edinburgh, 1989), p. 31.
2. Ibid., pp. 34, 37–8. In 1922, 'forty of Labour's forty-three candidates in Scotland were ILP members and many were actually sponsored by the ILP': also William Kenefick, *Red Scotland! The Rise and Fall of the Radical Left, c.1872 to 1932* (Edinburgh, 2007), pp. 184–6.

3. Kenefick, *Red Scotland!*, pp. 168–70.
4. J. Kemp, 'Red Tayside? Political change in early twentieth-century Dundee' in
   L. Miskell, C.A. Whatley and B. Harris (eds), *Victorian Dundee: Image and Realities*
   (East Linton, 2000), p. 151.
5. I. Donnachie, 'Scottish Labour in the Depression' in Donnachie et al. (eds), *Forward!*,
   pp. 49, 57. Including four ILP seats and Willie Gallacher's seat in West Fife, the left
   captured 42.4 per cent of the Scottish vote in 1935.
6. I.C.G. Hutchison, *A Political History of Scotland, 1832–1924: Parties, Election and Issues*
   (Edinburgh, 1986), pp. 249–65, 277, 285–7: see also I.C.G. Hutchison, 'Scottish
   politics' in C.M.M. Macdonald and E. McFarland (eds), *Scotland and the Great War*
   (East Linton, 1999), pp. 39–1.
7. W.M. Walker, *Juteopolis: Dundee and its Textile Workers, 1885–1923* (Edinburgh, 1979),
   ch. 9, p. 394; also W. Walker, 'Dundee's disenchantment with Churchill: a comment
   on the downfall of the Liberal Party', *Scottish Historical Review* 49 (1970), p. 91.
8. C. Whatley, 'The case of James Myles, the "Factory Boy", and mid-Victorian Dundee'
   in Miskell et al. (eds), *Victorian Dundee*, p. 95.
9. Kenefick, *Red Scotland!*, pp. 66, 69.
10. *The Scotsman*, 5 November 1890; *Advertiser*, 22 May 1893.
11. Walker, *Juteopolis*, p. 62.
12. Ibid., p. 161.
13. Kemp, 'Red Tayside?', p. 151.
14. Walker, *Juteopolis*, p. 230.
15. Ibid., p. 261.
16. A. Petrie, *The 1915 Rent Strikes: An East Coast Perspective* (Dundee, 2008), p. 7.
17. *Labour Leader*, 27 July 1895.
18. *Labour Leader*, 15 February 1902.
19. *Labour Leader*, 9 September 1905 and 26 January 1906. Walker noted that the
    Advertiser, 'which had never been generous to Labour candidates', was 'positively
    churlish' when it came to Wilkie: *Juteopolis*, p. 280.
20. *The Scotsman*, 19 January 1906.
21. *Labour Leader*, 20 July 1895.
22. *Labour Leader*, 27 July 1895. The Scottish vote accounted for 9.8 per cent of the total
    British votes polled (43,725) and MacDonald's share for Dundee was 3 per cent overall.
23. Walker, *Juteopolis*, pp. 264–9.
24. *Labour Leader*, 23 June and 6 July 1895.
25. *The Scotsman*, 2 October 1902.
26. Walker, *Juteopolis*, p. 195 n. 2.
27. Report on Black's first address after his selection as Labour candidate for Dundee,
    Labour Leader, 27 November 1902; and report on resolution by Dundee ILP
    'regretting the retirement' of Black, *Labour Leader*, 3 February 1905.
28. *Labour Leader*, 19 and 26 January, 2 and 9 February 1895.
29. *Labour Leader*, Black's Obituary, 2 February, and report on his funeral, 9 February
    1906.
30. *Labour Leader*, 6 June 1889. The Labour Representation Committee (LRC) was the
    title of the Labour Group in Parliament from February 1900 until it became the
    Labour Party in 1906. Local LRCs were also set up across England and Wales from
    that time, but the principle was pioneered in Scotland with the formation of the
    SWPECs – they later adopted the title LRC: see Kenefick, *Red Scotland!*, pp. 48–9.

31. *Labour Leader*, 27 November 1902.
32. Kemp, 'Red Tayside?', pp. 160–1.
33. *Dundee Year Book* (1906), p. 69.
34. *Labour Leader*, 17 and 31 October 1903.
35. *Labour Leader*, 12 and 19 December 1903. One of the other speakers was Mr George Foster, the ex-Colonial Secretary for Canada. The *Montreal Gazette*, 5 December 1903, reported that he made 'A Splendid Impression' on the people of Dundee at the Kinnaird Hall on Tuesday 2 December. He was later Sir George Foster, Canadian Minister for Trade and Commerce during the Great War: see also *Courier*, 3 December 1903.
36. *The Scotsman*, 3 December 1903.
37. *Labour Leader*, 6 January 1905. James Reid stood for Dundee Parish Council in 1895 along with nine others. He also became a town councillor in 1919: see also Walker, *Juteopolis*, p. 264.
38. *Labour Leader*, 26 May, 9 June and 7 July 1905.
39. *Labour Leader*, 1 September 1905.
40. C. Harvie, 'Before the breakthrough, 1886–1922' in Donnachie et al. (eds), *Forward!*, p. 14.
41. Kemp, 'Red Tayside?', p. 153
42. *Labour Leader*, 1 September 1905: Article by 'Cavroche' (pen-name of William Stewart, based on the character in Victor Hugo's *Les Misérables*).
43. Kemp, 'Red Tayside?', p. 153.
44. Ibid., p. 164.
45. Bob Stewart, *Breaking the Fetters: The Memoirs of Bob Stewart* (London, 1967), p. 43.
46. *The Scotsman*, 30 April 1908, noted that London had left the Scottish Labour Party to make the decision whether to run a candidate against Churchill. But Party leaders in London were nonetheless annoyed and embarrassed at the decision to challenge the Liberals. The same newspaper reported after the election that 'with the exception of Mr Keir Hardie, hardly a Labour member went to Mr Stuart's assistance': see *The Scotsman*, 11 May 1908.
47. Stewart, *Breaking the Fetters*, p. 47 n. 1.
48. Kemp, 'Red Tayside?', pp. 167–8.
49. *The Tocsin*, April 1909.
50. Kemp, 'Red Tayside?', p. 151.
51. *Glasgow Herald*, report on the political situation in Scotland and Dundee, 7 January 1910. The report also stressed that Dundee had been, since the passing of the Reform Act, 1832, 'an inviolate Liberal stronghold' until 1906, when the line of radical representation was broken and replaced by a 'more extreme party' in the form of Labour.
52. *Advertiser*, 2–5 May 1893.
53. E. Gordon, *Women and the Labour Movement in Scotland 1850–1914* (Oxford, 1991), p. 191.
54. *Dundee Year Book* (1904), pp. 84–5.
55. Gordon, *Women and the Labour Movement*, pp. 194–5: the union's formation was assisted by the Dundee Social Union, the ILP and the Women's Trade Union League, whose driving force was secretary Mary MacArthur.
56. *Dundee Year Book* (1907), p. 122.
57. Widely reported by the Scottish press from 14 December 1910.
58. *Advertiser*, 15 December 1910.

59. *Courier* and *Advertiser*, between 23 February and 20 March 1910; *The Scotsman*, 25 and 28 February, 11 and 25 March; *Glasgow Herald*, 26 February, 11 and 18 March 1911.
60. *Courier*, 20 and 21 December 1911.
61. *Forward*, 30 December 1911: also A. Bell, 'A Glorious Lesson in Solidarity? The Dundee Carters' Strike 1911' (unpublished MA dissertation, University of Dundee, 1999); and Kenefick, *Red Scotland!*, pp. 107–8.
62. Free Labour Bureau, Annual Reports: see *The Scotsman*, 15 June and 26 December 1911.
63. *The Scotsman*, 26 December 1911; see also *Glasgow Herald*, 20 and 25 December 1911, and for 'riots' during the carters' strike, 18 and 22 December 1911; *Advertiser*, and *Courier*, 26–30 December 1911. (During August 1911 the *Glasgow Herald* ran three leading editorials on the 'Epidemic of Strikes' taking place across Scotland and the danger posed by syndicalism (15–17, 26 August).)
64. *Courier*, 20 December 1911: see also Bell, 'A Glorious Lesson in Solidarity?', pp. 9–20. The troops of the Black Watch were never used in Dundee. But for the Labour movement this act could easily have been deemed provocative, given that workers had been shot and killed, and several others wounded, when troops opened fire on strikers at Llanelli and at Liverpool docks during August 1911: see S. Peak, *Troops in Strikes: Military Intervention in Industrial Disputes* (Nottingham, 1984), pp. 19–32; and E. Taplin, *The Dockers' Union: A Study of the National Union of Dock Labourers, 1889–1922* (Leicester, 1986), pp. 94–6.
65. The 1912 strike was a precursor to a much wider, protracted and well-organised strike by Dundonians and others across the east coast of Scotland in 1915: see Petrie, *The 1915 Rent Strikes*, pp. 46–9.
66. M. Brooksbank, *No Sae Lang Syne: A Tale of This City* (Dundee, 1968), pp. 3–4, 10, 20–1.
67. Reports from the *Courier* and the *Advertiser* between January and August 1912.
68. Kenefick, *Red Scotland!*, pp. 108–13; see also various reports from the *Courier*, *Advertiser*, *Scotsman* and *Glasgow Herald*, March–April 1912.
69. Gordon, *Women and the Labour Movement*, p. 195.
70. *Advertiser*, 5 November 1913 and 13–16 December 1913; *Glasgow Herald*, 9 and 13 December, reporting on railway carters' strike at Dundee.
71. *Courier*, 12, 14, 16–17, 22, 28 January; and 2, 7, 9–10, 16, 21, 24 February 1914.
72. G. Dangerfield, *The Strange Death of Liberal England* (London, 1997 edn), p. 319; also Kenefick, *Red Scotland!*, pp. 91–4.
73. Kenefick, *Red Scotland!*, p. 129.
74. Stewart, *Breaking the Fetters*, p. 51.
75. *Advertiser*, 8 November 1914.
76. *People's Journal*, 29 November 1915.
77. See Kenefick, *Red Scotland!*, pp. 149–51.
78. *The Scotsman*, 4 October 1916 and 17 July 1917; 22 June 1918.
79. W. Kenefick, 'War resisters and anti-conscription in Scotland: an ILP perspective' in Macdonald and McFarland (eds), *Scotland and the Great War*, pp. 59–80.
80. *The Scotsman*, 12 February 1916.
81. *Forward*, 28 April 1917.
82. Kenefick, *Red Scotland!*, pp. 159–62.
83. *Forward*, 23 February 1918; also Kenefick, *Red Scotland!*, p. 154.
84. *Advertiser*, 3 November 1924.

85. DUA, MS 270/1/1/1: Dundee Unionist Association Minute Book 1909–1936, 25 November 1918.

86. *The Scotsman*, 3 and 5 December 1918.

87. *The Scotsman*, 30 November 1918.

88. Figures calculated from election results in *The Scotsman*, the *Glasgow Herald* and the *Advertiser*.

89. Other candidates considered were local ILP Councillor John Carnegie and English Labour Councillor James Wilson (National Union of Railwaymen).

90. The National Council of the ILP asked the Dundee branch to release Wallhead in 1921 – almost certainly to free him to contest Merthyr. See *The Scotsman*, 5 October 1921.

91. *The Communist*, 4 November 1922.

92. Kenefick, *Red Scotland!*, p. 154.

93. Kemp, 'Red Tayside?', p. 151.

94. Kenefick, *Red Scotland!*, pp. 168–71.

95. I. McLean, *Legend of Red Clydeside* (Edinburgh, 1999), p. 204.

96. Lewis Grassic Gibbon and Hugh MacDiarmid, *Scottish Scene, or, the Intelligent Man's Guide to Albyn* (London, 1934), from 'Dundee', a 'Sketch' by Hugh MacDiarmid, pp. 158–63: Dundee's press monopoly included the *Courier and Advertiser*, the *Evening Telegraph*, the *People's Journal*, the *Scots Magazine*, the *People's Friend* 'and innumerable others'.

97. *Advertiser*, 30 November 1923.

98. DUA, MS 88/11/5: *The Tocsin* and letters to Joseph Lee from Philip Snowdon, 19 April 1909, and James Keir Hardie, 21 April 1909.

99. *Dundee Free Press*, 6 September 1926.

100. *Evening Telegraph and Post*, 4 November 1935.

101. *The Scotsman*, 11 and 16 February 1928: also Thomas Johnston, *Memories* (London, 1952), p. 100.

102. In Dundee between 1932 and 1947 only five individuals stood as ILP council candidates and they attracted little electoral support.

103. K.J.W. Baxter, '"Estimable and Gifted"? Women in Party Politics in Scotland c.1918–1955' (unpublished PhD thesis, University of Dundee, 2008), *passim*. For the involvement of women in the Labour and Communist Parties in the West of Scotland in the inter-war period, see N. Rafeek, *Communist Women in Scotland: Red Clydeside from the Russian Revolution to the End of the Soviet Union* (New York, 2008); A. Hughes, 'Fragmented feminists? The influence of class and political identity in relations between the West of Scotland Women's Suffrage Society and the Independent Labour Party in the West of Scotland, c.1919–1932', *Women's History Review* 14 (2005); and J.J. Smyth, *Labour in Glasgow 1896–1936: Socialism, Suffrage, Sectarianism* (East Linton, 2000).

104. Glasgow City Archives, CWS 1/39/6/24–51: Scottish Co-operative Women's Guild Annual Reports and Balance Sheets/Statements 1918–1945: 1918, p. 3 and 1935, pp. 90–5.

105. For a fuller discussion see Baxter, '"Estimable and Gifted"?', pp. 172–4 and 288.

106. Ibid., p. 83.

107. *Courier and Advertiser*, 14 November 1935.

108. *Courier and Advertiser*, 4 November 1931.

109. *Forward*, 29 October 1938.

110. *Forward*, 28 October 1906, and *The Tocsin*, October 1909.

111. Smyth, *Labour in Glasgow*, p. 206 and *passim*. NB: Smyth wrongly states that Glasgow was the only city council in Scotland to be controlled by Labour.

112. R. Rodger, 'Crisis and confrontation in Scottish housing, 1880–1914' in R. Rodger (ed.), *Scottish Housing in the Twentieth Century* (London, 1989), pp. 25–53, at p. 42; J. Melling, 'Clydeside rent struggles and the making of Labour politics in Scotland, 1900–1939' in Rodger (ed.), *Scottish Housing*, pp. 54–88, at p. 65.

113. Petrie, *The 1915 Rent Strikes*, pp. 46–9.

114. Quoted in B. Lenman and K. Donaldson, 'Partners' incomes, investment and diversification in the Scottish linen area, 1850–1921', *Business History* 13 (1971), p. 18.

115. See Myra Baillie, 'The Grey Lady: Mary Lily Walker of Dundee' in Miskell et al. (eds), *Victorian Dundee*, pp. 128–9.

116. See C. Whatley, D.B. Swinfen and A.M. Smith, *The Life and Times of Dundee* (Dundee, 1993), p. 151; and Baillie, 'The Grey Lady', pp. 128–9.

117. Dundee Social Union established the Dundee Restaurant for Nursing Mothers in 1909 – the first of its kind in Britain: see the Joseph Lee Collection: DUA, MS 88/11/5.

118. R.A. Cage, 'Infant mortality rates and housing: twentieth century Glasgow', *Scottish Economic and Social History* 14 (1994), pp. 77–92, at p. 80.

119. *The Scotsman*, 15 August 1936: see also *The Scotsman*, 5 October 1937.

120. D. Graham, 'The use of published population census burgh ward data for local population studies: Dundee, 1901–1971', *Local Population Studies* (1997), p. 58: see Table 4, 33.

121. Gibbon and MacDiarmid, *Scottish Scene*, pp. 158–63.

122. Gibbon and MacDiarmid, *Scottish Scene*; on Dundee's 'press monopoly', which included the *Courier and Advertiser* and its associated newspapers the *Evening Telegraph*, the *People's Journal*, the *Scots Magazine*, the *People's Friend* 'and innumerable others', see 'Dundee', a 'Sketch' by Hugh MacDiarmid, pp. 158–63.

123. *Courier*, 4 November 1936.

124. *Courier*, 25 and 27 February, 29 October and 2 November 1937.

125. Election results from the *Courier and Advertiser*, *passim*: see also Kenneth Baxter, 'Radical Toun or Conservative City? Women in Politics in Dundee c. 1922 to c. 1955' (unpublished Honours History dissertation, University of Dundee, 2003).

CHAPTER 9

Music and the People:
Dundee, c.1914–39

Ruth Forbes

In recent years, the role and function of music in nineteenth-century urban society has been the subject of numerous historical studies in Scottish, English and Welsh towns.[1] In the early twentieth century, patterns of musical activity continued to be influenced by these earlier developments. However, the period between the two world wars saw advancements in sound and communications technology, which alongside other social and economic developments, transformed the ways in which people experienced music.

In the decade preceding the First World War, Dundee already possessed a diverse musical culture.[2] However, while most sections of the community experienced music in some shape or form, the main beneficiaries of this musical culture were, arguably, the prosperous middle classes, who had the time and money to participate in a broader range of recreational activities. As in the nineteenth century, affiliation to a musical society such as the Dundee Amateur Choral Union or the Dundee Orchestral Society conferred cultural and social refinement, and membership remained restricted to the influential middle classes.[3] Although the Dundee Orchestral Society appears to have prioritised musical ability over social status, the long working hours and pitiful income levels of the working population conspired with the cost of instruments and tuition fees and anxieties about dress, behaviour and social acceptance, to exclude a large section of the community.[4] There were, however, some notable instances of social inclusion: for example, following the Education (Scotland) Act of 1872, the teaching of music to all children in local Board Schools had borne fruit in the high standard of children's choirs, and an expansion in the number of popular adult choirs from the 1880s onwards.[5]

The first decade of the twentieth century saw the culmination of the Victorian civic pride which had motivated the creation of a civic infrastructure into which various forms of cultural activity had been subtly interwoven.[6] The optimism of a new millennium also gave impetus to progressive ideas in town planning, and the formulation by City Engineer and Architect, James Thomson, of a series of plans, which included a new civic centre with a grand concert hall at its focal point.[7] However, against a background of declining trade and the consequent social problems of unemployment and slum housing, the allocation of public money on a grandiose city centre reconstruction project elicited justifiable criticism. Thomson's scheme was already floundering when, in April 1914, local jute magnate James Key Caird stepped into the breach, offering to pay £100,000 towards the cost of the City Hall. At this juncture, a brief examination of Caird's motives is illustrative. Caird had already donated towards a number of health and welfare institutions in the city; however, from 1912, he ratcheted up his donations to cultural institutions and international scientific endeavours.[8] While these actions indicate an element of continuity with those of an earlier generation of philanthropic industrialists, such as David Baxter and John Mitchell Keiller, their marked acceleration and changed focus suggest that he may have been influenced by the benefactions of Andrew Carnegie and the rationale which underpinned them.[9] Caird remained aware of local needs as well as wider developments, and by 1914, the need for a public hall of 'sufficient size and appropriate equipment' was clearly evident. The Kinnaird Hall, which had functioned as Dundee's main civic and concert hall for over half a century, was proving inadequate to the needs of Dundee's expanding audiences and the increasing number of larger musical ensembles. Moreover, its utilitarian facilities and drab appearance compared badly with other Scottish cities, and it is highly probable that the opening of Edinburgh's Usher Hall in March 1914 provided the catalyst for Caird's donation three weeks later.

As the town council proceeded hurriedly with the purchase and clearing of the site, Caird liaised with Thomson in formulating plans for the building, with the pragmatic Caird's concept of 'the maximum of usefulness and the minimum of ornamentation' ultimately prevailing over Thomson's more elaborate (and expensive) designs. The sense of urgency was portentous, as within three weeks of the foundation stone being laid on 10 July 1914, war broke out, delaying construction and pushing up costs, and Caird died in 1916. The new City Hall, renamed in Caird's honour, was finally completed in 1921. At 230 feet long, 82 feet wide and 50 feet high, with a capacity of up to 4,000, it was slightly longer than the average concert hall and accommodated a third more than the King's Theatre, hitherto the largest performance venue in the town. The smaller Marryat Hall (named after Caird's sister, Emma Marryat, who donated £75,000 following her brother's death) was incorporated at its right-hand side.

The first event held in the hall, on 3 September 1921, was not a grand opening concert but a political (Labour) meeting attended by an estimated 4,000 people, many of whom who were attracted by a desire to see inside the building. However, while a local press reporter praised the 'magnificent and spacious interior', he declared the most striking feature of the building to be the clarity of sound which enabled 'every word of the speakers [to be] heard with the most pleasing distinctness in all parts of the large building'.[10] While James Thomson attributed this to the proper proportions of length, width and height, and the absence of sound-distorting recesses within the building, he also hinted at an unplanned factor deep in the foundations, where the hollow spaces between supporting concrete pillars simulated the sounding board of a violin, creating a stereophonic effect.[11]

While Labour politician and experienced orator Ramsay MacDonald was the first to pay tribute to the hall, it was in the medium of music that its distinctive acoustic qualities were most readily appreciated, as the success of an initial series of six civic charity concerts confirmed. Such qualities brought out the best in audiences and performers. Indeed, the reviewer of a performance by the band of the 2nd Battalion of the Royal Scots observed: 'The crowd had a magnetic effect on the band, as they immediately improved on their recent visit.'[12] From the launching of the first series of international subscription concerts in October 1922, the hall's acoustics elicited praise from international performers, including violinists Fritz Kreisler and Mischa Elman, Russian tenor Vladimir Resing, Irish tenor John McCormack and Italian soprano Amelita Galli Gucci, all of whom described the Caird Hall as one of the finest in which they had ever performed.[13]

After the hiatus of war, the establishment of the Caird Hall gave an important kick-start to musical life in the city. The following year saw a surge in musical activity: for example, in the course of one week in February 1922 the Caird Hall hosted a concert by the Glasgow Orpheus Choir, a performance of Samuel Coleridge Taylor's 'Song of Hiawatha' by the Dundee Amateur Choral Union, an operatic concert, a grand concert, and a Saturday evening popular concert. At the King's Theatre, a week-long programme by the Carl Rosa Opera Company attracted capacity audiences.[14] The Caird Hall was officially opened by Edward, Prince of Wales in a brief, simple ceremony on 26 October 1923. The decision to eschew the expensive and ostentatious pageantry of earlier pre-war civic ceremonies – James Thomson handed a key to the Prince, who proceeded to unlock the main door, and decorations were confined to a few strategically placed flags and flowers – was determined largely by financial constraints and political sensibilities. That same year it had been considered necessary to spend £47,000 on Unemployment Relief, and the acute shortage of working-class housing was attracting extensive criticism in a forthcoming local election campaign. At the same time, the *Advertiser's* comment that 'the Caird Hall is sufficiently massive and dignified to speak for itself [hence it] needs no decoration', was consonant with Caird's vision of a living institution, 'adapted to the present day needs of an industrial city, and capable of adaptation to the varying requirements of a progressive community'.[15] Caird's vision was to prove accurate, as throughout the twentieth century the hall played a significant role in the musical life of the city, attracting internationally renowned musicians as well housing other cultural and political events.

The Great War marked the end of the era of civic pride and, with the death of Caird, the grand philanthropic gestures which accompanied it. In October 1919, Her Majesty's Theatre, Dundee's sole venue for drama, musical theatre and opera, closed after a campaign to establish a locally subsidised community theatre failed to attract sufficient investment.[16] At the same time, the town council's task of maintaining the existing cultural infrastructure was fraught with difficulty as every expense, from the purchase of imported Austrian chairs for the Caird Hall, to the organisation of civic concerts, was queried and criticised. In the case of the latter, the council's attempts at cost cutting backfired disastrously. In September 1921, the Caird Hall Committee entered into an arrangement with the conductor of the Dundee Orchestral Society, Alexander M. Stoole, to establish a series of six Sunday evening orchestral concerts.[17]

However, when the council's allowance of £90 failed to cover the minimum wage requirements of the Amalgamated Musicians' Union, the Caird Hall Committee sought to circumvent the extra expense by cancelling the series and organising a cheaper series of miscellaneous charity concerts by amateur ensembles.

When the musicians lodged compensation claims for breach of contract, the town council became embroiled in a protracted dispute in which Stoole's assertion that 'if one [musician] was paid all [forty-two] would require to be paid', was backed by the AMU's demand that equal treatment be given to each member. The musicians' stance came as something of a surprise to the town council who, up until this point, appear to have subscribed to the outmoded but nevertheless persistent concept of musicians as accomplished, temperamental domestic servants with neither the inclination nor collective power to assert their rights as employees.[18] This misjudgement proved to be a costly mistake, which ultimately concluded with the town council offering £110 to 'get out of the whole business'.[19]

The next venture into civic musical provision, the appointment of a city organist, met with greater success as, besides the reduced costs and complications of employing one individual, the undertaking was informed by past errors and contemporary practice. In March 1926, following an investigation of the position in other cities, the town council unanimously agreed to appoint a city organist at an annual salary of £50. In order to discourage local rivalries and avoid accusations of favouritism, canvassing for the post was prohibited, and Herbert Walton, organist at Glasgow Cathedral, was invited to make the selection.

Walton's choice of James Hinchliffe (b.1894) was an intelligent and popular one. Hinchliffe, a native Dundonian, was a prodigious young musician who had studied under his father, John Hinchliffe, a respected performer and teacher. At the time of his appointment in January 1927, Hinchliffe was already an accomplished soloist, accompanist and musical director with a broad experience in sacred and classical music and cinema accompaniment, as well as a developing knowledge of organ architecture and construction.[20] Any lingering doubts as to his appointment were put to rest by his proven abilities as a musical director and his long, unstinting dedication to the post. Yet, while Corporation concerts organised by Hinchliffe were consistently well attended and occasionally attracted capacity audiences, their core audience was largely drawn from the middle classes as well as a smaller number of musicians and dedicated listeners from all social classes.

Another source of civic musical provision which enjoyed a greater popular success, both in performance and audience terms, was that of instrumental bands. In the years preceding the First World War, there were approximately half a dozen brass and pipe bands actively based in the city. The outbreak of war had a significant impact on the nature and content of music, particularly on the bands, as the focus of activity shifted to patriotic concerts and military-style parades. Between September 1914 and December 1915, the *Dundee Year Book* listed thirty-four select concerts, the majority of which were benefits for war-related charities.[21] With their military associations, dress and repertoire, the bands presented the correct patriotic image, which was fully exploited in fund-raising and recruitment campaigns. Within a year, however, the loss of band members and audiences to military service and war work had resulted in the suspension of band activity at civilian level.

If the war curtailed musical activity in the civic sphere, it was to have a significant impact in the longer term, particularly in the realm of pipe music. The trend towards city pipe bands had been established well before the war: for example, in 1905, the formation of the Dundee Police Pipe Band, by a number of ex-soldiers in the force, marked the incorporation of the army piping tradition into civic institutional life. While the expansion of the British Empire had seen a number of young men pass through Scottish regiments where they received an intensive, arguably superficial, musical training,[22] the First World War saw an unprecedented level and rapidity of recruitment by regiments such as the Cameronians, the Gordon Highlanders, and the Highland Light Infantry, which by then had an established piping tradition. However, while the conditions of war did not produce great musicians, there were important social consequences, as many young men from the urban lowlands became infused with an interest and enthusiasm for pipe music which they carried back into civilian life.

The appeal of the pipes can be attributed to a number of factors. Firstly, they fulfilled an important psychological function. Over the course of the war, hundreds of pipers had been killed, as they formed the vanguard in numerous military assaults, a fact which inspired the pioneer of the remembrance movement, Earl Haig, to comment that 'the fallen [will] inspire others to learn the pipes and keep their music alive'.[23]

Learning the pipes thus became a form of memorialism, a way of allevi-ating the guilt of having survived. Secondly, membership of a pipe band also helped with the transition to normality, as the comradeship of war was transmuted into the sociability of civilian life. Lastly, and perhaps most importantly, was the music itself. Given that many ex-soldiers had experienced unspeakable trauma, the language of the pipes conveyed a complex of emotions, as well as providing a sense of cultural identity.

The end of the war saw a resumption of musical activity, as old bands were reformed and new ones, such as the McKenzie Pipe Band, founded.[24] After the disruptions of war,[25] Dundee's brass bands also resumed their activities with a renewed vigour and focus, and by the mid-1920s, the Sunday evening park concerts were attracting hundreds of young people. However, the council's haphazard organisation of them, and their refusal to grant £500, 'to put Dundee in a similar position to other communities', soon became a bone of contention with the Parks Committee and the bands themselves.[26] Matters came to a head in April 1926 when representatives of five bands threatened a mass strike unless the council dropped their 'oppressive' 7.5 per cent levy on collections and allocated an equal number of concerts, particularly in Baxter Park, to each band.[27] Amid an atmosphere of mounting industrial and political unrest and advance warning of a sympathetic protest by the neigh-bouring Forfarshire Band Association, the council promptly conceded the former demand, and pledged to resolve the latter.[28]

By enabling the bands to maximise their income from collections, the town council managed to maintain a source of cheap civic enter-tainment. Not surprisingly, the Parks Committee subsequently defended the bands' activities from all criticism. For example, when a delegation of ministers from the Dundee United Free Presbytery blamed the Sunday evening concerts for luring away a great many of the younger 'less robust' members of their congregations, members of the Parks Committee opined that it was equally possible to 'worship God in Baxter Park . . . as in a church', and moreover, that by attracting 'hundreds of young people to the parks', the bands kept them from 'wandering the streets' and indulging in less wholesome forms of recreation.[29]

However, the town council had another possible reason for culti-vating a good relationship with the bands. Despite advances in musical education (such as the establishment of the Schools' Music Festivals in 1920), throughout the inter-war years, the teaching of music within the state curriculum was limited to singing. The city's bands thus filled an important gap, providing a key source of free tuition in a range of instruments and relieving the municipal Education Department of any obligation to finance it. Many experienced band members, such as James Sword, Tommy Donaldson, Kenny McGregor and William Ogilvie, motivated by nothing more than a passion for music and a desire to pass it on, freely devoted their leisure time to teaching young inexperienced players, often through the auspices of the Boys' Brigade.[30]

While the Boys' Brigade, with its emphasis on drill, discipline and smartness, was linked to concepts of military service and good citizenship, many were undoubtedly attracted by the opportunities it afforded to obtain a musical education often denied to the boys of working-class families. Nevertheless, the growing interest and participation in musical activity also fuelled a demand for private tuition. In the first three decades of the twentieth century, the number of professional musicians and music teachers listed in the local directories rose steadily from eighty-seven to over a hundred, the majority of whom operated from premises in the west and centre of the city, with a smaller number in the suburbs of Lochee and Broughty Ferry.

For many full-time musicians, teaching formed part of a broader career which included employment as church organists, choirmasters, cinema accompanists, members of dance bands and solo performers. Teaching was also sensitive to variations in the economy, as experience of financial hardship often led to a drop in demand for non-essential services such as music lessons. One teacher, who had set up a studio in the High Street after returning from Newcastle during the General Strike, recalls how he 'did quite well at first', but a subsequent slump in business forced him to augment his income by working as a joiner for the Dundee Bedding Company. A growing demand for music lessons in the early 1930s enabled him to resume teaching full-time, until a decline triggered by the outbreak of the Second World War once more compelled him to take on another job as a clerk with the Imperial Tobacco Company.[31]

Significantly, whereas women were under-represented in most professions, they constituted over 40 per cent of the music teachers listed in the professional directories, and a majority of their pupils.[32] At a time when career opportunities for women remained limited, music teaching provided a measure of financial independence and also a means of supplementing the family income. Thus, given that the Boys' Brigade and instrumental bands were male preserves, in many lower-middle and upper working-class households which could generate sufficient income, private music tuition was reserved for girls.

While many ambitious musicians undoubtedly viewed teaching as a 'fall back' option, it was also regarded as a vocation, particularly in the case of women whose personal ambitions were sacrificed to the demands of family. An illustrative example is that of Matilda Marshall Bird (b.1891), who, at the age of sixteen, was obliged to decline a piano scholarship and embark on a teaching career alongside her father, John Bird, in order to support her five siblings. However, rather than begrudging a lost opportunity, Bird appears to have sublimated her ambitions in nurturing the talents of subsequent generations of female musicians.[33] While many women taught music at an elementary level, a significant number, including Bird, Nan Cordiner, May Robertson and Evelyn Reid, attained higher qualifications than many of their male colleagues, and enjoyed long and successful careers teaching to a high level.

The view that a musical education is vital for the visually impaired and that it is the role of a civilised community to help facilitate it, was evident in the policies of the Dundee Institution for the Blind, which sought to nurture the musical potential of its trainees. While the cultivation of musical skills was held to compensate for the lack of sight by sharpening the sense of aural perception, a musical education also paved the way for a career in music and the financial independence this provided. Hence one of the city's most popular choirmasters of the early twentieth century, Henry Marshall (b.1862), received his first music lessons while learning basket weaving there. After training as a piano tuner, Marshall progressed to the Royal Normal College for the Blind where he studied under a series of renowned teachers including Frits Hartvigson, who taught piano to Queen Alexandra. On returning to Dundee in the mid-1880s, Marshall applied for several organist-choirmaster posts; however, despite presenting impeccable references, he was repeatedly rejected in favour of sighted candidates. Marshall later recalled how experience of prejudice and the awareness that 'many had lost a situation because of it' motivated him to form the Dundee Select Choir, which subsequently gained a reputation for excellence in part-singing and produced several professional singers.[34] Besides his work as a church organist and choirmaster, Marshall was a successful teacher, and one of his most notable pupils, George Hutchison Millers (b.1880) – who also received his first lessons in music at the Dundee Institution for the Blind – went on to have a successful career as a church organist-choirmaster, and to hold the post of organist at the Kinnaird Hall for nine years.[35] Despite being labelled 'blind organists' by their obituarists, ultimately it was the talent and professionalism of Marshall, Millers and other musicians such as Robert Kilgour (b. c.1894), which enabled them to attract the patronage of pupils of all abilities, and maintain consistent commercial success. Moreover, Marshall's affirmation that 'a person without sight, and a very ordinary person at that, could conduct a choir' (emphasis original), which hinted at other social prejudices overcome, also resonated with a large section of Dundee's population.

Notwithstanding occasional dips in demand, such as that precipitated by the General Strike, the local musical economy not only weathered the recession but rose to an all-time high during the inter-war years. Paradoxically, the peak years of unemployment were paralleled by a growth in real incomes for many of those in work, and concomitantly, an increased consumption of musical products and services. The local trade directories of 1930–1 listed 102 musicians and music teachers, sixteen music and musical instrument sellers, four piano tuners and one bagpipe maker. While some musical instruments, especially bagpipes, fiddles and brass instruments, were obtained by loan, exchange or bequest, for those in receipt of a regular weekly wage hire purchase became a common method of obtaining traditional instruments and of enabling the uninitiated to experiment with new innovations and musical styles. For example, J.T. Forbes offered a full trial of a 3½ octave portable xylophone at terms of 3 shillings a week, and for 2s 6d, B.G. Forbes invited customers to try their hand at the Hill Billy guitar which, ostensibly, required 'no training whatsoever'. For less fortunate musicians struggling to eke out their weekly income, pawnbrokers (of which there were twenty-one listed in the 1930–1 trade directories) offered a means of safeguarding their instruments through a weekly cycle of hocking and redeeming. Ultimately, as customers failed to redeem their tickets, pawnbrokers became another source of cheap musical instruments.

Music sellers also developed various specialisms. By the mid-1930s, J.T. Forbes was importing Hohner accordions from Trossingen in Germany to the specifications of proprietor Charles S. Forbes and of Jimmy Shand, then employed as a salesman-demonstrator. Hohner subsequently went on to manufacture the prototype of the Shand Marino, which became intrinsic to Shand's success as the twentieth century's foremost exponent of Scottish country dance music. In the late 1930s, Larg's Piano Saloons advertised ten models of 'used and returned from hire' pianos, offering part-exchange or 'deferred terms', and Paterson's, Sons and Co., who specialised in gramophones, acted as agents for His Master's Voice and Columbia companies from the early 1920s onwards.[36]

One of the most important developments in the inter-war musical economy was the advent of radio. The transition of radio from the pastime of a few technical experts to the mass consumer market was rapid. In February 1923, a Modern Homes exhibition in the Caird Hall opened with a wireless demonstration, and among the various items on show, a 'wireless listening room' proved to be the most popular attraction. In a newspaper article entitled 'The Charm of Radio Music', a local commentator explained the merits of radio as a musical medium, citing the absence of 'jarring mechanical vibrations', and praising the tonal purity, volume and 'feeling of nearness and personality' it conveyed.[37] This growth in enthusiasm reflected a wider national trend. By 1925, the number of radio owners in Britain had risen to approximately two million, and the growing local market was indicated by the appearance of sixteen wireless operators and radio sellers in the Dundee trade directories and numerous advertisements for radio equipment in the local press.

Radio was particularly attractive to Dundee's population for a number of reasons. Firstly, after the initial outlay, it provided cheap musical entertainment for the entire family. The price of the cheapest ticket to a typical concert in the Caird Hall in 1923 was 2s 4d, which effectively prohibited the participation of large or average-sized working-class families, and making it a rare event for many others. Secondly, radio enabled people to listen to an eclectic range of music in their own homes, every night of the week if they wished, without having to alter their behaviour, dress or habits, free to respond as the music moved them.[38] Conversely, radio had its disadvantages. A wireless set was a costly and complex piece of equipment requiring skill and patience to set up. One labourer's daughter laughingly recalled how her father spent hours painstakingly assembling and tuning his new 'cat's whiskers' set, only to have the children stumble over it as they answered the call of nature in the middle of the night.[39]

Moreover, in contrast with the USA where a growing number of commercial radio stations were giving airtime to new styles of popular music, the BBC's monopoly on radio transmission resulted in a proliferation of instrumental music of an essentially conservative nature.[40] For example, in October 1938 (by which time an estimated 90 per cent of British households owned a radio set) a typical Saturday schedule included two programmes of organ music, three of orchestral music, a concert by the Kutcher Trio, two recitals of synthetic folk songs, thirty minutes of Scottish dance music, and concluded with a session by Ambrose and his Orchestra with songs from Evelyn Dall and Vera Lynn.[41] While such content may have failed to reflect the growing trend towards less sedate forms of popular music, the regular broadcasting of classical music also had a significant impact on local amateur societies, many of whom who were struggling to retain members and attract audiences.[42] In Dundee, where classical music was already acknowledged as the interest of a small but enthusiastic minority, the Dundee Orchestral Society attributed dwindling concert attendance to 'the abundance of music provided through the medium of wireless'.[43]

Not surprisingly, the staid musical content of radio programmes failed to appeal to many young people, who preferred to seek their entertainment outside the home, and the growing youth market was one which local entrepreneurs were quick to exploit. The inter-war years saw a significant growth in the number of dance halls, which became one of the most popular forms of music-based entertainment for younger members of the working class. One former worker at Valentine's postcard factory recalled how the workers would rush home at Saturday noon to change their clothes and descend on the dance halls, returning again later in the evening.[44]

Throughout the 1930s, 4d procured entrance to most dance halls, with some smaller venues, such as Joe Bell's Lochee Dance Hall, admitting regular customers 'on tick'.[45] Larger dance halls, such as the Locarno and the Palais, also taught dancing, with the proprietors travelling to London and Blackpool to pick up the latest dance movements which they subsequently introduced, along with their musical accompaniments, to Dundee patrons. Besides providing employment for local musicians, many dance hall owners engaged renowned jazz musicians from outside the International Celebrity Concert circuit. For example, the owners of the Palais, James and Helen

Duncan, secured Louis Armstrong for a gig there during his first visit to Scotland in 1933. The Duncans also were also involved in promoting a series of Sunday evening concerts in the Caird Hall, which included the bands of Jack Hylton, Henry Hall and Louis Levy.[46]

While dance halls were immensely popular with Dundee's working-class youth, the appeal of cinema cut across all barriers of age and class. The development of cinema was arguably the most important cultural phenomenon of the early twentieth century in local as well as global terms. For example, in 1930, Dundee, with its population of 175,000, had twenty-seven cinemas compared to 127 in Glasgow, thirty-nine in Edinburgh and fifteen in Aberdeen with their respective populations of 1,088,000, 438,000 and 167,000.[47] Before considering the importance of cinema in influencing musical tastes, it is worth examining the reasons for its particular predominance in Dundee. Since the end of the war, the desire to attract new industry to the town appears to have resulted in the greater accommodation of commercial forces, particularly in the area of leisure provision. In February 1936, for example, the town council granted planning permission to the Glasgow-based Green's entertainment firm to construct an 85-foot-tall concrete sign tower at their new super-cinema in the Nethergate, despite the vociferous objections of the Dundee Institute of Architects and the Dundee Art Society.

Two other factors in the popularity of cinema were the persistent evils of overcrowding, low pay and unemployment. Despite post-war goals of reducing Dundee's high levels of congested slum housing, at the end of the 1930s Dundee had a higher percentage of one- and two-roomed houses than any other Scottish city and several cases of multiple families living in one dwelling. For much of the population, the cinema provided an escape from a noisy, cramped home, and was often treated as an extension of such. Bill Ramsay, a former junior projectionist at the Pavilion Cinema in the Hilltown, recalls how large families would ensconce themselves on the rows of wooden benches and proceed to distribute nuts, oranges, cake, lemonade and whelks, obtained from a stall outside, throughout the show.[48]

The cinema environment was particularly hospitable to Dundee's poorer working class, for whom the dimmed lighting, warmth, continuous programmes and, particularly for the families of unemployed and low-paid shift workers, cheaper daytime prices and the practice of accepting jam jars and tea labels as admission fees, provided an affordable escape from grinding poverty, bad housing and lack of prospects. This phenomenon was paralleled in many other working-class towns, where the seemingly paradoxical consumption of cheap luxuries (such as visits to the movies) compensated for inadequate food, shelter and other basic necessities.[49]

Competition between Dundee's cinemas was intense, and managers sought to attract audiences through street advertising, window displays, and hiring people to act as cowboys and singing sheikhs. Besides providing an added attraction, music was an integral part of the cinema experience; from the pre-war years, when screenings of single-reel films were interspersed with 'turns' from local variety acts, to the silent epics of the early 1920s. The advent of longer films created the need for sound accompaniment, not only to help evoke the right mood and atmosphere, but also to sustain the attention of audiences accustomed to short bursts of entertainment. Films were often distributed with lists of suggestions and complex musical scores which challenged the most accomplished of musicians. For example, while working as organist at the Kinnaird Picture House, James Hinchliffe was given forty-eight hours to master 300 pages of music, including effects for storms, battles and other 'emotional experiences'. Music was also used imaginatively to publicise films. For example, in June 1925, the screening of J.B.L. Noel's documentary, *The Epic of Everest*, was preceded by a live performance by a band of Tibetan lamas, whose renditions of Buddhist monastic music on 10-foot *dung chen* horns elicited more attention than did the film itself.[50]

The need for live cinema accompaniment also created regular employment for local musicians. Larger city centre cinemas such as the Kinnaird, La Scala and the King's, employed orchestras ranging from twelve to eighteen in number, with smaller establishments hiring a pianist and occasionally a violinist and percussionist. The expense of maintaining large orchestras resulted in an increased dependence on organs, which were used to supplement the volume of orchestras and also for solo performances.[51] The Kinnaird Hall organ, which had been installed in 1864 as part of a general drive to promote musical culture and improve Dundee's civic image, entered its period of optimum use in the era of silent films. With its grand appearance and ability to mimic the effects of various instruments, the King's Wurlitzer organ, installed when the theatre was transformed into a super-cinema in 1928, provided an attraction in itself. A former patron recalls the sight of the organ 'rising majestically on its lift from the orchestra pit', as the dapper organist, Hill Cutler, 'bathed in the limelight', proceeded to lead the audience in the singing of contemporary popular songs, the words of which were projected on to the screen.[52]

With its badly synchronised and distorted sound track, the first talking picture shown in Dundee, *The Singing Fool* in 1929, was regarded as something of a novelty.[53] Within a few years, however, the installation of improved sound equipment had obviated the need for live accompaniment, and while some cinemas retained their orchestras for evening intermissions, there was a significant reduction in employment for local musicians. While established musicians such as F. Routledge Bell, leader of La Scala orchestra, and Henry Hollingworth, of the Regent's and King's orchestras, continued their respective careers as teacher of violin and leader of a regular cafe orchestra and occasional dance band, scores of musicians lost their jobs as a result of the transition to sound.[54] In 1982, Bill Ramsay recalled witnessing the sad spectacle of a violinist, clarinettist and trumpeter busking around a hat which displayed the sign, 'Out of work due to talking pictures.'[55]

For cinema audiences, however, the advent of talking pictures increased their exposure to a variety of musical styles. Local historian David Phillips (b.1914), attributed the larger than average attendance at an International Celebrity Concert by the Italian tenor Beniamino Gigli in October 1934 to the interest generated by the recent screening of a film, *Tell Me Tonight*, in which the Polish tenor Jan Kiepura sang several Italian arias. Both Phillips and a local press critic noted how vociferous calls from the 2,000-strong audience, including several members of Dundee's Italian immigrant community, elicited 'twice as many songs as the programme indicated', with Gigli's crowd-pleasing finale, 'O Sole Mio' 'bringing down the house'.[56]

Films and concerts often served to promote each other. On 15 January 1938, a concert by Paul Robeson in the Caird Hall coincided with the screening of two of his films, *King Solomon's Mines* and *Big Fella*, at four Dundee cinemas. In the latter Robeson sang three songs, 'Lazin'', 'Ma Curly Headed Baby' and 'You Didn't Oughta Do Such Things', which featured in his concert programme.[57] However, while exposure to artists and their material through the medium of cinema undoubtedly helped boost concert attendance, the appeal to Dundee audiences of artists such as Robeson and John McCormack merits further examination.

By the time he first appeared at the Caird Hall in 1927, the Irish tenor John McCormack was an established recording artist with a repertoire which encompassed light opera, German lied, drawing-room ballads, Italian serenata and traditional and modern Irish songs. Arguably, it was the inclusion of the latter which accounted for his appeal to Dundee's population, which in the 1920s, included a significant percentage of third- and fourth-generation Irish Catholics, many of whom retained their cultural identity through an adherence to the Catholic Church and a sympathy with Irish national ideals. In 1929, McCormack's rendition of César Franck's 'Panis Angelicus' was so well received that he was obliged to repeat it, and by his final concert in 1935, the enthusiastic response elicited by Irish standards such as 'Kathleen Mavourneen', Donald Ford's 'A Prayer to Our Lady', Thomas Moore's 'The Meeting of the Waters' and McCormack's adaptation of 'Londonderry (*sic*) Air' 'with words tenderly characteristic of his nation', led the reviewer to conclude that 'McCormack's admirers would be content to hear nothing from him but the wistful refrains of his native land'.[58]

However, McCormack's appeal also extended to serious musicians, and while one knowledgeable local singer attending McCormack's 1927 concert opined that some of the songs were 'cheap' and 'would not have been taken off anyone less famous', he concluded that McCormack's 'marvellous exhibition of breath control and self-expression' contributed to 'a wonderful night'.[59] Like many other performers on the international concert circuit, McCormack was skilled at adapting his material to suit the tastes and preferences of local audiences. For example, in 1930, the inclusion of 'Annie Lawrie' at the end of his Irish section was observably appreciated by a Dundee audience who, like McCormack himself, were the products of an integrated Scots and Irish heritage.[60]

Concert Programme by John McCormack, 30 October 1930[61]

1. Songs
    (a) Entlaubet ist der Walde   Old German (1536)
    (b) Alma del core
         (from 'La Constanza')   Caldara
         (words included)

2. Piano Solo   VITYA VRONSKI

3. Songs
    (a) Memnon (words included)   Arthur Foote
    (b) A Widow Bird Sare Mourning   Granville Bantock
    (c) A Cradle Song
        (words included)   Sir Hamilton Harty
    (d) There   Sir Hubert Parry
    Encores: Annie a-wooing
    Just For Today   Seaver

4. Irish Folk Songs
    (a) Song of the Fairy King
        (words included)   Arr. Stanford
    (b) I'd Roam the World Over
        (words included)   Arr. Wood
    (c) Una Ban (words included)   Arr. Hardebeck
    Encore: Machree
                                         Ernest Torrance

5. Piano Soli   VITYA VRONSKI

6. Songs
    (a) Luoghi sereni e cari   Donaudy
        (words included)
    (b) The Fairy Tree   Vincent O'Brien
        (words included)
    (c) Far Apart (*First time*)   Edwin Schneider
        (words included)
    (d) A Night Idyll   Raymond Loughborough
        (words included)
    Final Encore: Annie Lawrie

If McCormack's immense popularity can be attributed to his ability to cater liberally for public taste by bridging the gap between popular and classical music and by his appeal to residual cultural identities, the reasons for the massive drawing power of Paul Robeson are equally revealing. When Robeson first appeared at the Caird Hall in 1930, he too was an established international performer and recording artist. Yet, while a local critic commended Robeson's technique – 'he is a maestro of effective rubato and colour control [who possesses] rare beauty in his diction' – the most remarkable feature of his performance was his ability to touch 'receptive chords in the hearts of an audience', to which the critic attributed his 'sincerity, his deep-rooted interest in his race and sympathy with their sufferings' reflected in a repertoire of African-American spirituals. Such sympathy with the artist and his idiom had a local precedent in the reception extended to the Jubilee Singers, a touring party of emancipated slaves from Fisk University, Nashville, who visited the town during their European tour in 1873.[62] However, while the Jubilee Singers were credited with popularising the 'negro spiritual' in nineteenth-century Europe, Robeson's interpretation of songs wrought from displacement and oppression, such as 'Go down, Moses' and 'Water Boy', imbued the genre with a radical tone and contemporary relevance which resonated particularly strongly with working-class audiences.[63]

However, the qualities of the artist and the internationalist sentiments inherent in his material also appealed to Scots of all classes reared on Burns's notions of the dignity and essential worth of the common man – 'that man to man the world o'er shall brothers be, for a' that'. It is significant that a local reviewer of Robeson's first Dundee concert in 1930 discerned that the African-American ballad 'Steal Away' '[is] surely the negro equivalent of "Land o' the Leal"' as, from this period, Robeson became increasingly preoccupied with linking African songs to the indigenous music of other countries.[64] Moreover, while Robeson's decision to extend his 1934 concert programme to include such material was criticised in much of the English press, it was generally welcomed by Scottish, and particularly Dundee, audiences. Indeed, the local press noted that 'the innovation [of a broader programme] proved so successful, that to meet the demand in the cheaper areas, the organ gallery had to be extended to the platform'.[65]

Despite the absence of political comment, however, Robeson's deeply held convictions were not unknown to members of his audience. One former music teacher, whose parents attended Robeson's third Dundee concert in January 1938, recalls that her father, a self-taught violinist and committed socialist, was attracted equally by sympathy for Robeson's music and his staunch support for Republican forces fighting in the Spanish Civil War.[66]

Indeed, the strong empathy with Robeson, whose musical and political voices were inseparable, begs a re-evaluation of W.M. Walker's contention that Dundee's working-class population was 'too burdened by present anxieties to pursue politics [and sought relief] in entertainment not agitation'.[67] Indeed, while many nineteenth-century employers sought to harness the power of music to placate their workforces through the vehicle of works' soirées and benefit concerts, attempts by the jute manufacturing firm Cox Brothers to defuse escalating tensions over wage cuts in 1923 by holding concerts under the auspices of Camperdown Works Welfare Scheme, was branded by J.F. Sime of the Dundee and District Union of Jute and Flax Workers as a ploy to disguise Cox Brothers' sole concern with profit, regardless of the human cost.[68] And while an *Advertiser* reporter noted the absence of 'the music of the buzzers', 'the shrill shrieks of the horns' and the 'attenuated sound produced, compared with the usual babel, as striking proof that a lockout was in operation', the strike itself occurred against something of a musical backdrop.[69] At an 'open conference' held in Joe Bell's Casino Theatre, Lochee, a heated debate between Edwin Scrymgeour, MP and a thousand-strong crowd, was preceded by an impromptu concert and concluded with chanting, whistling and the singing of a strike song, 'Follow Me', by a large group of women.[70] Throughout this period, there were several instances of well-known tunes being appropriated to highlight political events and social grievances. For example, the evangelical hymn 'Jesus Loves the Little Children' was variously employed for strike and election ditties; the American popular song 'Bye, Bye, Blackbird' was adopted for a local parody on unemployment; and political poetess Mary Brooksbank's (b.1898) complaint of the exploited factory worker, 'The Jute Mill Song', borrowed its refrain, 'Oh dear me', from 'Auld Maid in a Garret', an older song bemoaning another issue (the lack of male partners) experienced by Dundee's disproportionately large female population.[71]

Amid widespread unemployment and social immobility, the unique ability of music to traverse space and time, and to give expression to a wide range of thoughts, feelings and aspirations, helped to keep people's hopes alive. Moreover, by providing an accessible conduit for political ideas, music could raise their consciousness as well as their spirits. Such a view would appear to contradict the argument of the Frankfurt School, that cinema, gramophone and radio were the means by which culture manufacturers inhibited the development of musical tastes by limiting choice.[72] Yet while Adorno and Horkheimer's theory helps to explain how an increasingly commercialised entertainment industry sought commodify popular music in order to exploit global markets, it is far from conclusive. Firstly, besides smacking of class prejudice and intellectual snobbery, their depiction of 'the man with leisure' as a passive and powerless consumer who 'has to accept what the culture manufacturers offer him' is contradicted by evidence that people of all social classes were actively engaged in the production and reception of music at many levels.[73] Undoubtedly, socio-economic factors continued to determine who could better afford musical instruments, tuition and gramophones, and gain access to elite musical circles. On the other hand, the development of sound and communications technology, the mass production of musical paraphernalia and the availability of hire purchase, allowed a greater number of people to draw from an increasing number of resources and influences. Secondly, while the US film industry exerted a strong influence on musical tastes, it was not necessarily a negative one. Indeed, rather than limiting choice, it can be argued that cinema and radio facilitated the development of diverse and sophisticated tastes by introducing different musical genres such as jazz, Latin American dance music, African-influenced rhythms and American popular song to greater numbers of people and making classical music more accessible to working-class audiences.[74]

Moreover, the assertions of contemporary Scots cultural commentators Hugh MacDiarmid and Lewis Grassic Gibbon, that American-based popular culture would precipitate the decline of indigenous traditions, were largely unfounded. Indeed, Grassic Gibbon's lamentation, in the closing pages of *Sunset Song*, of the supplanting of old Scots songs by American ones, was contradicted by the persistence of traditional musical forms.[75] From the First World War, city pipe bands entered a phase of growth and development which was sustained throughout the following decades, and the popularisation of Scottish accordion-based country dance music was also a twentieth-century phenomenon. The twentieth century also saw the continued growth of Gaelic song in towns with large Gaelic populations such as Glasgow and Inverness, and one of the most popular Gaelic songs of the late twentieth century, 'Morag of Dunvegan', was written by Neil Matheson, a Dundonian of Highland parentage, who had participated in local choirs and musical societies throughout the 1920s and 1930s.[76] Oral evidence also indicates the seamless co-existence of Scottish traditional music alongside modern popular genres. A former factory worker recalls sessions in her grand-parents' parlour at which three generations of fiddlers played pieces from the Logie Collection and strathspeys composed by her grandfather, while her grandmother played the piano and other family members counter-posed old Scots ballads with popular songs garnered from Hollywood musicals and gramophone records.[77]

It is perhaps fitting to conclude with an example which captures the essence of musical activity in Dundee in this period. In 1937, a group of voluntary reserve sailors travelling to the British Boat-pulling Championships whiled away the journey to London by improvising tunes on harmonicas and kazoos. On their return, this transitory group formed the Royal Naval Voluntary Reserve Harmonica Band, which comprised twenty-four harmonica players, two banjoists, a melodeon player, a drummer, a pianist and a vocal impersonator. While the band's self-styled 'conductor, guide and friend', J. Nisbet, had twelve years' experience as drum-major of the McKenzie Pipe, and also played bugle at the city's Armistice service, the remaining mill, foundry and shipyard workers who formed its membership had no musical training and played entirely by ear.[78] Practice sessions were held on board HMS *Unicorn*, where their rehearsal methods involved any individual who knew a particular tune playing it repeatedly until everyone had mastered it. By February 1938 they had amassed a repertoire of over two hundred items, spanning jazz, swing, Scottish, Highland, 'old time' and modern dance music, and old and new popular songs. Although the band's existence was short-lived – the RNVR's recreational activities were curtailed by the outbreak of the Second World War – its origins in cheap, improvised instruments, its eclectic repertoire and its unpretentious style prefigured the skiffle movement of the mid to late 1950s from which many of the bands of the 1960s evolved.

In concluding this general survey of musical activity in Dundee between the two world wars, it would be accurate to say that in many respects, patterns in Dundee reflected those of other urban communities in Scotland, England, Ireland and Wales.[79] However, while it is important to acknowledge the variety of individual experiences and tastes, musical life in Dundee continued to be shaped by the distinctive blend of economic, social and cultural variables which affected other aspects of life in the city. For this, arguably the most thoroughly working-class of Scottish cities, it was the reinvigoration of Scottish traditional music, the greater exposure to American cinema (and concomitantly, the soundtracks of Hollywood musicals) and the particular empathy with the evolving blues and country music of the poor North American underclass, which characterised this period in Dundee's musical history and which influenced audiences and musicians in the decades that followed.

NOTES

1. See, for example, R. Forbes, 'A study in music, community and identity in a late nineteenth-century Scottish town', *Journal of Victorian Culture* II (2006), pp. 256–80; also S. Gunn, *The Public Culture of the Victorian Middle Class* (Manchester, 1999); D. Russell, *Popular Music in England, 1840–1914: A Social History* (Manchester, 1987); and A.J. Croll, *Civilizing the Urban: Popular Culture and Public Space in Merthyr c.1870–1914* (Cardiff, 2000).

2. Music was a thriving feature of the local economy: in 1905, for example, the local trade directory listed fifteen music and musical instrument sellers, compared to five in 1885, and at ninety-three, the number of professional musicians was higher than ever before: *Dundee Directories*, 1884–85, 1904–05.

3. Patrons of the Dundee Orchestral Society in 1905 included Sir John Ogilvie, MP, prominent local employers and civic dignitaries, alongside composer Hamish McCunn, conductor Henry Wood and Professor of Music at Edinburgh University, F. Nieles: DCA, Records of the Dundee Orchestral Society (DOS).

4. A sample of 2,442 families surveyed for the DSU *Report on Housing and Industrial Conditions and Medical Inspection of School Children* (Dundee, 1905), p. 26 revealed over 2,161 living on less than 30 shillings a week.

5. That children in Dundee came to be taught through the medium of sol-fa, when the majority of schoolchildren in Britain were taught by ear alone, is partly due to the influence of Frank Sharp and Alexander Adamson, who were appointed teacher and Superintendent of Music to Board Schools respectively in 1874. Sharp also trained choirs in the town's industrial schools and on the *Mars* training ship for deprived and delinquent boys.

6. For example, the foundation of the Corn Exchange (later Kinnaird) Hall in 1858; the Albert Institute (encompassing a Free Public Library and Museum) in 1869; and the Victoria Art Galleries in 1889.

7. B. Harris, '"City of the future": James Thomson's vision of the city beautiful' in L. Miskell, C.A. Whatley and B. Harris (eds), *Victorian Dundee: Image and Realities* (East Linton, 2000).

8. Between 1895 and 1910, Caird donated £50,000 towards a cancer hospital, a sanatorium, a hospital for Women at Industry, and a rest home for elderly men. From 1912, he donated £10,000 to the British Association for the Advancement of Science on its visit to Dundee in 1912; £5,000 to the Royal Society; a donation of Egyptian

artefacts (acquired in 1907) to the museum of the Albert Institute in 1913; 270 acres of ground at Den o' Mains (Caird Park) at a cost of £25,000, also in 1913; £24,000 to Shackleton's Antarctic Expedition in 1914; and £100,000 towards construction of the new City Hall. *Dundee Year Book* (1916), pp. 53–5.

9. Carnegie, who coined the maxim 'A man who dies rich, dies disgraced', donated £37,000 for the construction of five library buildings in Dundee, the first of which was completed, and the remaining four designed, by James Thomson. The libraries opened in 1902, 1908, 1910 and 1911.

10. *Advertiser*, 5 September 1921.

11. The proximity of the building to sea level had necessitated the laying of reinforced concrete pillars at 12-foot intervals, many of which lay on the walls of the old town docks.

12. *Advertiser*, 3/4 November 1921.

13. McCormack was particularly effusive in his praise, repeatedly writing such comments as: 'How I wish they had this hall in Dublin' and 'Your beautiful hall still remains the envy of an Irishman. It is a jewel!' LHC, Caird Hall Autograph Book.

14. *Advertiser*, 7–13 February 1922.

15. *Dundee Year Book* (1914), p. 91.

16. *Advertiser*, 9 October 1919.

17. At this time, Stoole (b.1865) was one of the most respected and experienced musicians in the city. His father, James Stool (*sic*), a hydraulic engineer and founding member of the Dundee Instrumental Band, ensured that all his children received a musical education. Earlier in his career, Stoole held the posts of conductor of the Dundee Philharmonic and the Dundee Scottish Musical Societies, and in 1894, he helped establish the Dundee Orchestral Society. His younger brother Robert (b. *c*.1868) succeeded him as conductor of the DOS in 1935. LHC, Obituaries of A.M. Stoole, 22 February 1946, and R.O. Stoole, 11 February 1938.

18. The *Advertiser* also opined on the matter: 'Musicians, like others possessed of the artistic temperament, are difficult to handle': *Advertiser*, 5 Oct 1921. For a discussion of the origins and development of this concept, see T. Adorno, *Introduction to the Sociology of Music* (New York, 1976 [1962]), p. 58.

19. DCA, Report of Meeting of Law and Finance Committee, 25 February 1922.

20. John Hinchliffe (b.1864) moved to Dundee from Huddersfield in 1890 to take up the post of organist at St Paul's Parish Church. LHC, Obituaries of John Hinchliffe, 25 August 1925, and James Hinchliffe, 12 October 1970.

21. At one concert in March 1915, the Boy Scouts were drafted in to sell tickets and soldiers in uniform were admitted at half price. DCA, Records of DOS, 8 March 1915.

22. Archibald Campbell, 'The Highland bagpipe', *Piping Times* II, vol. 14, ch. 11 (August 1962), quoted in W. Donaldson, *The Highland Pipe and Scottish Society: Transmission, Change and the Concept of Tradition* (East Linton, 2000), p. 209.

23. Ibid., p. 317. Donaldson estimates that over a thousand pipers were killed or sustained wounds which, in some cases, led to premature death.

24. The McKenzie Pipe Band was founded in 1919 by Pipe-Major James McKenzie, a war veteran of the Argyll and Sutherland Highlanders. Membership consisted predominantly of ex-servicemen.

25. The band of the RNVR had been forced to abandon their instruments in Antwerp while fleeing a German attack, and only managed to retrieve them after the Armistice. LHC, Obituary of Robert B. Christie, 24 July 1971.

26. *Advertiser*, 22 April 1926.
27. The five bands were the RNVR, Dundee Trades Band, St Margaret's Brass Band, Dundee Premier Military Band and the Darktown Minstrels.
28. DCA, Council Minutes, April–May 1926.
29. DCA, Council Minutes, June 1926.
30. Sword, who had been a Pipe-Major in the 4th Battalion Black Watch during the First World War, later went on to form the Jute Industries Pipe Band in the early 1950s. Donaldson was Pipe-Major of the Camperdown, McGregor taught the Boys' Brigade, and Ogilvie was first Pipe-Major of the Dundee Pipe Band.
31. DOHP, Interview 39.
32. The female to male ratio is as follows: 30:87 in 1901–2; 42:96 in 1920–1; and 46:102 in 1930–1. The actual figure for female teachers is most probably higher. The Dundee Directories contain several single entries for female sibling partnerships operating from the same premises (although not for men). Moreover, many daughters of (and working alongside) listed male music teachers remain anonymous.
33. For example, in a card sent to Isabella (Ella) Kinmond, a day before a Royal College of Music exam, Bird wrote: 'There is a special reason why I wish you to come out on top, so do your utmost': LHC, Lamb Collection (LC) 235 (9), 26 April 1923.
34. One of Marshall's protégés, William Anderson, bassist with the Dundee Select Choir, went on to join the British Opera Company and perform regularly in radio broadcasts.
35. Marshall, who was born in Auchterarder, was blind from birth. Dundee-born Millers was blinded in a childhood accident. LHC, Obituaries of Henry Marshall, 19 December 1937, and George H. Millers, 18 September 1933.
36. *Courier*, 12, 14, 26 November and 1 December 1938.
37. *Advertiser*, 23 March 1923.
38. For a discussion of the inhibiting protocols of concert attendance, see C. Small, 'Performance as ritual: sketch for an enquiry into the full nature of the symphony concert' in A.L. White (ed.), *Lost In Music: Culture, Style and the Musical Event* (London, 1987), pp. 8–12.
39. DOHP, Interview 4.
40. This can be attributed in part to Director General John Reith's mission 'to educate, inform and entertain', but also to the BBC's agreement with the Musicians' Union to limit the use of gramophone recordings in favour of live broadcasts. For more detail, see D. Harker, *One for the Money: Politics and Popular Song* (London, 1980), p. 66.
41. Listings for the BBC's Scottish channel, *Courier*, 15 October 1938.
42. Between 1928 and 1936, the membership of the Dundee Orchestral Society dropped from fifty-four to thirty-four.
43. DCA, Records of DOS, 17 April 1936.
44. DOHP, Interview 4.
45. Bell (b.1879) owned the Casino Ballroom in Lochee and, at various points, the Broadway, Royal and Grand cinemas, and is credited with introducing the football pools to Dundee. His readiness to extend credit to customers and donate to worthy causes left him, on occasions, on the brink of debt. He lived in modest circumstances and died in Wellburn Home for the Aged on 21 August 1964. LHC, Obituary of Joe Bell.
46. At the time, Hall was leader of the BBC Dance Orchestra, and Levy was musical director for Gaumont Pictures.

47. D. Hutchison, '1900–1950' in B. Findlay (ed.), *A History of Scottish Theatre* (Edinburgh, 1998), p. 217.
48. *Evening Telegraph*, 24 February 1982.
49. See, for example, George Orwell's observations in *The Road to Wigan Pier* (London, 2001 [1937]), pp. 81–2.
50. *Advertiser*, 1 June 1925; LHC, LC 254 (6B): *Evening Telegraph*, n.d. 1960s.
51. T. Crampton, 'Music for the silver screen', *The Organist's Review* (November 1995), pp. 269–72.
52. LHC, LC 254 (6B).
53. *The Singing Fool*, starring Al Jolson, was essentially a silent film with subtitled dialogue into which recorded songs were incorporated.
54. LHC, Obituaries of F. Routledge Bell, 6 February 1957, and Henry Hollingworth, 10 December 1945. Routledge Bell was appointed teacher of violin by the Dundee Education Committee in 1932 and became a teacher at Dundee High School in 1942. The Hollingworth Trio played regularly at the tearoom of D.M. Brown's department store.
55. *Evening Telegraph*, 24 February 1982.
56. D. Phillips, *The Hungry Thirties* (Dundee, 1981), p. 93; *Courier*, 30 October 1934.
57. *Courier*, January 1938.
58. *Courier*, 26 March 1929 and 9 December 1935. McCormack, who was made a Papal Count in 1928, sang 'Panis Angelicus' at the Eucharistic Conference in Dublin (in 1932). The performance was broadcast throughout Ireland, Scotland, England and Wales. For more detail, see G. Ledbetter, *The Great Irish Tenor: John McCormack* (Dublin, 2003).
59. LHC, LC 285 (10), Programme notes of C.R., 27 February 1927. Alongside the Irish folk song, 'The Next Market Day', C.R. pencilled, 'one breath each verse'.
60. McCormack performed at the Caird Hall on four occasions: in 1927, 1929, 1930 and 1935. At his final concert, McCormack told the local press that his father, who was born in Galashiels, was the source of many of the Scots songs in his repertoire. *Courier*, 9 December 1935.
61. LHC, LC 285 (10).
62. The Jubilee Singers, who gave two concerts in the Kinnaird Hall in September/October 1873, had a repertoire of over a hundred songs: entry on the Jubilee singers in H. Wiley and S. Sadie (eds), *The New Grove Dictionary of American Music*, vol. 2 (London, 1986), p. 601.
63. 'Go Down, Moses' later featured in Preston Sturges's film about Depression America, *Sullivan's Travels* (1940); 'Water Boy' was a convict song.
64. M. Dubermann, *Paul Robeson: A Biography* (New York, 1998), p. 178.
65. Robeson's 1934 programme included the Scottish ballad 'Turn ye to me', Cecil Sharp's arrangement of the English folk song 'Oh, no John, no', a Mexican song, 'Encantadora Maria', and 'Ol' Man River' from Jerome Kern's *Showboat*. For the negative comments in the English press, see Dubermann, *Robeson*, pp. 178 and 626 n. 49.
66. Testimony of Mrs Rachel McGilchrist (interview by Ruth Forbes, Dundee, 2008). In December 1937, Robeson appeared at a rally in the Albert Hall in support of Basque refugee children. A week after the Dundee concert, on 23 January 1938, he travelled to Spain to sing for International Brigaders and Spanish Loyalists in training camps and base hospitals. Dubermann, *Robeson*, pp. 214–20. At this time, Dundee was supplying

a significantly large number of volunteers to the International Brigades. For comparative figures, see R. Baxell, *British Volunteers in the Spanish Civil War: The British Battalion in the International Brigades, 1936–1939* (London, 2004), p. 20 n. 103. For more detail on Scottish (including Dundee) volunteers, see D. Gray, *Homage to Caledonia* (Edinburgh, 2008).

67. W.M. Walker, *Juteopolis: Dundee and its Textile Workers, 1885–1923* (Edinburgh, 1979), p. 356.

68. *Advertiser*, 24 January 1923, 5 March 1923.

69. *Advertiser*, 23 March 1923.

70. *Advertiser*, 28 March 1923. For detail on the jute workers' strike of 1923, see Walker, *Juteopolis*, pp. 486–528.

71. The words of 'Bye Bye, Blackbird': 'Pack up all my cares and woes, Here I go, Singing low, Bye bye, blackbird' were replaced with 'We're the lads fae Norrie's pend, Never worked and we don't intend, Bye bye, Allan', a reference to the director of the Public Assistance Committee, Robert Allan. Phillips, *The Hungry Thirties*, p. 88. See 'The Jute Mill Song' and 'Strike Song' in M. Brooksbank, *Sidlaw Breezes* (Dundee, 1982).

72. M. Horkheimer and T. Adorno, *The Culture Industry: Enlightenment as Mass Deception* (London, 1973).

73. For a useful critique which addresses the Frankfurt School's failure to recognise the complexity and significance of popular music, see D. Kellner, 'Theodore Adorno and the dialectics of mass culture' in N. Gibson and A. Rubin (eds), *Adorno: A Critical Reader* (Oxford, 2002), pp. 86–109.

74. Note also the argument that the promotion of Latin American culture was part of a wider US strategy to shore up external markets following the Depression of the 1930s. See, for example, L. Shaw and M. Conde, 'Brazil through Hollywood's gaze: from the silent screen to the Good Neighbour Policy' in L. Shaw and S. Dennison (eds), *Latin American Cinema: Essays on Modern Gender and National Identity* (Jefferson, NC, 2005), pp. 180–208.

75. Grassic Gibbon wrote: 'You heard meikle of those old songs now, there were fine new ones in their places, right from America, folk said, and all about the queer blue babies that were born there, they were clever brutes, the Americans', *Sunset Song* (London, 1983 [1934]), p. 242. MacDiarmid also deprecated American-based popular culture for debasing language, hence undermining his aspirations towards a Scottish literary renaissance. L. Grassic Gibbon and H. MacDiarmid, *Scottish Scene, or, the Intelligent Man's Guide to Albyn* (London, 1934).

76. Matheson (b.1884) composed 'Morag a Dhun Bheagan' in 1959 at the age of seventy-five. The tune, which was first performed at the Edinburgh Festival by the Royal Marine Pipe Band in 1962, quickly became a Gaelic standard. LHC, Obituary of Neil Matheson, 16 July 1970.

77. *The Logie Collection of Original Music: Scottish Songs and Dance Music for Voice, Violin and Pianoforte*, compiled by J. Scott Skinner (1888); DOHP, Interview 4.

78. *People's Journal*, 5 February 1938.

79. See, for example, J. Rose, *The Intellectual Life of the British Working Classes* (New Haven, 2001), pp. 196–206.

CHAPTER 10

The 'Retreat' to Scotland:
The Tay Road Bridge and Dundee's Post-1945 Development

Jim Phillips

The Tay Road Bridge was opened with great but curious ceremony on 18 August 1966. It was a major engineering and industrial achievement, and a material embodiment as well as emblem of Dundee's modernisation. Its construction, over four years, cost £5 million and the lives of five workers, killed or drowned in three separate incidents: A. Bowness, on 27 April 1964, A. Keir, on 13 March 1965, and James Lennie, John McQueen and Donald Ross, all on 11 November 1965.[1] This feat of industrial modernisation, marred by the tragedy of the fatal human casualties, was marked in typically incongruent British ceremonial manner. Maurice McManus, Lord Provost of Dundee, and Willie Ross, Secretary of State for Scotland, welcomed the Queen Mother and an entourage of Lord Lieutenants and others of feudal rank who had no direct connection with the architectural, engineering, construction and labour processes that had made the bridge possible. The mild perversity of this situation is captured in still photographs of the ceremony, and a motion picture commissioned by Films of Scotland. The workers and other citizens of Dundee were kept well back from the chief celebrants and ceremonial dais by a line of police officers, and then watched as the Queen Mother and others were taken for a drive over to the Fife side and back again.[2]

The bridge's association with Dundee's modernisation is worth emphasising. It was embedded in the search for economic development that, in the spirit and practical application of the 1950s and 1960s, privileged road transport as the most efficient means of promoting and developing new forms of commercial and industrial activity. Progress necessitated new roads and peripheral industrial estates, and the running down and eventually the displacement of older industrial infrastructure. In Dundee this involved the wholesale reconstruction of the central waterfront area: the city's West Station was demolished, in the context of British Rail's Beeching-inspired contraction, and large sections of the docks were filled in, to accommodate new roads and the northern landing of the road bridge. This reconstruction encompassed an important paradox: a system of communications was established which erected substantial physical barriers – dual-carriage roads and bridge ramps – between Dundee and its diminished waterfront. In the process Dundonians were partly disconnected from their heritage as waterfront dwellers. This story is fairly well known, examined in Lesley Riddoch's excellent short film, *The Great Tay Road Bridge Mystery – Whodunnit?*, and featuring in the vigorous and engaging book, *Lost Dundee*, by Charles McKean and Pat Whatley.[3] The Tay Road Bridge encapsulated another paradox, however, which is less familiar than the disappearing waterfront story. It is embodied in the title of this chapter, 'The "Retreat" to Scotland'. This draws on the same essential stimuli as the disappearing waterfront – urban modernisation, the shift to road transport – but relates less to the physical and architectural character of Dundee and more to the city's position in the Scottish, UK and international economies. The Tay Road Bridge was devised and built as a contribution to the process of economic adjustment made necessary by the decline of jute, seen as aiding the vital task of industrial diversification by enhancing the movement of raw materials and finished goods, and expanding the reach and scale of the regional economy and local labour market. This was a central element in the 'de-globalisation' of Dundee, discussed by Jim Tomlinson in this volume's opening chapter, and which accelerated after the Second World War.

There remained, of course, very powerful international elements in Dundee's post-1945 economy. Jute was still a central factor, and industrial diversification involved significant inward investment, notably by US manufacturers, including NCR (then makers of cash registers), Timex (watches), Veeder-Root (electrical and mechanical counting machines) and Holo-Krome (socket screws), operators of four of the largest seven establishments on Dundee's industrial estates in 1965–6.[4] But this refocused international economic configuration, and the new industrial mix, were products of 'regional policy', the range of central government initiatives and measures that encouraged economic activity in areas of the UK that had been over-reliant on declining 'traditional' export sectors, generally established in the nineteenth century and peaking in importance before 1914, of which Dundee and jute was an acute example. These central government measures involved a strong emphasis on state aid to business, through developing infrastructure, including factory premises and improved physical communications. The emphasis now was on connecting Dundee to a different form of international economy than the 'traditional' variant based on cheap jute imports and 'soft' imperial exports, one focused instead on the production and sale of high-value-added consumer goods, like the cash registers and watches produced by NCR and Timex. This brought Dundee into closer connection with other parts of Scotland and the UK, placing greater emphasis on internal communications. The paradox that emerges, then, through the Tay Road Bridge story, is of Dundee becoming less outward-looking, and less international in its economic scope, as the twentieth century progressed. It was in this sense that Dundee 'retreated' to Scotland after 1945.

The discussion that follows consists of two parts: the structural economic and political features that shaped Dundee's 'retreat' to Scotland, including the longer pre-1945 history of the Tay Road Bridge; and the detailed elements of the bridge's eventual construction, which highlight the difficulties of effecting Dundee's closer post-1945 Scottish integration. The 'retreat' was strategically sound, but not straightforward, weakened by Dundee's relative political weakness after 1945. The bridge was constructed with economic functionality as the central public rationale. Dundee's civic leaders pressed central government to support the project financially because of its intended impact in widening the local labour market and shortening the distance between manufacturing enterprises, particularly those new to the city, and their suppliers and customers. A Scottish Television documentary, broadcast originally on the day of the bridge's opening, captured this economic functionality emphasis, describing the road link as offering 'its own special contribution to the renaissance of the city', with the 'speedier communications for industry and tourism', enabling Dundee to look beyond the 'jute, jam, journalists and little else' legacy 'to a bright, vibrant future'.[5] Dundee leaders further argued that the bridge would offer a strategic link in long-distance north–south road communications.

But the UK government, through the Scottish Office, was not persuaded by this, seeing the bridge as servicing localised needs only, leaving Dundee and neighbouring authorities to fund construction through loans to be serviced essentially by tolls on users. Here was Dundee's limited political strength. The Scottish Office assessment was reasonably accurate, and in perhaps at least the first two decades of its existence the bridge in reality was of highly limited economic utility. Partly this related to the details of its location, with a city central landing point, remote from the road north, to the new industrial estates on the Kingsway and points beyond. This central location, bringing users immediately into the heart of the city, suggests indeed that the bridge was more important as a symbolic statement of Dundee's modernity, in keeping with the argument – articulated by Charles McKean and others – that the city was being remade in the 1960s. The bridge was designed to help Dundee to retreat to Scotland: it was perhaps also devised as a means of assisting the city's retreat from the troubled urban, social and industrial inheritance of the nineteenth and earlier twentieth centuries. The analysis utilises, among other items, Scottish Office and Ministry of Transport files, Dundee town and city council records, the papers of E.D. Morel, MP for Dundee from 1922 to 1924, material from the Population Census, and contemporary business reports and academic surveys.

THE PROMISE OF THE TAY ROAD BRIDGE

In the introductory chapter of this book Jim Tomlinson argues that there were three distinct phases in the drawn out twentieth-century response to the decline of jute: the inter-war period; the 1940s to the 1960s; and the 1970s onwards. The construction of the Tay Road Bridge slots into the middle phase, of managed economic change and industrial diversification, but there were important inter-war developments also. These prefigured the bridge's eventual construction, establishing if in rudimentary form the structural economic and political features that encouraged Dundee's closer Scottish integration as the twentieth century progressed. Three economic features associated with the bridge were recurrently highlighted and appear at various points in this discussion: industrial diversification; regional policy; and an enlarged regional economy and local labour market.

Dundee's civic leaders wanted a road crossing of the Tay immediately after the First World War, and tried to secure Ministry of Transport support for this venture,[6] with careful lobbying undertaken from 1922 to 1924 by the city's Labour MP, E.D. Morel. The bridge at this point was conceived by James Thomson, City Architect, as part of a comprehensive plan for Dundee's development,[7] including the Kingsway ring road, and local authority housing estates, initiated with the Logie scheme in 1919.[8] Thomson's proposal for the road crossing involved utilising the piers of the old Tay Railway Bridge , destroyed in the famous fatal storm of 1878, with a north landing west of the city centre. George Baxter, City Engineer, regarded these piers as unfit for such purpose, and opposed Thomson's proposal as unsafe.[9] The difference of opinion between Baxter and Thomson was reported in the local press,[10] and seems to have diminished the Ministry of Transport's ultimate interest in the project, although Sir Henry Maybury, the Ministry's Director General of Roads, having visited Dundee and been recurrently cajoled by Morel, persuaded the Treasury to fund exploratory engineering work to the sum of £10,000. This was some way short of the estimated cost of constructing the bridge itself, thought to range from between £660,000 to just under £1 million.[11]

Dundee's leaders had been encouraged to think that central government support would be forthcoming by a slightly curious reference to the Tay in a speech made at Hounslow by Sir William Joynson-Hicks, the Conservative government's Minister of Health, in October 1923. This implied that to counter rising unemployment the government would support constructing a Tay road crossing, to employ between six and seven thousand of Dundee's currently idle industrial workforce. Dundee responded by asking that the government contribute 75 per cent of the overall costs of construction.[12] Morel then spent much time vainly persuading the local authority to moderate its request, lest the government be deterred from offering any assistance.[13] In any event a combination of pressures – notably the Thomson–Baxter disagreement and the local authority's reluctance to undertake the level of borrowing required to meet its share of the costs – resulted in a falling off of interest in the bridge in Dundee until the early 1930s. In the context of the rapid escalation of unemployment in Dundee as elsewhere, arising from the major diminution of international trading activity that followed the 1929 Wall Street Crash, the revived Tay Road Bridge campaign from 1931 understandably mobilised the 1920s emphasis on employment creation.

The multiplier effect was now noted, with the incomes of those engaged in constructing the bridge generating further economic activity in the city. But there was also a new and more sophisticated emphasis on the Tay road crossing's potential place in the development of the UK's national economic infrastructure, as part of a chain of bridges and other connections to establish a 'Great East Coast Trunk Road' from southern England to northern Scotland.[14] This reflected the presence and influence of Tom Johnston, Morel's Labour successor as an MP in the city until 1929, Lord Privy Seal in the 1929–31 Labour government – having fought and regained his Stirling seat in 1929 which had been lost in 1924 – and later, as Secretary of State for Scotland in Winston Churchill's Second World War coalition government, the principal ministerial architect of post-1945 regional policy.[15] Johnston encouraged Dundee to work more closely with adjacent local authorities, to maximise regional political and financial support for the bridge.[16] Immediate prospects of progress vanished in the financial crisis of August and September 1931, which led to the Labour government's collapse and the subsequent election of a 'National' – and Conservative-dominated – government that sought to endure the Depression by cutting public expenditure.[17] But the Johnston advice to widen regional support was heeded by Dundee's civic leaders, and the more sophisticated rationale extended in the second half of the 1930s by a Tay Road Bridge (Local Authorities) Joint Committee, established by Dundee, Fife and Angus in 1934. This generally emphasised the 'closer economic and social integration' of eastern Scotland that a road crossing would stimulate, and picked out the particular potential advantages of expanding the regional economy and stimulating the growth in Dundee of new industries. Fruit canning and confectionery, for instance, would be brought closer to Fife's berries and sugar beet.[18]

These larger imperatives – regional policy, industrial diversification and enlarging the regional economy – assumed even stronger prominence in the case for the Tay Road Bridge that was made by Dundee after 1945, as it attempted to bring itself into closer alignment with the rest of Scotland in the context of jute's continuing decline. The Lord Provost of Dundee, Garnett Wilson, pressed the UK government both during and immediately after the Second World War to see that the adoption of new industries in the city would greatly be encouraged by the establishment of a Tay road crossing.[19] John Muir, Secretary-Organiser of Dundee

Trades and Labour Council, articulated the same perspective in correspondence in 1946 with Joseph Westwood, Secretary of State for Scotland.[20] The structural context here was the 1945 Labour government's commitment to regional economic development, encouraging the creation of employment in areas of the UK that had been disfigured in the 1920s and 1930s by the decline of the 'traditional' industries of coal, metals, heavy engineering, shipbuilding and textiles. The government's Distribution of Industry Act made provision for subsidised 'advance' factories, industrial estates and other incentives to encourage firms to establish new manufacturing operations.[21] In Scotland this work was encouraged by the Scottish Council for Development and Industry (SCDI), an organisation which drew its core support from private sector industry and commerce, although it was partly funded also by local authorities and trade unions. The main remit of the SCDI was to foster inward investment, and it successfully identified US firms and the electronics sector in particular as principal tools in diversifying the Scottish economy after 1945.[22]

This strategy has been criticised, establishing Scotland as a 'branch-plant' economy with low-skilled 'screwdriver' jobs and a precarious future, as research, development and strategic investment decisions were taken elsewhere.[23] Eventually – in the 1970s and then especially in the 1980s and 1990s – this resulted in US firms leaving Scotland, relocating usually to lower wage cost environments in Asia. This was the experience of Dundee, most bitterly in recent memory with Timex, which reduced its employment commitments radically in the city in 1983, and then left altogether after a lengthy wage dispute in 1993 with its remaining employees, who were locked out and then sacked. But it is not clear that there were any realistic alternatives to this approach after 1945, and Dundee, as elsewhere, benefited for more or less the span of one human generation's working life from the employment created through the regional policy framework established and developed after 1945. Some of the implications of this, including new opportunities for women, and the impact on jute manufacturers of the higher wages offered by the US firms, are discussed elsewhere in this book. The 'bifurcated' and highly gendered labour process adopted by Timex, examined by Bill Knox and Alan McKinlay in Chapter 11 below, with skilled male workers producing components until 1983 that were then assembled by unskilled female workers, illustrates the multi-dimensional character of US enterprise in

Dundee. The skilled men enjoyed significant variety in their work, and a substantial degree of autonomy. Women found their work routinised and to some extent alienating, but their working environment was clean and safe, and in this respect at least the US firms were model employers, with a tendency also to consult employees about working practices and production methods that contrasted greatly with the authoritarian managerial tradition of jute. The new industries were, in short, from the perspective of employees and labour, significantly preferable to the jute industry, with its low pay, dirty and noisy working conditions, sometimes draconian management and often conflict-ridden industrial relations. The new industries also contributed, it is worth reiterating, to a wider mix of economic activity in Dundee. The city's industrial profile certainly shifted significantly between 1945 and the mid-1960s, with a broader range of types of firm, with multinationals, including the US multinationals, alongside the pre-1945 family and other local businesses. One basic but telling measure of this shift is the composition of the Board of Directors of Dundee Chamber of Commerce in 1966. This was evenly split with four names each from the old and the new: W.W. Duncan of Jute Industries, James Bruce of W.C. Grant & Co. Ltd. and the Association of Jute Spinners and Manufacturers, H.C. Scarlett of Dundee Linoleum, and T. Parnell of Caledon Shipbuilding and Engineering; and then C.S. Webb of NCR, E.C. Lowson of Holo-Krome Ltd., R.H. Smith of EMI Astral, and A.C. Bastable of Ferranti.[24]

The Dundee Chamber of Commerce was generally optimistic about the city and its prospects in the mid-1960s, but in its publications at least maintained some wariness too, with a particularly anxious eye on government economic and regional policy, and placing great store on the continual improvement in links with other parts of Scotland, including through the Tay road crossing. This, it was emphasised, would give Dundee 'four sides for the first time, instead of three', and establish the city as 'the principal centre in East Scotland'.[25] The perennial general concern was the ongoing contraction of jute, and the corresponding importance of renewing recurrently the city's industrial and employment base. In 1951 the population of Dundee was 177,340. This had risen to 182,978 in 1961. The segment of the population that was in employment was more or less identical in these two census years: 48.8 per cent in 1951, and 48.9 per cent in 1961.[26] This pattern of stagnant or only marginally increasing economic activity worried policy makers and business leaders in Scotland in the early 1960s. The predominant view was that significant and fairly rapid employment growth – as opposed to the largely unchanging Dundee position – was required to close the gap in wealth and welfare with other parts of the UK. This was articulated in the 1961 Toothill Report, authored by the managing director of Ferranti, and sponsored by the SCDI. This argued for a further diversification of Scottish industry through establishing 'growth points', achievable by state investment in infrastructure – roads, bridges and airports – and adjustments in the provision of incentives to private industry.[27] The key issue was raising the rate of economic growth in Scotland so that it matched that of the UK as a whole: this necessitated creating employment at a faster rate in Scotland than in the UK as a whole, especially in higher growth, consumer-based and value-added sectors. This required a net growth of 15,000 new jobs in Scotland each year, rather than the net growth of 5,000 jobs being achieved in the early 1960s.[28] Lord Polwarth, SCDI chairman, flattered readers of the *Dundee Chamber of Commerce Journal* by telling them that Dundee had been highly successful in attracting the right type of new employment, with between five and six thousand employed in US firms. This was twice the proportionate Scottish average for US employment, and a sign of Dundee's potential as an 'industrial growth point',[29] although this potential required careful nurturing. In this respect Polwarth, who was politically close to the Conservative government that was toiling its way towards defeat in the October 1964 general election, was pleased to point to the 1963 White Paper, *Central Scotland.* This responded to Toothill and, more significantly, popular social disquiet arising from the escalation of unemployment in 1962–3,[30] by proposing investment in growth-related infrastructure. Roads were singled out, and explicit references to the economic benefits arising from the Forth and Tay Road Bridges, both under construction, were included.[31] A Tay road crossing would perhaps have brought Dundee 'closer', for instance, to valuable skilled and semi-skilled labour resources in Fife. In this connection it might be noted that the small Fife Tayside burghs of Newport and Tayport contained a total of 1,840 economically active men in 1961, a potentially useful 3.4 per cent addition to the number of economically active men in Dundee itself. Five hundred and sixty of these Newport and Tayport men were skilled manual workers, and a further 160 were semi-skilled.[32] There is one objection to this hypothesis, however, which will be raised in greater detail in the final section of this chapter: the Newport and Tayport workers already had public transport access to the Dundee labour market through the rail link. Adding to this existing connection with a road crossing might have appreciably expanded the potential scale of the city's labour market. But the eventual consequence, with the rail link cut in 1969 and replaced rather than supplemented by the road crossing, probably served merely to stabilise rather than expand the supply of Fife labour to Dundee.

This was the general structural economic and regional policy context within which debates about the Tay Road Bridge had been developing in the 1950s, although the Conservative government's reference to this in the 1963 White Paper was almost entirely disingenuous. It implied that the bridge was a key element in an integrated government plan. The tortuous history of discussions relating to the bridge in the 1950s and early 1960s, which can be traced through documentary material in Scottish Office, Ministry of Transport and City of Dundee archives, indicates otherwise. Some tantalising proposals emerged, notably a suggestion in 1955 that the existing Tay and Forth bridges both be converted for dual road and rail use. This was supported by the SCDI but, with the combination of timbering for roads and steaming railway engines, was ruled out as impossibly hazardous by officials at the British Transport Commission.[33] The crucial issue – underlining central government's limited strategic interest in a Tay road crossing – eventually emerged in a meeting in May 1957 between Scottish Office ministers, including the Secretary of State, John Maclay, and the various Fife, Angus and Dundee local authorities concerned with the bridge. The local authorities pressed the national, strategic case for the Tay road crossing, to connect the south with the north. Maclay's response was simple: no such national case existed, for the bridge offered only a 'local connection' between Dundee and Fife.[34] Maclay's officials agreed. A.N. Sutherland of the Scottish Home Department noted in July 1957 that the road journey from Edinburgh to Dundee via a Forth road crossing and Perth would be just six miles longer than the road via the Forth, Fife and a Tay crossing to Dundee, and with tolls in place very little 'through traffic' from south to north would use the latter route.[35] The Scottish Office position was reinforced by the Treasury and Board of Trade, where officials were particularly adamant that ongoing efforts to manage the decline of jute should not extend to central government support for a Tay

Road Bridge.[36] In public, however, the government remained emollient, the Scottish Office accepting later in 1957 a proposal from Dundee that a week-long traffic survey be conducted, to establish the origins and destinations of vehicles that might potentially make use of a Tay road crossing.[37] Three points were identified: the Tay ferry crossing, the Perth–Dundee road at Bullionfield, and the Perth–Forfar road at Scone. The survey, in August 1958, suggested that just over one-third of all users would be likely to use the bridge. This proportion was swollen by the presence in the survey of Tay ferry traffic. Much less than one quarter of those surveyed at Scone, 6,163 of 28,494, on the extant north–south thoroughfare, were potential bridge-users.[38] This appears to have consolidated the 'local connection' view in the Scottish Office,[39] and sealed the outcome that eventually materialised in the winter of 1960–1: government support would only take the form of a loan of roughly one-third of the construction costs. The remainder would have to be borrowed by local authorities from other sources, with all borrowings to be repaid from toll levies.[40]

This eventuality disappointed the bridge's advocates, and burdened Dundee and the other local authorities concerned with the legacy of debt and tolls, which were abolished in February 2008, and – as the final section explores – the requirement to build as cheaply as possible. But the goal of an enlarged regional economy, first articulated after the Second World War in the *Tay Valley Plan* of 1950,[41] could still be pursued with enthusiasm. The bridge appeared to burnish the promise implicit in Polwarth's emphasis on Dundee as a 'growth centre' and the Chamber of Commerce's vision of the city as East Scotland's business core. Several contributors to the Chamber's December 1965 *Journal*, notably N.T. Carne of NCR, and Jock Bruce-Gardyne, the Conservative MP for South Angus, emphasised the manner in which the bridge would broaden Dundee's economic opportunities. Carne referred to the strengthened links with Fife and its electronics sector, and his hope that Dundee would become, among other things, a 'centre for management training'. Bruce-Gardyne, whose other writings and public utterances indicated a preoccupation with industrial unrest in western Scotland, duly noted that the bridge would bring employers to a city with much to offer business, including a 'skilled labour force with a splendid labour relations record'.[42] As the opening ceremony approached, the Earl of Dundee, a Conservative, and George Thompson, Labour MP for

Dundee East and Cabinet Minister, both writing in the Chamber's *Journal*, reiterated the importance to the expanding regional economy of the bridge, with enhanced links to Fife and further encouragement to 'modern manufacturing enterprise', including multinational firms. Displaying the same type of opportunism evident in the Conservative government's 1963 White Paper, Thompson added that the bridge advanced the same aim as his government's National Plan for Scotland,[43] of widening the labour market in pursuit of higher economic growth, particularly through the expansion of high value added manufacturing goods.[44]

LOCAL CONNECTION AND POLITICAL WEAKNESS

It should be clear that in the genesis of the bridge much store had been placed on its role as a strategic national link, between points at long distance south and north of Dundee, and as a means of enlarging the local and regional economy, notably by shrinking road journey times between Fife and the city's northern industrial estates. In this manner the bridge would bring Dundee closer to Scotland, and further encourage the process of industrial diversification that was mitigating the slow but unremitting decline of jute. This thinking was fairly pervasive in the early 1960s, even permeating the Board of Trade in Whitehall.[45] Arguments about the strategic national importance of the Tay crossing and the industrial opportunities it created were weakened, however, by one fundamental physical feature: the site of the bridge's northern landing, in the centre of Dundee. Journeys to the north, whether to outlying industrial estates, or towards Arbroath or Forfar and thence Aberdeen, were impeded by the city centre. This flaw was identified by, among others, Ove Arup, the engineer, who had submitted alternative plans to Dundee, in a letter to the Minister for Transport, Ernest Marples, in January 1961. Arup's rejected plan landed the bridge significantly further east, on the Stannergate, just a few hundred metres from the eastern end of the Kingsway, providing easier access, he claimed justifiably, to the new industrial estates as well as routes north of the city.[46]

The decision to locate the bridge centrally emerged as a result of three related factors. First, the King William IV dock was known by the Bridge Joint Committee in the late 1950s to be available for sale by the Dundee Harbour Trust,[47] and it was on this central site, once filled in, that the bridge was landed. Second, this offered the shortest and, not surprisingly perhaps, the cheapest potential span across the river from the spot of high ground chosen on the Fife shore to accommodate river traffic. Cost was very clearly a factor, especially once it became clear that the local authorities would have to finance the project without central government support other than loans. This much was happily conceded by the Tay Road Bridge Joint Board in the glossy and illustrated celebratory publication that appeared in the summer of 1966, which noted also that economies had been pursued in the construction of the crossing. Duncan Logan (Contractors) Ltd. of Muir of Ord, in the Black Isle, submitted the lowest bid. It arrived in Dundee by plane, fifteen minutes before the deadline elapsed: 'The Board accepted it on the spot, and half an hour later a letter had gone to the contractors to tell them so.'[48] The absence of direct state funding arguably reflected Dundee's relative political weakness, in Scotland and the UK, which Jim Tomlinson refers to in this book's introductory chapter, and this perhaps shaped the third element in the bridge's physical position: the city's civic leaders strongly favoured a central northern landing. Arup alleged that this reflected the 'parochial interests of Dundee traders', who feared that the city would simply be by-passed by a bridge carrying traffic between south and north.[49] He may have been right, although the central location also served the ambition of some civic leaders, perhaps buoyed by a sense of the city's political marginalisation, to modernise the heart of Dundee. In this connection there is the suggestion, articulated by Charles McKean in Lesley Riddoch's film, that civic leaders consciously wished to erase Dundee's nineteenth-century industrial manifestations, with their associated social difficulties and human miseries, by positioning the city as the most modern in Britain. The massive concrete and steel structure across the Tay, '7,365 feet long, the longest river crossing of any road bridge in Britain',[50] was of core importance in this process of urban reconstruction: a utilitarian landing a mile or so to the east of the city centre – as Ove Arup proposed – would have diminished its impact substantially.

Initial experience underlined the Scottish Office's misgivings about the bridge as a strategic national link. It also indicates the ambiguous manner of its impact as a driver of further industrial diversification, and strengthens the suggestion that the importance of the bridge probably resided in symbolic rather than economic utility terms. In 1969 a cost–

benefit analysis, published in the *Scottish Journal of Political Economy*, estimated that the bridge had secured significant 'primary' savings for its users in the Perth–Fife–Tayside area: fewer miles to travel meant more time for leisure or other purposes, and on average a smaller number of accidents. The 'secondary' or 'spill over' savings, however, in terms of wider improvements experienced by non-users as well as users, chiefly in terms of the economic development stimulated by the existence of the bridge, were much harder to pin down.[51] The bridge's limited short-term industrial impact is partly revealed through comparing the different details on residence, economic activity and transport that appeared in the *Sample Census*, conducted on 10 per cent of households in 1966, just before the bridge opened, and in the *Population Census* of 1961 and 1971. In the five-year span from 1966 to 1971 it appears that the total level of employment fell in Dundee, from 92,690 jobs to 87,000, although the relative number of those working in Dundee but who were resident outside of the city had very rapidly more than doubled, from 5.8 per cent in 1966 to 12.3 per cent in 1971.[52] Dundee's civic leaders had worried about the possibility of depopulation from time to time, and during the talks with Tom Johnston about the road crossing in 1931 Fife had been invited to share a burden of funding the scheme precisely because of the benefits it was expected to derive from additional ratepaying population.[53] Yet the bridge did not necessarily leak large numbers of Dundonians to Fife: the population of Newport increased significantly between 1961 and 1971, by 11.9 per cent, to 3,719, but Tayport shrank, from 3,151 to 2,897.[54] In Newport and Tayport the combined number of economically active males was also falling, from the 1,840 previously noted for 1961, to 1,685 in 1971. This is not suggestive of communities in the throes of rapid, bridge-fuelled expansion. Indeed the only really marked shift in employment and residential patterns in these burghs arising from cross-Tay links stemmed from the severance of the railway connection, with the closure of the branch line through Newport to Tayport in 1969. Six hundred of Newport's 1,230 persons in employment travelled to work in 1966 by train, but only twenty did so in 1971, presumably having first motored or cycled to Dundee or Leuchars. It might safely be deduced that many of Newport's 1966 railway commuters switched to private car, for travel across the new bridge, with the number of the burgh's residents journeying to work by car jumping from 230 in 1966 to 690 in 1971.[55] It is this rough congruence of 600

Newport rail commuters in 1966 and 690 Newport car commuters in 1971 that points to the broad conclusion that might be made about the bridge's moderate economic functionality: it stabilised rather than widened the size of the local labour market in Dundee, offsetting the loss of the rail links to parts of north-east Fife.

The enlarged proportion of workers travelling into Dundee from outside is in fact better explained by three related factors: an acceleration of changes in employment structures; the significant growth of some adjacent Angus settlements; and increased car ownership. Academic commentators noted the declining level of employment in unskilled manual sectors, notably in jute and other 'traditional' industries, including shipbuilding, at the time,[56] and this trend features elsewhere in this book. There was a consequent increase in the relative importance of white collar and professional positions, and these were more likely to be filled by commuters from affluent outlying communities, many of whom were private motorists. The various structural changes are perhaps encapsulated in the remarkable growth of Monifieth, immediately to the east of Dundee in Angus. This small burgh's population was relatively stable from 1951 to 1961, rising marginally from 3,419 to 3,474, and then more than doubling to 7,635 in 1971.[57] The number of persons in employment who lived in Monifieth increased by about 75 per cent in the second half of this growth decade, from 1966 to 1971. But the segment of these persons who travelled to work by car increased more rapidly, by 150 per cent, so that 46 per cent of all Monifieth residents in employment were using private cars to get to work in 1971. This was a particularly vivid illustration, it should be emphasised, of a more general trend to private car usage in the UK, with 1970 approximately the point where the number of zero-car and one-car households converged, at about 45 per cent of all households in each case, and a significant volume of two-car households – 10 per cent of all households by 1975 and 20 per cent by the early 1990s – began to emerge.[58] This trend was highly evident in Dundee itself, where in 1966 just over 50 per cent of the city's resident workers travelled to work by bus, and of the remainder more journeyed by foot, 23.6 per cent, than by car, 19.7 per cent. Within five years 27.8 per cent were travelling by car, 21.1 per cent by foot, and 45.7 per cent – still predominant but clearly in retreat – by bus.[59] This was not a case, in other words, of more people gaining employment and stimu-lating enlarged industrial activity because of access to private road transport, but essentially a larger portion of a stable or stagnating Dundee workforce travelling in cars, and the construction of the bridge contributed to this. This observation is further sustained by evidence on traffic crossing the new road link. In the year from August 1966 a total of 2,112,379 cars and commercial vehicles up to 30 hundredweights (roughly 1,500 kilograms or 1.5 tons) and 173,208 commercial vehicles over 30 hundredweights used the bridge. This latter category – the type of large road vehicles that would be associated with significant commercial and industrial freight activity – constituted 7.41 per cent of overall traffic, with a daily average of 475 crossings of this type.[60] This arguably represented an important phenomenon, with business users utilising a new opportunity. On the other hand, there is little evidence that heavy commercial traffic increased significantly thereafter, and the vast majority of crossings – of which there were 3.5 million by 1971 – continued to be undertaken by private motorists. In this sense the Scottish Office's emphasis on the bridge as essentially a local connection was probably sound, particularly as user numbers peaked in the summer months of July and August.[61] In predicting a healthy future for the bridge in 1966 the Earl of Dundee had warned about the possible hazard inherent in the pricing of tolls, with a higher rate for heavy traffic operating as a particular potential deterrent to longer-distance usage,[62] and the Road Haulage Association complained about this to the Tay Bridge Joint Board in 1966. A significant portion of correspondents to the bridge authorities over the years that followed were road hauliers and other business users complaining about the differentiated heavy traffic rate. A number of these indicated that they would use the bridge more frequently if the heavy traffic toll was reduced or scrapped.[63] It was not.

This prompts the speculative thought that perhaps the needs of business in Dundee, and particularly those of manufacturing firms on the northern industrial estates, were not particularly served by the bridge, although clearly the ability to bring people – workers, mainly, including those who had lost the opportunity to travel by rail, and perhaps some visiting executives, associates and customers – from Fife, was an advantage. However, the movement of materials – components and other parts, and then finished goods – continued essentially to flow in and out of the city on a west–east axis. Exports not exiting via the small and declining port of Dundee would be sent via Perth rather than the Tay Road Bridge, to the docks of Grangemouth, Leith or Glasgow and, from 1969, the container terminal at Greenock.[64] Containerisation of cargo traffic, indeed, was a sudden and revolutionary innovation in the 1960s that took many of the parties engaged in port transport by surprise.[65] It was certainly largely unheralded as a possibility in the 1950s as the authorities in Dundee began marshalling financial provision for the Tay Bridge. Maybe the millions borrowed for the road crossing could have been invested in reconstructing the waterfront to the betterment of industrial function in Dundee? A container terminal would certainly have offered valuable service to the US manufacturers whose goods were, after all, primarily aimed at West European and Scandinavian as well as UK markets in the 1960s and 1970s.[66]

US business users themselves, however, offered only praise for the bridge. Harold A. Neff, President of Holo-Krome, one of the largest US firms in the city, addressed the first meeting of the Dundee Chamber of Commerce following the opening of the new crossing. Neff's comments ranged across the various themes that have comprised this chapter: the importance of industrial change to the city of Dundee, and the role of regional policy and overseas enterprise, notably US firms, in effecting this process of change. Neff knew his audience, of course, and spoke to its regional pride and dignity when concluding his speech by talking about the Tay Road Bridge as a very powerful expression of local self-help and independence. In the US, he lamented, a bridge of such economic importance and physical magnitude would have been 'heavily financed' by the government.[67] This was an unwitting reiteration of Dundee's relative political isolation in the 1960s. Efforts to bring the city closer to Scotland and the UK, to compensate for the decline of jute, were hampered by this isolation, which the Tay Road Bridge – the cheapest route, the cheapest build, the central northern landing – acutely embodied.

E 32 Murrayfield Properties' enticing perspective for the new Overgate in 1968. Burke's concept ess bleak than his earlier one, but now included a tall block of offices at the town end. ge from the Charles McKean library)

E 33 A c.1950s (undated) proposal for a Tay Road Bridge by Maunsell & Partners. The ferry ur remained untouched, and whereas the Earl Grey dock was to be used for landfall and ng, part of the William IV dock was retained, and the inner part proposed for a helicopter n. (Image from the Charles McKean library)

PLATE 34 The Overgate during demolition. (a, top) Witnesses to the creation of the Angus Hote
(Courtesy D.C. Thomson) (b, above) Aerial view of the demolition of the Overgate at the juncti
with Long Wynd, looking beyond to the West Port. It conveys some sense of the density of this
district, and how lanes and closes extended behind – even though much of the latter had been fi
up with industry. (Copyright D.C. Thomson)

PLATE 35 (*Above*) Gardyne's Land, High Street (the centre building) after conversion to a backpacker's hostel in 2006. This complex of structures, incorporating a thirteenth-century well, sixteenth-century beams, seventeenth-century staircase and early eighteenth-century panelled room, is Dundee's premier 'anchor of memory' of its days as a Renaissance port. (Copyright Charles McKean)

PLATE 36 (*Left*) Woman at work in a jute mill in the 1960s. Around this time men for the first time became the majority of workers in the industry. (Michael Peto Collection, University of Dundee Archives)

PLATE 37 Woman jute worker in the 1960s. This picture does not convey the dirty (and noisy) atmosphere of the mills. (Michael Peto Collection, University of Dundee Archives)

PLATE 38 The coronation of Elizabeth II in 1953 evokes a popular response in a jute mill owned b Malcolm Ogilvie & Co. (Malcolm Ogilvie Collection, University of Dundee Archives)

PLATE 39 George Dutch Davidson, Ullalume 1900, pen & ink drawing. Davidson was one of the ing artists of the Dundee Celtic Revival until his tragic death at the age of only 21. pyright Dundee Art Galleries & Museums)

PLATE 40 (*Left*) Dudley D. Watkins, Lord Snooty, original artwork from *The Beano* 1940, pen & ink drawing. (Copyright D.C. Thomson & Co. Ltd)

PLATE 41 (*Above*) Artists at Valentines, 1940s. (Courtesy of a private collection)

PLATE 42 (*Right*) For his postgraduate work at Duncan of Jordanstone College, sculptor David Mach created this extraordinary Carpet of Leaves at Camperdown Park, 1978. (Copyright University of Dundee Museum Services, Duncan of Jordanstone College Collection)

INDEPENDENT LABOUR PARTY.

𝔓𝔞𝔯𝔩𝔦𝔞𝔪𝔢𝔫𝔱𝔞𝔯𝔶 𝔈𝔞𝔫𝔡𝔦𝔡𝔞𝔱𝔢𝔰.

PLATE 43 From the *Labour Leader*, Christmas Edition, December 1894 (page 13): James MacDonald's photograph (*left*) was one of twelve depicting twelve of the Independent Labour Party's parliamentary candidates to appear in this special edition of the newspaper. This is probably one of the first examples of photography being used by the *Labour Leader* (very few photographs were used before 1914).

TE 44 (*Right*) Recruitment poster n the *People's Journal*, 14 August .: this made a direct appeal to 1 British and Scottish patriotic iment as the willing recruits ked to Britannia while the spirit Robert the Bruce looked on rovingly.

THE TOCSIN

An Illustrated Labour and Socialist Journal

| No. 1 | APRIL, 1909 | One Penny |

FOREWORD.

THIS is the first number of "The Tocsin." It is the result of much earnest desire, a of no less earnest endeavour, on the part of various representatives of Labour, Sociali Trade Union, Co-operative, and kindred movements in Dundee and District, a whatever be the fate of this modest, and yet not unambitious little venture, we can look ba with pleasure to many acts of sacrifice and disinterested service which we found inexpressit grateful. The Guarantors, who so nobly stepped into the breach—in character half Curti half Mæcenas — have placed us under a debt of more than gratitude. We thankfu acknowledge the active assistance of the members of the Women's Freedom League, and all others, named and unnamed, who have so generously helped.

If, as you very well may, you should discover the paper to be deficient in any respec we can but crave your indulgence for what is the product of limited leisure, and of by means unlimited finance. We shall endeavour after betterment in each succeeding issue. From the Working Classes of the community we not only ask for sympathetic suppo but we claim it. From our political opponents we should desire that courteous consideratic which we shall endeavour to extend. For ourselves we shall make effort to abstain from a personalities. In argument it is not necessary to garrotte your antagonist; the touch of ev a buttoned foil may prove as effective as the blow of a bludgeon. "The Tocsin," we tru shall always ring with a sufficient clarity of tone.

Let us be charitable—this is but a difficult world, and truth may lie at the end of ma and devious ways.

Let us write with a full remembrance of the weight of words.

Let us be cheerful. "The Tocsin" shall not only sound to one wild note of warnir or alarm. Ye shall have ringing of changes and carillons; bob-majors and grandsi triples. We shall toll a passing-bell, we trust, for many an iniquitous custom. Ye ladies and gentlemen, with your permission, we hope to ring you yet a mad merry peal at tl passing of this sad, old, outworn, unsatisfactory system and scheme of things.

Let us be magnanimous—as they to whom victory, if yet distant, is still not qui invisible. For our cause, if the world do but hold, defeat can only be temporary. With are the inexhaustible reinforcements of the yet unborn.

Here then is the first number of "The Tocsin." THE EDITOR.

PLATE 45 Front page of the first edition of *Tocsin* produced and published in Dundee in 1909: *Too* variously included reports on 'Town Council Matters' by councillor John Reid, 'Parish Council Affairs' by James Gordon, 'School Board Notes' by Agnes Husband, and reports on the activities o the Dundee Branch of the Women's Freedom League. Alex Wilkie wrote a weekly column on Parliamentary matters, and free legal advice was offered by locally based solicitor J. Grafton Lawso: Throughout there are many references to the work of the Independent Labour Party. (Joseph Johnston Lee Collection, Dundee University Archives)

GENERAL STRIKE AFTERMATH

CERTAIN newspaper proprietors have decided that non-union labour only will in future be employed in the production of their publications, which means that many members of the Printing Trade Unions who loyally supported the General Strike cannot obtain employment or reinstatement with these firms without giving up what our forefathers fought for—the right to membership of a Trade Union.

We appeal for your support to combat and defeat this attack on the Printing Trade Unions by refusing to purchase any of the following publications :—

GEORGE OUTRAM LIMITED—

Glasgow Herald
Evening Times
Bulletin
Weekly Herald

JAMES HEDDERWICK & SON—

Evening Citizen

ABERDEEN NEWSPAPERS LIMITED—

Aberdeen Press and Journal
Evening Express

THOMSON-LENG (GLASGOW AND DUNDEE)—

The Dundee Advertiser and Courier
The Weekly News
The People's Journal
The People's Friend
The Weekly Welcome
The Sunday Post
The Saturday Post
The Evening Telegraph
The Adventure

Fairyland Tales
The Mascot
My Weekly
Red Letter
The Rover
Topical Times
The Wizard
People's Friend Library
White Heather Novels
Ivy Stories

Save in regard to the general stoppage decided upon by the British Trades Union Congress the proprietors of the foregoing publications had no known quarrel with their employees as workers, nor had they any grievance against the Unions.

Thus, because of their loyalty to the Trades Union Congress and their sympathy with the Miners, the Printing Trade Unions are not now recognised by the proprietors of the above publications.

This Leaflet is fully endorsed by the General Council of the Scottish Trades Union Congress.

(Signed) Wm. Elger, Secretary.

Published by National Society of Operative Printers and Assistants.
National Society of Electrotypers and Stereotypers.
Society of Litho Artists, Designers, Engravers, and Process Workers.
Scottish Typographical Association.

E 46 This leaflet was produced by trade unionists in the associated printing trades in Scotland rotest against the employers' decision not to reinstate workers who had taken part in the General e in 1926 in support of the miners. This campaign was also supported by the Scottish Trades n Congress. (Kinnear Local Book Collection, Dundee University Archives)

DUNDEE ELECTOR

FIRST ISSUE.   DUNDEE, JANUARY 1906.

COUNCILLOR ALEXANDER WILKIE.

THE PEOPLE'S CANDIDATE.

Every VOTE given to WILKIE

MEANS A VOTE FOR

REAL SOCIAL REFORM.

PLATE 47 The first issue of the *Dundee Elector*, January 1906; this particular copy is signed by Alexander Wilkie. (By kind permission of the Wellgate Library Dundee)

E 48 View possibly take from the newly built Tower building, showing elements of the city
re with the vast railway marshalling yards, which were shortly afterwards dispensed with.
wn Copyright: RCAHMS. Licensor www.rcahms.gov.uk)

E 49 Aerial shot showing the central landing point of the Tay bridge. (Copyright RCAHMS.
oduced courtesy of J.R. Hume. Licensor www.rcahms.gov.uk)

PLATE 50 (*Above*) Workers'
occupation of the Timex
Factory. (Copyright D.C.
Thomson)

PLATE 51 (*Right*) A close-up of
a female worker showing the
delicate and intricate skills
involved in watch assembly.
(Copyright D.C. Thomson)

PLATE 52 (*Above*) The female assembly line. Note the presence of male supervisors (Copyright D.C. Thomson)

PLATE 53 (*Left*) A sociable and seemingly chaotic female assembly line. (Copyright D.C. Thomson)

PLATE 54 Female assembly line, disciplined and organised. (Copyright D.C. Thomson)

PLATE 55 Female worker employed on the most demanding part of the job. (Copyright D.C. Thomson)

PLATE 56 Dundee – view from Dental Tower, 1983. This photograph captures the mix of old and ‌ around the city centre. (Turner–McKinlay Photographic Collection, University of Dundee hives)

PLATE 57 The Caird Hall in revolutionary garb. BBC film making: *An Englishman Abroad*, 1983. (Turner–McKinlay Photographic Collection, University of Dundee Archives)

PLATE 58 NUPE protestors outside Fife Health Board headquarters, Glenrothes, 1984. The 1980s were notable for the scale of opposition to the policies of the Thatcher government in Dundee and much of Scotland. (University of Dundee Archives)

PLATE 59 Gordon Wilson, SNP MP for Dundee East, campaigns for a 'yes' vote in the 1979 referendum on devolution for Scotland. (Gordon Wilson Collection, University of Dundee Archiv

NOTES

1. DCA, Tay Road Bridge Joint Board Minutes (hereafter TRBJB), 30 November 1965.

2. Tay Road Bridge Joint Board, *40th Anniversary: A special edition booklet to commemorate the 40th Anniversary of the Tay Road Bridge* (Dundee, Tay Road Bridge Joint Board, 2006); *Tay Road Bridge*, produced by Campbell Harper Films for Films of Scotland, directed by Henry Cooper (1967).

3. *The Great Tay Road Bridge Mystery: Whodunnit?* Written and presented by Lesley Riddoch; produced and directed by Charlie Stuart; Feisty Productions with Fresh Film and Television (2007); C. McKean and P. Whatley with K. Baxter, *Lost Dundee: Dundee's Lost Architectural Heritage* (Edinburgh, 2008).

4. A.M. Carstairs, 'The nature and diversification of employment in Dundee in the twentieth century' in S.J. Jones (ed.), *Dundee and District* (Dundee, British Association, 1968), p. 334.

5. *The Road and the Miles*, Scottish Television, 1966, http://ssa.nls.uk/film.cfm?fid=T1141; thanks to Carlo Morelli for this reference.

6. NAS, DD4/302: Note of interview between Road Board and City of Dundee delegation, 11 February 1919.

7. DCA, Minutes of Dundee Town Council, 'Town Planning: Comprehensive Plan and Report', submitted to Meeting of Housing and Town Planning Committee, Dundee, 13 January 1919.

8. C. McKean and D. Walker, *Dundee: An Illustrated Architectural Guide* (Edinburgh, 1993), p. 17.

9. London School of Economics, E.D. Morel Papers (hereafter LSE Morel), Baxter to Morel, 19 January 1924; thanks to Jim Tomlinson for this and other Morel references.

10. NAS, DD4/302: clippings from *Courier*, 30 October and 5 November 1923.

11. LSE Morel, Maybury to the Lord Provost, Dundee, 16 June 1924.

12. NAS, DD4/302: Town Clerk, Dundee to Joynson-Hicks, 16 October 1923.

13. LSE Morel, Morel to Lord Provost, Dundee, 18 January 1924.

14. NAS, DD4/303: Conference between Lord Privy Seal, Tom Johnston, and Scottish Local Authorities concerned with a bridge across the Tay, 5 May 1931. This conference was attended by the Secretary of State for Scotland, Willie Adamson, and the Minister of Transport, Herbert Morrison.

15. C.H. Lee, *Scotland and the United Kingdom: The Economy and the Union in the Twentieth Century* (Manchester, 1999), pp. 106–7.

16. NAS, DD4/303: Conference between Lord Privy Seal and Scottish Local Authorities, 5 May 1931.

17. R. Skidelsky, *Politicians and the Slump* (London, 1994 [1967]).

18. NAS, DD4/303: Tay Road Bridge (Local Authorities) Joint Committee, *The Case For the Tay Road Bridge* (Dundee, City Chamberlain's Department, October 1936), pp. 12–13.

19. Garret Wilson, *The Making of a Lord Provost* (Dundee, 1947), pp. 95–7.

20. NAS, DD4/3432: John F. Muir to J. Westwood, 19 November 1946.

21. J. Tomlinson, *Democratic Socialism and Economic Policy: The Attlee Years* (Cambridge, 1997).

22. P. Payne, 'Scottish Council (Development and Industry)' in Michael Lynch, *The Oxford Companion to Scottish History* (Oxford, 2001), pp. 574–5.

23. W. Knox, 'Class, work and trade unionism in Scotland' in A. Dickson and J.H. Treble (eds), *People and Society in Scotland*, vol. 3: *1914–1990* (Edinburgh, 1994), p. 111.

24. *Industry and Commerce in the Dundee Region. Dundee Chamber of Commerce Journal* (hereafter *Dundee Chamber of Commerce Journal*) (June 1966), pp. 100–1.

25. *Dundee Chamber of Commerce Journal* (September 1965), p. 451; (March 1965), p. 346.

26. General Register Office, Edinburgh (hereafter GRO), *Census, 1951, Scotland. Occupation and Industries.* (Edinburgh, HMSO, 1956) Table 6, 'Occupation and Industrial Status'; *Census, 1961, Scotland. Occupation and Industry County Tables: Dundee, Clackmannan and Fife* (Edinburgh, HMSO, 1966), Table 1, 'Occupation and Status'; *Census, 1961, Scotland. Population, Dwellings, Households: Cities of Glasgow, Edinburgh, Aberdeen, Dundee* (Edinburgh, HMSO, 1963).

27. Committee of Inquiry appointed by the SCDI under the Chairmanship of J.N. Toothill, *Report on the Scottish Economy* (Edinburgh, SCDI, 1961).

28. SCDI, Campsie House, Glasgow: SCDI Executive Committee Minutes, 11 July 1962, 'Programme For Growth'.

29. 'The target within Scottish sights: Lord Polwarth discusses the opportunities and problems', *Dundee Chamber of Commerce Journal* (March 1964), pp. 19–21.

30. J. Phillips, *The Industrial Politics of Devolution: Scotland in the 1960s and 1970s* (Manchester, 2008), pp. 19–27.

31. *Central Scotland: Programme for Development and Growth*, Cmnd. 2188 (London, HMSO, 1963).

32. GRO, *Census, 1961, Scotland. Occupation and Industry: Dundee, Clackmannan and Fife*, Table 5, 'Socio-Economic Group of Economically Active Males'.

33. NAS, DD4/3432: C. Macrae, Secretary, SCDI, to T.F.S. Hetherington, Scottish Home Department, 14 May 1952; W.A. Christianson, Engineer, Victoria Street, London, to the Secretary, SCDI, 9 May 1955; and J.S. Campbell, British Transport Commission, to A.C. Cowan, 8 June 1955.

34. NAS, DD4/4373: Meeting between Secretary of State for Scotland and Local Authorities concerned with Tay Road Bridge, 20 May 1957.

35. NAS, DD4/4373: A.N. Sutherland, Scottish Home Department, 'Proposed Crossing of the Tay at Dundee', 16 July 1957.

36. TNA: PRO T224/288: A.K. Ogilvy-Webb, 'Dundee Jute Industry', EA (57) 76, 9 July 1957.

37. NAS, DD4/4373: Meeting of Scottish Office and Local Authority officials to discuss the Tay Bridge project, 25 October 1957.

38. DCA, TRBJB, 8 September 1958.

39. NAS, DD4/4373: Meeting between Secretary of State for Scotland and Local Authorities concerned with Tay Road Bridge, 11 December 1959.

40. DCA, TRBJB, Sub-Committee, 23 December 1960.

41. R. Lyle and G. Payne, *The Tay Valley Plan: A Physical, Social and Economic Survey and Plan for the Future Development of East Central Scotland* (Dundee, East Central [Scotland] Regional Planning Advisory Committee, 1950).

42. 'The Dundee Region's Year of Opportunity', *Dundee Chamber of Commerce Journal* (December 1965), pp. 529, 531.

43. *The Scottish Economy, 1965 to 1970: A Plan For Expansion*, Cmnd. 2864 (London, HMSO, 1966).

44. *Dundee Chamber of Commerce Journal* (June 1966), pp. 111–13, 117.

45. TNA: PRO BT 303/155, IM/3646/O: 'Jute Goods. Protection – The Next Step', April 1963.

46. NAS, DD4/4941: Ove Arup to Ernest Marples, 30 January 1961.

47. DCA, TRBJC, 11 November 1959.

48. Alastair Borthwick, *The Tay Road Bridge* (Dundee, Tay Road Bridge Joint Board, 1966), pp. 3, 11.

49. NAS, DD4/4941: Ove Arup to Ernest Marples, 30 January 1961.

50. Borthwick, *Tay Road Bridge*, inside title page.

51. N.R. Gillhespy, 'The Tay Road Bridge: a case study in cost-benefit analysis', *Scottish Journal of Political Economy* 16 (1969), pp. 167–83.

52. GRO, *Sample Census, 1966, Scotland. Workplace and Transport Tables* (Edinburgh, HMSO, 1968), Table 7, 'Working Population by Means of Transport to Work'; *Census, 1971, Scotland. Workplace and Transport Tables* (Edinburgh, HMSO, 1974), Table 8, 'Working Population by Means of Transport to Work'.

53. NAS, DD4/303: Conference between Lord Privy Seal, Tom Johnston, and Scottish Local Authorities concerned with a bridge across the Tay, 5 May 1931.

54. GRO, *Census, 1961, Scotland. Population, Dwellings, Households. East and Central Counties* (Edinburgh, HMSO, 1963); GRO, *Census, 1971, Scotland. Scottish Population Summary* (Edinburgh, HMSO, 1973).

55. GRO, *Sample Census, 1966* Table 7, and *Census, 1971*, Table 8.

56. A.D. Campbell, 'The economic structure of the Tayside region' in Jones (ed.), *Dundee and District*, pp. 337–46.

57. GRO, *Census, 1961, Scotland. Population, Dwellings, Households. East and Central Counties; Census, 1971, Scotland. Scottish Population Summary.*

58. Information gratefully received by the author from Stephen Cragg of SIAS Transport Planners, using Department for Transport-published data.

59. GRO, *Sample Census*, Table 7, and *Census, 1971*, Table 8.

60. DCA, TRBJB, 14 September 1967.

61. DCA, TRBJB, 2 February 1972.

62. *Dundee Chamber of Commerce Journal* (June 1966), p. 113.

63. DCA, A/1/13/16/2: Tay Road Bridge – Tolls and Traffic Correspondence, and Toll Charges and Objections.

64. Phillips, *Industrial Politics of Devolution*, p. 59.

65. M. Levinson, *The Box: How the Shipping Container Made the World Smaller and the World Economy Bigger* (Princeton, 2006), *passim* but especially pp. 127–49.

66. N. Hood and S. Young, *Multinationals in Retreat: The Scottish Experience* (Edinburgh, 1982).

67. *Dundee Chamber of Commerce Journal* (September 1966), pp. 181–6.

The Union Makes us Strong?
Work and Trade Unionism in Timex, 1946–83

Bill Knox and Alan McKinlay

For over fifty years the central belt of Scotland has been a major recipient of multinational investment, but, in spite of this, the history of foreign direct investment remains unwritten. This silence has created a lacuna in our understanding of the development of the Scottish economy since 1945, as, for much of the post-war period, first American – and then Japanese – companies were regarded as vital not just to employment creation, but also to the modernisation of the Scottish manufacturing base. The first significant series of American arrivals occurred between 1945 and 1955 with consolidation to 1965; a second wave of American inward investment, based on microelectronics, was largely complete by 1973. However, through to the late 1980s the American presence suffered major closures, especially in engineering. From the early 1980s Japanese consumer and microelectronics firms have established assembly operations, with the 1990s witnessing the troubled beginnings of aggressively globalising businesses from other Pacific-rim nations. Throughout all these shifts in the demography of multinational inward investment, American firms have remained dominant in terms of employment, constituting a continuing and important element of the Scottish manufacturing base. And yet there are few fine-grained studies that focus on the experiences of particular firms or factories, and still fewer that draw on employers' association or union archives or interview material. By drawing on such material we can examine the grassroots struggles to maintain the integrity of the 'American model', on the one hand, and to develop effective trade union representation inside the factory. This takes us beneath the surface of existing survey material on industrial relations which relies almost exclusively on accounts by managerial respondents. Thus, this chapter will concentrate on three interrelated main themes: the dynamics of work organisation in Timex, union organisation and collective bargaining. In terms of the latter we pay particular attention to two watershed moments in the history of the company's operations in Dundee; the 1972 autoshop dispute and the 1983 occupation of the Milton factory.

The UK Time Company was established in 1946, becoming Timex in 1954. Timex was attracted to Scotland by the prospects of long-term growth, regional aid, clean air and access to a large regional workforce habituated to factory production. The first few years were modest and based in converted farm buildings. In spite of these humble beginnings, steady expansion of output and employment characterised Timex's first decade. By the early 1960s the plant employed over 1,500 people, rising to over 2,500 by 1965. Product diversification, notably the production of the Polaroid Swinger camera, was paralleled by rapid employment growth to 4,200 in 1968, peaking at around 6,000 in the first half of the 1970s.[1]

In Timex, family networks were critical in securing employment: 'our kids would work at Timex . . . at least one of our children worked at Timex, if not two. Aunties, uncles, nephews, [and] when it closed it was whole families.'[2] By the mid-1960s the earnings of Timex workers exceeded that of other local employees, with skilled engineers earning around 25–35 per cent more than their counterparts in NCR or Veeder Root. As one worker put it:

I earned good money – my bairns were never short o' a holiday, school claes. I was never poor or anything like that, because Timex paid no bad wages, because we made them good. It wisnae because Timex wanted to gie the money awa' – they were a stingy firm – but they were forced through militancy.[3]

During the immediate post-war years Timex in America shifted from the mass production of fuses and other war materials to the mass production and mass marketing of mechanical watches. Indeed, Joachim Lehmkuhl, the chairman of the parent company, US Time, publicly stated that he aimed to become 'the Henry Ford of the American Watchmaking industry'.[4] The micromechanical advances of wartime production were fundamental to Timex's post-war production strategy: near total product standardisation, the use of novel alloys, a reduction in the number of parts used and so the simplification of manufacturing operations, the use of pin-lever rather than jewel actions, and maximum mechanisation to reduce the scope for human error and to minimise labour costs.[5] These new materials and techniques produced robust watches capable of matching jewelled-lever watches in terms of quality and reliability. Jewellers, wedded to a notion of the superiority of craftsmanship over mass production, refused to stock Timex watches, forcing the company to innovate in marketing, advertising and distribution. By the early 1960s Timex had cornered the domestic American market for low- to mid-priced watches, a market that it had effectively created.[6] Mass manufacturing was based on four stages: gear and pinion, flat parts, spring making, and case making. These parts fed a three-stage assembly process: movement assembly, sub-assembly, final assembly, and test and despatch.[7] Designing highly routinised work processes predicated on managers' assumptions about the 'nimble fingers', self-discipline and attentiveness of women was, of course, hardly new.[8] Initially, production demanded that the operators gained experience and a fairly extensive knowledge of the complete production process.[9] But the need for operator experience and ingenuity faded quickly from the mid-1950s. American firms often used assembly lines to pace labour, but few achieved the stability of Timex.[10] In Timex, machine pacing was particularly intense in the all-female assembly departments during the plant's first decade. As one woman assembler put it:

> You were like a battery hen. You just sat on all these lines and all these watches were coming down in containers. The atmosphere was good but it was very strict – you daren't look up or get caught talking.[11]

Tasks were highly routinised, often taking no more than an instant or a few seconds to complete. The target for a typical assembly task – inserting balance wheels into casings – was 8,000 per shift.[12] One female Timex line employee worked on the next stage of assembling balance wheels from these 'kits':

> It was very boring – you worked on a machine that had a wee die and you just put the balance wheel in and the wee bitties on top

of them and then pulled this handle. It went with a swish of air
– and you just sat and done that all day long. Every day felt like
a month.[13]

Tasks that required the assembler to develop a feel for the task were
prized for their difficulty. One assembler recalled that her favourite job
was done using an eye loop to prise open the back of the mechanism:

> open it a little bit with your finger . . . ye would get your tweezers
> up – then pick up the part that you had to put in – and ye just
> fitted it in – the holes were really dead tiny . . . you couldnae
> really see the holes but you knew it was in because it would just
> slip intae the socket sortie thing – that was really interesting – I
> liked that little job.[14]

Better still were the final assembly and testing stations. Fixing back plates
and ensuring that the watch functioned required the assembler to
develop rudimentary diagnostic skills and learn how to cannibalise other
watches.[15] There was no managerial recognition that there were any
significant distinctions between tasks or that some operators developed
meaningful tacit skills. Confronted by a woman who claimed that her
task required experience and skill, a senior manager responded, 'I could
get chimpanzees to do the job.' This woman, a veteran of munitions
factories and Dundee's jute mills, reflected that this dismissive response
was more accurate than the manager appreciated:

> and really I went on a machine in Timex and to be successful you
> would've had to be a fucking chimpanzee because the machine
> was so made that you would've needed at least four-feet-long
> legs, six-feet-long arms and a two-feet body.[16]

All assembly tasks had set hourly production targets. Machine pacing
and a sequential labour process maintained strict discipline: 'you had to
keep the line moving. If you were too slow it meant the person next to
you couldn't work. That was a pressure. Some girls worked on their
nerves'. But if this pressure could generate 'bitchiness' it also encouraged
them to provide relief and assistance if a workmate was struggling: 'if
they were having a bad day you would help them out'.[17] In the decade to

the mid-1960s, management retained almost complete unilateral control over production standards. A failure to meet targets meant that assemblers were given an ultimatum, produce or leave Timex.[18] There is some evidence that bonus standards were tight until a series of wildcat strikes in the late 1960s forced management to accept that contested productivity standards should be subject to negotiation and re-timing and that this could be triggered by the workgroup, not solely by management.

Supervision was tight: the ratio of supervisors to workers was never less than one to twelve in the assembly areas. Particularly in the plant's first decade, management was able to enforce strict discipline. In November 1952, Patricia Thomson was dismissed for running on hearing the lunch-bell, contrary to her departmental manager's orders.[19] Random quality inspections combined with the direct, tangible presence of supervisors on the line increased the pressures on the workforce. One worker complained in 1965 that the manager of the field repair department 'stands over them when they are working sometimes with a stop watch in his hand. He makes sarcastic remarks and threatens to fire them, in other words, they are under great pressure.' Such managerial interventions short-circuited any process of collective bargaining and, indeed, undermined the authority of supervisors. Two wildcat strikes in quick succession by the department's 'eighty girls' testified to the breakdown of the formal rules of collective bargaining and the stewards' inability to exercise any influence further up the managerial structure. In such a situation, union stewards and the foremen had common cause in their search to re-establish their authority on the line. The shop stewards suggested that all local grievances and infractions of company rules should be dealt with by the foreman in the presence of the steward: 'the Departmental manager to stay away as much as possible'. One late 1960s study of high labour turnover among women electronics workers concluded that the greatest single source of dissatisfaction was disrespectful supervisors whose arbitrary use of sanctions was perceived as a way of disguising their poor co-ordination of production.[20] It is impossible to overstate the gendered nature of supervision in Timex. Women assemblers used banter to negotiate, challenge or ridicule male supervisory authority.[21] As one put it:

There were no men on the line, other than your supervisor. And if your head looked up from the assembly line, he just came along and pushed it down again. So you had to knuckle down. There was this one supervisor and he was so full of his own importance . . . his nose was always in the air and he was always looking to get on to somebody. . . . So we had the chairs with metal legs, . . . and I had a habit of sitting with my legs wrapped round them. And he got on to me this one day and started a fit of laughter . . . that I just couldn't stop. I ended up on my back and tears were running down my face. And he said, I'm sorry, I didn't think I would affect you like that. But I was laughing, I wasn't crying.[22]

And again:

There were some great bosses at Timex but you always had the odd few that really wielded a stick. I think their bark was worse than their bite. . . . Having so many women underneath them, it was a male thing, 'aw these bloody women, they never do what they are told', but it was the odd few. Most of the gaffers were good.[23]

While assembly supervisors were overwhelmingly male, there was one notable exception, 'one lady that ruled the roost', Marion McMillan, from the mid-1950s until the early 1970s.

If you worked for her you were a Marion McMillan girl. She was like the headmistress in *Annie*. She was like the head of the orphanage: you didn't cough unless Marion told you to; you didn't run unless Marion told you to. That was old Timex. . . . [A]s the years went by it got to be a better place to work, the rules were still there, but the people wouldn't accept Marion McMillan as the headmistress any more. She had lorded it over people, but it was young girls that worked under her. Married women worked for her, gave her respect, but you were not one of her girls.[24]

For the line worker, to breach quality standards was to risk 100 per cent inspection of every item they produced, a key part of the supervisor's armoury. This involved a supervisor 'right on the shoulder' of the assembler. This ensured not only that the individual could not earn their production bonus but also jeopardised the throughput that their workmates' earnings depended upon: 'you'd be speaking too much for his liking. The inspector would pay more attention to your work. She would pick up your work and say that there was a bit of fluff on it and put on a flag and then we would have to do 160 until she lifted the flag. That was one of the worst bits of your job.' This limited the assemblers' ability to work at their own pace, to assist – or be helped – by others. 'That was tension', because it exposed the worker to supervisory reprimand for failing to maintain their output over several days.[25]

MEN'S WORK

Timex men and women overwhelmingly worked at quite different kinds of jobs and in separate locations. The vast majority of men were skilled engineers who provided the tools for the assembly operation in Dundee and, indeed, other parts of the corporation's international operations. Skilled engineering work was very accurate but also predictable and largely undemanding. In the production department, engineers were responsible for routine maintenance: 'if you put in one drill you are gonnae put in a hundred drills. The only time that I enjoyed the work was when you had a change-over – you had to strip the machine down to basics then build it back up as a completely different piece part – different cams, different set-ups, different pick-ups.'[26] High degrees of accuracy were demanded by mass production. As such, American mass manufacturers developed extensive training programmes to transform Scottish engineers accustomed to the flexibility and improvisation demanded by heavy industry into toolmakers attuned to the precision demanded by mass production.[27]

The division between men's and women's tasks was not simply about location and skill. Men enjoyed a high degree of control over the nature and pace of their work that was quite different to the regulated, fast-paced work of women assemblers. The Milton autoshop was organised so that engineers alternated between day and night shifts. The engineers' custom was that the majority of demanding tasks were completed by the day shift so that:

the night-shift guy just coasted it – he could sit down and read books and newspapers and fall asleep if that's what you felt like doing . . . Because the machines were automated and just kept churning out the product and an inspector would go round every hour and check the quality and if it was OK he'd put on a green ticket. If you got a red ticket you would just switch off and the dayshift guy would fix it and you would dae the same for him when you were on night-shift.[28]

Skilled engineers would also manipulate their workloads to create free time at work:

we would be given an allowance. If a machine broke down we would be given a certain number of hours to fix that certain machine. But management wasn't that clever because . . . you would start a job and be minutes away from finishing that job and you would stop, just leave it dangling. We would leave all these jobs dangling . . . so people would accumulate enough hours to do nothing for an entire week . . . We did have quite tough targets, but the clever guys knew how to get around these targets.[29]

Male work in Timex was, then, quite different from female work: it was primarily skilled, supervision was relaxed, and there was limited time pressure. Earnings were largely controlled by the men or, at least, they were much more negotiable than for females.

TRADE UNIONS AND COLLECTIVE BARGAINING

A chronic shortage of skilled engineers forced American companies to recognise the Amalgamated Engineering Union (AEU) and, indeed, to use the union as an informal recruitment agency.[30] In Dundee this process was eased by the role that the engineering union and the city's Trades Council had in the Corporation's post-1945 drive to modernise and diversify the region's industrial base. The AEU's priority was securing employment for skilled men.[31] From the outset, however, *all* American inward investment was consistently anti-union and, at most, grudgingly accepted, if not tolerated, union membership and representation. Thus, any gains in union effectiveness were secured in spite of company opposition, often as the outcome of protracted disputes.[32] From its arrival in Dundee, Timex reluctantly accepted some kind of union presence inside the factory, although this did not extend to an acceptance of formal collective bargaining, or endorsing a specific union as the privileged representative of the workforce. While there was no formal recognition of a role for shop stewards, management was nudged towards a grudging acceptance that some form of union representation was inevitable. The Timex employment contracts – which were much more formal and comprehensive than was common in British manufacturing – reassured new hires that 'there shall be no discrimination by anyone representing the Company in a Supervisory capacity against any Employee because of the Employee's membership in a Trade Union'.[33] But the firm went no further in guaranteeing an individual's right to union representation or specifying an agreed procedure giving voice to any collective grievance.

The first few years of union organisation in Timex were fitful, with irregular communication between the plant and the union's local official. Indeed, the plant's first convener resigned in 1951, after less than a year in post, due to the lack of support from his workmates.[34] Two years later union organisation was still inadequate – patchy steward organisation and an enforced over-reliance on inexperienced representatives – to deal with a firm that was 'now adopting a "get tough" policy, tightening up in relation to production'.[35] Individual female bonus was set unilaterally by management and the union had no oversight of earnings across the factory as a whole. Women assemblers were transferred between jobs, even if this reduced their earnings, and management reduced bonus targets abruptly and without consultation.[36] For the male steward representing the largely female inspection department, 'his girls' were underpaid and this was a reflection of their poor union organisation. In May 1952, he reported, 'I have managed to get a girl to take over the position in the inspectors' department.' His delight was short-lived, however, as 'the girl' steward resigned her post within six weeks. Without a steward to collect union dues, members could soon slip deeply into arrears. So extensive was this problem that the beleaguered steward resorted to simply writing off these arrears so that he could begin to re-unionise the department.[37] Equally, Timex was careful to exclude known union activists, a policy which provoked a three-month overtime ban in the winter of 1952–3.[38] However, there was no real solidity or depth to union infrastructure, especially in female-dominated areas, although there had been some modest gains in female steward numbers. The AEU was beginning to appreciate the extent of its limited bargaining power inside Timex.[39]

National AEU campaigns to win the male labourer's rate for women workers were critical in galvanising, if not accelerating, local union efforts to recruit women and increase the number of female shop stewards.[40] The union's 1955 wage claim met with entrenched employer hostility to any concessions that would give women parity with any group of male workers. For female activists, the employers' rejection caused 'much discontent among our women members owing to the unsatisfactory settlement. . . . Women resented receiving less wages for higher skill than for sweeping the floor – the male labourer's rate.'[41]

Until the early 1960s, the overwhelming impression is of the fragility of union organisation among Timex's female workers. Female shop stewards were typically young and inexperienced, often teenagers who had just joined the union.[42] Two new twenty-year-old stewards in Department 1520 – movement assembly – reported to the AEU that they had asked management how the bonus system worked: 'they had been shown masses of papers and figures' but remained none the wiser.[43] Further, there were no elections for female stewards before 1966, which suggests that the key problem was identifying volunteers rather than choosing between rival candidates. Inevitably, there was a high turnover rate among such novice female stewards.[44] Male stewards, by contrast, were elected, almost always skilled, generally in their late twenties to their mid-thirties, and held office for more than three years. They tended to have well-defined workgroup constituencies, seldom numbering more than thirty members. Female stewards, on the other hand, represented much larger and less well-defined workgroups, sometimes numbering as many as 140 members. All of these factors combined to make the task of the young female steward much more difficult than her older and more experienced male counterpart. One indicator of the importance of these demographic differences between male and female stewards is that during the surges in employment that typified Timex between 1953 and 1968, male membership density and levels of steward representation were maintained, while female membership and steward numbers lagged by several months. Membership turnover placed an enormous administrative burden on a patchy and largely inexperienced lay organisation.[45] No less important, but much more difficult to demonstrate, was how these levels of labour instability made it difficult for the young female stewards to develop their skills in a gradual manner to consolidate their authority on the assembly lines.

The existence of union representation did not necessarily presume a supportive membership. The dismissal of the Camperdown factory's female convener, 'Sister Brown', and another steward, Mrs Black, in 1956, did not trigger any concerted protest from the workers, despite the union's assertion that the reasons given for dismissing two long-service employees – 'negligence' and 'aiding and abetting' – were spurious. In less than a month the loss of key stewards plunged the factory's union organisation into 'a state of chaos'; a serious problem during a period of short-time and redundancies.[46] Model changes were always preceded by an abrupt tightening of all aspects of labour discipline, as management became uncompromising and stringent in punishing recalcitrant workers. Phasing out one product line entailed internal labour transfers; something which raised issues of equity, especially if there was a potential loss of earnings for transferees. The union had not secured procedural authority in labour transfers, far less over redundancy selection. Inevitably, this combination of issues breached the informal rules of the workplace and caused 'a great deal of discontent'.[47] There is little doubt that this was a strategic move by Timex management to reduce worker representation during a significant period of factory reorganisation. This abrupt loss of effective union representation for women assemblers coincided with a retooling of the plant in readiness for the introduction of new electronic clocks. The AEU lost any realistic hope of representing female workers facing redundancy or over the definition and bonus levels for new tasks.

Local women activists were acutely aware that while national wage campaigns could generate membership numbers, durable union organisation and robust representation depended upon building up a cadre of experienced female shop stewards.[48] However, before 1970, the shop steward's main responsibility was organisation rather than representation. Stewards had to ensure that all eligible individuals had joined and that their members' contributions were up to date. This was no small task. Although national and local recruitment campaigns achieved positive results, membership gains were gradually eroded if shop stewards proved unequal to the task of checking subscription cards and effectively representing their constituents. The most important gains in female union organisation followed in the wake of spontaneous shop floor protests about arbitrary or unfair management, particularly when this was associated with a specific manager.[49] As a result, through the mid-1960s female union membership and steward representation became more firmly established in Timex; indeed, by 1967, some largely female departments were now accepted by management as de facto closed shops.[50]

A 'MALIGN INFLUENCE BROODING OVER THE CITY'?[51]

For workers drawn to Timex by the prospect of high earnings, the embryonic state of the plant's bonus system was always a pressure point. The rapid employment growth and product diversification of the mid-1960s again opened up the piecework system to intense shop floor pressure. Comparability disputes rippled across the factory. The most intense and protracted were those of the autoshop machine setters, who pursued the same basic rate as the factory's aristocrats, the toolroom engineers. Toolroom workers enjoyed a differential in basic rate of approximately 10–15 per cent. Dundee's colossal autoshop comprised over five hundred machines producing high volumes of standard components for local and, increasingly, international production. By the late 1960s the Dundee autoshop was at the core of Timex's international production system. Management pacified the well-organised, assertive autoshop workers by a combination of high bonus rates and the easy availability of overtime. But this was never a stable settlement and, in any case, ran counter to the craft engineers' default bargaining strategy of *always* securing the highest possible basic rate, as this was factored into overtime and holiday payments, sick pay and pensions. In other words, high bonus earnings or overtime represented, at most, short-term gains: the long-term aim was *always* to consolidate ad hoc concessions by management into the basic rate. In 1968–9 the autoshop workers struck twice, for two and three weeks respectively, for parity in wage rates with the toolroom. Timex did not yield to this pressure, fearing that it would accelerate pattern bargaining across the factories. Informal strikes by setters and steward negotiations around bonuses may have narrowed the gap in earnings, but it never achieved parity with the toolroom rate. The engineers also used covert methods of increasing their earnings. As one steward explained:

> What we did was create our own bonus schemes where we would delay production in order to get overtime at the week-ends. . . . [A] worker would say to me, 'we need overtime on the week-ends because it is coming up to Christmas' and I would go to the broken machine and I simply wouldn't fix it on time. I would then go to the manager and say that we need to come in one week-end to fix it. In this way I would create bonuses for the other workers through being able to work overtime.[52]

The setters argued that changes in product design, finer tolerances, and the higher-quality finishes required by the new Timex electric watches, combined to make their work comparable to that of toolmakers in terms of variety, complexity and autonomy. Such formal comparability claims made little headway, however. In every dispute, the stewards struggled to regain their lead and to use their qualified leadership as a bargaining tool. More potent than walk-outs were a host of workgroup tactics that interrupted workflows or indirectly challenged supervisory power and authority. Few or none of these guerrilla tactics were led by shop stewards. The custom was that the setters kept their machines running during breaks and shift handovers. Simply by switching their machines off for a few minutes the setters seriously disrupted production, but without loss of earnings. This long-running dispute inevitably sucked supervisors into daily controversies. Specifically, supervisors retaliated by tightening up time discipline, a process that required their intervention several times daily. Supervisors looked to working charge hands to assist by ensuring their workmates returned to work promptly. This placed the charge hands in a difficult position and one in which they had few sanctions: 'their disciplinary powers are limited to breaking up groups in conversation, seeing that the men start when break times are over. Charge hands have disciplinary powers up to the point of verbal warning, he has no powers of suspension, dismissal, written incident report or final warning.' Drawing charge hands into this war of attrition simply raised the stakes by compelling supervisors to formally discipline workers for trivial, individual incidents, a response that carried the risk of further escalation.[53] Timex factory management pronounced itself 'rather perturbed about the way this situation had developed and felt the Shop Stewards, the Union, and the Management were losing control so far as the members were concerned'.[54]

Comparability disputes were not restricted to elite male, skilled groups. Rather, comparisons with the earnings of other female assembly workers were used by Timex stewards. Where union arguments based on equity or the difficulties of recruiting experienced female labour failed, shop stewards warned that Timex should expect surges of labour turnover as women moved to other factories.[55]

In the late 1960s, a concession to one male skilled group set off a chain reaction across the Timex factories.[56] Timex management was perplexed by the AEU's inability to maintain discipline over its membership, especially the female assemblers. The personnel manager reported 'that the girls had walked out . . . He felt it was wrong for any body of people to walk out the way they did without consulting with the Shop Stewards and the Trade Union officials.'[57] Indeed, far from being a reflection of militant shop steward leadership, it seems likely that these disputes triggered a sharp growth in the number of female stewards.[58] But the growth in female representation did not necessarily signify anything more than a spread of workgroup 'voice', and was not matched by improved strategic co-ordination inside the Timex union.[59] The AEU secured a pre-entry closed-shop agreement with Timex in 1968, a reflection of the union's success in gaining 100 per cent membership and the gradual extension of the scope and depth of collective bargaining over the previous decade. For the steward leadership, the nature of union organisation and collective bargaining differed significantly between the two plants. The Milton plant was well organised, led by politically articulate stewards, 'the Praetorian Guard': 'it was sort of homogeneous – it moved together. It was one of the jewels in the crown of the AEU.'[60] Similarly, the Milton plant was, argued Gordon Samson, AEU convener, more organised than Camperdown. For Samson, 'women are harder to rouse on some factory-wide issues, but quick to rise on matters affecting their department. When roused the difficulty is finding an acceptable compromise, because they want 100 per cent.'[61] Given the routinised nature of the tasks of female labour, there was little opportunity for women to bargain in terms of their skill. Equally, the importance – and success – of highly informal forms of representation and bargaining placed the workgroup at the forefront of shop floor politics, *not* the union.

The Milton toolroom was the fulcrum of union organisation from 1959, the year that the AEU first secured a comprehensive bargaining process that assigned stewards a legitimate and defined role. Over the next decade the toolroom workers became the cornerstone of organising efforts across the Timex factories. However, there was a paradox in the toolmakers' role in union organisation. Firstly, sectional representation favoured skilled male workers – such as toolmakers – over female assembly workers so that the male to female steward ratio was as much as thirty to one. Secondly, although toolmakers were important in pulling together factory-wide union organisation, their bargaining practices remained highly sectional. Thus, there were no moments or issues in which skilled engineers used their bargaining power to press an issue specific to female assembly workers. This reflected the particularity of the toolroom contract, their specialised work, and the careful socialisation of novice craftsmen into a strong group culture. All toolmakers received the same wage rate: there were no differentials and no productivity bonus. The onus was precision and problem-solving, not efficiency. All incoming toolmakers had to adjust to much finer tolerances in their work and to find their place in an informal control of work flows and pace that was completely controlled by the toolmakers themselves, virtually without reference to management. Thirdly, the toolmakers – always and everywhere an occupational group with a highly developed sectional identity – confirmed their sense of their elite, male status by their awareness that the workforce resented their elitism, their dominance of the union's bargaining agenda, and their determination to promote their own interest at all costs. The toolroom was the heart of the engineering union in Timex. The highly skilled nature of their job reduced the pressure for production. The toolmakers exercised considerable control over their work, and an acute self-awareness of their shared responsibility to maintain their craft status and their bargaining power. Equally, their location made it relatively straightforward to ensure effective and stable shop steward representation.[62] One toolmaker of thirty years' experience reflected that they 'were not popular with the rest of the workforce. The tool-makers stuck together to fight for better conditions, they were not backed up by the shop floor workers.'[63]

Timex management were prepared to give ground on bonus and overtime but, in the early 1970s, on the strategic issue of technical change, they adopted a much firmer line.[64] Generally, American-owned companies were much more reluctant than British manufacturers to bargain over non-pay issues such as recruitment, manning levels or capital investment.[65] Timex had introduced new automatic setting machines in their French plant. Compared to existing technology, this new automatic production system required no more than monitoring and occasional adjustment. The machinery could be operated round the clock with minimal supervision outside the day shift. New technology threatened the autoshop workers' considerable bargaining power and with it their position in the factory's earnings hierarchy and any prospect of achieving parity with the toolroom. Moreover, the new machinery threatened the autoshop engineers' perception of themselves as elite, precision engineers, equal in skill and status to toolmakers. The new technology, recalled local union official Harry McLevy,[66] 'upset their . . . feeling that they were sortie untouchable. Here was this thing that could do their work . . . it didnae need them for sixteen hours.' This technology threatened not just the entire setting department but also challenged the principle of union regulation of work organisation more generally. For the union's factory leadership, the critical strategic consideration was protecting the principle of negotiating the terms of technological change, *not* preventing production innovation or preserving specific contracts indefinitely. Further, the steward leadership wished to use this moment to ensure that productivity gains were not monopolised by specific workgroups but shared by the workforce as a whole. Moreover, the rewards for productivity gains need not be thought of solely in terms of cash but could be shared in terms of training, upskilling and job security.

Management were receptive to such wider terms because of the upsurge in demand for Timex watches. However, none of this broader bargaining agenda progressed far. The autoshop workers refused to budge from their pursuit of their own jobs, terms and conditions. Equally, the autoshop workers appreciated that the sheer scale of efficiency savings left ample room for a local settlement in which they were the sole beneficiaries. In reply, management insisted that technical innovation would proceed and offered only redeployment and some protection against short-term loss of earnings for displaced engineers, far short of their ambitions. But short-term financial compensation only confirmed the autoshop workers' fears that their long-run bargaining power, status and earnings were irreparably damaged. The bitter two-week dispute crumbled acrimoniously – some strikers returned to work – and, rather than risk a collapse of organisation and their authority, the stewards returned to work, even though Timex restarted workers selectively, a process that exposed individual stewards to victimisation. Even this defeat was weighed in terms of the long-term strategic position of the steward leadership. The alternative to 'an orderly retreat' was to risk the collapse of the union infrastructure, in which stewards would confront 'people scabbin', a lot of Doubting Thomases on the floor'. Even so, this 'orderly retreat' was achieved at considerable short-run cost to union organisation and to victimised stewards.[67] Only one striker – John Kydd – remained excluded by Timex. Kydd mounted a daily one-man picket for over year before he was reinstated. His vigil was supported by a levy organised by the shop stewards. Kydd's victimisation was a rallying point that minimised internal union dissension and reaffirmed the need for a combative union ready to confront a Timex management prepared to single out one man for such discrimination.

The autoshop dispute proved to be a watershed in the development of workplace trade unionism and the nature of collective bargaining in Timex. From 1972 the shop stewards' strategy gradually gained a coherence based on a centralised leadership. The factory convener, John Kydd, was a member of the Communist Party until 1978 and his personal and political networks tied Timex to struggles such as UCS and the miners' strikes. The steward leadership aimed to socialise stewards, especially novices, to see their activities as representing not just their immediate workgroup but also a factory-wide union strategy. This was a difficult balancing act: all the bargaining experience of Timex demonstrated that the company would respond to immediate pressure in terms of bonus but resist any across the board rate movements.

> Everybody wis fighting, fighting and there was a stormy period of disputes in the Timex – just to get a reasonable wage. Timex's profits were so phenomenal at that time it wisnae hard to argue for money.[68]

One apprentice engineer in the mid-1970s recalled his first exposure to this militancy:

> We weren't blameless. In the 1970s there were a lot of industrial disputes and . . . I remember the first time I went to the main factory. It was a Friday and the shop steward came in with golf clubs and everyone said, 'We'll be on strike this afternoon.' And I said, 'How do you know?' 'The shop stewards have their golf clubs with them.' So, we would strike and we would be out for

the afternoon. We had a lot of that in the 1970s and I remember being amazed by this. Every week we seemed to be losing a half-day's pay when everyone went out to the pub or played golf. That kind of thing only lasted for around two years. Then the union started taking a hard line on that.[69]

Kydd's reinstatement marked a shift towards greater centralisation and discipline among the stewards. In the Milton plant stewards assembled in the canteen every morning break to speak to their peers about a political issue selected from the newspaper, the better to hone their negotiating skills and, in some cases, to reinforce the link between factory and national politics. On the other side of the coin, factory management, personified by Graeme Thompson, accepted factory-wide bargaining as a way of reducing local disputes and establishing the broad parameters of factory discipline. The basic thrust of management strategy was to maintain production continuity. In terms of time management, for instance, the managers agreed that disciplinary procedure would only be invoked if an individual was late by more than 100 minutes or more than five times per month. This shift towards factory-wide collective bargaining reduced, but never eliminated, sectional bargaining. In 1974, for instance, mass action won significant gains in wages and forced management to withdraw any threat of dismissals. In the same year and for the first time Timex threatened closure of its Dundee operations in response to a strike, although this was met with the equally novel warning by shop stewards that this would lead to factory occupations.[70]

The centralisation of collective bargaining was now focused on the entire Dundee operation, rather than particular departments. From 1974, *all* industrial disputes, no matter how small or short-lived, provoked a management response that questioned the viability of the complete Dundee operation.[71] The stakes were raised for all disputes.

'THIS FACTORY IS NOW UNDER NEW MANAGEMENT': THE 1983 MILTON OCCUPATION[72]

Timex now is now not really Timex as it was.[73]

The first, tentative move into electronics sub-contracting was in 1978–9, when Timex began the manufacture of chassis for IBM computer monitors and a limited volume of computer-chips.[74] This diversification was accompanied by the reduction of mechanical watch production. More importantly, Timex corporate management decided in 1981 that the mechanical watch's demise was imminent and that remaining production would be concentrated in France at the expense of the restive Dundee and Portugal factories.[75] The AEU was uncertain about the direction of Timex's strategy but it was clear that jobs in mechanical watch-making were extremely vulnerable.[76] The pressure to diversify Dundee's product range increased: none were complete successes, some verged on the farcical. Perhaps the most damaging, however, was the collapse of the Nimslo 3D camera project, which had been prepared for large-scale production by Dundee engineers, a collapse that put some 400 jobs at immediate risk.[77] In late 1982 the Dundee plants had their first experience of lay-offs and short-time working since the company's arrival in 1946.[78] Nevertheless, the union had rebuffed a frontal attack on its organisation, had defended the pre-entry closed shop, and had managed to extend its role in policing how any redundancy policy was to be implemented.[79] However, there were no illusions that this was anything more than an 'uneasy peace'.[80]

In early 1983 Timex announced a call for 1,900 voluntary redundancies, centred on the skilled workforce. Management were well aware that there was likely to be widespread opposition to redundancy. And in the spring of 1983 the Milton management became conscious that preparations were afoot for an occupation. Factory management turned a blind eye to sleeping bags being brought in and wall plates being produced to secure the doors.[81] The moment of the occupation was uneventful: there was no attempt by management or the police to halt the process or to wrest control back from the workforce. The carefully hand-written 'Occupation Rules' were plastered all over the plant: all stewards were to meet at 8.30 each morning, as well as the start of their shift; all workers were to be punctual for the start of their shift; that the plant was to be kept clean and tidy; and no alcohol was to be brought in and any drunkenness would not be tolerated.[82] All aspects of the occupation were organised in great detail, especially in terms of public relations. There were to be no impromptu comments to the press, all press statements were prepared and approved by the stewards' committee; all speakers were to follow the same, prepared script. The stewards' consistent theme was that the occupation was a fight to defend not just jobs in the Milton factory but employment in Timex in particular and Dundee more generally. Internally, the stewards argued that nobody should apply for voluntary redundancy: 'We are only interested in retaining the right to earn a dignified livelihood and are not interested in severance payments.'[83]

The Dundee Trades Council issued a special issue of *The Voice*, which summarised the main campaign themes: firstly, the Timex workforce had been efficient and innovative and was being abandoned by a heartless, short-sighted multinational management; secondly, retrenchment at Timex would have a major and immediate effect on Dundee's economy; thirdly, the company had provided much of the skills training for the city, and if that was lost then this would be a body-blow to the long-term viability of the city's manufacturing base; and, fourthly, this was not a politically motivated occupation but one that was forced on a workforce with no alternative. Mass redundancy, then, hit at the city's economy and the working-class past, present and future. *Only* the Timex workers could be trusted with the plant's future.[84]

The occupation started to crumble after three to four weeks with between twenty-four and fifty Milton workers applying for voluntary redundancy. Across the workforce as a whole, management had all but secured the required volunteers for redundancy. The stewards' capacity to protect all jobs had been undercut by the choices of their constituents. The six-week occupation ended with a negotiated agreement and an orderly return to work. Timex agreed to follow a full consultation process but the union was compelled to accept a reduction in the workforce of 425, sweetened only by the company's token gesture that there would be no compulsory redundancies.[85] Timex negotiators knew that this was a meaningless concession given the number of applications they had received for voluntary severance. This was to prove a devastating blow to union organisation and authority inside Timex.

The end of the 1983 occupation signalled a decisive shift to mass consumer electronics.[86] The plant now had to re-skill the workforce for outsourced assembly of printed circuit boards and, in contrast to the long boom until the end of the 1970s, forage for work. 'The company has never recovered from the fact that the union took over their factory.'[87] The Thompson regime was replaced by a management team enlisted from mass electronics companies, particularly from Philips. In industrial relations terms, the key figure was Barry Lawson, who became the Dundee plants' operational manager. From the first, Lawson was a controversial figure. He announced his arrival to shop stewards by boasting that the shots which killed the socialist president of Chile, Salvador Allende, were fired from his garden. In the decade after the defeat of the 1983 occupation, management adopted a much harder line. The stewards' committee was acutely aware that it could no longer mount factory-wide campaigns and the best it 'could hope for was individual, tactical wins over individual managers'.[88]

CONCLUSION

There is a simple way to tell the Timex story and that is as a story of strategies, of capital and labour, of power and resistance. And that is a compelling story not least because that is the way that key actors, especially shop stewards, thought, acted and interpreted the dynamics of collective bargaining from 1972 onwards. However, there is another version of this story that is less heroic, which speaks to gender and sectionalism. The ownership of skill was male-bounded and defended resourcefully by dedicated toolroom activists, who enjoyed wages and privileges out of reach of the other, mainly female, workers in Timex. Thus, trade union bargaining practices remained highly sectional with few moments or issues in which skilled engineers used their bargaining power to press a concern specific to female assembly workers. With little history of workplace solidarity, workers were ill-equipped to conduct factory-wide agitation or action. It was little wonder that the 1983 occupation should end in an inglorious defeat. However, as a result of the action displaced skilled men were transferred onto production lines, where they performed assembly tasks that had not just been thoroughly routinised and tightly supervised but which were *always* considered as women's work. The skilled engineers, therefore, did not just lose their jobs, their power-base and the informal privileges accrued over decades, they were also emasculated. Milton transferees even became objects of pity among some of their female colleagues. In the long run, the masculine form of union organisation had been the undoing of worker power in Timex, but there is also the fact to consider that in such a contest for economic survival multinational capital has inherent advantages over labour. The strategic ability to switch production to other sites throughout the world has made it almost impossible for workers and their organisations to combat management decisions that adversely affect their livelihoods. The historically divided workforce of Timex's Dundee operations could only offer token resistance to a strategy that needed to be confronted by organised labour on a global level.

ACKNOWLEDGEMENTS

We gratefully acknowledge the invaluable help of Charlie Malone, Abertay University; and Rhona Rodger, of the McManus Art Gallery, for arranging access to the interviews for the play *On the Line*. Alan McKinlay would also like to thank his 2008 students who conducted additional interviews.

NOTES

1. *Courier*, 11 January 1983.
2. A. Gardner, Interview, 12 March 2008, p. 7, University of St Andrews Oral Histories (UST/OH).
3. McManus Art Gallery, Dundee (MAG), uncatalogued deposit: J. Kydd, Interview, 10 October 1994, pp. 3, 12.
4. 'Making the most of time', *Nation's Business* (September 1968).
5. H. Uyterhoeven and F. Knickerbocker, *Timex Corporation* (Cambridge, MA, 1972).
6. A. Glasmeier, *Manufacturing Time: Global Competition in the Watch Industry* (New York, 2000), pp. 179–90; D. Yankelovich, 'New criteria for market segmentation', *Harvard Business Review* 42 (1964), p. 355; M.E. Barrett, 'Time marches on: the worldwide watch industry', *Thunderbird International Business Review* 42 (2000), pp. 349–72.
7. Timex, 'Manufacturing/Assembly Process' (n.d., *c.*1965).
8. H. Bradley, *Men's Work, Women's Work: A Sociological History of the Sexual Division of Labour in Employment* (Cambridge, 1989), pp. 168–9; M. Glucksmann, *Women Assemble: Women Workers and the New Industries in Inter-War Britain* (London, 1990), pp. 61–2.
9. DCA, GD/AEU/2/34: AEU National Survey, 'Women's Wages – Engineering Industry', 9 September 1955.
10. W. Knox and A. McKinlay, 'American multinationals and British trade unions, c. 1945–74', *Labor History* 51 (2010) [forthcoming].
11. MAG, DM.OR.47: Anon., female assembler, Interview, 24 October 1994.
12. MAG, DM.OR.48: Ingrid Welsh and Sheena Webster, Interview, 11 October 1994.
13. MAG, T/94/D17.OR.46: Anon., female sub-assembler, Interview, 24 October 1994, p. 3.
14. MAG, uncatalogued deposit: Anon., Interview, 10 November, 5 December 1994.
15. MAG, DM.OR.48: I. Welsh, S. Webster, Interview, 11 October 1994, p. 6.

16. R. Macaulay, 'The radical conservatism of the Scots' in C. Fought (ed.), *Sociolinguistic Variation: Critical Reflections* (Oxford, 2004), pp. 187–9.

17. UST/OH: A. Lowe, Interview, 6 March 2008.

18. DCA, GD/AEU/2/31: AEU Dundee District Secretary to District Organiser, 12 December 1967.

19. DCA, GD/AEU/1/25: AEU, Dundee DC, Minutes, 5, 11 November 1952.

20. R. Wild and A. Hill, *Women in the Factory: A Study of Job Satisfaction and Labour Turnover* (London, 1970), pp. 35, 40–3.

21. A. Pollert, *Girls, Wives, Factory Lives* (London, 1981), pp. 141–4, 151–5; R. Cavendish, *Women on the Line* (London, 1982), pp. 86–90.

22. UST/OH: A. Lowe, Interview, 6 March 2008.

23. MAG, uncatalogued deposit: A. Roberston, Interview, 17 October 1994.

24. UST/OH: A. Gardner, Interview, 12 March 2008.

25. UST/OH: A. Gardner, Interview, 12 March 2008.

26. MAG, uncatalogued deposit: J. Kydd senior, Interview, 10 October 1994.

27. Anon., 'Teething troubles of American plants abroad', *Anglo-American News* 22:5 (May 1955), pp. 204–5.

28. MAG, uncatalogued deposit: W. Leslie, Interview, 20 September 1994, p. 9.

29. UST/OH: C. Malone, Interview, 26 March 2008.

30. A. Carstairs, 'The nature and diversification of employment in Dundee in the twentieth century' in S.J. Jones (ed.), *Dundee and District* (Dundee, British Association, 1968), p. 326.

31. See DCA, GD/AEU/2/11.1: Dundee Corporation, 'New Industries Committee'; *Courier*, 18 October 1946.

32. J. Gennard and M. Steuer, 'The industrial relations of foreign-owned subsidiaries in the United Kingdom', *British Journal of Industrial Relations* 9 (1971), pp. 143–59; W.W. Knox and A. McKinlay, 'Working for the Yankee dollar: American inward investment and Scottish labour, 1945–70', *Historical Studies in Industrial Relations* 7 (1999), pp. 1–26.

33. *Your Job with UK Time* (c.1948), p. 14; more generally, see D. Forsyth, *U.S. Investment in Scotland* (New York, 1972), p. 160.

34. AEU, Dundee DC, Minutes, 30 March 1949; DCA, GD/AEU/1/22, 23: 7 March 1950.

35. AEU, Dundee DC, Special Meeting re UK Time, 23 April 1953.

36. DCA, GD/AEU/1/26: AEU, Dundee DC, Minutes, 23 April 1953.

37. DCA, GD/AEU/2/34: AEU steward, Milton to AEU District Organiser, 11 May, 19 June 1952.

38. DCA, GD/AEU/1/25: AEU, Dundee DC, Minutes, 9 December 1952.

39. DCA, GD/AEU/1/27: AEU, Dundee DC, Minutes, 12 October 1954.

40. C. Wightman, *More than Munitions: Women, Work and the Engineering Industries 1900–1950* (London, 1999), pp. 176–9.

41. DCA, GD/AEU/1/28: AEU, Dundee DC, Minutes, 31 March 1955.

42. DCA, GD/AEU/1/29: AEU, Dundee DC, Minutes, 24 January 1956.

43. DCA, GD/AEU/1/32: AEU, Dundee DC, Minutes, 1, 22 December 1959.

44. For an extreme example, see DCA, GD/AEU/1/36: AEU, Dundee DC, Minutes, 29 October 1963.

45. J. Bell, 'Stability of membership in trade unions, *Scottish Journal of Political Economy* 1 (1954), p. 5; P. Findlay and A. McKinlay, '"Restless factories": shop steward organisation on Clydeside, c. 1945–70', *Scottish Labour History* 39 (2004), p. 4.

46. DCA, GD/AEU/1/29: AEU, Dundee DC, Minutes, 13, 31 March 1956.
47. DCA, GD/AEU/1/37: AEU, Dundee DC, Minutes, 7 January, 28 April, 2 July 1964.
48. DCA, GD/AEU/1/30: AEU, Dundee DC, Women's Sub-Committee, 30 April, 18 November 1957.
49. DCA, GD/AEU/1/38: AEU, Dundee DC, Minutes, 14 September, 5 October 1965.
50. DCA, GD/AEU/1/40: AEU, Dundee DC, Minutes, 31 January 1967.
51. Lord Provost W.K. Fitzgerald commenting on a strike of 130 Milton screw setters, *Courier*, 25 November 1971.
52. UST/OH: C. Malone, Interview, 26 March 2008.
53. DCA, Finnigan to AEU, District Secretary, 24 January 1967.
54. AEU Dundee DC, Company Files, 'Timex': Petrie to Brown, 1 May 1968; for similar processes in Burroughs, Cumbernauld, see W.W. Knox and A. McKinlay, 'Bargained Americanization: workplace militancy and union exclusion c. 1945–1974' in M. Kipping and N. Tiratsoo (eds), *Americanisation in Twentieth Century Europe: Business, Culture, Politics*, vol. 2 (Lille, 2001), p. 400.
55. Glasgow City Archives, TD1059/17/1/3: Dundee and District Engineering Employers' Association, Minutes, 3 November 1964.
56. DCA, GD/AEU/2/31: AEU, Dundee District Secretary to General Secretary, 15 August 1968.
57. DCA, GD/AEU/2/31: AEU, Dundee District Secretary to District Organiser, 9 January 1968.
58. DCA, GD/AEU/12/1/41: AEU, Dundee District Committee, Minutes, 16, 30 April 1968.
59. DCA, GD/AEU/12/1/41: AEU, Dundee District Committee, Minutes, 2 July 1968.
60. MAG, HH/Timex/94/DM.OR.50: H. McLevy, Interview, 12 October 1994, p. 3.
61. MAG, uncatalogued deposit: G. Samson, Interview, 'Social Trends Project', June 1987.
62. E. Batstone, I. Boraston and S. Frenkel, *Shop Stewards in Action: The Organisation of Workplace Conflict and Accommodation* (Oxford, 1972), pp. 143, 222–3.
63. MAG, uncatalogued deposit: 'George', Interview, 'Social Trends Project', June 1987.
64. See G. Martin and M. Dowling, 'Organizational transformation and HRM in a multinational context: a tale of two companies' in I. Beardwell (ed.), *Contemporary Developments in Human Resource Management* (Montpellier, 1996).
65. P. Buckley and P. Enderwick, *The Industrial Relations Practices of Foreign-Owned Firms in Britain* (London, 1985), p. 58.
66. MAG, uncatalogued deposit: H. McLevy, Interview, 12 October 1994.
67. *Courier*, 26, 27 November, 2 December 1971.
68. MAG, uncatalogued deposit: J. Kydd, Interview, senior, 10 October 1994, p. 12.
69. UST/OH: C. Malone, Interview, 26 March 2008.
70. *The Scotsman*, 14, 16 March 1974; *Courier*, 13 April 1974.
71. *Courier*, 15, 22 September 1979, 7 March 1982.
72. Placard over main gate to the Milton factory, see *Courier*, 20 April 1983.
73. MAG, uncatalogued deposit: D.R. Whyte, Interview, Social Trends.
74. *Courier*, 3 February 1982.
75. *Fortune*, 27 January 1983.
76. Confédération Générale du Travail, 'Besançon: Special Redeployment', 9 November 1982; J. Stopford, and L. Turner, *Britain and the Multinationals* (London, 1985), p. 143.
77. *Courier*, 20 December 1982.
78. *Courier*, 7 December 1982.

79. *Courier*, 23 October, 10, 19 November 1982; and *The Scotsman*, 31 March 1983.
80. *Courier*, 2 April 1983.
81. MAG, uncatalogued deposit: C. Malone, Interview, 23 September, 4, 24 October 1994; *Courier*, 8, 9 April 1983.
82. 'Occupation Rules', 25 April 1983.
83. Press Statement, 19 April 1983.
84. Dundee Trades Council, *The Voice* (n.d., *c.* April 1983).
85. E. Byrne Lee, 'The Timex Dispute, Dundee 1983' (unpublished MA Honours dissertation, University of Edinburgh, 1984), p. 43; *Courier*, 7, 18, 19 May 1983.
86. *Technology Magazine*, 9 January 1984.
87. MAG, uncatalogued deposit: F. Alexander, Interview, 1987 Social Trends.
88. MAG, uncatalogued deposit: Anon., Interview, 1987 Social Trends.

CHAPTER 12

City of Discovery?
Dundee since the 1980s

Jim Tomlinson

Greatly aided by the influx of multinational companies after 1945, recorded unemployment in Dundee was below the Scottish average in the 1950s and 1960s, and at below 3 per cent the figure emphasises how far the city had economically improved from the dark days of the 1930s. While net emigration increased, the total population of the city rose between 1951 and 1961 and was then stable until 1971. These employment and population trends suggest that the city was participating substantially in the post-war 'golden age' of the British economy. This relative buoyancy was despite the troubles of jute; after the stability of much of the 1950s and early 1960s, the industry again came under pressure in the late 1960s, as polypropylene challenged jute in many uses. The radical rebuilding of the city centre in the 1960s was linked to an optimistic frame of mind, which saw the city as having started on a path of successful modernisation, and it was widely believed that the rebuilding would entrench and reinforce this process. As Jim Phillips emphasises in 'The "Retreat" to Scotland: The Tay Road Bridge and Dundee's post-1945 Development', Chapter 10 above, the optimism surrounding the opening of the Tay Bridge in 1966 was emblematic of this perception that, underpinned by new communications, the city was set fair to flourish. Some allowance must be made for official boosterism on such occasions, but this optimistic tone is also evident elsewhere. Thus Carstairs, an academic commentator, in his contribution to the 1968 British Association volume on the city, endorsed the view that the local economy had proved 'resilient, flexible, capable and willing to expand'.[1] In 1970 the President of the local Chamber of Commerce noted: 'Over the last ten years, with the exception of one or two periods, there has been a general expansion in the area and if we may, without complacency, congratulate ourselves a little, it was a story of remarkable success.'²

One telling reflection of contemporary assumptions can be found in the 1970 official publication, *Tayside: Potential for Development*.³ Here it was suggested that Dundee could build on its post-war success by becoming the hub of an expanded 'City Region' with a population in that region potentially doubling from around 375,000 to 750,000 between 1971 and 2001. Within this, the city population would perhaps rise from 180,000 to 300,000.

This was not to happen; the city's population fell after 1971, and by 2001 (ignoring boundary changes) was down to 145,000 (Table 12.1). We may see this gap between vision and reality as a fine example of futurologist's hubris, but more important is to understand why that vision was not realised, and the answer lies in one of the 1970 document's key assumptions: the projected future expansion of manufacturing employment. To support the increase in total population the report envisaged the proportion of the workforce in manufacturing rising slightly from 34 per cent to 37–38 per cent of a much larger total by 2001.⁴ In fact, this proportion fell dramatically to 10 per cent (of a slightly smaller total) by the end of the twentieth century (Table 12.2). This, of course, was the manifestation of that process of de-industrialisation, highlighted in Chapter 1 above as a key twentieth-century trend in the city. The central issue in this chapter is how the city responded to

TABLE 12.1
Dundee population 1951–2007

Year	Population
1951	177,340
1961	182,978
1971	182,521
1981	177,545
1991	155,550
2001	145,560
2007	142,170

Source: Census; for 2007, General Register Office Mid-year Estimates.

TABLE 12.2
Employment in Dundee by sector in 2007 (sectors with more than 5 per cent of total)

Mainly Private Sector	Percentage of workforce
Wholesale and retail trade	15.8
Manufacturing	10.3
Real estate, renting and business activities	8.9
Transport, storage and communication	7.7
Hotels and restaurants	6.3
Construction	5.3
Mainly Public Sector	
Health and social work	14.7
Public administration and defence; social security	13.2
Education	10.6

Derived from: Dundee City Council, About Dundee 2008 (Dundee, 2008)

that de-industrialisation, as both its inescapability and its radical implications became evident, especially from the 1980s.

DE-INDUSTRIALISATION AND THE RESPONSE

Nationally de-industrialisation became a central political topic from the 1970s, as the recession of that decade exposed the weaknesses of significant parts of British manufacturing. These weaknesses were variously interpreted at the time, but for most commentators it was taken as given that any decline in manufacturing could and should be reversed.[5] The precise time when that assumption was commonly abandoned is hard to specify, but the collapse in manufacturing in the Thatcher slump at the beginning of the 1980s seems to have been a key moment in increasingly making the continued relative decline of manufacturing understood as a trend to be accepted, if rarely to be celebrated.[6]

As noted in Chapter 1, Dundee saw a rapid decline of manufacturing from the early 1970s, with losses in jute coupled to the retreat of the multinationals. Timex started its rundown of employment in 1974, when it had peaked at over 6,000 workers, falling to 3,900 by 1981, and contracting further to 2,000 in 1983, when there was a bitter dispute over redundancies. Final closure came in 1993, with a further major dispute, precipitated by the sacking of 340 workers, overwhelmingly women.[7] In NCR the peak year for employment was 1970, and this fell continuously and even more rapidly over the next decade, to below 1,000 by 1980.[8] This overall manufacturing decline accelerated in the early 1980s, generating a sharp increase in unemployment, which saw the claimant rate increase to 17 per cent by 1986. In 1980 a conference called in response to growing unemployment in the city, entitled 'Dundee Industry', heard from both a government minister ascribing the problem to long-term 'industrial decline' and 'loss of competitiveness' and the Labour leader of the council ascribing it to government policy. But both assumed that the key issue in restoring employment and posterity was to restore industrial growth.[9]

But very soon the terms of debate were noticeably shifting, and the results of this are symbolised by the 'rebranding' of Dundee as 'The City of Discovery' in 1982.[10] This rebranding had many roots. The title chosen was a punning reference to the ship of that name, whose return and display in the city where it had been built was at the core of a new 'heritage' strategy, and simultaneously to the desire of the city to build up industries based on scientific discovery, especially in electronics and life sciences. Both these strands were grounded in elements of the city's history going back much earlier than the 1980s, though only in that decade would they come together to provide the underpinnings for a new approach to the city's future.

The growing emphasis on heritage was part of a national cultural shift towards a growing interest in 'the past', a shift which has been much analysed by historians and cultural commentators.[11] In Dundee the heritage to be celebrated focused on Dundee's links with the sea, and Dundee and textiles.[12] Both of these elements had been represented in museums in the city – in the main city museum, the Albert Institute (renamed the McManus in 1986), but also in the Dudhope Technical Museum (opened in 1900). One of the stimuli to action in the 1970s was the threat of closure and dispersal of the machinery collection of the second of these institutions, at a time when interest in industrial archaeology was growing.[13]

But it was 'Dundee and the sea', focused on the RRS *Discovery*, which was to provide the first and most important element in the heritage strategy. *Discovery* was built in Dundee, and it was from there she sailed to the Antarctic with Scott in 1912. She was languishing in St Katherine's Dock in London, and in 1985 the newly formed Dundee Heritage Trust acquired her for the city. *Discovery* was to become the city's most important tourist attraction.

The story of *Discovery* is not just a story of local initiative, but inter-woven with a broader shift in national economic thinking and policy. Drawing on the example of the National Enterprise Board, the Scottish Development Agency was established in 1976.[14] Initially much of the SDA's focus was on traditional industrial policy, helping to stimulate industrial investment by subsidies. It owned 25 million square feet of factory space, acted as a venture capitalist, and had overall responsibility for attracting new investment into Scotland. While Labour nationally remained in power until 1979, the Agency helped to fill the alleged 'finance gap', but its expenditure in this regard was trivial. It also became increasingly involved in major urban projects, which was in line with the general trend of policy in relation to social deprivation from the 1970s onwards.[15] In Dundee, the Agency led an elaborate 'Area Initiative', the Dundee Project (signed November 1982), which grew into 'a major attempt to revitalise the economic life of the city', but with a clear emphasis on training and skills rather than direct employment provision.[16]

The SDA, and its successor body, Scottish Enterprise, was to be important for both the heritage and high technology components of the 'city of discovery'. Crucially for the former, the Agency saw revitalisation of the waterfront as central to the city's overall improvement. This was coupled to the Scottish Office's designation of an Enterprise Zone consisting of six sites in the city, including a large part of the waterfront, in 1984.[17] Revitalisation of the waterfront was most plausibly based on tourism, and within that *Discovery*, returned to Dundee in 1986, was central. In 1993 it was relocated adjacent to the newly built Discovery Point, aided by profits obtained from one of the other occupants of the Enterprise Zone, Tesco, itself to become an important part of the local economy in the following decades.[18] The Dundee Heritage Trust also established the Verdant Works as an award-winning jute museum, opened in 1996. By 2006 it was calculated that tourism was employing 5,000 people in the city, with an annual turnover of £430 million, the top attractions being Camperdown Wildlife Centre, Sensation (the Dundee Science Centre), and the *Discovery*.[19]

The second aspect of the 'city of discovery' was 'high technology' industry. Again, this had roots in the city's history, but emerged as a distinct sense of being the basis of a new over-arching strategy for the city's future only in the 1980s.

One of these roots was development of a substantial university sector. The University of Dundee had roots going back to the University College founded in 1881 on money from the Cox family. It merged with St Andrews in 1897, but moved towards greater autonomy when becoming Queen's College in 1953, before becoming entirely separate in 1967. While expanding in the 1960s and 1970s in the wake of the Robbins Report on higher education, it still only had 3,000 students in 1981, and the following few years saw a crisis as the Thatcher government cut spending on universities, with Dundee being especially hard hit.[20] But the beginning of the 1990s, with the successful fight to keep a dental school, inaugurated two decades of rapid expansion. From very small beginnings in biochemistry, Life Sciences emerged as a key area of research, with eventually 800 staff, including several Nobel prize winners. The University also merged with Duncan of Jordanstone Art College in 1994, and this too has contributed very much to the City of Discovery reinvention.[21]

Abertay became a university in 1994, and grew to about a third of the size of Dundee University in the early 2000s. It evolved from the Dundee Institute of Technology, previously the Dundee College of Technology, which was founded in 1888. Abertay focuses on vocational subjects, including an emphasis on entrepreneurialism, but is best known for its computer arts and computer games technology research and teaching. It is also home to the Dundee Business School.

By the beginning of the twenty-first century this expansion of the universities has given them an economic weight in the city which is among the highest of any place in Britain. Total student numbers for the two universities plus Dundee College reached almost 40,000 in 2007, with over 5,000 staff.[22] Their impact is magnified by the fact that academic salaries are high (the average full-time academic salary is in the top 15 per cent of the income distribution nationally), but universities also provide a significant number of other jobs, ranging from higher professional to manual. This expansion has been driven by a number of forces. Especially since the 1960s there has been a powerful 'science lobby' which has claimed that more expenditure on science and scientific research and development, and more trained scientists and technologists, is the route to faster economic growth, and university expansion has been an important consequence of that notion.[23] Such ideas helped the separation of Dundee University from St Andrews in the 1960s, and its subsequent growth, which was uninterrupted, though at variable pace, except during the public spending cuts of the early 1980s.[24] Under New Labour, expansion was aided by a continuation of that lobby's effective activities, helping to secure Research and Development as one area of continued government 'industrial policy', alongside a target to expand higher education to reach a 50 per cent participation rate. By 2009 it was evident that this era of expansion was over, but the scale and character of any contraction were still to be decided.

Links between the universities and local industry are very important. On the electronics side, the new industries, such as game software, grew out of both the universities sector and existing industry. Duncan of Jordanstone provided key stimulus on the design side of gaming development, while Abertay provided major inputs on the software engineering side. But there were also links with the post-war American electronics incomers, NCR and Timex. NCR had always had a significant research and development component to its activities in Dundee, alongside manufacturing, and this provided opportunities for local students to develop ideas before they were spun out into separate companies. Timex played a different role, as a provider of rudimentary but extremely cheap home computing capacity, with budding entrepreneurs in the 1980s able to obtain extraordinarily cheap Spectrum machines which the Timex factory produced under licence.[25] One of the key firms to emerge from this environment was VIS, with initial financial support from the Prince's Trust. The company's main site is in Dunfermline (initially chosen as halfway between the designers from Duncan of Jordanstone and the software engineers in abundant supply in Edinburgh), but it continues with a small base in Dundee.

The biggest employer in this sector in Dundee by 2009 was Realtime Worlds, founded in 2002 by Dave Jones, creator of the highly successful Grand Theft Auto and Lemmings games. By 2009 it had grown to employ over 200 staff.[26] One characteristic of such firms is that they employ mostly highly skilled people, and this has led them to sustain close links with the universities, with courses closely aligned with company requirements.

Both because it consists largely of small firms, and because it fits poorly into the Standard Industrial Classification used to define industrial sectors, it is difficult to say how big the digital media (including games, software development and communications technology) industry is. The matter is also complicated by the fact that economic data is compiled for very different geographical areas – Dundee City, Dundee City Region and Tayside.[27] A 2007 survey suggested that there were over 300 companies in this sector in Tayside, employing 3,500 people, a figure which had increased by 52 per cent since 2002. Of these jobs, 93 per cent were full-time, and 80 per cent taken by men. Output was estimated to be £185 million, with exports of £50 million.[28] It is estimated that 70–80 per cent of this activity was in Dundee City.[29] On this basis, the industry made up about 3 per cent of employment in the city in 2007. However, its contribution cannot be judged solely by the number of jobs. These jobs are likely to be well-paid, and therefore generate significant spending in the local economy. In addition, the reason such industries tend to cluster together is in part linkages to higher education institutions, but also linkages with other similar firms, creating what economists call agglomeration economies. This means that once a critical mass of firms exists, they provide a strong incentive for other firms to locate nearby, and this appears to have occurred in Dundee. Other things being equal, this suggests that further significant growth in this sector is possible in the future.

The other 'knowledge-based' industry which flourished in Dundee from the 1990s was life sciences. Here the links with the universities are even closer than in the case of digital media, given the research-intensive nature of the activity, which means that much of the underpinning to the commercial sector has to come from publicly or charity funded work. Many of the companies involved are direct 'spinouts' from academic research, one example being Cyclacel Ltd, founded in 1996, which has over 70 staff, 60 per cent with PhDs, and which specialises in researching, developing and commercialising cancer drugs.[30]

Thus, alongside the major developments within Dundee University noted above, the 1990s and early 2000s saw the commercial life sciences sector grow rapidly, especially on Dundee Technology Park, on the western edge of the city; on Dundee MediPark (adjacent to Ninewells Hospital), and on the Dundee Technopole (adjacent to the University). As in digital media, the sector is characterised by a large number of small firms, whose precise scale and impact are difficult to pin down. A survey of activity in 2007 suggested that life sciences in the Dundee City Region employed 4,300 people, almost four times the figure of 1,100 in 1997. This was done by sixty-five organisations, a ninefold increase from the seven of 1997.[31] How much of this activity was in Dundee City is hard to gauge exactly. Given the close links with the universities, it is likely that the proportion was at least as high as for digital media, though it is notable that there is significant manufacturing activity in this industry outwith Dundee, such as at the GlaxoSmithKline plant in Montrose, though employment there has fallen from its 1990s peak.[32]

If we estimate employment in the city in this sector at around 3,000 in 2007, this would mean it accounted directly for about 3.5 per cent of total employment. As with digital media, this relatively small figure may be misleading as to the significance of life sciences. The evidence suggests it was the fastest growing area of economic activity in the decade up to 2007, and the agglomeration economies involved provide a basis for further expansion. The industry also generates substantial local spending from the high incomes paid to its employees. It is also clearly highly synergetic with the universities, embedding a cluster of sophisticated activity in the local economy.

These two 'new' industries are not isolated in the local economic structure. While most large-scale manufacturing by multinationals has ended (except in the case of Michelin, where high weight–value ratios in transporting tyres keep production in Dundee, close to European markets), NCR retains a significant research facility in the city. While the company ended all manufacturing locally in 2009, its continued presence suggests that 'high-tech' companies beyond digital media and life sciences can find good reason to stay.

Ever since the 1930s the city has been aware that to attract and retain 'new' industries it must make itself attractive to potential incoming companies and their employees. The straightforward investment subsidies to companies of post-war 'industrial policy', which served Dundee so well in the 1950s and 1960s, largely died out in the 1980s. But subsidies for research and development, for infrastructure and commu-nications continue to be important, and Dundee has been significantly aided by such money, coming from Edinburgh, London and Brussels. Alongside financial inducements, and to attract and retain managers and highly paid professionals in the new sectors, the city has strongly encouraged the development of cultural and leisure facilities. The area around the eastern end of the Perth Road has been designated a cultural quarter, including the Repertory Theatre and Dundee Contemporary Arts. These have both been successful in providing high-quality venues, Dundee Contemporary Arts having become a major exhibition centre for contemporary art as well as proving an 'arts' cinema. Dundee Contemporary Arts is also significant in emphasising the close co-operation between the universities and the city; Dundee Contemporary Arts was jointly funded by the University of Dundee and the city council. The recognition of a symbiotic relationship between local higher education and the city's prosperity is a striking feature of recent history. It is further evident in the co-operation over the project to bring a branch of the Victoria and Albert Museum to the city, which achieved initial agreement in 2009.[33]

Cultural activity should not, of course, be seen as just an adjunct to 'proper' industry. On the one hand, expenditure on cultural and leisure pursuits grew significantly in the boom years from the mid-1990s, so these sectors have become major forms of economic activity and employment in their own right. On the other hand, the boundaries between artistic/cultural and 'high-tech' activity have become blurred – as in, for example, the high-quality design embodied in computer games. The rhetoric of a new 'creative class' may be overblown, but there is no doubt that the changes in the city since the 1980s, and especially since the 1990s, have brought into being a wide spectrum of new kinds of creative economic activity, where that term embraces everything from drug discovery to contemporary art installations.[34] The 'city of discovery' has certainly brought about the growth of prosperous activities in parts of the city. However, the barriers to the generalisation of this prosperity can partly be gauged from the data on average incomes. In April 2007 median earnings for all full-time employees in the city stood at £413, 93.7 per cent of the Scottish average, and close to the bottom of the Scottish ranking of geographical areas.[35]

CHANGING EMPLOYMENT PATTERNS

In assessing the impact of these 'new' activities on the city as a whole, we need to note economic activities which have *not* grown much in the city – what might be seen as lost opportunities. By far the most important of these is North Sea Oil. Today it seems self-evident that Aberdeen would become the onshore base for Scotland's oil industry. But when the industry began in the 1960s it was widely assumed that Dundee would become a major beneficiary of this discovery. An official report of 1978 is worth quoting at length on the perspective almost a decade after the first major finds were made:

> In the Tayside region the level of involvement in offshore work has been disappointing in the light of the physical advantages. The two main ports of Dundee and Montrose are well placed in relation to the fields in the middle North Sea . . . and appear to have no significant cost disadvantages as supply bases compared with Aberdeen and Peterhead. The latter two, however, have been much more successful despite the fact that, initially at least, Dundee harbour was physically more suited to the offshore industry's requirements. Two reasons which may explain Dundee's relative lack of success are the absence of good air communications, and an original lack of interest on the part of the authorities concerned in attracting oil-related business to the city . . . Total oil-related employment in wholly related companies in Dundee, in early 1977, was just over 500 – not a negligible figure, but small in relation to the area's need for new employment.[36]

The first of the two reasons suggested for Dundee's unattractiveness to oil companies is relatively straightforward. Aberdeen's Dyce Airport seems to have provided a convenient base for the expansion of air communications, including helicopters flying to the rigs. Dundee's Riverside Airport was much less established and more physically restricted.[37] How far politics affected the outcome is more controversial. It seems clear that initially central government favoured Dundee, with the Scottish Secretary in the late 1960s, Willie Ross, defending this preference on the basis that 'success leads to success. You can't hold back success', a view based on the extent to which Dundee was seen to have adapted to the economic changes of the 1950s and 1960s.[38] Suggestions that the local council lacked an interest in attracting oil are unproven, as are beliefs that corruption in the city council repelled potential investors.[39] Whatever the reasons, the failure to attract significant oil activity has had a huge impact in Dundee. Before North Sea Oil, Aberdeen and Dundee were broadly similar in population size; by the end of the twentieth century Aberdeen had in excess of 200,000 inhabitants, over a third more than Dundee. Oil has transformed Aberdeen economically; where in the 1950s and 1960s it had a precarious economy, heavily reliant on fishing, it has enjoyed a 'boom town' experience since the 1970s, albeit with all the fluctuations characteristic of a place dependent on the oscillating price of a primary product.

While oil is unambiguously a new industry, finance is a long-established activity, which nationally (in both Scotland and the UK) expanded enormously in the long upswing after 1992. Dundee has long had a presence in international finance, most notably as a pioneering centre for the investment trust in the late nineteenth century. One of these pioneers, the Alliance Trust, continues to have a presence in the city, and built a brand-new building to house over 200 staff, opened in 2009. The trust is a major financial institution, with FTSE 100 status.[40] However, finance has overall remained a small part of the economy, with around 3 per cent of local employment – far less than, for example, Edinburgh. The limited impact of this industry may reflect the absence in Dundee of those agglomeration economies which may still characterise this industry, despite its reputation for footlooseness. Of course, limited reliance on this sector (and the fact that Alliance Trust does not operate in the more speculative aspects of finance) may have helped to protect the city's economy in the crisis from 2007. Nationally the growth of financial services was one of the forces which underpinned the extraordinary redistribution of income to the wealthy, with both the top 1 and 5 per cent of the income distribution doubling their share of the national income in a generation, and returning Britain to inequality levels close to those before 1913.[41] But given the limited role of these services in Dundee, this has had little direct impact on the local economy.

In the years from the 1990s, significant employment expansion in the private sector has come in private sector retail and distribution services, though in common with national trends, the retail sector became more concentrated, with the growth of Tesco in particular, which grew to be the largest private sector employer in the city.[42] Another major employer was D.C. Thomson, the most long-standing, stable source of private sector jobs, a company which on the face of it thrived on producing a resolutely old-fashioned set of products, newspapers and magazines, though it spread its investments widely, including into a range of newer media.[43] Its commitment to new technologies was shown by its major participation in 'Scotland on Line', Scotland's first internet provider.

But by far the most striking shift in employment, as employment in manufacturing has declined, has been the growth of the public sector, with the expansion of the NHS and education, in both the school and college sector, and the universities. The official categorisation of employment does not use a private/public sector distinction, but the public sector component probably lies between 35 and 40 per cent (Table 12.2).

Under the Conservatives between 1979 and 1997 the growth in NHS spending for the country as a whole was below the long-term (1950–2004) trend of 3.7 per cent per annum, at 3.1 per cent, but still substantial; in what was to become the greatest boom in spending ever seen in the NHS, this figure rose to 8.1 per cent per annum between 2000 and 2001 and 2004 and 2005.[44] Locally, this was reflected in the Tayside NHS Trust becoming the largest employer, above all through the continued expansion of Ninewells, though other services also contributed. Total employment in Tayside NHS (which includes Dundee) grew by around 40 per cent during the boom after 1992 (from 10,301 FTEs in 1993, to 14,099 in September 2008). This growth was especially fast between 2001 and 2005.[45]

The story of education is somewhat different. Here, under the Conservatives, spending had grown very slowly, at 1.5 per cent per annum (the long-term trend was 4 per cent), but again in Labour's second term, after 2001, there was a striking surge, the annual rate of increase rising to 6.1 per cent.[46] As in health, this policy included a huge expansion of capital projects in these two sectors, alongside big increases in employment levels. In Dundee the rise in education spending was evident in both the school and college sector and in the two universities, though physically the impact on universities was most apparent, with both the University of Dundee and Abertay putting tens of millions into new buildings on their campuses. More sustained was the expansion of employment (Table 12.2).

Other public sector employment expansion, especially by the city council, reflects (as does that in health and education) the fact that the public sector now embraces some of the most labour-intensive activities in the economy, where labour-saving productivity gains are very hard to achieve. The imperative to 'take labour out' which has been so powerful in driving up labour productivity (and diminishing employment) in manufacturing is simply not possible in most of the public sector.

Dundee, like many post-industrial parts of Britain, has thus become highly dependent on public sector employment – a kind of 'regional Keynesianism' not sufficiently stressed in most accounts of contemporary Britain. The effects of this are complex. Within its aggregate affect on the local labour market, it has undoubtedly favoured the employment of women, who are much more strongly represented in the public sector than in 'new' industries such as digital media. Thus it has allowed Dundee to continue to be a relatively good place for female employment opportunities, following the demise of jute and the multinational electronics firms which previously provided a large number of such jobs. Public sector employment is also now relatively well-paid compared with the private sector, though as much of this reflects the contracting out to the private sector of low-paid jobs previously done 'in-house' by public sector employers, it is perhaps of more statistical than substantive significance.

As suggested in Chapter 1, the growth of public employment can be seen as a key component of the 'de-globalisation' of the city, making its economic fortunes much more reliant on political decisions in London and Edinburgh, and much less (at least directly) on the vagaries of the international economy. In the years from the mid-1990s those political decisions made public sector employment the key underpinning for the employment of most Dundonians, however much the new industries provided an important dynamism to the local economy.

THE WELFARE OF THE PEOPLE

What has happened to the welfare of the local population of Dundee in the years of 'the city of discovery'? The strategy of focusing on new 'high-tech' industries and creating an environment which would attract and retain workers in those industries is in accord with Scotland-wide strategies.[47] But such strategies are necessarily problematic. As Turok has suggested, the danger is that 'The focus on high value jobs and top quality living environments for highly skilled and resourceful people is a narrow basis for urban revitalisation and growth. It will do little directly to improve the life chances of people outside the creative class, ie poor, low skilled and workless groups, and it may even cause harm through gentrification of inner-urban areas and displacement of low-income households.'[48]

How do developments in the recent history of Dundee relate to such criticism? It should be stressed that the high-profile 'rebranding' of the city and the production of 'Visions' may give a misleading sense of the city council's role, much of which undoubtedly is focused on what has come to be called social inclusion, and reducing deprivation. Thus 'partnerships' to reduce social exclusion and deprivation are an important part of the city's policies.[49] Nevertheless, these grand plans, 'rebrandings' and visions have shaped policy, and the spending of money.

In the context of these 'reinventions', how have the inhabitants of the city fared? The availability of work, and the wages and conditions of work, remain central to most people's welfare. The long upswing in the national economy since 1992 undoubtedly reduced unemployment in Dundee; while the claimant count seriously understates the figure, it gives a broadly accurate picture of the trend. But for recent years we also have the benefit of careful estimates of the real level of unemployment based on calculations which add to the official data working-age people who are receiving incapacity benefit, but who in a fully employed economy would find employment.[50] These calculations give estimates of 16.9 per cent for January 2002 (claimant count 7.6), falling to 11.4 per cent in January 2007 (claimant count 4.1). This data clearly suggests a continuing serious unemployment problem in the city even at the end of the 'NICE' period, though a problem which has been reducing in line with national macroeconomic buoyancy. However, it puts Dundee in a significantly better position than five other Scottish areas. This may reflect the fact that the worst areas for unemployment across Britain tend to be areas of previous large-scale concentrations of heavy male manual work (coalmining, shipbuilding, iron and steel), which was not Dundee's position. One other notable feature of this calculation is that it suggests that a significant proportion of this 'hidden unemployment' is female; while the official rate shows a ratio of 3.5:1 between men and women, the 'real' rate has a ratio of only 1.2:1. This may perhaps be a hidden legacy of the high employment rates of women in the city, dating back to jute and the post-war American multinationals, with a residue of older women who lost jobs and never regained employment. Also significant for the economic fortunes of women has been the concentration of employment growth in part-time work. Between 1999 and 2005 the total number of women employees increased three times as fast for women as for men. About two-thirds of this increase for women was in part-time jobs.[51] Views on the significance of such trends are highly controversial: did they reflect an accommodation of employers to women's desired patterns of 'work-life balance', or an absence of the full-time jobs that women would have preferred if they had been available?[52]

Broader evidence on social conditions in Dundee comes from the 2006 Scottish Index of Multiple Deprivation (SIMD). This index adds together data about income, employment, health, education, accessibility, housing and crime to derive a summative figure, which is used to assess relative deprivation. The conceptual underpinning of this is the notion of relative poverty, expanded to embrace a range of activities of which the poor are deprived. It is also relative in the sense that it describes the position of each aspect covered relative to the others, not the absolute level of deprivation. The SIMD uses 'data zones' of approximately 750 people, and ranks these from the most to the least deprived.[53] Dundee had 179 of these zones, and 53 of these ranked within the 15 per cent most deprived in Scotland. These covered 28.9 per cent of the city's population. In a Scottish context this suggests that Dundee is less seriously deprived than Glasgow and Inverclyde, but above all other areas.[54]

One clear indicator of the challenges faced by Dundee in the early twenty-first century is the levels of economic inactivity and dependence on benefits. In 2008 Dundee City came twenty-seventh out of the ranking of thirty-two Scottish local authorities for the proportion of the adult population in employment, with 73 per cent.[55] This low proportion is part of a long-term trend, as shown in Table 12.3. It correlates with high levels of dependence on benefits, as suggested by the calculations on unemployment noted above, which seek to take on board the scale of claims for disability allowances.[56] The implications for welfare of these patterns are suggested by data on household incomes. The figures cited above on median earnings put Dundee about 6 per cent below the Scottish average, while the household data suggests an 11 per cent gap with the Scottish mean.[57] One final measure of the state of the local economy at the end of the boom under New Labour gives a rather more optimistic indication, at least in relative terms. The number of sixteen to nineteen-year-olds Not in Education, Employment or Training (NEETs) was 9.4 per cent, below the Scottish average of 10.4 per cent.[58]

TABLE 12.3
Population changes in Dundee 1971–2001, percentages (post-1996 boundaries)

	Percentage change in Dundee	Percentage change in Scotland
Total population	-21.31	-3.07
Population of working age	-17.91	1.93
Persons in employment	-27.84	1.75
Ratio of those in employment to population of working age	-8.54	-0.12

Source: census data, collated by I. Turok, 'Urban policy in Scotland: new conventional wisdom, old problems?' in M. Keating (ed.), Scottish Social Democracy (Brussels, 2007), p. 146.

An issue which continued to be both hugely significant for the welfare of its inhabitants, but also the site of key tensions and battles, was housing. At the peak of municipal ownership in the 1980s, Dundee council owned over 70 per cent of the local housing stock, but from that peak the local authority's role as a landlord rapidly diminished, as the stock was sold to sitting tenants or housing associations.[59] Increasingly, public sector housing was only for the most socially deprived, especially the unemployed.[60]

The strategy of regeneration involves attracting more middle-class residents, a policy reinforced by the loss of 17,000 largely better-off households when local government was reorganised in 1996, with the city council regaining a full range of powers. To try and raise its council tax base the city pursued a policy of 'increasing the number of new houses built in the higher council tax bands and demolishing the identified surplus housing to improve overall quality of the City's housing stock'.[61] Between 1999 and 2004 there was a drop of 3,000 properties in the lowest band (A) and a rise of 1,900 in the higher bands (D and above).[62]

There is a strong incentive for the council to demolish multi-storey blocks because they get capital grants from the Scottish Government to do so, and lose responsibility for recurrent maintenance expenditure. This has arguably led to a smaller-scale repeat of the 1960s experience of demolition breaking up communities, even though these multi-storey blocks (while generally in better condition than the slums of the 1960s) do not conform to any contemporary ideal of housing. From the early part of the new century there were major private sector residential developments on the waterfront. This was clear evidence of the process of gentrification of the city housing stock, as council ownership became very much residualised.[63] Housing continues to be expensive, but housing benefit is paid from national not local public funds, and acts therefore as an 'inflowing' subsidy for private sector landlords.[64]

Housing is the area where the long-standing trend for local authorities to lose power to central government is most apparent. This broad trend means that the capacity of any city to shape its own future is limited. Nevertheless, it is worth asking how far the authorities in Dundee have successfully found opportunities to improve local conditions.

Local politics in Dundee in the 1960s and 1970s has become notorious for corruption.[65] In the 1980s the struggle with central government over housing, coupled to the twinning of the city with Nablus on the West Bank, emphasised the strength of the left in local politics.[66] The battles over the rundown of Timex, which had become a bastion of union power in the city, also emphasised an understandable local belief that industrial employment was crucial to the city. But at the same time, in the early 1980s, there were emerging new forces on the Left in the city who coupled a concern with social deprivation and poverty with a recognition that a new direction had to be sought.[67] Thus the 'city of discovery' relied, among other things, upon a shift in local politics, a 'new urban socialism' which was a feature of the 1980s. By the beginning of the twenty-first century the notion of cities as central to economic prosperity was being revived across Scotland, so that by 2004 it was being claimed that 'Scotland's cities are vital to driving the overall economic health of Scotland'.[68] To some degree this is a return to a 'vision' of the 1960s, with the then planners' enthusiasm for 'city regions'.[69] Dundee's own 'City Vision' of 2003, which developed the trajectory of the 'city of discovery', led to substantial grants from the Scottish executive under the 'Building Better Cities' initiative.[70]

DUNDEE AND THE BIGGER PICTURE

Almost as soon as the scale of competition to jute and the social problems of the city became widely recognised in the early twentieth century, radical plans for improvement of the city were put forward.[71] The post-war years have seen a plethora of such plans, from the Tay Valley Plan of 1950, the City plan drawn up by Dobson Chapman in 1952, through to the 'Vision' of 2003.[72] These plans have had little in common. Those of the 1950s and 1960s saw major physical redevelopment strongly guided by public authorities as the key to a prosperous future. By the end of the twentieth century there was much more reliance on the private sector, both in physical improvement and economic policy – hence the terminology of 'vision' rather than 'plan'. Paradoxically, however, this fading of the social democratic dream of publicly managed economic and social improvement has been accompanied by a striking trend towards much greater reliance on public sector employment.

Most of this expansion has come from nationally funded services (the NHS, universities), or the increased national subventions to local services (especially education). The city's own revenue base has been hit hard by the loss of population (both through boundary changes and emigration), and the demographic shift towards a larger elderly population; but also the size of the non-working group among those of working age – the hidden as well as recorded unemployed. Paradoxically, also, the city now has lots of commuters who contribute little to its revenues, a major unintended consequence of improvement in the local transport infrastructure since the time of construction of the Tay Road Bridge.[73] By 2001 18,000 people a day were commuting into the city, compared with 5,500 of a much larger working population in 1951.[74]

The national redistribution to the rich over the last generation has not helped Dundee. But the redistributions from the generality of taxpayers to the poor have, underpinning some economic improvement for most Dundonians, even those without employment.[75] This shift was very much underpinned by national macroeconomic buoyancy, making enormously increased public spending politically possible, along with rising incomes. But the 'real unemployment' level and SIMD data emphasise the limits to Dundee's capacity to overcome the end of Juteopolis in the quarter of a century after the initiation of the city of discovery.

The success of local efforts to improve conditions in the city has been, ever since 1945, in large measure dependent upon national macroeconomic conditions. The post-war boom of the 1950s and 1960s aided the sustaining of the revival initially brought about by the Second World War. The travails of the 1970s and 1980s reflected the failures of national macroeconomic policy of those decades. Britain's exit from the ERM in 1992 began a long upswing in the economy which lasted until 2007, and provided a much more favourable national economic environment for Dundee. However, some aspects of that period were double-edged in their local impact. In particular, in a fashion similar to that before the First World War, the inhabitants of Dundee gained benefits from 'globalisation' in the form of a flood of cheap imported manufactured goods, as they had gained from the flood of cheap food before 1913; but both periods also saw local employment hit by international competition, and this is one cause of the de-industrialisation which, as stressed above, represented the key challenge to the city's prosperity.

The growth of public sector employment, coupled with the entrenchment in the city of new, 'high-tech' industries, meant that it was much better placed to withstand the recession which began in 2008 than it was to deal with the global economic collapse of the 1930s. But this enhanced economic security was, of course, a matter of degree. Political decision making in London and Edinburgh, in a context of perceived fiscal crisis, would still have great impact on the city, however intelligent the city's own efforts proved.

NOTES

1. A. Carstairs, 'The nature and diversification of employment in Dundee in the twentieth century' in S.J. Jones (ed.), *Dundee and District* (Dundee, British Association, 1968), p. 320.
2. DCA, Minutes of Meetings of the Directors of Dundee Chamber of Commerce, 12 June 1970. Optimistic views of the whole of Scotland's economic performance in the 1960s were common: see, for example, N. Buxton, 'The Scottish economy, 1945–79: performance structure and problems' in R .Saville (ed.), *The Economic Development of Modern Scotland 1950–1980* (Edinburgh, 1985), pp. 52–3, 55–7; C. Lythe and M. Majmudar, *The Renaissance of the Scottish Economy?* (London, 1982), p. 188.
3. A. Campbell and D. Lyddon, *Tayside: Potential for Development* (Edinburgh, HMSO, 1970). The 1966 economic *Plan* for Scotland proclaimed that 'the general condition and prospects of the Dundee area, and particularly of the city itself, offer the most promising feature of the whole North-East'. It was recognised that the future of jute was likely to be further contraction; 'But despite this, Dundee itself has an impressive record of post-war successes in modern fast-growing industries and now has a substantial labour force skilled in the requirements of precision engineering.' The *Plan*

suggested the possibility and desirability of the city expanding to a population of a quarter of a million (from around 150,000), to create a substantial self-sustaining 'city-region': Secretary of State for Scotland, *The Scottish Economy 1965 to 1970: A Plan for Expansion*, Cmnd. 2864 (1966), para 199.

4. Campbell and Lyddon, *Tayside*, p. 104.

5. F. Blackaby (ed.), *Deindustrialization* (London, 1979); R. Bacon and W. Eltis, *Britain's Economic Problem: Too Few Producers* (London, 1976).

6. R. Rowthorn and J. Wells, *De-industrialization and Foreign Trade* (Cambridge, 1987).

7. *The Times*, 7 May 1983, 9 May 1983, 9 July 1983, 4 September 1984.

8. N. Hood and S. Young, *Multinationals in Retreat: The Scottish Experience* (Edinburgh, 1982), pp. 106–13.

9. City of Dundee District Council, *Dundee Industry: One Day Conference 23 October 1980* (Dundee, 1980), pp. 1–3, 7–9.

10. This became 'One City, Many Discoveries' in 2008.

11. A sceptical view, sharply expressed, is P. Wright, *On Living in an Old Country* (1985; 2nd edn, Oxford, 2009); R. Hewison, *The Heritage Industry: Britain in a Climate of Decline* (London, 1987). C. Di Domenico and M. Di Domenico, 'Heritage and urban renewal in Dundee: learning from the past when planning for the future of a post-industrial city', *Journal of Retail and Leisure Property* 6 (2007), pp. 327–39.

12. Recognition of the importance of D.C. Thomson and the theme of 'Dundee and graphic journalism' has not so far led to any concrete actions: C. Lythe, A. Walker, M. Edwards and D. Ross, *Dundee Heritage Trust: The Beginning* (Dundee, DHT, 1997), p. 13.

13. The Abertay Historical Society (founded in 1947) was important in providing initiative on this issue: Lythe et al., *Dundee Heritage Trust*, pp. 10–11.

14. N. Hood, 'The Scottish Development Agency in retrospect', *Three Banks Review* 171 (1991), pp. 4–5.

15. Hood, 'Scottish Development Agency', pp. 9–10.

16. H. Morison, *The Regeneration of Local Economies* (Oxford, 1987), p. 180; for assessment of the impact of this partnership on the Whitfield area of Dundee, T. Begg, *Housing Policy in Scotland* (Edinburgh, 1996), pp. 156–8.

17. Lythe et al., *Dundee Heritage Trust*, p. 13.

18. Department of the Environment, *Enterprise Zone Information 1989–1990* (London, HMSO, 1993).

19. *Scottish Economic Statistics 2008*, Table 3.6; Scottish Enterprise, *Dundee City Region* (prepared by Oxford Economics, 2009), p. 72.

20. D. Southgate, *University Education in Dundee, 1881–1981* (Edinburgh, 1982).

21. K. Baxter, M. Rolfe and D. Swinfen, *A Dundee Celebration* (Dundee, University of Dundee, 2007).

22. DCC, *Dundee Economic Development Plan 2008–2011* (Dundee, City Council, 2008), p. 13; Rolfe in Baxter et al., *Dundee Celebration*, pp. 55–9 estimates Dundee University alone brought a total injection of £0.5 billion per annum (including student spending) by 2007.

23. K. Gannicott and M. Blaug, 'Manpower forecasting since Robbins: a science lobby in action', *Higher Education Review* 2 (1969), pp. 56–74; D. Edgerton, *Science, Technology and the British Industrial 'Decline' 1870–1970* (Cambridge, 1996).

24. A re-amalgamation with St Andrews was raised as a serious possibility in this cutback period: TNA: PRO UGC 7/1085 University of Dundee, 1983.

25. Interview conducted by Jim Tomlinson with Chris van der Kuyl, 5 November 2009.

26. Scottish Enterprise, *Dundee City Region*, p. 66.

27. The Dundee City Region includes the city, Angus, Perth and Kinross, and NE Fife. Tayside is the same, minus NE Fife.

28. Scottish Enterprise, *Dundee City Region*, pp. 65–6. This data is for Digital Media; a wider category, commonly used, is Digital Media and Enabling Technologies, which embraces TV, music and publishing, and here the evidence suggests much less expansion: ibid., pp. 64–5.

29. DCC, *Dundee Economic Development Plan*, p. 14.

30. www.cyclacel.com (accessed 21 December 2009).

31. Scottish Enterprise, *Dundee City Region*, p. 74.

32. A. Petrie with C. Whatley, *The Glaxo: 50 Years in Montrose* (Montrose, GlaxoSmith Kline, 2002).

33. The city's own McManus Gallery and Museum was also subject to major redevelopment, re-opening in 2010.

34. R. Florida, *The Rise of the Creative Class* (New York, 2004); for sceptical views on this, see for example E. Peck, 'Struggling with the creative class', *International Journal of Urban and Regional Research* 29 (2005), pp. 740–70.

35. *Scottish Economic Statistics 2008* (Edinburgh, 2008), Table 4.19. The figure for men was 89.6 per cent, for women 95.4. It is notable that the highest income sector is manufacturing, reflecting the decline in routine production, and the movement into much more sophisticated products.

36. Scottish Economic Planning Department, *Economic Impact of North Sea Oil* (Edinburgh, HMSO, 1978), p. 53.

37. W. Mackie, 'Impact of North Sea Oil on the North East of Scotland, 1969–2000: A Historical Analysis' (unpublished PhD thesis, University of Aberdeen, 2001), pp. 118–19, 220, 396.

38. Ibid., p. 120.

39. Interview conducted by Jim Tomlinson with Alex Stephen, Chief Executive of Dundee City Council, 1991–2009, 11 November 2009.

40. C. Munn, *Alliance Trust: A Short History 1888–2008* (Dundee, Alliance Trust, 2009). The Alliance Trust and the Second Alliance Trust merged in 2006 to become Alliance Trust PLC.

41. M. Savage and K. Williams (eds), *Remembering Elites* (Oxford, 2008), p. 1.

42. DCC, *About Dundee 2008* (Dundee, 2008), p. 14.

43. There is very little published material on D.C. Thomson, though there is an informative website at www.londonfreelance.org/rates/owners/_dct.html. There is a great deal of material on the company's industrial relations in the 1950s to 1970s in the National Archives, resulting from its strongly anti-union policies, which date back to the aftermath of the 1926 General Strike: TNA: PRO LAB 10/1508, PREM 11/556.

44. J. Hills, T. Sefton and K. Stewart (eds), *Towards a More Equal Society? Poverty, Inequality and Policy since 1997* (Bristol, 2009), pp. 6, 41.

45. NHS Tayside in NHS Scotland Workforce Statistics.

46. Hills et al. (eds), *Towards a More Equal Society?*, pp. 6, 41.

47. DCC, *Dundee: A City Vision* (Dundee, 2003); Scottish Executive, *Smart Successful Scotland* (Edinburgh, 2001).

48. I. Turok, 'Urban policy in Scotland: new conventional wisdom, old problems?' in M. Keating (ed.), *Scottish Social Democracy* (Brussels, 2007), p. 155.

49. DCC, *A City Vision*, especially pp. 16–18.
50. C. Beatty, S. Fothergill and R. Powell, *The Real Level of Unemployment 2007* (Sheffield, Sheffield Hallam University, 2007); C. Beatty, S. Fothergill, T. Gore and A. Green, *The Real Level of Unemployment 2002* (Sheffield, Sheffield Hallam University, 2002).
51. Scottish Enterprise, *Economic Review Tayside*, p. 43
52. S. Macrae, 'Constraints and choices in mothers' employment careers: a consideration of Hakim's Preference Theory', *British Journal of Sociology* 54 (2003), pp. 317–38.
53. Scottish Executive, *Scottish Index of Multiple Deprivation* (Edinburgh, HMSO, 2004).
54. DCC, *Scottish Index of Multiple Deprivation 2006: Dundee City Council Analysis* (Dundee, 2007), pp. 2–3.
55. Scottish Enterprise, *Dundee City Region*, p. 47.
56. Scottish Enterprise, *Economic Review Tayside*, p. 48 suggests incapacity claimants were 9 per cent of the adult population in Dundee in 2006, compared with a Scottish average of 7.4 per cent.
57. *About Dundee, 2008*, p. 12. Because of the different bases of calculation, these figures can only be regarded as suggestive.
58. Scottish Enterprise, *Economic Review Tayside*, p. 49.
59. S. Glynn, 'Home truths: the myth and reality of regeneration in Dundee', Edinburgh, Institute of Geography Online Paper Series: GEO-132: www.geos.ed.ac.uk/homes/sglynn/Home_Truths.pdf
60. J. Wadsworth, 'Eyes down for a full house: labour market polarisation and the housing market in Britain', *Scottish Journal of Political Economy* 45 (1998), pp. 376–92.
61. City Corporate plan, cited in DCC, *Population Matters* (Dundee, City Council, 2004), p. 10.
62. DCC, *Population Matters*, p. 25.
63. S. Glynn, 'Getting rid of the ugly bits: the myth and reality of regeneration in Dundee, Scotland' in S. Glynn (ed.), *Where the Other Half Lives: Lower Income Housing in a Neoliberal World* (London, 2009), ch. 5.
64. Nationally, housing costs for average working-class households rose in the late twentieth century, but there is no local data on this: A. Offer, 'British manual workers: from producers to consumers, c.1950–2000', *Contemporary British History* 22 (2008), p. 551.
65. *Courier*, 14 March 1980. This major corruption case involved an ex-Lord Provost, Tom Moore, and an ex-Councillor, James Stewart, alongside John Maxwell, a developer. The charges related to the period 1959–75. All three were sentenced to five years' imprisonment, but both Moore and Stewart were freed on appeal. See *Courier*, 7 February 1980 to 14 March 1980, and 20 June 1980. Note that such corruption was not uncommon in this period, with parallels in the redevelopment of Newcastle, for example.
66. Linked to this was the role of George Galloway, a key figure in the local Labour Party before his departure in 1983: D. Morley, *Gorgeous George: The Life and Adventures of George Galloway* (London, 2007).
67. Interview with Alex Stephen.
68. Scottish Executive, *The Framework for Economic Development in Scotland* (2004), p. 25, cited in Turok, 'Urban policy in Scotland', p. 148.
69. Campbell and Lyddon, *Tayside*.
70. I. Turok, 'Scottish urban policy: continuity, change and uncertainty post-devolution' in C. Johnstone and M. Whitehead (eds), *New Horizons in British Urban Policy* (Aldershot, 2004), pp. 123–4.

71.   C. McKean and P. Whatley with K. Baxter, *Lost Dundee: Dundee's Lost Architectural Heritage* (Edinburgh, 2008), pp. 162–6, 182–9. B. Harris, '"City of the Future": James Thomson's vision of the city beautiful' in L. Miskell, C.A. Whatley and B. Harris (eds), *Victorian Dundee: Image and Realities* (East Linton, 2000), pp. 169–84.

72.   McKean and Whatley, *Lost Dundee*, Part III; G. Lloyd and J. McCarthy, 'Dundee: a city discovering inclusion and regeneration' in C. Couch, C. Fraser and S. Percy (eds), *Urban Regeneration in Europe* (Oxford, 2003), pp. 61–5.

73.   Jim Phillips, 'The "Retreat" to Scotland: The Tay Road Bridge and Dundee's post-1945 Development', Chapter 10 above.

74.   DCC, *Population Matters*, p. 13: *Census, 1951, Occupations and Industries*, p. xl.

75.   For the national pattern of redistribution, see Hills et al. (eds), *Towards a More Equal Society?*, pp. 35–44.

Index